FAULT-TOLERANT COMPUTING
Theory and Techniques

FAULT-TOLERANT COMPUTING
Theory and Techniques
Volume II

DHIRAJ K. PRADHAN, Editor

University of Massachusetts

PRENTICE-HALL
Englewood Cliffs, New Jersey 07632

Library of Congress Cataloging-in-Publication Data
Main entry under title:

Fault tolerant computing : theory and techniques.

Includes bibliographies and index.
1. Fault-tolerant computing. I. Pradhan, D. K.
QA76.9.F38F38 1986   004.2   85-23238
ISBN 0-13-308230-X (v. 1)
ISBN 0-13-308222-9 (v. 2)

Editorial/production supervision: Nancy Milnamow and Diana Drew
Cover design: Edsal Enterprises
Manufacturing buyer: Gordon Osbourne

Printed in the United States of America

10 9 8 7 6 5 4 3 2 1

ISBN 0-13-308222-9 025

Prentice-Hall International (UK) Limited, *London*
Prentice-Hall of Australia Pty. Limited, *Sydney*
Prentice-Hall Canada Inc., *Toronto*
Prentice-Hall Hispanoamericana, S.A., *Mexico*
Prentice-Hall of India Private Limited, *New Delhi*
Prentice-Hall of Japan, Inc., *Tokyo*
Prentice-Hall of Southeast Asia Pte. Ltd., *Singapore*
Editora Prentice-Hall do Brasil, Ltda., *Rio de Janeiro*
Whitehall Books Limited, *Wellington, New Zealand*

CONTENTS

Chapter 2
DESIGN FOR TESTABILITY   **95**

E. J. McCluskey, *Stanford University*

Chapter 3
FAULT SIMULATION   184

Y. Levendel, *Bell Laboratories*

P. R. Menon, *Bell Laboratories*

Chapter 4
CODING THEORY FOR FAULT-TOLERANT SYSTEMS   265

B. Bose and J. Metzner, *Oregon State University and Oakland University*

Chapter 5
CODING TECHNIQUES IN FAULT-TOLERANT, SELF-CHECKING, AND FAIL-SAFE CIRCUITS   *336*

Yoshihiro Tohma, *Tokyo Institute of Technology*

Chapter 6
ARCHITECTURE OF FAULT-TOLERANT COMPUTERS   *417*

D. Siewiorek, *Carnegie-Mellon University*

Chapter 7
FAULT-TOLERANT MULTIPROCESSOR
AND VLSI-BASED SYSTEM COMMUNICATION
ARCHITECTURES

467

D. K. Pradhan, *University of Massachusetts*

Chapter 8
SYSTEM DIAGNOSIS

577

C. R. Kime, *University of Wisconsin*

PREFACE

Fault-tolerant computing has evolved into a broad discipline, one that encompasses all aspects of reliable computer design. Diverse areas of fault-tolerant study range from failure mechanisms in integrated circuits to the design of robust software.

High reliability in computer design was first achieved through so-called fault-avoidance techniques; these involved computer design which used high-quality, thoroughly tested components. Sometimes, simple redundancy techniques were employed to achieve limited fault tolerance. Automated recovery techniques were seldom used as there was little confidence in the hardware. The drastically increased reliability requirements as well as the increased computer speed quickly made manual recovery obsolete. One example of this is the 1964 *Saturn V* launch computer, which had a reliability requirement of only 0.99 for 250 hours; this compares to the late-1970s FTMP and SIFT computers, with reliability requirements of 10^{-9} failures per hour over the 10-hour mission time.

Besides ultrahigh-reliability needs, fault-tolerant computing is driven by other key factors, such as ultrahigh availability, reduced life-cycle costs, and long-life applications. A good illustration is the ESS system of Bell Telephone, which has an availability requirement of only 2 minutes downtime per year. Because reduction of the life-cycle costs of commercial computers has become a major objective of manufacturers, fault-tolerance techniques have become increasingly important, such as using low-cost error-correction/detection codes and maintenance processors like those utilized in systems such as the IBM 3081 and Sperry 1100/60 models. Still another major thrust behind strong development of fault-tolerant computing are the long-life applications. A prime example here is the very high survival probability warranted in spacecraft computers such as the one planned for the upcoming *Galileo* spacecraft.

Other major factors influencing growth and development of fault-tolerant computing include the intangible trade-offs between the lack of high reliability and the loss of computational power, including gaining consumer confidence. This is to say that a loss of availability of a supercomputer, even during a small amount of time each day, can actually result in a loss of computing energy equivalent to the entire throughput of a mainframe computer. Also, we cannot afford to overlook the critical point that the wide use of computers now makes it essential that they be not only highly available, but especially, reliable, so as to heighten their acceptance and use by the general public. A good example here is the ultimate goal of "paperless" offices and banks—impossible to achieve without the availability of low-cost, highly available, *and* highly reliable computers.

The design of reliable computers is actually much more complex than the design of other complex human-made objects (robots, airplanes, etc.). Perhaps this can better be grasped by looking at one statement in the *IEEE Spectrum* (Oct. 81, p. 41): "Information-processing errors can occur through a failure lasting a billionth of a second in one of the hundreds of thousands of digital components that switch billions of times a day." It is no exaggeration to say that fault-tolerant computer design requires a real understanding of a large and complex set of interrelated subjects. The goal of this book, then, is to provide a strong, broad base for general understanding. Particularly emphasized is the theory itself, as well as how the theory works to pave the way for the implementation of practical techniques.

Basic to the design of reliable computers is the availability of defect-free parts. Effective testing strategy becomes critically important to determine the presence or absence of defects and faults. This book's first three chapters are devoted to an in-depth focus on three major aspects of the testing of integrated circuits: test generation, fault simulation, and design for testability.

Test generation for digital circuits is one of the oldest areas of study in fault-tolerant computing. But this field has had to undergo rapid revamping to keep pace with the nearly revolutionary changes in circuit technology. The factors affecting the test generation problems are twofold, while the number of components that can be supported on a chip is increasing. The chip itself is becoming susceptible to a more diverse variety of failures, ranging from internal opens and shorts to encapsulation and bonding failures. Sounder understanding of these failures has yielded newer fault models, such as bridging faults, stuck-open faults, and crosspoint faults. Abraham and Agarwal's opening chapter gives us this necessary current perspective of the testing and test generation area. Not only is a good overview of the basic theoretical issues presented, but various practical state-of-the-art test generation algorithms such as PODEM, function testing, and random testing are also included.

With limited internal access to increasingly complex circuits, the test generation problem is a most untenable one. The use of testability as a *design criterion* is one particularly successful solution to this "testing problem." Dubbed "design for testability," this area has received much current attention, especially since the introduction by IBM in the late 1970s of the level-sensitive scan design (LSSD). Various techniques and issues involved in the design for testability area are given a very thorough treatment in the chapter by McCluskey.

The third chapter, written by Levendel and Menon, gives a highly useful and easy-to-understand treatment of the principles as well as the practices of the area known as fault simulation—a most practical technique for both test generation and test validation.

One interesting tool, used to depict the failure characteristic of components over time, is the "bath-tub" curve. What this implies is that a large initial failure rate is likely for components for a short duration, known as the "burn-in period." Following this, the components may experience a failure rate which is small, if steady, all through their operational life. Then the failure rate rapidly increases because of wear-out and the like. Therefore, a small probability of component failure exists during the useful life. The following two chapters go into detail as to the theory and techniques involved in the design of circuits which are fault tolerant. To begin with, error-correcting and error-detecting codes have been used quite successfully, providing low-cost error control. The chapter by Bose and Metzner provides a sharp, concise treatment of the theory and application of error-correcting codes at the subsystem level, such as RAMs and ALUs. Following this, Tohma's chapter yields a well-delineated view of the error-detection/correction techniques available at the gate level for the design of fault-tolerant and self-checking circuits.

The issues of organization and architecture of computers are key ones to the design of fault-tolerant computers. The next two chapters tackle these issues. The chapter by Siewiorek gives an in-depth survey of various existing fault-tolerant architectures. Included here is a discussion of a broad range of fault-tolerant architectures, incorporating those that are available commercially. It should be noted that the recent computer architecture thrust has been concerned with the area of multiprocessors and distributed processors. One can say nothing less than that it is expected that the next generation of computers will consist of innovative interconnections of multiple computing elements. Fault-tolerance issues in interconnecting multiple computing elements therefore will inevitably receive increasing attention. The chapter by Pradhan provides an overview of various architectures which are suitable for yielding robust interconnections between computing elements. Also discussed are some of the recent research results in the area of fault-tolerant VLSI (very large scale integration) and WSI (wafer-scale integration) interconnections.

With this feasibility of interconnecting a large number of computing elements to build an integrated system, the issue of *self*-diagnosis becomes a critical one. Self-diagnosis techniques have already become commercially feasible with the use of maintenance processors with computers such as the IBM 3081, Honeywell DPS 88, and Sperry 1100/60. These maintenance processors, although logically built and electronically separate, are located with the mainframe; they are capable of performing both diagnosis and recovery. Other commercial systems, such as those DEC has employed, take the form of remote computers that perform automated diagnosis.

An elegant theory, known as system diagnosis, provides an understanding of various fundamental relationships in the framework itself when computing elements that can test other computing elements. Kime's chapter gives a very comprehensive overview of the various models developed and their results.

Determining the reliability of ultrareliable systems through life testing is an awesome task. For example, in order to test that the failure probability of an FTMP system does not exceed 10^{-9} for a 10-hour mission, 10 million computer-years would be required. In other words, this translates to running 1000 FTMP computers for 10,000 years. Consequently, analytical and simulation techniques provide our only other practical alternatives. Stiffler's chapter examines this analytical approach and provides a detailed overview of the CARE III technique.

Although a major body of theory of software fault tolerance is not yet in place, the problem of software fault tolerance is one not to be taken lightly. That is, one significant cause of system failure can be attributed to software failure. As an illustration, both the *Apollo* and the Space Shuttle missions were aborted at least once because of software failures. Reliability in software has been achieved primarily through fault-avoidance techniques, principally because software faults are design errors (as opposed to wear-out faults experienced by hardware). Although software reliability increases with its heightened use, the possibility exists of an unforeseen combination of environmental factors causing catastrophic failure. Redundancy techniques, analogous in principle to those found in the design of fault-tolerant hardware, have been formulated to avoid such catastrophes. Although deceptively simple, these techniques can be very difficult to implement because of the intrinsic complexities of the software itself. Because these inherent problems make software reliability a new, important, and distinct area of research, it is well surveyed by Hecht and Hecht in the book's final chapter.

This book is intended to be both introductory and suitable for advanced-level graduates. It is suggested that the chapters be selected in different combinations to provide courses with different orientations.

Course Topic	Chapter Combinations
Introduction to fault-tolerant computing	7, 1, 3, 5, and 10
Testing and diagnosis	1, 2, 3, 5, and 8
Fault-tolerant hardware design	7, 1.1, 1.2, 2, 4.1–4.3, 4.6–4.9, 5, 6.1–6.4
Fault-tolerant system design	7, 4, 5, 6, 8, 9, and 10
Theoretical issues in fault-tolerant computing	1, 2.1, 2.5, 2.6, 4, 5, 6.1, 6.6–6.9, 8, 9, and 10.1–10.4

Chapter 6

ARCHITECTURE OF FAULT-TOLERANT COMPUTERS*

D. Siewiorek

6.1. INTRODUCTION

Historically, reliable computers have been limited to military, industrial, aerospace, and communications applications in which the consequence of computer failure was significant economic impact and/or loss of life. Reliability is of critical importance in situations where a computer malfunction could have catastrophic results. Examples include the Space Shuttle, aircraft flight control systems, hospital patient monitors, and power system control.

Reliability techniques have become of increasing interest for general applications of computers because of several recent trends. A few of these trends are listed below.

Harsher environments: With the advent of microprocessors, computer systems have left the clean environments of computer rooms for industrial environments. The cooling air contains more particulate matter. Temperature and humidity vary widely and are frequently subject to spontaneous changes. The primary power supply may fluctuate, and there may be more electromagnetic interference.

*Adapted from "Introduction to Part II: The Practice of Reliable System Design," in D. Siewiorek and R. Swarz, *The Theory and Practice of Reliable System Design,* Digital Press, Bedford, Mass., 1982, pp. 323–344.

Novice users: As computers proliferate, the typical user is less sophisticated about the operation of the system. Consequently, the system has to be more robust, including toleration of inadvertent user abuse.

Increasing repair costs: As hardware costs continue to decline and labor costs escalate, a user cannot afford to have frequent calls to field service. Figure 6.1.1 depicts the relationship between hardware purchase price and the addition of reliability, maintainability, and availability features. Note that as hardware cost increases, service costs decrease, due to less frequent and shorter field service calls.

Larger systems: As systems become larger, there are more components that can fail. Since the overall failure rate is directly related to the failure rates of the individual components, fault-tolerant designs may be required to keep the overall system failure rate at an acceptable level.

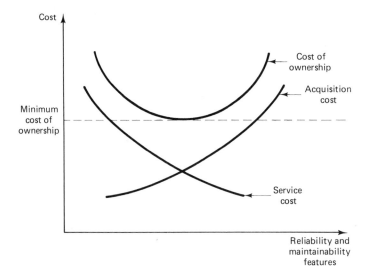

Figure 6.1.1 Cost of ownership as a function of reliability and maintainability features.

The ultimate system goals affect design philosophy and design trade-offs. The costs of fault tolerance must be traded off against the cost of an error. Error costs include downtime as well as actions based on incorrect computation. Table 6.1.1 lists some of the system goals affecting design trade-offs. Is the system to be highly reliable or highly available? Do all outputs have to be correct or only data committed to long-term storage? How familiar must the user be with the architecture and software redundancy? Is the system dedicated so that attributes of the application can be used to simplify fault-tolerance techniques? Is the system constrained to use existing components? Even if the design is new, what is the cost and/or performance penalty to the user who does not require fault tolerance? Is the design stand-alone, or are there other processors that can be called upon to assist in times of failure?

TABLE 6.1.1 SYSTEM GOALS
DETERMINE DESIGN PHILOSOPHY

Reliability versus availability
Grain of correctness
    Correct data output
    No loss of data
Transparency to user
Dedicated or general purpose
New design or add-on
    Penalty to nonreliability user
Stand-alone or multiple processor

TABLE 6.1.2 TWELVE COMPUTER SYSTEMS GROUPED ACCORDING TO
THE APPLICATION TAXONOMY[a]

General-purpose commercial systems	High availability	Long life	Critical computations
VAX-11/780	Tandem	STAR	C.vmp
IBM S/360-S/370-4300 family	Pluribus	Voyager	SIFT
	ESS		FTMP
Univac 1100/60			
	Intel 432		

[a]Note that a system is not necessarily uniquely defined by one application area.

In this chapter we discuss briefly attributes of 12 fault-tolerant computer systems that have been built. To provide a framework for that discussion, the systems will be grouped by application (see Table 6.1.2).

6.2. Application Types

Four different application types have been identified (paraphrased from [RENN80]). The applications are ordered by increasingly stringent reliability requirements.

General-purpose commercial systems. High-performance general-purpose computing systems are very susceptible to transient errors (due to close timing margins) and permanent faults (due to their complexity). As performance demands increase, fault tolerance may be the only recourse to building commercial systems with sufficient mean time to errors (MTTE) to allow useful computation. Occasional errors that disrupt processing for several seconds are tolerable as long as automatic recovery follows. Table 6.2.1 lists some general-purpose computing systems, their mean time to crash (MTTC), mean number of instructions executed (MNIE) between crashes, and percentage of failure due to hardware/software/unknown. For example, the data taken from a 6-month evaluation period of the Cray-1 [KELL76] indicated an

TABLE 6.2.1 NUMBER OF INSTRUCTIONS EXECUTED BETWEEN SYSTEM
CRASHES FOR SEVERAL MAINFRAME SYSTEMS

System	MTTC (h)	MNIE ($\times 10^{10}$)	HW (%)	SW (%)	%unknown
B5500 [YOUR72]	14.7	2.6	39	8	53
Chi/05 (Univac1108) [LYNC75]	17	6.7	45	55	—
Dual 370/165 [REYN75]	8.86	28	65	32	3
SLAC [CAST82]	20.2	23	73	22	5
PDP-10 [CAST82]	10	4.3	—	—	—
CRAY-1 [KELL76]	4	190	—	—	—

MTTC of 4 h and an average repair time of 25 minutes. Each repair period represents a loss of over 10^{12} instruction executions. Example systems considered in this category are the DEC VAX-11/780, IBM S/360-S/370-4300 family, and the Univac 1100/60.

High availability.   High-availability systems share resources where the occasional loss of a single user is acceptable, but a system-wide outage or common data base destruction is unacceptable. These systems are most frequently oriented toward special-purpose computing, executing programs whose demands can be anticipated.

Hamming-coded memory, bus parity, time-out counters, diagnostics, and software reasonability checks are the primary redundancy techniques. Thus coverage is low. In multiple-processor systems, however, the fault can be isolated once it is identified, and the system can continue operation, perhaps in a degraded mode. Examples of high-availability systems include Tandem, Pluribus, ESS, and the Intel 432.

Long life.   Long-life systems such as unmanned spacecraft cannot be manually maintained over the system operating life (frequently 5 or more years). Often, as in spacecraft encounters with planets, the peak computational requirement is at the end of system life. These systems are highly redundant, with enough spares to survive the mission with the required computational power. Redundancy management may be performed automatically (e.g., on board the spacecraft) or remotely (e.g., from ground stations). STAR and Voyager are examples of long-life spacecraft systems.

Critical computations.   The most stringent requirement for fault tolerance is in real-time control systems, where faulty computations can jeopardize human life or have high economic impact. Computations must not only be correct, but recovery time from faults must be minimized. Specially designed hardware is employed with concurrent error detection so that incorrect data never leave the faulty module. A simple example is C.vmp, a triply redundant microprocessor. SIFT and FTMP are examples of avionic computers designed to control dynamically unstable aircraft. Their design goal is a failure probability of less than 10^{-9} for a 10-h mission.

6.3. GENERAL-PURPOSE COMMERCIAL SYSTEMS

6.3.1. VAX-11/780

The reliability, availability, and maintainability program (RAMP)* of the VAX-11/780 32-bit computer is representative of contemporary general-purpose computing design. Some RAMP features are defined in the system architecture and must appear in every implementation. Other features are implementation specific.

The VAX architecture defines three types of exceptions: aborts, faults, and traps. *Aborts* are the most severe form of exception. When an instruction is aborted, the machine registers and memory may be left in an indeterminate state. Because system state is destroyed, the instruction cannot be correctly restarted, completed, simulated, or undone.

Faults, on the other hand, leave the machine registers and memory in a consistent state. Once the fault is eliminated, the instruction may be restarted and the correct results obtained. Faults restore only enough state to allow restarting. The state of the process may not be the same as before the fault occurred.

Finally, a *trap* occurs at the end of the instruction causing the exception. The machine registers and memory are consistent and the address of the next instruction to execute is stored on the machine stack. The process can be restarted with the identical state as before the trap occurred.

Exceptions are defined for overflow/underflow and other violations of arithmetic operations (trap), reserved instruction/operand/addressing mode usage, memory management violations (fault), memory errors (e.g., correctable data, nonexisting memory), backplane bus parity and protocol violations, and machine check (abort). The machine check is the most damaging exception. It is triggered when internal CPU error-checking circuitry detects an exceptional condition. The processor may be restartable if the exception is related to redundant logic whose sole purpose is to improve machine performance (e.g., instruction cache, instruction look-ahead buffer).

An archetypal implementation of a VAX-11 is illustrated in Fig. 6.3.1. The central processing unit (CPU) is connected to memory and I/O devices by a backplane bus. I/O devices reside on either the Unibus or Massbus. The Massbus is a high-speed block transfer bus used primarily for block-oriented mass storage devices such as disks and tapes. Bus adapters convert Unibus or Massbus protocols to the backplane bus protocol. Two standard options are the floating-point accelerator (FPA) and the writable control store (WCS). The WCS supports microcode changes and can also be used for microdiagnostics. The console subsystem is a small computer that provides control

---

*IBM uses the acronym RAS for reliability, availability, and serviceability, while Univac uses the acronym ARM for availability, reliability, and maintainability.

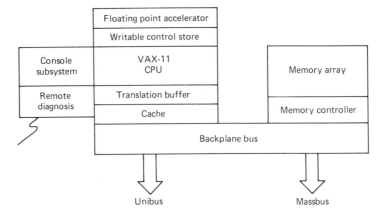

Figure 6.3.1 Archetypical VAX-11 implementation.

(halt, restart, initialize, etc.) over the CPU, as well as access to internal system registers. There is a set of internal system registers associated with each subunit (i.e., cache, memory, translation buffer, backplane, etc.). In general, each subunit is associated with up to four types of registers: configuration/control, status, data, and diagnostic/maintenance. The configuration/control register contains information on the state of the element (e.g., checking enabled, reporting enabled, etc.). The status register contains flags summarizing the state of the element, including error reports. Data registers capture relevant information about the system state when an error was detected (e.g., address used on cache look-up when a cache parity error was detected). Finally, the diagnostic/maintenance register contains control and status information relative to checking the error-detection/correction logic. The console subsystem has a mass storage device containing the main system bootstrap code and some diagnostics. The console subsystem also has access to the visibility bus, which makes almost 600 internal logic signal values visible to the microdiagnostics.

The main memory is protected by error-correcting code (ECC) and has a battery back-up option that preserves the contents of memory over short-term power failures. Finally, a port is provided for remote diagnosis (RD). The RD port provides all functionality of the console subsystem to a remote site.

Remote diagnosis (RD) is an integral part of the VAX-11 maintenance philosophy. A typical VAX-11 maintenance scenario is as follows. Disk resident, user mode diagnostics would periodically execute under the VMS operating system. The goal of User Mode diagnostics is to exercise and detect functional errors in memory, Massbus adapters, (MBAs), Unibus adapters (UBAs), device controllers, and device drives. Errors, reported by user mode diagnostics or hardware check circuits, would prompt a customer call to the diagnostic center (DC). The customer replaces the removable disk media with a diagnostic and scratch disk, turns a key on the front console to Remote, and calls the DC (note that unauthorized access is not possible). The DC engineer calls the customer's processor, logs onto the system, and begins to execute a script of diagnostics. Micro- and macrodiagnostics can be loaded from the diagnostic

TABLE 6.3.1 COMMON VAX RAMP FEATURES

Feature	Example	Benefit	Aid MTTF	Aid MTTR
Processor consistency checking	Arithmetic traps, memory address protection, limit checking, reserved opcodes	Limits damage due to hardware or software errors	No	Yes
Interval timer	1-μs resolution	Used by diagnostics to test time dependent functions	No	Yes
Disk error-correcting codes	RP05, RP06, and RK06 detect all errors up to 11 bits and corrects single burst up to 11 bits	Tolerates transient and media-related faults	Yes	Yes
Peripheral write-verify checking hardware	Read after write followed by comparison	Error detection	No	Yes
Track offset retry hardware	Upon error, disk retries read. If retry fails, disk head is offset for retry		Yes	Yes
Bad block handling	VMS removes bad disk blocks from use		Yes	Yes
On-line error logging	Records exceptional conditions in an error log, including time and system state	Aids permanent and intermittent fault isolation	No	Yes

TABLE 6.3.2 VAX-11/780 RAMP FEATURES

Feature	Details	Benefit	Aid MTTF	Aid MTTR
FAULT INTOLERANCE				
Airflow	Blowers	Lowers chip junction temperature	Yes	No
LSI	Memory chips	Fewer chips, hence fewer boards; more reliable per function over SSI/MSI; lower power consumption, hence cooler junction temperatures	Yes	Yes
Cabling		Fewer pluggable connectors to fail	Yes	Yes
Sensors and indicators	Power loss	Protects system from damage due to emergency conditions	Yes	Yes
Modular power supply		Easy replacement	No	Yes
FAULT TOLERANCE				
Main memory	8-bit ECC per 64-bit word	Tolerates transient and permanent failures; logging of error information allows quick fault isolation	Yes	Yes
Control store	3 parity bits, one per each 32 bits of control store	Provides tolerance of transient errors as well as partial isolation to the failing chip	No	Yes
Translation buffer	Two-way set associative. Six parity bits for each set: three over 16-bit tag, valid, modify, and 4-bit protection; three over 21 bits of page frame number	Provides faulty chip isolation; tolerates transients by recalculating TB contents; tolerates permanent failures by disabling one set	Yes	Yes
Cache	Two-way set associative. Seven parity bits per set: three over 12-bit tag and valid bit; four over 32 data bits (byte parity)	Provides faulty chip isolation; tolerates transients by refetching cache contents; tolerates permanent failures by disabling one set.	Yes	Yes

TABLE 6.3.2 (cont.)

Feature	Details	Benefit	Aid MTTF	Aid MTTR
Synchronous back-plane interconnect (SBI)	Two parity bits: one over 32-bit data/address field, one over 12 bits of control information	Detection of errors and isolation to faulty bus port; transients tolerated by bus-level retry	No	Yes
	Silo (a first-in, first-out queue) captures last 16 bus cycles	Used to isolate faulty chips	No	Yes
Unibus adaptor	Parity on data paths and Unibus map	Provides faulty chip isolation; transients tolerated by retry	No	Yes
Massbus	Data and control bus lines parity	Provides faulty chip isolation; transients tolerated by retry	No	Yes
Watchdog timer	In LSI-11 console processor	Detects hung machine and allows automatic restart	No	No
Clock margining	Change clock speed	Aids isolation of timing problems	No	Yes
Maintenance registers	SBI fault/status	Aids fault isolation	No	Yes
	SBI silo comparator			
	SBI error			
	SBI time-out address			
	SBI maintenance buffer			
	Translation parity			
Visibility bus	Internal signals made available to the console or microdiagnostics	Aids fault isolation	No	Yes
Remote diagnostic module	Load/examine critical machine registers	Provides remote, expert trouble-shooting	No	Yes
	Single-step sequencer			
	Clock margining			
	Error status registers readable over ID bus			
	Access to visibility bus			
	Microdiagnostics loadable into writable control store			

disk and executed, the error log can be examined, memory locations deposited or examined, and so on. If the diagnostic disk is not operable, the diagnostics can be loaded from the console subsystem mass storage device or downline-loaded over the phone. The DC will attempt to isolate the failure to a subsystem. If the CPU is faulty, the diagnostic on the console subsystem mass storage device would be executed to verify the CPU status.

The DC would advise the local field service office as to the failing subsystem. Upon arrival at the customer's site, field service would replace the faulty board and reverify the system. If the failing subsystem were the CPU, microdiagnostics would be loaded into the writable control store.

RD has at least three major advantages: (1) faster mean time to repair (MTTR), especially when the problem is of a trivial nature and can be resolved over the remote diagnostic link; (2) faster resolution of difficult problems, because the person at the DC is an expert in VAX system fault determination; and (3) greater certainty that the repair person is sent to the site with the correct part in hand.

All diagnostics can be run either at the site or remotely. There is a "building block" approach. First, the console subsystem verifies its own operation. Then the system hardcore (CPU, backplane interconnect, and memory controller) is checked by loading microdiagnostics into the writable control store. Macro-level tests on the I/O bus adapters and peripheral controllers are next run, followed by peripheral device diagnostics.

Functional-level tests, that is, isolation to the failing major unit, can generally be performed on-line with the operating system. Field-replaceable units can then be determined by stand-alone fault-isolation diagnostics. Automatic on-line error logging is an integral part of every VAX system. A snapshop of the system is taken upon a CPU, memory, I/O, or software error.

Table 6.3.1 lists the RAMP features common to different VAX implementations. The benefit of each feature is listed as well as an indication of whether the feature improves mean time to failure (MTTF) and/or MTTR. Table 6.3.2 continues the list of RAMP-related-model specific features for the VAX-11/780. More details can be found in Chapter 8 of [SIEW82c].

6.3.2. IBM S/360-SI/370-4300 Family

Table 6.3.3 depicts the evolution of IBM's maintenance strategy. Techniques are listed for a representative machine from each major era. The techniques can be loosely grouped into three major areas: internal hardware error-detection circuits, diagnostics (including software and microcode), and display (e.g., lights, error logs, tracing, etc.). The IBM strategy has evolved from *failure recreate* to *failure capture*. Prior to the S/370, the IBM customer engineer attempted to recreate the failure by rerunning diagnostics, sometimes in conjunction with varying voltage and clock frequency, until the failure reoccurred. The system was placed in a tight programmed loop to produce a continuous failure condition for analysis. In failure capture, hardware circuits detect errors, and information about the current status of the machine state is logged for

TABLE 6.3.3 EVOLUTION IN IBM'S MAINTENANCE STRATEGY

Machine	Era	Techniques
650	Late 1950s	Six internal checkers Stand-alone diagnostics on punched cards Light and switch panel
1401	Early 1960s	20 internal checkers Stand-alone diagnostics Light and switch panel
S/360-50	Mid 1960s	75 internal checkers OLTEP (Online Test Executive Program) Microdiagnostics Log fault data to main memory; EREP (Error Recording and Edit Program) for outputting logged data Maintenance panel
370/168 Mod 3	Early 1970s	Error-detection circuits OLTEP Microdiagnostics for fault isolation Service processor, including trace unit—trace up to 199 fixed and 8 movable logic points over 32 machine cycles for intermittent or environmental faults
303X	Mid 1970s	Error-detection circuits OLTS (Online Functional Tests) Console and processor microdiagnostics EREP Scope loops Support processor, including trace and remote (telephone) access to log data and trace information
4341	Late 1970s	Error-detection circuits 25,000 shadow latches Support processor—error logging and environmental monitoring

subsequent analysis. A historical perspective on IBM reliability, availability, and serviceability (RAS) is provided in [HSIA81].

Droulette [DROU71] describes in detail the RAS features of the IBM System/360–System/370. The goal is high availability with minimized impact of failures. Four stages of corrective action are identified, each with successively larger impact on users; transparent recovery (e.g., instruction retry, I/O retry, retrieve fresh copy from secondary storage), one user affected (e.g., selective termination of task executing at time of error), multiple users affected (e.g., reinitialize system), and down (e.g., repair activity required). The successively higher severity stage recovery structure is common in systems with high-availability goals or in real-time data processing environments where temporary loss of data is tolerable.

Table 6.3.4 illustrates the features in the IBM 4300 series. The hardware error-detection, error-correction, and error-monitoring circuits described in Table 6.3.4 are used in the following maintenance scenario. The support processor displays a diagnostic code. A customer engineer is called. Upon arriving, the customer engineer examines the error information on the system diskette, executes diagnostics from the system diskette, and uses the support processor to monitor results. If the customer engineer requires further information, he or she can telephone a central data base (called RETAIN) with the latest service aids and failure data from other sites. A field technical support center specialist can use the telephone link to monitor remotely and/or control diagnostics on the 4341.

TABLE 6.3.4   IBM 4300 SERIES RAS

Error-detection/correction circuits
  Single-bit error correction/double-bit error detection in main memory.
  Data path parity.
  Store and fetch memory access protection
  Instruction retry (4341 only). On an error, processor performs a retry and, if unsuccessful, loads the machine check interrupt. Options include hardstop on error, no retry (but log-out), disable error report, and stop after log-out. During instruction execution, data in certain machine facilities are saved. Prior to instruction reexecution these data are restored.
  Disk error correction.
  I/O retry at both processor and disk controller level.
  Peripheral unit power-off signal (4341 only).
  Disk self-test.
  Voltage margin under program control.
  Relocatable control storage.
  Level-sensitive scan design (LSSD).
  Microdiagnostic location to field-replaceable unit (FRU) 80% of time.
  Halt or trace on address or data match comparisons can be made on any reference, I/O reference, data store, or instruction fetch.
Support processor
  Separately powered.
  Separate system diskette for microcode loading, system error logging, and storage of microdiagnostics.
  Sensors for monitoring of power variances, temperature fluctuations, and electrostatic discharge (4341 only).
  For both retriable and unretriable errors, the support processor performs an internal log-out. Each log-out has an identifier used to specify the number of log-outs to date.
  Support processor-generated eight-digit reference code guide to failing unit. Reference code logged on diskette and display console.
  Display console and data link functions for remote support facility (RSF).
Remote support facility
  Remote monitoring (especially of error registers) and control.
  Remote initiation of diagnostics.
  Remote examination of error log on system diskette.
  Distribute microcode updates.

6.3.3. Sperry Univac 1100/60

Since the introduction of the Sperry Univac 1108 in 1965, the Sperry Univac 1100 series has continued to evolve. ARM (availability, reliability, and maintainability) at Univac emphasizes on-line error detection and has been incrementally enhanced with:

Parity on main memory and processor general registers

Parity on I/O channels and I/O controllers

Parity on cache

ECC on main memory

Maintenance panel

Maintenance controller using scan compare to allow comparison of processor state after each clock cycle to known correct data on magnetic tape

Maintenance processor to read/write CPU registers

As Table 6.3.5 and Fig. 6.3.2 indicate, parity on multibit logic and duplication of random logic are the primary error-detection techniques employed in the 1100/60. Based on the assumption that most errors are transients, recovery consists primarily of retry (Table 6.3.6). Rather than attempt a number of retries immediately after an error is detected, the 1100/60 pauses so that the source of a transient (e.g., power supply instability, etc.) dies out. The pause can be from 5 ms to 5 s in 1-ms increments. The pause value is set to cope with site-dependent conditions. If repeated retries are unsuccessful, the maintenance processor in multiprocessor configuration can read the program state (i.e., registers) in the faulty processor and transplant the state into another processor in a software/user transparent manner. The error-detection logic composes 15% of the total CPU logic.

TABLE 6.3.5 ERROR-DETECTION HARDWARE
IN THE UNIVAC 1100/60

Memory
    Double error-detecting code on memory data
    Parity on address and control information

Cache: parity on data, address, and control information

I/O unit: parity on data and control

CPU
    Parity on data paths
    Parity on control store
    Duplication and comparison of control logic

Hard failures are tolerated in main memory through ECC, in cache through performance degradation, and in the writable control store by retrieving the microinstruction from a backup storage device and by inverting the bits if required for a bit to match a stuck-at value.

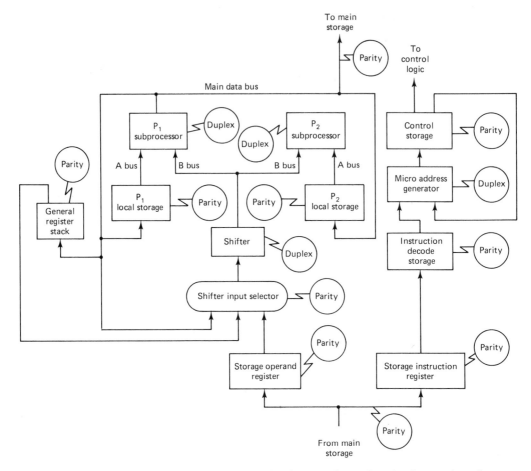

Figure 6.3.2   Block diagram of the 1100/60 microexecution section, showing sample applications of fault-detection techniques. (Adapted from [BOON80].)

TABLE 6.3.6   ERROR RECOVERY IN THE UNIVAC 1100/60

Memory
   Single error-correction code on data
   Retry on address or control information parity error
Cache
   Retry on address or control information parity error
   Disable portions of cache on data parity errors
I/O unit: Retry on data or control parity errors
CPU
   Retry on control store parity error
   Invert sense of control store
   Macroinstruction retry

An integral part of the 1100/60 ARM philosphy is the system support processor (SSP). The SSP combines many of the features of the IBM 4341 support processor and the VAX-11/780 console subsystem. With the advent of low-cost microprocessors, it became cost-effective to concentrate into a support processor the functionality that was traditionally provided by front-console switches and maintenance panels. Once the basic functionality was provided for system control, expansion to ARM functionality naturally followed. A support processor typically consists of a 50K- to 100K-instruction per second processor, a small amount of nonvolatile ROM (e.g., 4K words), RAM (up to 256K words), secondary storage (i.e., floppy disk), remote access port, and interfaces to buses and control signals internal to the CPU. Table 6.3.7 lists some of the functionality associated with support processors [KUNS80].

TABLE 6.3.7 USES OF SUPPORT PROCESSORS

System console
System boot
System quick test of boot path
Error logger
Diagnostic tool
    Microdiagnostics
    Scan/set/compare internal state
    Fault injection
    Remote diagnosis
Error recovery
    Writable control store reload
    Transplant state to another processor
    Reconfiguration

The 1100/60 has an automatic error log, a built-in logic analyzer, and programmable power supplies for margin testing. More information can be found in [BOON80].

6.4. HIGH-AVAILABILITY SYSTEMS

6.4.1. Tandem

Tandem Computers, Inc., was founded in 1974 for the purpose of building high-availability computer systems for commercial transaction processing. The Tandem 16 is the first commercially available, modularly expandable system designed specifically for high availability. Design objectives for the system included:

- "Nonstop" operation wherein failures are detected, components reconfigured out of service, and repaired components configured back into the system without stopping the other system components.

- No single hardware failure can compromise the data integrity of the system.
- Modular system expansion through adding more processing power, memory, and peripherals without affecting applications software.

Tandem is composed of up to 16 computers interconnected by two message-oriented Dynabuses as depicted in Fig. 6.4.1. Figure 6.4.1 uses the PMS (processor, memory, switch) notation of [SIEW82a]. A loosely coupled architecture was selected over a tightly coupled, shared-memory architecture since it was felt that the former allowed for more complete fault containment. Built-in hardware includes

> Check sums on Dynabus messages
> Parity on data paths
> Error-correcting code memory
> Watchdog timers

All I/O device controllers are dual-ported so that they can be accessed by an alternate path in case of processor or I/O failure. For more details, see [KATZ77].

Upon this hardware structure, the software builds a process-oriented system with all communications handled as messages. This abstraction allows blurring of the physical boundaries between processors and peripherals. Any I/O device or resource in the system can be accessed by a process, no matter where the resource and process reside.

Data integrity is maintained through the mechanisms of I/O *process pairs*. One I/O process is designated as primary, the other as backup. All file modification messages are delivered to the primary I/O process. The primary sends a message with checkpoint information to the backup so that it can take over if the primary's processor or access path to the I/O device fails. Files can also be duplicated on physically distinct devices controlled by an I/O process pair on physically distinct processors. All file modification messages are delivered to both I/O processes. Thus, in the case of physical failure or isolation of the primary, the backup file is up to date and available.

Consider an example given in [BART81] of I/O process pairs as depicted in Fig. 6.4.2. Initially, all sequence numbers (SeqNo) are set to zero. The requester sends a request to the server. If the sequence number is less than the server's local copy, a failure has occurred and the status of the completed operation is returned. Note that the requested operation is done only once. Next, the operation is performed and a checkpoint of the request is sent to the server backup. The disk is written, the sequence number incremented to one, and the results checkpointed to the server backup, which also increments its sequence number. The results are returned from the server to the requester. Finally, the results are checkpointed to the requester backup, which also increments its sequence number. Now consider failures. If either backup fails, the operation completes successfully. If the requester fails after the request has been made, the server will complete the operation but be unable to return the result. When the requester backup becomes active, it will repeat the request. Since its sequence number is zero, the server test at step 2 will return the result without performing the

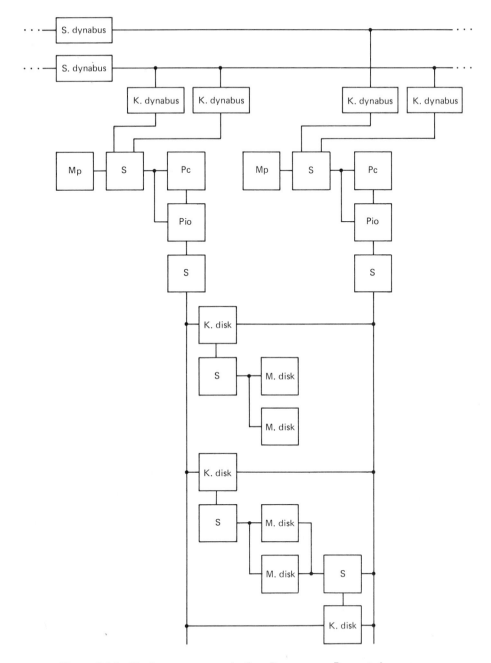

Figure 6.4.1 Tandem system organization. P, processor; Pc, central processor; Pio, I/O processor; M, memory; Mp, primary memory; S, switch; K, control.

Step	Requester SeqNo = 0	Requester Backup SeqNo = 0	Server SeqNo = 0	Server Backup SeqNo = 0
1	Issue request to write record ————		————————→	
2			If SeqNo < MySeqNo, then return saved status	
3			Otherwise, read disk, perform ——→ operation, check-point request	Saves request
4			Write to disk SeqNo = 1 ————→ checkpoint result	Saves result SeqNo = 1
5	←————		—Return results	
6	Checkpoint results ——→	SeqNo = 1		

Figure 6.4.2 Sample process-pair transactions.

operation again. Finally, if the server fails, the server backup either does nothing or completes the operation using checkpointed information. When the requester resends the request, the new server (i.e., the old server backup) either performs the operation or returns the saved results.

User applications can also use the process-pair mechanism. Consider "nonstop" application program A in Fig. 6.4.3. Program A starts up a backup process Ab in another processor. There are also duplicate file images, one designated primary and the other backup. Program A periodically (at user specified points) sends checkpoint information to Ab. Ab is the same program as A but it knows that it is a backup program. Ab reads checkpoint messages to update its data area, file status, and program counter. Ab loads and executes if the system reports that A's processor is down (i.e., error message sent from A's operating system image or A's processor fails to respond to a periodic "I'm alive" message). All file activity by A is performed on both the primary and backup file copies. When Ab starts to execute from the last checkpoint, it may attempt to repeat I/O operations successfully completed by A. The system file handler will recognize this situation and send Ab a successfully completed I/O message. Ab periodically asks the operating system if a backup process exists. Since one no longer does, it can request the creation and initialization of a copy of both

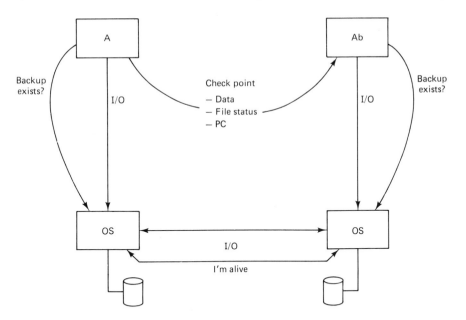

Figure 6.4.3 Shadow processor in tandem.

the process and file structure. More information on the operating system and the programming of nonstop applications can be found in [BART78].

Maintenance is the key to restoring redundant operation. The longer a repair action takes, the more likely that a second failure will bring the system down. To minimize maintenance time, Tandem averages one field support person for each customer. A remote diagnostics system provides more expert backup for the customer.

Networking software exists that allows up to 255 geographically dispersed Tandem systems to be interconnected. Tandem applications have included order entry, hospital records, bank transactions, library transactions, semiconductor manufacturing, airline systems, and inventory systems. By the end of 1981, over 1500 Tandem processors had been installed for 460 customers.

6.4.2. Pluribus

Pluribus was conceived in 1972 by Bolt, Beranek and Newman (BBN) as a modular, highly available multiprocessor for the ARPAnet IMP (interface message processor) task. As depicted in Fig. 6.4.4 the system is composed of three types of buses: processor, memory, and I/O. Memory, processors, and bus arbiters are off-the-shelf components without modification. Up to two CPUs with their own local memory occupy a processor bus. Shared memory and I/O devices reside on separate buses. Communications between buses are via "bus couplers." Each bus coupler can map part of the address space on one bus to physical addresses on another bus. Any number of processors, shared memories, and I/O buses can be interconnected via bus couplers.

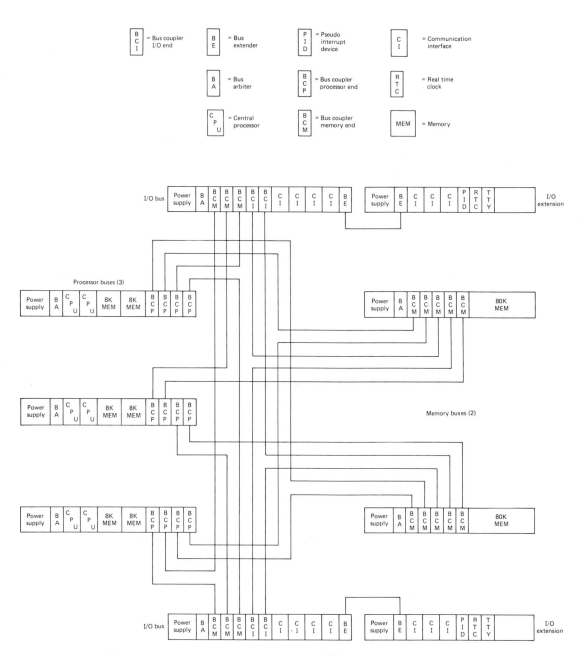

Figure 6.4.4 Logical organization of a typical Phiribus system, showing interconnections of the distributed switch (bus coupler) structure. (Adapted from [KATS78].)

The local memory acts as cache for code and temporary data. The shared memory is used for shared system data, interprocess communications, redundant copies of local code, and less frequently used system code.

Interprocessor control is via a special set of registers in the I/O address space. A processor accesses these registers on another processor's bus by establishing a path via an I/O bus consisting of a forward path through an I/O bus coupler and a backward path through the target processor's I/O bus coupler.

The major form of interprocess communication is via the pseudo-interrupt device (PID). The PID is a hardware priority queue that exists on the I/O bus. When polled by a processor the PID returns the highest-priority number in the queue and deletes the number. The PIDs are typically used to schedule processes. Each number corresponds to a process that can be run on any processor. I/O devices (upon completion of an operation) or processes can enter numbers into the PID. Thus, in a dedicated, special-purpose application, the PID eliminates the overhead in context swapping and scheduling associated with interrupts and system monitor calls. In order to work in a real-time application, however, the system's programmer has to ensure that the PID is polled frequently enough that no I/O information is lost. In the IMP application the highest-speed device has to be serviced within 400 μs of its request. Since the worst case would be when all processors simultaneously started executing a new task, the code is divided into strips. Each strip represents a task that, once started, runs to completion. There is no temporary context between tasks. Each strip requires at most 300 μs to execute, ensuring the necessary frequency of PID interrogation.

Division of an application into strips places a significant burden on the application programmer. The interprocessor communication mechanisms would have to be rethought if the Pluribus were to be used in a general-purpose environment. More details on Pluribus can be found in [KATS78].

Most of the Pluribus fault tolerance is achieved at the software task level. A relatively long period between fault occurrence and fault detection was acceptable due to the nature of the IMP task. The several levels of protocol in the ARPAnet, each with its own error detection and recovery, means that the Pluribus need not concentrate on data integrity. If a failure in a Pluribus occurred, all the in-progress messages would be buffered at other ARPAnet nodes until positively acknowledged. These messages would eventually be rerouted past the failed Pluribus. Even if the subnet protocol failed to complete the message transmission reliably, the host-to-host protocol would retry the entire message transmission.

Thus the application required only that the Pluribus recover gracefully from a failure. This goal can be achieved by quick system reinitialization with omission of questionable components. The Pluribus IMP software utilizes:

Periodic software checks, including diagnostics

Redundancy in data structures

Watchdog timers that must constantly be reset by software.

The multiprocessor structure allows for maximum performance when there are no failures (i.e., the periodic checks are estimated to degrade performance by only 1%) and maximum assistance when there are failures (i.e., by focusing all resources on reaching a consensus on a failure-free configuration).

The network structure allows for remote diagnosis from the network control center (NCC). Even in the case of total destruction of memory contents, the Pluribus can request the code be transmitted from the NCC or other Pluribuses in the network. Any transitory messages lost will be restored via the retransmission mechanism in the various levels of protocol.

It is well known that the best system diagnostic is the normal execution of programs. Frequently, normal execution will stress the system in ways not reproduced by diagnostics (this is especially true for I/O or timing-sensitive problems). The "friendly" environment provided by the IMP application allows the Pluribus to rotate hardware into use. Any problematic hardware will only appear as a transient to the system since the offender will quickly be configured out.

The Pluribus represents a cost-effective fault-tolerant architecture that takes fullest advantage of the characteristics of its application environment (i.e., real-time applications where data loss and brief outages are tolerable). The Pluribus is operational in the ARPAnet and has achieved a measured factor-of-5 improvement in unavailability (0.32%) over previous-generation IMPs (1.64%) [KLEI74].

6.4.3. ESS Processors

The electronic switching systems (ESSs) developed by Bell Telephone Laboratories over the last two decades are the most numerous fault-tolerant digital systems. The ESSs handle routing of telephone calls through central offices. They have an aggressive availability goal: 2 hours downtime in 40 years (i.e., 3 minutes per year) with less than 0.01% of the calls handled incorrectly.

The Bell System has collected data on the historic trends of causes of system downtime [TOY78]. Twenty percent is attributed to hardware. Good diagnostics and trouble-location programs can help minimize hardware-induced downtime. Fifteen percent was attributed to software. Software deficiencies included improper translation of algorithms into code or improper specifications. Thirty-five percent of downtime was attributed to recovery deficiencies. These deficiencies can be caused by undetected faults or incorrect fault isolation. The remaining 30% is attributed to human procedural error.

Telephone switching has many properties in common with the Pluribus ARPAnet IMP application's real-time routing of information. There is some natural redundancy in the network and in the data (i.e., a telephone user will redial if he or she gets a wrong number or is disconnected). However, there is a user aggravation level that must be avoided: users will redial as long as it does not happen too frequently. Note, however, that the thresholds are different for failure to establish a call (moderately high) and disconnection of an established call (very low). Thus a staged failure recovery process is followed, as depicted in Table 6.4.1.

TABLE 6.4.1   LEVELS OF RECOVERY IN AN ESS SYSTEM

Phase	Recovery action	Effect
1	Initialize specific transient memory	Affects temporary storage; no calls lost
2	Reconfigure peripheral hardware; initialize all transient memory	Lose calls in process of being established; calls in progress not lost
3	Verify memory operation, establish a workable processor configuration; verify program, configure peripheral hardware; initalize all transient memory	Lose calls in process of being established; calls in progress not affected
4	Establish a workable processor configuration; configure peripheral hardware; initialize all memory	All calls lost

A substantial portion of the complexity of an ESS system is in the peripheral hardware. Since the telephone switching application leads to a substantially different organization from general-purpose computers, a brief description of a typical system will be given. More details can be found in [KULZ77].

Figure 6.4.5 depicts a typical long-distance ESS office. Various types of analog and digital telephone trunks enter the office. A transmission interface converts the different types of signals into 8-bit pulse-code-modulated (PCM) signals that are used in the time-space-time (TST) switch. The information received over one line is retransmitted over another line after routing via interchanging of time slots (time portion of TST), switching of buses (space portion of TST), and interchanging of time slots. The information is changed back to analog or digital signals by the transmission interface.

Signal processors scan the telephone trunks for any change in status, thus relieving the central control (CC) of this simple but time-consuming task. An interoffice signaling channel provides an independent channel (in addition to the telephone trunks) over which ESS offices communicate.

Finally, the central control provides overall system control, administration, call processing, and system maintenance. System maintenance includes automatic isolation of faulty units, defensive software strategies, and support for rapid repair. The CC instructions reside in the program store (PS) while transient information (e.g., telephone calls, routing, equipment configuration) is held in the call store (CS). The auxiliary unit (AU) bus interfaces to disk and magnetic tape mass storage.

The primary redundancy technique employed in the ESS processors for tolerating failures has been duplication. Figure 6.4.6 illustrates a system with duplicate CC, CS, PS, and their associated buses. Assuming that only one of each component is required for a functional system, there are 64 possible system configurations.

Duplication can be used not only for toleration of hard failures but also for error detection, provided that both units are executing in synchronization and there is a

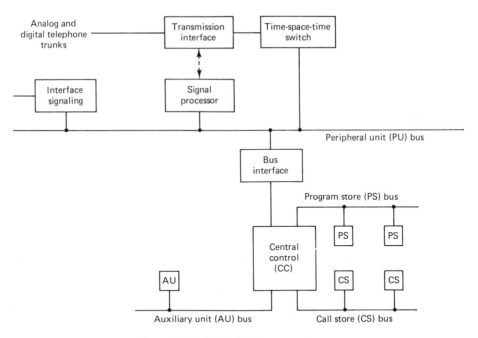

Figure 6.4.5 Typical ESS system diagram.

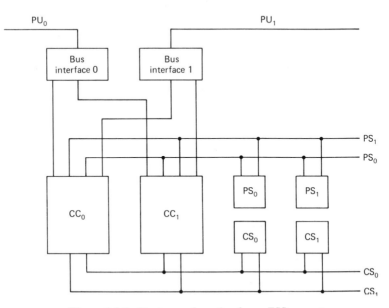

Figure 6.4.6 Duplex configuration for an ESS computer.

mechanism for matching their results. A historical summary of the ESS systems is given in Table 6.4.2 together with the processors used in each system.

Table 6.4.3 sketches the attributes of the ESS processor family, which are summarized below. The No. 1 ESS processor was the initial proving ground for the duplicate-and-match philosophy. It can be shown that the mean time to failure (MTTF) of a duplex computer, where only one computer has to work for the system to be working and where the switchover upon failure to a simplex computer is assumed perfect, is

$$MTTF = \frac{\mu}{2\lambda^2}$$

where λ is the failure rate of a computer and μ is the repair rate. The No. 1 ESS processor was specified to handle up to 65,000 telephone lines in a large metropolitan telephone office. This requirement led to a relatively large, 12,000-gate processor built from diode transistor logic. The failure rate of the No. 1 ESS processor was too large to meet the MTTF goal. Thus the system was divided into six subsystems, as depicted in Fig. 6.4.6: peripheral unit (PU), central control (CC), call store (CS), program store (PS), call store bus (CSB), and program store bus (PSB). If the failure rate for subsystems is identical, the mean time to failure is approximated by

$$MTTF = \frac{6\mu}{2\lambda^2}$$

where λ is the failure rate of the entire computer and μ is the repair rate. For a constant λ and μ, the division into subsystems has improved MTTF by a factor of 6. The major form of fault detection and location in the central computer is duplication and matching. Both CCs operate in synchronism. Two matched circuits compare 24 bits of internal state during each 5.5-μs machine cycle. There are six different sets of internal nodes that can be monitored, depending on the instruction being executed. A mismatch generates an interrupt which calls fault recognition programs to determine which half of the system is faulty. Information can be sampled by the matchers and retained for later examination by diagnostic programs. The program store employs a Hamming code on the 37 data bits. There is also parity over address plus data. The call store has one parity bit on address and data and another parity bit just on address. Both the program store and call store automatically retry operations upon error detection.

After a fault has been detected, the system configuration logic attempts to establish various combinations of subunits. First a configuration is established and a sanity timer started. A sanity program is then executed. The sanity program is similar to a maze that the hardware must transverse before the sanity timer times out. If a time-out occurs, the reconfiguration logic generates a new configuration to be tried.

The No. 2 ESS processor computer was specified to handle 1000 to 10,000 telephone lines. Due to its smaller size, cost was more of an issue than in the ESS-1 system design. Thus there was only one subsystem composed of central computer,

TABLE 6.4.2 SUMMARY OF INSTALLED ESS SYSTEMS

System	Number of connected telephone lines	Year introduced	Number installed	Processor used in system	Comments
ESS–1	5000–65,000	1965	1000	No. 1 ESS	First digital processor; it had separate control and data memories
ESS–2	1000–10,000	1969	500	No. 2 ESS	
ESS–1A	100,000	1976		No. 1A ESS	Four to eight times faster than No. 1 processor
ESS–2B	1000–20,000	1975	500	No. 3A ESS	Combined control and data store.
ESS–3	500–5000	1976		No. 3A ESS	Microcoded, emulates No. 2 processor

TABLE 6.4.3 SUMMARY OF ESS PROCESSORS

Processor	Year introduced	Complexity (gates)	Unit of switching	Matching	Other error detection/correction
No. 1	1965	12,000	PS, CS, CC, buses	Six internal nodes, 24 bits per node; one node matched each machine cycle; node selected to be matched dependent on instruction being executed	Hamming code on PS Parity on CS Automatic retry on CS, PS Watchdog timer Sanity program to determine if reorganization lead to a valid configuration
No. 2	1969	5,000	Entire computer	Single match point on call store input	Diagnostic programs Parity on PS Detection of multiword accesses in CS Watchdog timer
No. 1A	1976	50,000	PS, CS, CC, buses	16 internal nodes, 24 bits per node; four nodes matched each machine cycle	Two parity bits on PS Roving spares (i.e., contents of PS not completely duplicated, can be loaded from disk upon error detection) Two parity bits on CS Roving spares sufficient for complete duplication of transient data Processor configuration circuit to search automatically for a valid configuration
No. 3A	1975	16,500	Entire computer	None	On-line processor writes into both stores m-of-$2m$ code on microstore plus parity Self-checking decoders Two parity bits on registers Duplication of ALU Watchdog timer Maintenance channel for observability and controllability of the other processor 25% of logic devoted to self-checking logic and 14% to maintenance access.

program store, call store, and appropriate buses. The design required 5000 gates of resistor–transistor logic. Only one point, the input to the call store, was matched. Thus it might take 10 to 100 μs for an internal error to manifest itself as a mismatch. Upon mismatch the on-line processor runs error-detection programs in an attempt to locate a hard failure. If the failure is detected, control passes to the standby processor. Program store is 22 bits wide and is protected by parity. Program words have odd parity, while data words have even parity. Thus any attempt to execute data as program would be detected. In addition, logic circuits detected multiword accesses. The control store was 16 bits wide and employed no error-detection codes. A watchdog timer was also employed for error detection. The watchdog timer would be set at various places in the program flow. If an error occurred, the chances are that the program would not be able to reset the watchdog timer before it zeroed.

The No. 1A processor was meant to be replacement for the No. 1 ESS in large offices. It was used in the 1A ESS and 4 ESS systems. Constructed from bipolar, small-scale integration, it was from four to eight times faster than the No. 1 ESS processor. The program store was now in read-write memory with a disk for backup. There were two matched circuits which compared 24 bits each 700-ns machine cycle. There were 16 internal nodes, four of which were matched every machine cycle. The 24-bit-wide program store was protected by two parity bits. Program store was not fully duplicated. Instead, two 64,000-word blocks of memory were used as roving spares. Backup disk storage made it possible to regenerate information in the failed unit. The two parity bits were interlaced so that double adjacent errors were detected. The call store contained transient data which would be difficult to regenerate. Thus the call store was duplicated and protected by two parity bits. There was separate processor configuration hardware in each central computer. Upon a time-out of a timer, the system would be reset, initialized, and reconfigured.

The No. 3A processor was designed to handle 500 to 5000 telephone lines in low-cost applications. The central control was microprogrammed and the No. 3A could emulate the No. 2 ESS. The call store and program store were combined in one main memory with an access time of 1 μs (this is to be compared to the 6-μs access time in the No. 1 ESS). The entire system was duplicated. However, there was no matching operation. Instead, self-checking circuits were used to detect and isolate failures. This led to improved diagnostics over previous ESS designs. The standby processor would be halted, but its memory would be updated on writes. Parity errors on reads would automatically switch to the other main memory. An internally detected error would cause switching to the standby processor. Approximately 25% of the 16,500 gates in the No. 3A ESS processor were devoted to self-checking circuits.

Table 6.4.3 summarizes the attributes of the ESS processor family. More details can be found in [TOY78].

6.4.4. Intel 432

The Intel 432 is a modular architecture in which performance and/or reliability can be incrementally improved. The basic hardware organization of the 432 is shown in Fig.

6.4.7. The central system is composed of three different module types: an interface processor (IP), a generalized data processor (GDP), and a memory. These modules are connected together via a packet bus. The GDP module is the central processing unit in the machine. It provides the basic computation power of the 432 with a capability-based logical addressing structure to provide a secure software run-time environment. For a complete description of the processor architecture, see [INTE81]. The GDP module is composed of the processor and an interface (e.g., BIU) between the local processor bus and the system-wide packet bus. The IP module provides an interface between an independent I/O system and the central 432 system. The IP is responsible for managing all I/O traffic and providing a protected, capability-based interface into the central system. The IP module contains the processor, the interface to the I/O system, and the interface between the local processor bus and the system-wide packet bus. The memory module provides control of a dynamic RAM memory array and an interface on to the packet bus.

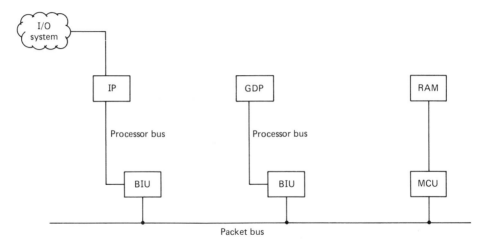

Figure 6.4.7   Basic 432 hardware organization. GDP, generalized data processor; IP, interface processor; BIU, bus interface unit; MCU, memory control unit.

The packet bus provides a high-speed central system communications channel. The bus is a message-based multiprocessor bus, composed of 16 data, 3 control, and 3 arbitration lines. A variable number of bytes can be transmitted as a function of bus transaction type. The bus not only supports processor-to-memory transfers, but also supports transfers directly between modules (e.g., processor to processor). The packet bus is the only intermodule communications channel. There are no interrupts or any other independent signals between modules.

Figure 6.4.8 illustrates how a 432 system can be expanded to provide increased processing and I/O power as well as increased memory space and communication bandwidth. The expansion is achieved solely through VLSI chip replication and is totally transparent to the software system.

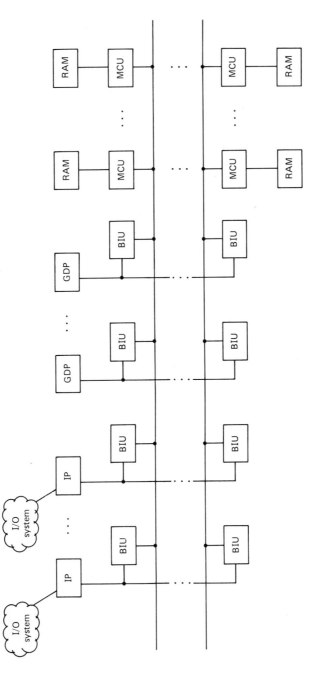

Figure 6.4.8 Expanded 432 configuration.

Error detection mechanisms are separated into four distinct categories based on the type of operation they are designed to cover.

Transfer of information: Information flow is covered by either 2-bit odd/even interlaced parity or duplication.

Storage of information: A Hamming code over the 32 bits of data storage plus the address of the storage location detects and corrects errors.

Transformation of information: Whenever data undergo transformation in the 432 system, error detection is available by complete duplication. Additional circuitry, also duplicated, is used to compare results. Figure 6.4.9 illustrates the concepts behind functional redundancy checking (FRC). One of the pair is selected as master, the other as checker. The master has its comparison logic disabled and is responsible for carrying out normal operation. The checker disables its outputs and monitors the outputs of the master. The checker is responsible for duplicating the operation of the master and using its comparison circuitry to detect any inconsistency.

Protocols: Each bus is provided with a time-out to protect against errors in the bus protocol.

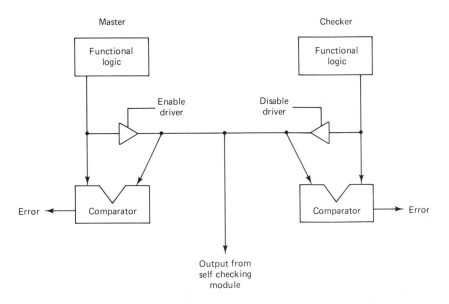

Figure 6.4.9   Functional redundancy checking.

Figure 6.4.10 depicts a multiprocessor 432 system with resources dedicated to providing fault detection. More details can be found in [SIEW82b].

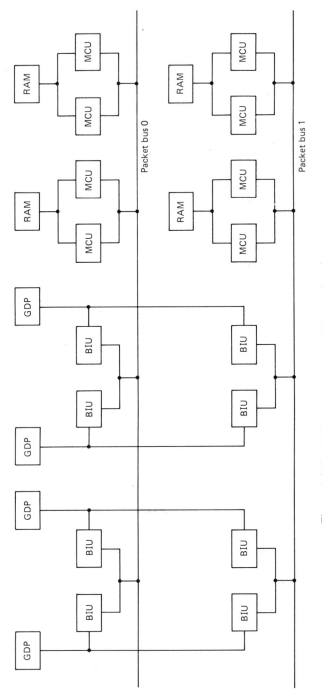

Figure 6.4.10 Multiprocessor system with error detection.

6.5. LONG-LIFE SYSTEMS

6.5.1. Spacecraft Systems

Spacecraft are the primary example of systems requiring long periods of unattended operation. Unlike most other applications, spacecraft must directly control their environment, including electrical power, temperature, and even stability. Thus one must treat all aspects of a spacecraft (e.g., structural, propulsion, power, analog, and digital) when designing for reliability.

Spacecraft missions cover a range from simple (e.g., weather satellites in low earth orbit) to sophisticated (e.g., deep-space planetary probes passing through uncharted environments). Some points in the range are low-earth-orbit sensing, low-earth-orbit communications or navigation, low-earth-orbit scientific, synchronous-orbit communication, and deep-space scientific. For nondemanding missions, system reliability goals are met through reducing complexity and simplicity of design. Before examining the reliability techniques used for more demanding missions, let us first explore an archetypical spacecraft.

A typical spacecraft can be divided into five subsystems:

Propulsion: This system provides the means for controlling the stability and orientation (e.g., attitude) of the spacecraft. Multiple, often redundant, chemical or pressurized gas thrusters are used most frequently. Occasionally, spacecraft employ a spin for stability instead of the active control implied by thrusters.

Power: The generation and storage of electrical energy must be closely monitored and controlled since all other spacecraft systems rely on electricity to operate. Most often, spacecraft electrical systems are composed of solar cells and battery storage. The batteries are used to ride through loss of sun or loss of orientation periods. Control of solar cell orientation, battery charging, power transients, and temperature is the most frequent, time-consuming task for the spacecraft computers.

Data communications: Communications is divided into three, often physically distinct, channels. The first is commands from the ground to the spacecraft over the uplink. It is even possible to reprogram a spacecraft computer over the uplink. The other two channels are from the spacecraft to the ground (e.g., downlinks). One downlink carries data from the satellite payload and the second carries telemetry data about the spacecraft subsystems (e.g., temperature, power supply state, thruster events, etc.).

Attitude control: A dedicated computer is often used to sense and control the orientation and stability of the spacecraft.

Command, control, payload: All aspects of spacecraft control are usually centered in a single command/control computer. This computer is also the focus for recovery from error events. Recovery may be automatic or under control from the ground via uplink commands.

Typically, each of these five subsystems is composed of a string of elements. Table 6.5.1 depicts seven stages in a representative power subsystem. Solar panels are physically oriented by tracking motors. Power is delivered to the spacecraft via slip rings (such as those used on the armature of motors). A charge controller automatically keeps the batteries at full potential. A power regulator smooths out voltage fluctuations while a power distributor controls the load connected to the power subsystem. At each stage in the string, redundancy is used to tolerate anticipated fault modes. To save complexity, the output of a string is usually all that is reported via telemetry.

A typical maintenance procedure would be as follows. When a failure has been detected, the spacecraft automatically enters a "safe" or "hold" mode. All nonessential loads on the power subsystem are shed. Normal mission sequencing and solar array tracking are stopped. The spacecraft is oriented to obtain maximum solar power. Meanwhile, the ground personnel must infer what possible failures could cause the output behavior of each of the strings. A possible failure scenario is selected as most likely and a reconfiguration (e.g., "work around") of the spacecraft subsystems devised. A command sequence implementing the "work around" is sent to the satellite. Depending on the severity of the failure, this entire procedure may take days, or even weeks, to complete.

Spacecraft fault responses vary from automatic in hardware for critical faults (e.g., power, clocks, and computer), to on-board software for serious faults (e.g., attitude and command subsystems), to ground intervention for noncritical faults. Faults can be detected by one of several means:

Self-tests: Subsystem fails self-test, such as checksums on computer memories.

Cross-checking between units: Either physical or functional redundancy may be used. When a unit is physically duplicated, one is declared on-line and the other as monitor. The monitor checks all the outputs of the on-line unit. Alternatively, there may be disjoint units capable of performing the same function. For example, there is usually a set of sensors and actuators for precision attitude control. Attitude may also be less precisely sensed by instruments with other primary functions. The less precise calculation can be used as a sanity check on the more precise units.

Ground-initiated special tests: These are used to diagnose and isolate failures.

Ground trend analysis: Routine processing and analysis of telemetry detects long-term trends in units that degrade or wear out.

6.5.2. Voyager

Table 6.5.2 depicts the major features of each spacecraft subsystem for JPL's Voyager. Voyager is a deep-space probe used in the Jupiter and Saturn planetary fly-bys [JONE79].

Figure 6.5.1 displays the interconnection of subsystems on the Voyager spacecraft. Standby redundancy is used in all but the sensor payload. The standby spares are "cross-strapped" so that either unit can be switched in to communicate with other

TABLE 6.5.1 TYPICAL POWER SUBSYSTEM

Element	Tracking solar array	Solar array drive	Slip-ring assembly	Charge controller	Batteries	Power Regulation	Power Distribution
Redundancy	Extra capacity Series/parallel connections of individual solar cells allows for graceful degradation	Redundant drive elements and motors	Parallel rings for power transfer	Automatic monitoring and control of battery charge state	Series/parallel connections Diode protection	Redundant spares	Automatic load shedding

TABLE 6.5.2 ATTRIBUTES OF THE VOYAGER SPACECRAFT

System characteristics	Propulsion	Power	Data communications	Attitude control	Command and payload
Planetary probe three-axis stabilized Mission life: 7 years	Hydrazine thrusters	Three radioactive thermal generators 430 W at Jupiter	Downlink, 2 Uplink, 1 Two antennas (high gain and low gain)	Redundant sun sensors and Canopus (star) trackers	Command rate: 16 bps Redundant computers, 4K words each Data storage on board

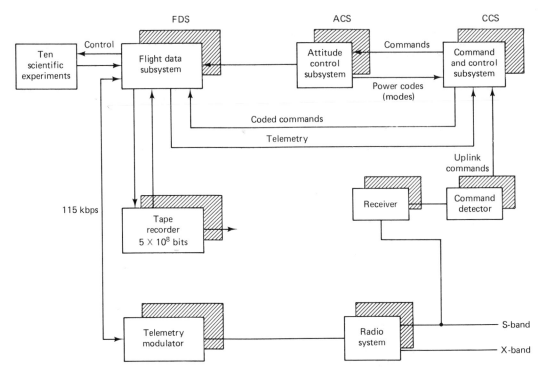

Figure 6.5.1   Voyager system block diagram.

units. This form of standby redundancy is called "block" redundancy in that redundancy is provided at subsystem level rather than internal to each subsystem. The attitude control subsystem (ACS) is composed of redundant computers; one is an unpowered standby spare. The command and control subsystem (CCS) is also a redundant computer, but the standby is powered and monitors the on-line unit. Cross-strapping and switching allow reconfiguration around failed components. The CCS executes self-testing routines prior to issuing commands to other subsystems. Tables 6.5.3 and 6.5.4 list the error detection mechanisms in the Voyager attitude control and command control subsystems. Memory is only 4K words. The tape recorders are used for storage of scientific data only. New programs for memory have to be loaded from the ground.

A list of typical redundancy techniques used in contemporary spacecraft is:

Propulsion: redundant thrusters. Multiple valves for propellant flow control. Automatic switchover based on excessive attitude change rates. Multiple commands required to initiate any firing sequence.

Power: redundant solar cell strings, batteries, power buses. Automatic load shedding.

Data Communications: redundant transponders. Digital error detection and correction techniques. Switch from directional to omni antennas for backup.

TABLE 6.5.3 ERROR DETECTION IN VOYAGER
ATTITUDE CONTROL SUBSYSTEM

CCS fails to receive "I'm healthy" report every 2 s
Loss of celestial (sun and Canopus) reference
Power supply failure
Fail to rewrite memory every 10 h
Spacecraft takes longer to turn than expected (thruster failure)
Gyro failure
Parity error on commands from CCS
Command sequence incorrect
Failure to respond to command from CCS

TABLE 6.5.4 ERROR DETECTION IN VOYAGER
COMMAND AND CONTROL SUBSYSTEM

Hardware
   Low voltage
   Primary command received before preceding one processed
   Attempt to write into protected memory without override
   Processor sequencer reached an illegal state
Software
   Primary output unit unavailable for more than 14 s
   Self-test routine not successfully completed
   Output buffer overflow

Attitude Control: redundant sensors, gyros, and momentum wheels. Automatic star reacquisition modes.

Command and Control: hardware testing of parity, illegal instructions, memory addresses. Sanity checks. Memory checksums. Task completion timed. Watchdog timers. Memory write protection. Reassemble and reload memory to map around memory failures.

Table 6.5.5 lists typical redundancy in spacecraft subsystems as a function of mission.

The Voyager missions were lower-cost substitutes for a "Grand Tour" mission. The Grand Tour was to take advantage of the alignment of the five outer planets of the solar system. In support of the Grand Tour mission, the Jet Propulsion Laboratory (JPL) designed and breadboarded a self-test and repair (STAR) computer [AVIZ71].

6.5.3. STAR

Figure 6.5.2 depicts the architecture of the STAR computer. Data communication between the units is over two four wire buses: memory-out (M-O) and memory-in (M-I) bus. There are both read-only (ROM) and read/write (RWM) memories; sepa-

TABLE 6.5.5 TYPICAL REDUNDANCY IN SPACECRAFT SUBSYSTEMS AS A FUNCTION OF MISSION

Mission subsystem	Low-earth-orbit sensing	Low-earth orbit navigation or communication	Low-earth-orbit scientific	Synchronous-orbit communications	Deep-space scientific
Propulsion		Station-keeping maneuvers via ground commands → Redundant thrusters and leak detection			Backup system Leak detection and automatic switching
Power		Redundant batteries Low-voltage detection and load shedding →		Overload protection Low-voltage dropout	Overload protection
Data communication		Redundant links →		Low-rate telemetry and commands	Redundant data and command channels Omni antennas for backup
Attitude control	← Safe hold and ground fix →			Automatic	Automatic
Command and payload		Multiple repeaters	Fault tolerant on board data processing	Multiple repeaters and graceful degradation	High-reliability design

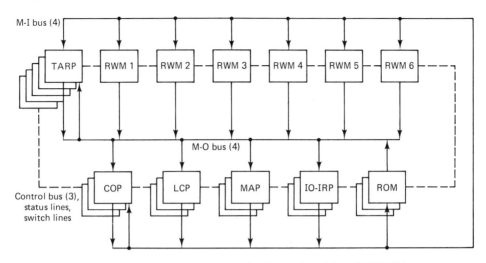

Figure 6.5.2   STAR computer organization. (Adapted from [AVIZ71].)

rate processors for instruction sequencing (COP), logical operations (LOP), arithmetic operations (MAP), I/O (IOP), and interrupts (IRP); and a test and repair processor (TARP). The philosophy used in STAR was to detect errors at interfaces to blocks and replace blocks upon failure. Redundancy techniques were used that were appropriate to each block. Data are composed of 28-bit words with an appended 4-bit residue code, transmitted in eight successive nibbles over the four-wire buses. Instruction operation codes are divided into three bytes, each encoded as a 2-out-of-4 code. Duplication is used to detect errors in the logic processor and read/write memories. Each unit reports 2 bits of status (e.g., unit output active, disagree with bus for duplicate units, operation completed, and internally detected fault) to the TARP. The TARP monitors both the memory buses for correctly encoded information and the status bits from the various units. The unit status bits can only assume specific sequences during fault-free operation. Any deviation indicates an error. Upon error detection, the TARP directs reconfiguration—and recovery. Reconfiguration is achieved by power switching of spare units. Recovery is accomplished by resetting the program counter and internal registers to values stored by software at user-specified "rollback points." The TARP is critical to the error detection, reconfiguration, and recovery activities and hence is implemented in hybrid redundancy with three active, majority-voting copies and two standby spares that can replace any copy that disagrees with the majority output.

6.6. CRITICAL COMPUTATIONS

6.6.1. C.vmp

C.vmp (for "computer, voted multiprocessor") is a triplicated microprocessor system designed for real-time control environments. The design goals for the system included the ability to tolerate permanent and transient faults; fault survival should be transparent to user software; no lost time due to recovery from faults; use of off-the-shelf components; and dynamically trading performance for reliability.

To be consistent with the design goals of modularity and software transparency, bus-level voting was selected as the major fault tolerance mechanism. That is, voting occurs every time the processors access the bus to either send or retrieve information. There are three processor–memory pairs, each pair connected via a bus as depicted in Fig. 6.6.1. A more precise definition of C.vmp would therefore be "a multiprocessor system capable fo fault-tolerant operation." C.vmp is, in fact, composed of three separate machines capable of operating in independent mode executing three separate programs. Under the control of an external event or under the control of one of the processors, C.vmp can synchronize its redundant hardware and start executing the critical section of code.

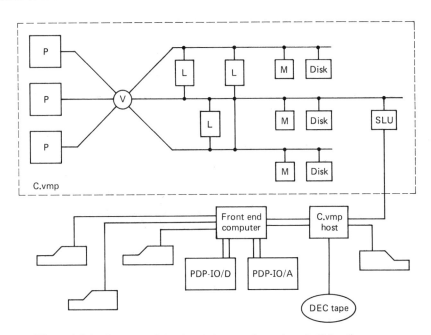

Figure 6.6.1   C.vmp configuration and connection to host facilities. P, processor; V, voter; L, parallel I/O unit; M, memory; SLU, console terminal serial line unit.

With the voter active, the three buses are voted on and the result of the vote is sent out. Any disagreements among the processors will, therefore, not propagate to the memories, and vice versa. Since voting is a simple act of comparison, the voter is memoryless. Disagreements are caught and corrected before they have a chance to propagate. The voter may be totally triplicated if desired. With voter triplication even the voter can have either a transient or a hard failure and the computer will remain operational. In addition, provided that the processor is the only device capable of becoming bus master, only one bidirectional voter is needed regardless of how much memory or how many I/O modules are on the bus. Voting is done in parallel on a bit-by-bit basis. A computer can have a failure on a certain bit in one bus, and, provided that the other two buses have the correct information for that bit, operation will continue. There are cases, therefore, where failures in all three buses can occur simultaneously and the computer would still be functioning correctly.

Bus-level voting works only if information passes through the voter. Usually, the processor registers reside on the processor board and so do not get voted upon. The PDP-11, for example, has six general-purpose registers, one stack pointer, and one program counter. However, after tracing over 5.3 million instructions over 41 programs written by five different programmers and using five different compilers, the following average program behavior was discovered [LUND77].

1. On the average a register gets loaded or stored to memory every 24 instructions.
2. A subroutine call is executed, on the average, every 40 instructions, thus saving the program counter on the stack.
3. The only register that normally is not saved or written into is the stack pointer. To maintain fault tolerance the system must periodically save and reload the pointer.

Thus normal program behavior can be counted on to keep the registers circulating through the voter.

The multiplexed paths through the voter are shown in Fig 6.6.2. Part (a) shows the case for the (unidirectional) control lines. Signals generated by the processor are routed from bus receivers to multiplexers which allow either signals from all three buses, or signals from bus A only, to pass to the voting circuit. The output of the voting circuit always feeds a bus driver on external bus A but is multiplexed with the initially received signals on buses B and C. This arrangement allows all three processor signals to be voted on and sent to all three external buses; the signal from processor A only to be "broadcast" to all three external buses; and the independent processor signals to be sent to the separate external buses, albeit with extra delay on bus A.

1. *Voting mode:* The transmitting portion of each of the three buses is routed into the voter, and the result of the vote is then routed out to the receiving portion of all three buses. In addition to the voting elements the voter has a set of disagreement detectors. These detectors, one for each bus, activate whenever that bus has "lost" a vote. By monitoring these disagreement detectors, one can learn about the types of failures the machine is having.
2. *Broadcast mode:* Only the transmitting portion of bus A is sampled, and its contents are broadcast to the receiving portions of all three buses. This mode of operation allows selective triplication and nontriplication of I/O devices, depending on the particular requirements of the user. The voter has no idea which devices are triplicated and which are not. The only requirement is that all

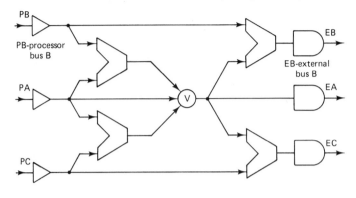

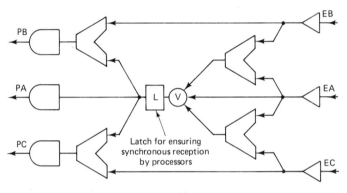

(a)

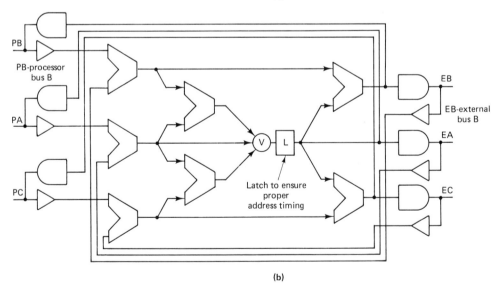

(b)

Figure 6.6.2 (a) C.vmp unidirectional voter multiplexing; (b) C.vmp bidirectional voter multiplexing. (Adapted from [SIEW78].)

nontriplicated devices be placed on bus A. To handle nontriplicated devices two extra lines are added to bus A.

3. *Independent mode:* Buses B and C are routed around the voting hardware. Bus A is routed to feed its signals to all three inputs of the voting elements. In this mode C.vmp is a loosely coupled multiprocessor. Switching between independent and voting modes allows the user to perform a performance/reliability trade-off.

The unidirectional control signals generated by devices on the external buses are handled the same way as processor signals, except that the direction (external-processor) has been changed.

Figure 6.6.2b shows the more complex case of the bidirectional data/address lines. Two sets of bus transceivers replace the sets of receivers and transmitters used before, and another level of multiplexing has been added. The signals received from both sets of transceivers are fed into a set of multiplexers that choose which direction the signals are flowing. After passing through the set of multiplexers and the voter circuit, the voted signal goes through a latch which ensures that bus timing specifications are met. From there the signals pass onto the opposite bus from which they were initially received. (Note that the drivers on the receiving bus are disabled to avoid both sinking and sourcing the same signal.)

A major goal in the design of C.vmp was to allow dynamic trade-off between reliability and performance. Ideally, when reliability is of less importance, the machine should be able to split into a loosely coupled multiprocessor capable of much greater performance. Conversely, when reliability becomes crucial, the three processors ought to be able to resynchronize themselves and resume voting. Consideration of dynamic voting mode control led to the following features.

1. In transiting from voting to independent mode, a simple change in the multiplexing control signals causes the next instruction to be fetched and executed independently by the three processors.

2. To ensure proper synchronization of all processors in transiting from independent to voting mode, a delayed transition forces an interrupt, presumably after each processor has had ample time to execute a WAIT instruction. (WAIT halts the processor until an interrupt occurs.)

Two bits are provided in the voter control register for voter mode control. The first, a read-only bit, monitors the state, returning 0 if voting, and 1 if not. The other, a read/write bit, chooses the desired mode. Each processor has a copy of the voter control register, and a vote is taken on the mode control bit. This control register is accessed like any I/O device register, as a specific memory location.

There are two levels of synchronization used in C.vmp to keep the three processors in step: bus signal synchronization and processor clock synchronization. The first type of synchronization deals with the bus control signals. The voter uses RPLY to synchronize the three buses, as it is asserted by an external device (memory and I/O devices) once every bus cycle. Thus processors can stay in step if they receive RPLY concurrently.

Perhaps the most critical timing problem encountered in the design of C.vmp was the synchronization of the four phase processor clocks, and also the memory refresh timing oscillators. This part of the design was left untriplicated in C.vmp due to its very small size, hence high reliability, relative to the rest of the machine.

An important parameter in the design of fault-tolerant computers is the amount of performance degradation suffered to obtain greater reliability. In a triplicated architecture such as C.vmp, the obvious loss of two-thirds of the available computing power is unavoidable. This was the reason C.vmp was made flexible enough to switch between voting (fault-tolerant) mode and independent (high-performance) mode. However, this fundamental loss due to triplication is not the only loss; the voter cutting and buffering all the bus lines introduces delays of 80 to 140 ns in the signals between the processors and the memories.

A second stage for measuring performance was to run a set of test programs with representative mixes of instructions and addressing modes. A degradation in performance of about 16 to 19% can be expected compared to a standard LSI-11. Issues in synchronization of asynchronous events, initialization, online repair, and handling of nonredundant devices are reported in [SIEW78].

C.vmp executes programs approximately 15% slower than the nonredundant LSI-11's from which it is constructed. It exhibits a mean time to crash that is five to six times greater than a nonredundant LSI-11 measured in the same environment. C.vmp executes an unmodified version of the DEC RT-11 operating system. Although composed of almost 150 SSI chips in a wire-wrap version, the voter has been reimplemented in a custom LSI chip with four bus lines per 48-pin package, thus decreasing voter complexity to approximately 10 custom LSI chips plus 20 SSI chips.

6.6.2. SIFT and FTMP

SIFT (software-implemented fault tolerance), designed by SRI International [WENS72, WENS78], and FTMP, designed by Draper Labs [HOPK78], are intended for real-time control of aircraft. Due to concerns over fuel efficiency and performance, the aircraft of the future will be dynamically unstable. The loss of computer control for even a few milliseconds could lead to disaster. Thus these experimental systems are designed for a failure probability of 10^{-9} during a 10-h mission. An interesting problem arises from this reliability goal: How does one verify that the systems meet their design specification? 10^{-10} failures per hour translates into 1.14 million operating years before failure. The approach taken in SIFT is to mathematically prove the correctness of the system software.

As the name implies, software-implemented fault tolerance relies primarily on software mechanisms to achieve reliability. The hardware consists of independent computers communicating with other computers over unidirectional serial links. Thus for N computers there are $N(N-1)$ links. The SIFT software is divided into a set of tasks. The input to a task is produced by the output of a collection of tasks. Reliability is achieved by having tasks done independently by a number of computers. Typically, the correct output is chosen by a majority vote. If all copies of the output are not identical, an error has been detected. Such errors are recorded for use by the executive for determining faulty units and system reconfiguration. Voting is performed only on the input data to tasks rather than on every partial result. Thus the tasks need to be only loosely synchronized (e.g., to within 50 μs).

Figure 6.6.3 depicts the distribution of tasks among three processors. Application task A receives its input from task B. Task A receives the majority voted input from three copies of task B provided by the executive. When task A finishes, it places its output into a buffer so that the executive can provide the majority voted data as input to the next task. The number of processors executing a task can vary with the task and even with the execution instance of the task.

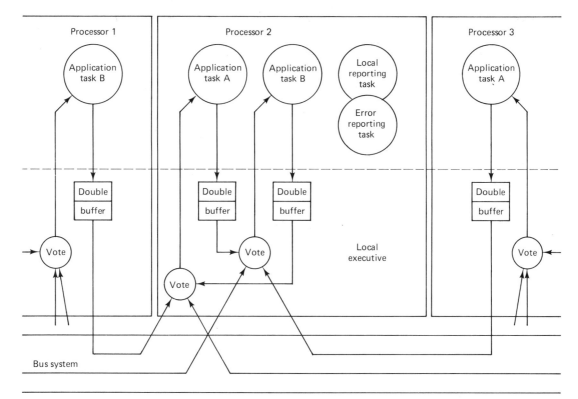

Figure 6.6.3   Arrangement of application tasks within SIFT configuration. (Adapted from [WENS78].)

The SIFT project had to solve a number of challenging problems, including distributed clock synchronization, reaching consensus on system health in the presence of faults, and the mathematical proof of software correctness [WENS78].

In an approach somewhat similar to SIFT, the space shuttle computer [COOP76, SKLA76, AWST81] employs software voting in a five-computer complex. The computer complex is responsible for guidance, navigation, and control; system management; payload management; and prelaunch and preflight checkouts. Four of the five computers are used as a redundant set during critical mission phases. The fifth computer performs noncritical tasks and acts as a backup to the primary system. The control outputs of the four primary computers are voted on at the control actuators. In addition, each computer listens to the outputs of the three other computers and compares those signals with its own via software. If a computer detects a disagreement, it signals the disagreeing computer. The received disagreement detection signals are voted on in the redundancy management circuitry of each computer. If the vote is positive, the redundancy management unit removes its computer from service. Up to two computer failures can be tolerated in voting mode operation. After the second failure, the system converts to a duplex system that can survive one additional computer failure by using comparison and self-tests to isolate the failure. The fifth computer contains a backup flight software package written by Rockwell International; the primary software package was written by IBM. These separate software packages minimize the probability of a common software bug.

Whereas SIFT takes a software-intensive approach to fault tolerance, FTMP takes a hardware-intensive approach. Figure 6.6.4 depicts the structure of FTMP. The

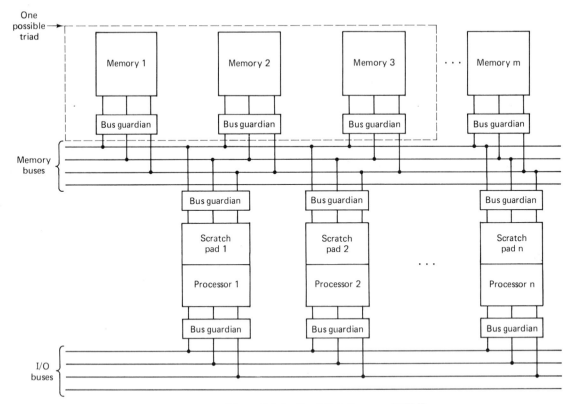

Figure 6.6.4 Simplified diagram of FTMP.

basic elements are processor–memory pairs (P, processors; SP, scratchpad memory), I/O units, and common memory modules. A set of redundant serial buses interconnects the elements. Basic elements combine into triads as controlled by status information in the bus guardians (BGs). Application software is divided into tasks. A task is initialized when a processor–memory triad reads input data, and perhaps code, from a common memory triad. The bus guardians are set up so that the processors read from the appropriate three common memories over the appropriate three buses. Each common memory drives a different active bus. All processors read in data in bit-serial synchronization. The bus guardians vote on the information prior to loading it into scratchpad memory. The processors then independently execute the program. Upon completion, the output data are written into the common memory triad, with each processor driving a different active bus and each memory module voting on the contents of the three active buses.

When an element of a triad fails, its status is detected by the voting mechanism and can be configured out by reprogramming the bus guardians. The reprogramming is done by reconfiguration management software. Thus any element can serve as a spare for any triad. More than one processor–memory and/or common memory triad can exist at the same time, but only one active bus triad.

Problems addressed by FTMP include design of a tightly synchronized, redundant, fault-tolerant clock; triad reconfiguration in a distributed system containing failures; physical isolation to prevent fault propagation; and systematic exercising of all elements [HOPK78].

6.7. SUMMARY

In this chapter the architecture of 12 fault-tolerant computers has been briefly sketched. As indicated in the introduction, there will be a growing demand for fault-tolerant systems as our society becomes increasingly dependent on computers for day-to-day operation. Indeed, one airline has estimated that it loses up to $20,000 per minute of downtime in its computer reservation system. As the cost of downtime and errors increases, we will see more and more effort devoted to toleration of failures. As in any engineering discipline, there are design trade-offs between the cost of implementation and the cost of failure. The challenge is, then, to couple the potential of new technology with fault-tolerant techniques to produce increasingly better systems.

REFERENCES

[AVIZ71] Avizienis, A., G. C. Gilley, F. P. Mathur, D. A. Rennels, J. A. Rohr, and D. K. Rubin, "The STAR (Self-Testing and Repairing) Computer: An Investigation on the Theory and Practice of Fault-Tolerant Computer Design," *IEEE Trans. Comput.*, vol. C-20, no. 11, pp. 1312–1321, Nov. 1971.

[AWST81] "Velocity, Altitude Regimes to Push Computer Limits," *Aviation Week Sp. Technol.,* pp. 49–51, Apr. 6, 1981.

[BART78] Bartlett, J. F., "A 'NonStop' Operating System," *Hawaii Int. Conf. Syst. Sci.,* 1978.

[BART81] Bartlett, J. F., "A NonStop Kernel," *ACM 8th Symp. Operat. Syst. Principles,* Pacific Grove, Calif., vol. 15, no. 5, pp. 22–29, Dec. 1981.

[BOON80] Boone, L. A., H. L. Liebergot, and R. M. Sedmak, "Availability, Reliability and Maintainability Aspects of the Sperry Univac 1100/60," *Dig., 10th Annu. Int. Symp. Fault-Tolerant Comput.,* Kyoto, Japan, pp. 3–8, Oct. 1–3, 1980.

[CAST82] Castillo, X., S. R. McConnel, and D. P. Siewiorek, "Derivation and Calibration of a Transient Error Reliability Model," *IEEE Trans. Comput.,* vol. C-31, no. 7, pp. 658–671, July 1982.

[COOP76] Cooper, A. E., and W. T. Chow, "Development of On-Board Space Computer Systems," *IBM J. Res. Dev.* vol. 20, no. 1, pp. 5–19, Jan. 1976.

[DROU71] Droulette, D. L., "Recovery through Programming System/360-System/370," *Proc. Spring Joint Comput. Conf.,* pp. 467–476, 1971.

[HOPK78] Hopkins, A. L., Jr., T. B. Smith III, and J. H. Lala, "FTMP—A Highly Reliable Fault-Tolerant Multiprocessor for Aircraft," *Proc. IEEE,* vol. 66, no. 10, pp. 1221–1239, Oct. 1978.

[HSIA81] Hsaio, M. Y., W. C. Carter, J. W. Thomas, and W. R. Stringfellow, "Reliability, Availability, and Serviceability of IBM Computer Systems: A Quarter Century of Progress," *IBM J. Res. Dev.,* vol. 25, no. 5, pp. 453–465, Sept. 1981.

[INTE81] "The Intel 432 System Summary," Intel Corp., Aloha, Oreg., 1981.

[JONE79] Jones, C. P., "Automatic Fault Protection in the Voyager Spacecraft," Jet Propulsion Laboratory, California Institute of Technology AIAA Paper 79-1919, Pasadena, Calif.

[KATS78] Katsuki, D., E. S. Elsam, W. F. Mann, E. S. Roberts, J. G. Robinson, F. S. Skowronski, and E. W. Wolf, "Pluribus—An Operational Fault-Tolerant Multiprocessor," *Proc. IEEE,* vol. 66, no. 10, pp. 1146–1159, Oct. 1978.

[KATZ77] Katzman, J. A., "A Fault-Tolerant Computing System," Tandem Computers, Inc., Cupertino, CA, 1977.

[KELL76] Keller, T. W., "CRAY-1 Evaluation Final Report," Los Alamos Scientific Laboratory, Dec. 1976.

[KLEI74] Kleinrock, L. and W. F. Naylor, "On Measured Behavior of the ARPA Network," *Proc. AFIPS NCC,* vol. 43, pp. 767–778, 1974.

[KLEI76] Klein, M. R., "Microcircuit Device Reliability, Digital Detailed Data," Reliability Analysis Center RADC MDR-4, Summer 1976.

[KULZ77] Kulzer, J. J., "Systems Reliability—A Case Study of No. 4 ESS," in *System Security and Reliability,* Infotech State of the Art Report, pp. 186–188, 1977.

[KUNS80] Kunshier, D. J., and D. R. Mueller, "Support Processor Based System Fault Recovery," in *Dig., 10th Int. Symp. Fault Tolerant Comput.,* Kyoto, Japan, pp. 197–301, Oct. 1–3, 1980.

[LUND77] Lunde, Å, "Empirical Evaluation of Some Features of Instruction Set Processor Architectures," *Commun. ACM,* vol. 20, No. 3, pp. 143–153, Mar. 1977.

[LYNC75] Lynch, W. C., W. Wagner, and M. S. Schwartz, "Reliability Experience with Chi/OS," *IEEE Trans. Softw. Eng.,* vol. SE-1, no. 2, pp. 253–257, June 1975.

[RENN80] Rennels, D. A., "Distributed Fault-Tolerant Computer Systems," *Computer,* pp. 55–65, Mar. 1980.

[REYN75] Reynolds, C. H., and J. E. Kinsbergen, "Tracking Reliability and Availability," *Datamation,* vol. 21, no. 11, pp. 106–116, Nov. 1975.

[SIEW78] Siewiorek, D. P., V. Kini, H. Mashburn, S. R. McConnel, and M. M. Tsao, "A Case Study of C.mmp, Cm*, and C.vmp: Part I—Experiences with Fault Tolerance in Multiprocessor Systems," *Proc. IEEE,* vol. 66, no. 10, pp. 1178–1199, 1978.

[SIEW82a] Siewiorek, D. P., C. G. Bell, and A. Newell, *Computer Structures: Principles and Examples,* McGraw-Hill, New York, 1982.

[SIEW82b] Siewiorek, D. P., and D. Johnson, "A Design Methodology for High Reliability Systems: The Intel 432," Chapter 18 in *The Theory and Practice of Reliable System Design,* D. Siewiorek and R. Swarz, Digital Press, Bedford, Mass., 1982.

[SIEW82c] Siewiorek, D. P., and R. Swarz, *The Theory and Practice of Reliable System Design,* Digital Press, Bedford, Mass., 1982.

[SKLA76] Sklaroff, J. R., "Redundancy Management Technique for Space Shuttle Computers," *IBM J. Res. Dev.,* vol. 20, no. 1, pp. 20–28, Jan. 1976.

[TOY78] Toy, W.N., "Fault-Tolerant Design of Local ESS Processors," *Proc. IEEE,* vol. 66, no. 10, pp. 1126–1145, Oct. 1978.

[WENS72] Wensley, J. H., et al., "SIFT-Software Implemented Fault Tolerance," *Proc. AFIPS Fall Joint Comput. Conf.,* pp. 243–253, 1972.

[WENS78] Wensley, J. H., L. Lamport, J. Goldberg, M. W. Green, K. N. Levitt, P. M. Melliar-Smith, R. E. Shostak, and C. B. Weinstock, "SIFT: Design and Analysis of a Fault-Tolerant Computer for Aircraft Control," *Proc. IEEE,* vol. 66, no. 10, pp. 1240–1255, Oct. 1978.

[YOUR72] Yourdan, E., *Design of On-Line Computing Systems,* Prentice-Hall, Englewood Cliffs, N.J., 1972.

PROBLEMS

6.1. Compare and contrast the dual processor approaches to redundancy as exemplified by Tandem, Bell ESS No. 1, and Intel 432 functional redundancy checking. Specifically comment on cost, performance, fault detection ability, and fault latency (i.e., time between fault occurrence and detection).

6.2 Create a Markov model for dual redundancy. Assume that the system fails only when both computing elements have failed. Include the effects of fault detection and repair. (Note that a successful repair activity restores the system to a nonfailed state. Thus the model has a transition from the one failed processor state to the no-failed processor state.) Explain how the model differs for the Tandem, Bell ESS No. 1, and Intel 432 functional redundancy checking architectures. Calculate the availability (i.e., the probability of being in nonfailed state) for the Tandem architecture assuming a computing element failure rate, λ, of $1000/10^6$ hours and a repair rate, μ, of $\frac{1}{4}$ h.

6.3. Compare and contrast the triplicated approaches to redundancy as exemplified by C.vmp, SIFT, and FTMP. Comment on cost, performance, fault detection ability, and fault latency.

6.4. Create a Markov model for triplicated redundancy. Assume that the system fails only when two or more computing elements fail. Include the effects of fault detection and repair. Explain how the model differs for the C.vmp, SIFT, and FTMP architectures. Calculate the availability for C.vmp assuming a computing element failure rate, λ, of $1000/10^6$ h and a repair rate, μ, of $\frac{1}{4}$ h.

6.5. Estimate the cost and fault detection coverage (i.e., percent of logic protected) for reliability, availability, and maintainability features for the general-purpose commercial computers VAX-11, IBM 4341, and Univac 1100/60.

6.6. Discuss the impact of technology evolution (e.g., small-scale integration to medium-scale integration to large-scale integration) on fault-tolerant architectures. In particular, contrast the STAR (circa 1970) with the Intel 432 (circa 1980).

6.7. Pick one of the 12 architectures described in this chapter and discuss how you would improve its design. Contrast the cost, performance, fault detection ability, and fault latency of your design with the original design. How have you taken advantage of the technology evolution? Create a Markov model for both architectures. Plot a graph using values of failure rate, λ, and repair rate, μ, that indicates the region in which your design is superior to the original design.

Chapter 7

FAULT-TOLERANT MULTIPROCESSOR AND VLSI-BASED SYSTEM COMMUNICATION ARCHITECTURES

Dhiraj K. Pradhan

7.1. INTRODUCTION

The evolution of fifth-generation computers makes it clear that traditional sequential computer architecture will soon see a striking departure—overtaken by newer architectures which use mulitple processors as the state of the art. This particular thrust is enhanced by developments in integrated circuit (IC) technology, creating a widening gap between the technological advances and the architectural capabilities that can exploit these fully. As a result, much recent research has focused on these new architectural innovations, especially those created by interconnecting multiple processors/processing elements.

These architectures, existing and emerging, can be categorized as to their degree of integration and processor granularity, illustrated in Table 7.1.1. As seen, the multicomputer systems extend from geographically distributed networks, where a handful of computers are connected over long distances, up to the very large scale integration (VLSI) systems, which interconnect a large number of simple processing cells all on a single chip. Fault-tolerance is of critical importance, in the class of highly integrated systems, which is the focus of this chapter.

Achieving reliable operation also becomes increasingly difficult with the growing number of interconnected elements, and correspondingly, the increased likelihood of faults that can occur. In addition to reliability and availability improvement, the motivation for fault tolerance stems from the factor of yield enhancement in VLSI environment. Low yield is a problem of increasing significance, as circuit density

TABLE 7.1.1   NETWORK STRUCTURES

Degree of integration	Processor granularity	Network examples	Interconnection technology
Low	Large	Long-haul networks	Satellite packet radio
Medium	Medium	Local area networks	Loop Bus
Medium	Medium	Multiprocessor systems	Bus Loop Shared memory Tree Multiple bus
High	Small	VLSI-based systems	Binary tree Cube Multiple bus Mesh Reconfigurable network

grows. One solution suggests improvement of the manufacturing and testing processes, to minimize manufacturing defects. However, this approach is not only very costly but also quite difficult to implement, because of the increasing number of components that can be placed on one chip. However, incorporating redundancy for fault tolerance also provides a practical solution to this yield problem as well. Yield is enhanced by accepting circuits—in spite of certain defects—by means of restructuring through redundancy, as opposed to having to discard the circuit altogether.

In the design of any fault-tolerant system, the key architectural consideration becomes the system interconnection. An example is the aircraft control systems, where it has been well recognized [HOPK78] that both ease of reconfiguration and sustained access to the surviving elements depends entirely on the system communication structure, which is the central subject of this chapter. In general, this chapter surveys various approaches that have been developed for design of fault-tolerant network architectures that can be utilized in a wide range of closely coupled systems—systems including certain VLSI-based ones.

This chapter examines the strengths and weaknesses of architectures such as the shared bus interconnection, ring networks, completely interconnect networks, tree networks, and so on, from the standpoint of fault tolerance. Also discussed are the various techniques available that make these networks robust and fault tolerant. Surveyed here, too, are some of the newer and more novel network architectures that contain the properties of fault tolerance and the ability to interconnect a very large number of elements.

VLSI technology has many promising applications, including the design of special-purpose processors as an interconnected array of processing cells on a single chip, as well as the design of supercomputers that use wafer-scale integration technology. These two factors, in conjunction, possess the potential of major innovations in computer architecture. One principal aspect of these architectures that is explored here is how fault tolerance can well be incorporated into such systems. Discussed here is the problem of using redundant cells so as to achieve the elements of fault tolerance, yield enhancement, testability, and reconfigurability.

The purpose of this chapter is to delineate certain fault-tolerance concepts by considering a broad range of network architectures. This chapter is organized into different sections corresponding to various networks; these networks are ordered according to the network processor granularity. Specifically, the opening sections treat those networks of large processor granularity such as shared bus, shared memory, and loop. The focus here is on the solutions to various reliability-related problems. Only those architectural aspects that relate directly to the fault tolerance of these networks are discussed. The later sections examine networks of progressively smaller processor granularity, concluding with a section on multiprocessing cell single chip/wafer architectures. Networks discussed in the latter sections represent more novel and innovative approaches to interconnecting a large number of processing elements, in the context of projected technological trends.

7.2. RELIABLE SHARED BUS DESIGN

Most fault-tolerant multiprocessors designed to date used shared (time-division multiplexed) bus structures for interconnection [HOPK78, TOY78, SIEW78, MANN80]. The shared bus, therefore, is certainly an important interconnection for multiprocessors, although it is mostly suitable for interconnecting a small number of modules. The chief attractiveness of the bus structure lies in both its simplicity and cost effectiveness.

From the point of view of fault tolerance, however, shared bus structures are particularly vulnerable to single-point failures. However, several design alternatives are available that eliminate these potential bus failure problems. This section reviews these design alternatives, as well as their respective effectiveness against various failures. Also discussed here are some of the reported techniques for the design of redundant bus structures. This section is concluded with examples of various bus structures: the FTMP bus, and the proposed MIL STD-1553 and IEEE Standard 802.4 buses, which have been designed specifically with robustness as a factor.

The basic organization of a shared bus is shown in Fig. 7.2.1. Typically, a shared bus connects a number of modules of various types (processors, memories, input/output units, etc.) Some of the modules both transmit and receive data, whereas others simply receive data. Only one module is allowed to transmit on the bus at any one time, although more than one module can receive. Also, only one of the modules, at any given time, initiates and orchestrates the bus transmission; this module is called the *bus master*. When several modules require bus transmission, a certain arbitration mechanism is used in order to decide which module should gain access to the bus. Such arbitration is performed using either a centralized or distributed mechanism. A

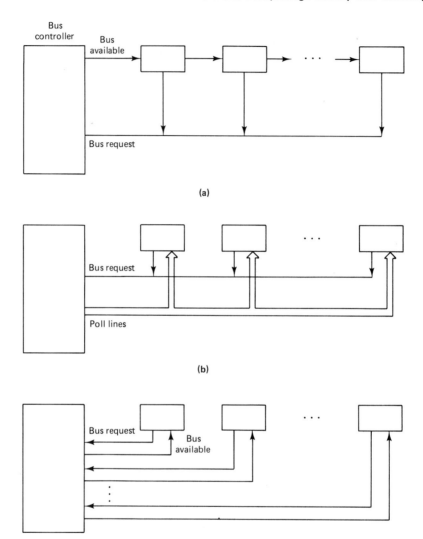

Figure 7.2.1   Shared bus networks: (a) daisy chain; (b) polling; (c) independent requesting.

special module called a *bus controller* is used in performing centralized arbitration. In a distributed arbitration, all the modules requesting the bus use the same arbitration protocol to decide independently who gains control of the bus.

Also, the shared bus design uses certain synchronization protocols to perform *handshake* functions between the bus master and the other modules involved in the transmission—the *bus slaves*. Specifically, these protocols allow the modules to determine when the bus is ready for transmission and when the transmission is complete.

The principal sources causing bus failures can be broadly classified into the following categories:

1. Control failures
2. Synchronization failures
3. Bus connection failures

The following elaborates on the failures listed above and discusses possible design techniques that provide safeguards against these failures.

7.2.1. Control Failures

Critical to overall bus reliability is the selection of appropriate control and synchronization strategies. There are, in general, two types of bus control organizations: centralized and distributed.

In the *centralized bus*, different modules send the request for the bus to the bus controller. Then the bus controller signals the module whose request has been granted, using certain control lines. So a centrally controlled bus can be seen to be especially vulnerable to bus controller failure.

This problem is somewhat alleviated in the *distributed bus*. A distributed bus typically uses serial transmission where data and control information are transmitted serially as messages or tokens. Here, bus arbitration is usually performed by those modules themselves trying to access the bus. The modules determine who has the bus by using some common arbitration protocol. Techniques used for implementing distributed arbitration protocols include token passing for sharing the control of the bus, and collision detection to detect bus conflicts (see Example 2). Thus no single module failure need completely disable the bus control function. However, in the distributed bus there is always the possibility that a failed module may not release the bus or that it may try to access the bus illegally. The solutions to such a situation are either to isolate the failed module, or to switch to a spare bus. These actions can be performed more easily in a centrally controlled bus. Also, the type of bus control failures encountered depends on the particular bus allocation technique being used, as illustrated below.

Conceptually, there are three basic bus allocation techniques: the daisy chain, polling, and independent requesting [THUR81]. These are illustrated in Fig. 7.2.1 featuring centrally controlled buses. Of these three techniques, the daisy chain appears to be most vulnerable to failure, whereas the independent request technique is the least vulnerable.

In the *daisy chain* (used, for example, in the DEC Unibus), there is a single bus grant line which carries the bus grant signal. This signal is generated by the bus controller, in response to a bus request when the bus is not busy. The bus grant signal then propagates through the modules; thus modules that did not request the bus simply pass the signal to their successor. When the bus grant signal arrives at a module that requested the bus, the module blocks the signal from propagating any further and then asserts the bus-busy line and gets control of the bus. When the module has completed its use of the bus, it releases the bus grant signal, which then passes on to the next module. A module failure can have serious consequences. For example, a failed module may not allow the bus grant signal to propagate, thus effectively not allowing the bus to be accessed by modules of lower priority. Also, a failed module can generate and propagate a false bus grant signal, thus creating a bus conflict. Furthermore, in this daisy chain scheme it is very difficult to remove a failed module (for off-line repair) or even just to isolate the failed module. To do so would require rewiring the bus grant line so that it bypasses the failed module.

The *polling* technique, on the other hand, is less prone to some of the failures discussed above. The polling is usually implemented by using a common bus request line, together with one or more poll lines. A module that requires access to the bus asserts the bus request line and then monitors the poll lines for its poll code to appear. Access to the bus is gained when the corresponding poll code appears. The poll codes are usually generated by the bus controller or by the last module that controlled the bus. Thus a failure of the poll lines or of the modules constitutes potential single-point failures.

However, a failed module can be denied any access to the bus fairly easily; this is accomplished by ensuring that the poll codes that correspond to the failed module are never placed on the poll lines. Also, removal of a failed module can be performed with relative ease without affecting other modules.

Finally, the *independent request* technique uses for each module a separate bus request line and a separate bus grant line. Since here there are no shared control lines, a control-line failure may cause minimal damage. Also, removal of a failed module requires minimal changes in the connections. Thus the independent request techniques can be considered to be the most robust of the three techniques.

So, in designing a robust bus structure, one must pay particular attention to the selection of the appropriate bus control and allocation strategy.

7.2.2. Synchronization Failures

Synchronization failures as well as their effects are varied. The following discusses first the various synchronization failures, and then goes into design techniques that protect against these potential failures. Synchronization-related failures can occur because of a wide range of causes. Two major sources can arise because of clock-skew and improper design of handshake protocols. *Clock-skewing failure* is the misalignment of data and clock cells at the receiver when data and clock signals are carried on separate lines. This is illustrated in Fig. 7.2.2 and occurs because of differential transmission and gate delays, noise, and possible variation in clock speed as well as in rise and fall time [STON82] of data and clock lines.

A common technique that has been used to overcome this problem is the use of *self-clocking codes*. Some of the most frequently used codes in serial communication are the NRZ (nonreturn to zero), RZ (return to zero), and Manchester II codes, illustrated in Fig. 7.2.3. Of these three codes, the RZ and Manchester II codes are

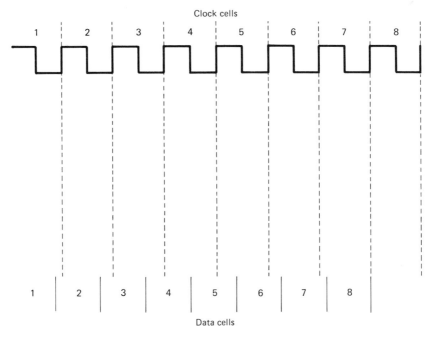

Figure 7.2.2   Clock-skewing failure.

self-clocking in that the clock information forms an integral part of the encoded waveform. For both of these codes, there is a transition in each cell, irrespective of the data bit. Thus the receiver is easily synchronized by using the transitions in the data cells. In addition, the Manchester II code has the added feature of built-in error-detection capabilities. This error-detection capability is provided for by the fact that a 0-to-1 change (and vice versa) would require a double change in the signal levels within one data cell. This is obviously a highly unlikely occurrence—any noise is more likely to change the bit into an invalid signal, shown in Fig. 7.2.4.

The other advantage of Manchester II codes is the lack of any dc component (i.e., the cumulative sum of voltage levels in any bit stream is 0). This allows for transformer coupling in the bus interface design. As we discuss later, transformer coupling provides some natural fault isolation. Some of these considerations have prompted the adoption of Manchester II codes in the MIL-STD-1553 bus (see Example 1).

Other synchronization errors occur because of improper design of handshake protocols. There are basically two types of handshake protocols that are used in parallel buses: the synchronous technique and the asynchronous technique. The *synchronous* technique uses a global clock for synchronization. Here, all of the modules are synchronized by using a global clock; thus any changes in the address and data lines are allowed to occur between two successive clock pulses. As a result, this scheme is susceptible to clock skewing; in addition, a failure of the clock itself can

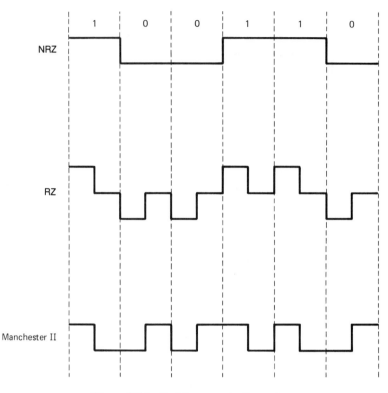

Figure 7.2.3 Serial communication codes.

be catastrophic. Therefore, this technique is used only when a small number of modules with identical speeds are connected in close spatial proximity.

In the *asynchronous* technique, synchronization is achieved between the transmitter and the receiver by the exchange of certain special signals. These signals and their analogs are typically referred to as *address-valid* and *data-accept* signals. These signals may be carried over two separate lines and are used as follows.

The sender first asserts the address-valid signal after placing the data and the address on the bus. This address-valid signal causes other modules to examine the address lines. The designated receiver, upon recognizing its address, reads the data from the bus and then asserts the data accept line to signal this. There are two potential synchronization failures possible here. These failures are commonly referred to as *duplicate data* and *missing data errors*.

The duplicate data error can occur when the sender holds up the address-valid signal for too long. This can cause the same data to be read twice, as shown in Fig. 7.2.5a. On the other hand, if the receiving module holds the data-accept signal for too long, subsequent data from the transmitting module can be lost, as shown in Fig. 7.2.5b.

A solution used commonly to avoid these two problems (e.g., in the DEC

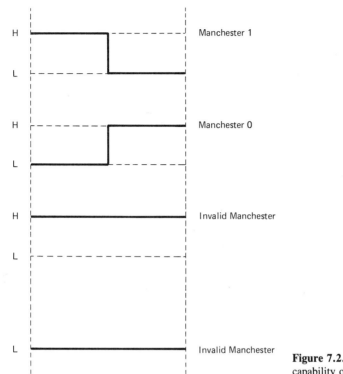

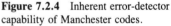

Figure 7.2.4 Inherent error-detector capability of Manchester codes.

Unibus) is to interlock the address-valid and data-accept signals, as shown in Fig. 7.2.6. Here the address-valid signal is lowered by the transmitter immediately after it recognizes that the data-accept signal has been raised. This eliminates the possibility of reading the same data twice (duplicate data error). Similarly, the missing data problem can be eliminated if the data-accept signal is lowered immediately by the receiver, as soon as it detects that the address-valid signal has been lowered by the transmitter. Interlocking schemes can somewhat slow down the bus; therefore, in some designs, these signals are only partially interlocked.

In general, then, various techniques are available for minimizing the possibility of errors due to synchronization. The basic penalty for ensuring error-free synchronization is the maximum speed at which the bus can be operated. The use of self-clocking codes requires a higher bus bandwidth (compared to the non-self-clocking codes) to achieve the same information rate. Similarly, interlocking requires a longer period to complete transmission.

7.2.3. Bus Connection Failures

Bus connection failures can occur in bus interface and in bus lines: of these two types of failures, perhaps bus line failures are less likely since the bus lines are passive devices.

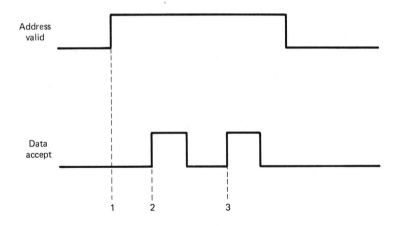

1. Source raises the address-valid signal after placing data and address on the bus.
2. Destination raises the data-accept signal after reading the data from the bus.
3. Destination reads the data from the bus second time and raises the data-accept signal again.

(a)

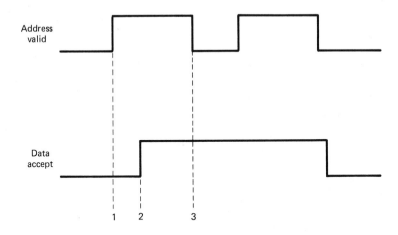

1. Source raises address-valid signal after placing data and address on the bus.
2. Destination reads the data from the bus and raises the data-accept signal.
3. Source places the second data item on the bus and raises the address-valid signal. This second data item is lost as the destination has not lowered the data-accept signal yet.

(b)

Figure 7.2.5   (a) Duplicate data error; (b) missing error data.

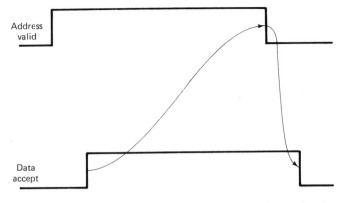

1. The address-valid signal is lowered by the source as soon as it recognizes that the data-accept signal has been raised.
2. The data-accept signal is lowered by the destination as soon as it recognizes the lowering of the address-valid signal.

Figure 7.2.6   Interlocked scheme.

Other important issues in the design of robust bus connections include grounding- and shielding-related problems [STON82]. For instance, noise that is due to ground currents is caused by the inevitable differences in the ground potential between two widely separated modules connected by a bus. Similarly, improper shielding can cause bus noise because of external radiation. Various solutions to these problems have been discussed [STON82].

The effect of a bus interface fault can be local or global, depending on the type of interface design as well as on the type of faults. Several types of bus interface circuits can be found. Some of the more commonly used interface hardware includes transformer coupling, open-collector connections, and tri-state connections.

Transformer couplings, which are used primarily for serial buses, use one or more transformers, illustrated in Fig. 7.2.7. Although these transformer couplings are limited in terms of speed, they possess a certain natural robustness. Also, extra electrical isolation can be provided between the module and the bus by using additional transformers, as shown in Fig. 7.2.7. So a fault in the module may have a minimal impact on the bus. One other important advantage of transformer coupling is its ability to eliminate certain external noises such as ground noise, discussed earlier.

Other techniques of bus interfacing include the open-collector technique and the tri-state technique, which is found more in the metal-oxide-semiconductor (MOS) logic. In this the possibility of a fault causing a permanent short between the bus line and the bus driver always exists—a development that can have serious consequences. On the other hand, a permanent open fault may be of less concern because it will only disconnect the module.

One possible solution to these bus interface and bus line faults is to incorporate redundant buses, as done in the FTMP computer (see below). Designing fault-tolerant

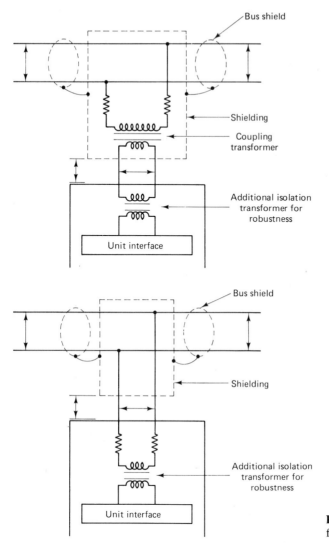

Figure 7.2.7   Bus interface using transformer coupling.

bus interconnections that use redundant buses becomes quite attractive when the bus structure is serial. This technique, though, is not cost-effective for parallel bus structures. Therefore, several other techniques that incorporate redundancy into bus structures have been proposed in [CART71], [ROTH67], and [PARH79]. In these, the basic strategy is to use a limited number of spare bus lines and switch these alternate bus lines, in the event of a fault, using specially designed switches.

An attractive feature of the switching techniques is that they can be used to switch out faulty address and control lines in addition to faulty data lines. Also, a faulty module can be more easily disconnected from the bus. Thus it is possible to make a fault-tolerant bus structure without replicating all the bus lines.

From the point of view of bus hardware and interface failures, a notable example of redundant robust bus design can be found in the FTMP (fault-tolerant multi-processor) computer [HOPK78]. This computer is designed using the technique of replicated redundancy in all its modules (processors, memories, and I/O units), buses, and bus-interface hardware. In this, an active configuration consists of several triads, where each triad is made up of sets of three identical modules that are connected to three different buses. Each of these three modules can receive data from all the buses, but can transmit data to only one of the buses. The three active buses in the triad carry three identical copies of the same data that have been generated independently by three different modules. The assignment of active modules to active buses for the purpose of transmission is done in a quasi-static manner and is reconfigurable so as to allow for fault recovery. Specialized hardware units perform the task of this reconfiguration and these are referred to as *bus guardians* (BGs) and *bus isolation gates* (BIGs). Associated with each module is a pair of BG units which connect the module to the buses through a set of BIG units, illustrated in Fig. 7.2.8. These bus guardians perform several key functions, which include monitoring the status of the associated module, switching out the module if the module becomes faulty, and reconfiguring the bus connection when a fault is detected.

Briefly, BG units function as follows. There are two power switches for each module; each is controlled by a different BG unit. For this module to be ON, both of

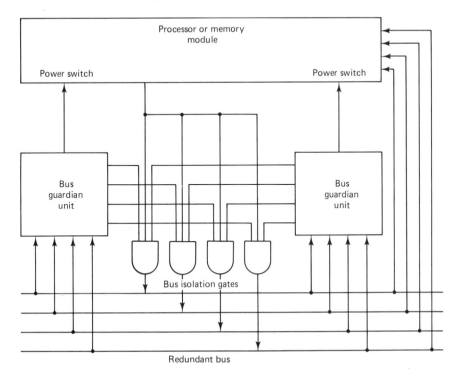

Figure 7.2.8   FTMP bus interface.

these switches have to be ON simultaneously. In other words any one of the two BG units can switch the module OFF, thus disconnecting the module. This guarantees that both BG must concur on the status of their associated module for the module to be active. Additionally, the BG units control to which bus the module may be connected. The BIG units are designed so that for a transmission (from the module onto the bus) to be possible, both BG units must select the same bus at a given time. This type of dual redundancy ensures that as long as at least one of the BG units is functional, the effect of any failure need not be catastrophic since, at worst, the module gets switched off. The system is thus fault tolerant for a large class of faults, including faults in the buses as well as in the BIG units. (Having redundant buses allows the BG units to switch out a bus if the bus itself or the BIG unit connected to the bus becomes faulty.) However, success of this fault-tolerant design depends greatly on the ability of BG units to function independently. This requires careful design of BG units with proper isolation and separate power sources.

This section concludes with a discussion of inherent fault tolerance in two other bus designs: the MIL-STD-1553 and IEEE 802.4 buses. (The MIL-STD-1553 data formats are used in FTMP bus design.)

Example 1.   The bus standard, MIL-STD-1553, was developed by the U.S. Air Force to provide a standard for reliable bus design. This has found significant use in Air Force applications. Later versions of this design include the MIL-STD-1553a and MIL-STD-1553b bus [MILI78]. These are serial buses; the basic hardware is a twisted pair, shielded to provide protection against radiation. The maximum operation speed is specified as 1 million bits per second. All communication is performed using serial, fixed-length words.

The bus is centrally controlled by the bus controller. However, there can be more than one module that is capable of controlling the bus, although at any one time, only one bus controller can be active. All transfers on the bus are performed in half-duplex mode in that the flow can occur in only one direction at a time. The modules, generally, are of three types: the bus controller, the remote terminal, and the sub-system with remote terminal. The remote terminal is only capable of receiving or transmitting data and does not possess any control capability, whereas the subsystems have both terminal and bus control capability.

The built-in design features to achieve high reliability include the following:

1. Manchester II encoding
2. Time-out and fail-safe properties
3. Transformer coupling
4. Provision for redundant buses

The basic word formats used for data and control words are shown in Fig. 7.2.9. A word consists of 20 bits, of which 3 bits are used for synchronization and 1 for parity. The synchronization code consists of two $1\frac{1}{2}$-bit-wide signals, as shown in the figure. Thus the synchronization code is not a valid Manchester code. The synchronization code is therefore easily distinguished from other bits. The command and

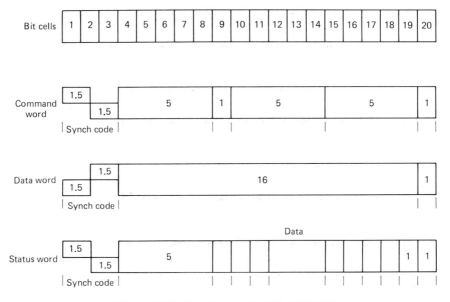

Figure 7.2.9   Word formats for MIL-STD-1553.

status words, though, have the same synchronization code, easily distinguished from each other by using the direction of flow. (The command word is always sent from the controller, whereas the status word is always sent to the controller.) For the sake of robustness, the terminal always acknowledges a command word with a status word back to the controller. Also, all transfers are done under the direction of the bus controller.

A time-out mechanism is built into the system. The maximum response time is assumed to be 12 μs. In the event that there is no response to a command word within 14 μs, a time-out mechanism is invoked which may result in a retry or in any other suitable action. Also included in the design is a fail-safe mechanism that prevents any terminal from using the bus for more than 800 μs. This built-in feature disconnects the terminal automatically when the bus is used for more than 800 μs.

Other high-reliability features include transformer coupling and a provision for redundant buses. One or more alternate buses can be provided which can be switched in in the event of faults. This switching can be performed by the bus controller using special command words.

Example 2.   The IEEE 802.4 is a proposed bus standard and is part of the IEEE 802 family of standards for local area networks [IEEE 85]. These standards deal with physical and link layers as defined by the ISO open system interconnection model.

The proposed bus standard IEEE 802.4 is a distributed bus utilizing the token-passing access method. The token passing is performed from module to module in a logical ring. The modules are organized in the ring in descending order of the module addresses. The node requiring access for the bus waits for the token to arrive and then gets control of the bus. It then initiates transmission and when the transmission is complete, it passes the token to its sucessor. Therefore, in steady state there are two phases: the data transfer phase and the token transfer phase. The token is passed from node to node in a logical ring. In addition to the nodes in the ring, there can be other nodes on the bus. These nodes cannot receive the token and hence can act only as bus slaves. This is illustrated in Fig. 7.2.10. Here nodes 10, 8, 5, and 3 are in the logical ring and therefore can act as bus masters. Nodes 2 and 11 are not in the logical ring and hence cannot initiate transmission.

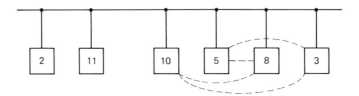

Figure 7.2.10   Logical structure of IEEE 802.4 bus.

All data and control information is encapsulated in a standard frame. There are three basic types of these frames:

1. Control frame
2. Data frame
3. Management data frame

The control frame further consists of the following types:

1. *Token*: When a node is finished transmitting its data, it passes the token to the next node in the ring.
2. *Claim-token*: When a node has not received the token for some time and there has been no activity on the bus during this duration, the node sends a claim-token frame to notify other nodes that it is going to generate a token.
3. *Solicit-successor*: When a node wants a successor to whom it will pass the token, it sends this frame. The frame contains the address of the sender.
4. *Set-successor*: When a node wants to be the successor of a particular node in the logical ring, it sends this frame to that node. This frame is a response to a solicit-successor frame.
5. *Who-follows*: When a node wants to find out the address of the node that immediately follows its successor, it sends this frame. This frame contains the address of the present successor of the sending node.
6. *Resolve-contention*: When a node observes multiple nodes responding to its query, at the same time it sends this frame. This frame initiates a bus contention resolution algorithm among the nodes.

Various bus protocol functions defined by the standard are described below. Each node in the logical ring is capable of all the following functions.

1. Lost token recovery
2. Distributed initialization
3. Token-holding timer
4. Limited data buffering
5. Node address recognition
6. Frame encapsulation and token formation
7. Frame check sequence generation and frame checking
8. Valid token recognition
9. New member addition
10. Node failure error recovery

Fault recovery mechanisms.   The IEEE 802.4 standard is capable of recovering from certain faults which can be induced by either communication or module failures. Various fault conditions from which recovery can occur are listed below.

1. Multiple tokens
2. Lost token
3. Token-pass failure
4. "Deaf" station
5. Duplicate addresses

These various fault conditions occur in different circumstances and are handled by the protocol, as described below.

The token is passed from module to module in a numerically descending order. The token is released by a module if either the token-holding timer runs out, or if the module does not have any more messages to transmit.

After passing the token, the sender monitors the medium to be certain that its successor has received the token. If the sender hears a valid frame following the token, it assumes that the successor has received the token and is transmitting. If the sender does not hear a valid frame from its successor, it monitors the medium for an extra four time slots. If, during these four time slots, it does not hear anything, it assumes that the token has been garbled and needs to be retransmitted. But if it hears another noise burst or a valid frame, it assumes that the successor has received the token.

If even after the second transmission of the token, the successor does not respond, the sender assumes that the successor has failed. It then sends a who-follows frame with the failed successor's address in the data field. All modules compare this address with the address of their predecessor. The station that finds a match responds to the sender with a set-successor frame. This module then becomes the new successor of the token holder. The sender then passes the token to its new successor. If necessary, this procedure is repeated. However, if this does not work, the sender sends a solicit-successor frame, asking any module in the network to respond to it. If there are any operating nodes in the system, they respond and after a bus contention resolution algorithm (described below), the logical ring is reestablished.

If all attempts at soliciting a successor fail, the sender assumes any or all of the following:

1. All modules have failed.
2. The medium is broken.
3. The module's own receiver has failed (deaf station).

Under such conditions, the sender stops attempting to maintain the logical ring. Also, if the module detects any faults in itself, it can remove itself from the ring by sending a set-successor frame, containing the address of its successor to its predecessor.

On the other hand, if the token holder, after having sent a solicit-successor frame, hears from multiple modules, it sends a resolve-contention frame. All modules that are involved in the contention process delay a period of time before sending the set-successor frame. The idea is to make the highest addressed node win the contention. This is because the token is to be passed around in the ring in a descending order of addresses. Each of the contending nodes delays for an amount of time, which is determined by the one's complement of the first 2 bits of their respective addresses. The higher addressed nodes thus delay the least and send their set-successor frames earlier than the lower addressed nodes. In the delay state, any module that hears the transmission of another module drops out of the contention process. It is quite possible that two or more modules have the same value in the 2 bits and thus delay the same amount. To take care of this problem, the procedure is repeated with the next 2 remaining bits for the remaining modules. This procedure continues until all the address bits have been exhausted. In the end, the module with the highest address wins and becomes the successor of the token holder. However, if two modules are mistakenly assigned the same address, they both might filter through the contention process using the same delays and may not resolve. To take care of this possibility, a final resolution pass is taken, using a 2-bit random number. Hopefully, the two modules will produce different values and one of them will finally win the contention. The module that loses at this stage becomes aware of the duplicate address situation and informs its network management of this problem.

Finally, the bus is also capable of recovering from a lost-token situation as described below: If the token is lost, there will not be any activity on the bus. Each node has an *inactivity timer* which expires if the inactivity period is long enough. When a node senses its inactivity timer going off, it transmits a claim-token frame. (It could very well have generated a token at this point. But this is not done because it is quite possible that the inactivity timer of the other nodes might also expire soon, and they would also generate tokens. To avoid this, the module sends the claim-token frame.) As before, other modules might transmit the claim-token frame at the same time. This is then taken care of by using the bus contention resolution algorithm.

Thus the IEEE Standard 802.4 bus maintenance protocols are able to detect and recover from a variety of multiple concurrent errors. The error recovery mechanisms are elaborate and appear quite feasible. But many other fault situations still need to be accounted for. The duplicate address detection mechanism detects duplicate addresses only if the modules with duplicate addresses have reached the final stage of the bus contention resolution algorithm. This implies that they have to be the highest addressed nodes. Therefore, the question arises: Is there a reasonable way to detect duplicate address nodes, that are not the highest addressed, among the contending nodes? Furthermore, if two duplicate address nodes that have reached the final stage of the resolution algorithm produce the same random number coincidentally, how is this taken care of? The assumption here is that, most likely, they will produce different random numbers. But the random number is only a 2-bit random number; thus the probability that both nodes will generate the same number is quite high. This is especially true if the random number generation technique is not statistically independent. One problem that seems to be overlooked is the possibility of a node never releasing the token. This could well happen if the *token-hold timer* for a node becomes faulty and the timer never expires. These faulty situations have to be taken care of by higher-level protocols.

In summary, although a shared bus is prone to single-point failures, various techniques can be employed to make the bus structure robust and fault tolerant.

7.3. FAULT TOLERANCE IN SHARED-MEMORY INTERCONNECTIONS

Shared-memory interconnections are frequently used in tightly coupled multiprocessors. In these, all data shared by the processors are stored in the shared memory, so all interprocessor communications are routed through this shared memory. The shared memory is usually realized by using multiple memory modules. This enhances the memory bandwidth and reduces the vulnerability to failure. Each processor may also have a private memory. Notable examples of fault-tolerant computers that use shared-memory interconnection are C.Vmp [SIEW78] and the Pluribus [KATS78] system.

Four basic types of interconnection structures are used to interconnect processor and memory modules:

(a) Common bus shared memory
(b) Crossbar-switch shared memory
(c) Multibus/multiported shared memory
(d) Multistage interconnection networks

These are illustrated in Fig. 7.3.1.

In the common bus interconnection, all processor–memory transfers are time-division multiplexed; therefore, the bus bandwidth is a severely limiting factor to the

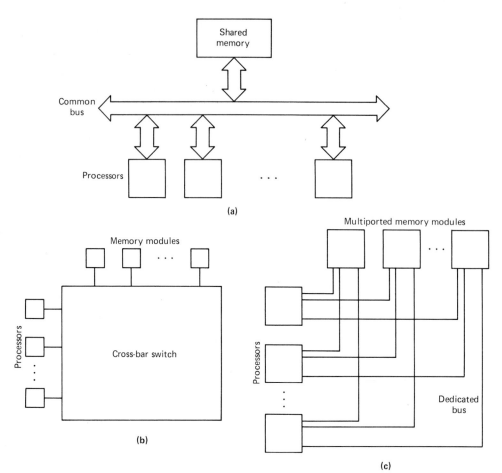

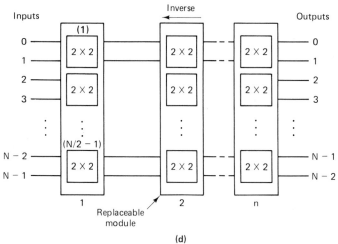

Figure 7.3.1 Shared-memory interconnections: (a) common-bus shared memory; (b) cross-bar-switch shared memory; (c) multibus/multiported shared memory; (d) multistage network.

overall throughput. The crossbar switch, on the other hand, allows simultaneous connections between all nonoverlapping processor–memory pairs. All of the arbitration/priority logic is incorporated into the crossbar switch itself. The multibus/multiported memory interconnection uses a dedicated bus (link) to connect each processor–memory pair. Here each memory module is multiported and the arbitration/priority logic is embedded at the memory I/O ports.

The multistage networks are built by using a large number of simple (usually 2 × 2) switches. These switches are arranged in a multiple stage, as shown in Fig. 7.3.1d. Different patterns of interconnections between the inputs and outputs are realized through various combinations of the switch settings. In general, these networks can be broadly classified into two categories, discussed below.

7.3.1. Nonblocking Networks [BROO83]

A network is said to be nonblocking in the strict sense or *strictly nonblocking* if any desired connection between unused inputs and outputs can be established immediately without interference from any arbitrary existing connections. A network is said to be nonblocking in the wide sense or *wide-sense nonblocking* if any desired connection between two unused inputs and outputs can be established immediately without interference from arbitrary existing connections, provided that the existing connections have been inserted using some routing algorithm (peculiar to the network). If the algorithm has not been followed, some attempted connections may be blocked.

Thus a nonblocking network is any network that can provide all possible combinations of input/output connections. Also, given some combination of already established interconnections between a subset of inputs and outputs, the network is able to establish a new path between any unconnected input/output pair, without altering the paths already established. The three-stage networks proposed by Clos [CLOS53] and Cantor [CANT71] are examples of nonblocking networks.

7.3.2. Rearrangeable Networks [BROO83]

A network is said to be *rearrangeable* when a desired connection between unused inputs/outputs may be temporarily blocked, but can be established if one or more existing connections are rerouted or rearranged. A network is said to be *blocking* if there exist interconnection patterns that will prevent some additional desired connections from being established between unused inputs/outputs, even with rearrangement of the existing connections. Compared to nonblocking networks, blocking networks are simpler to design and control. All shuffle-exchange-based networks are examples of blocking networks.

In considering the effects of faults in the shared memory systems, one has to consider faults both in the interconnection logic and in the memory modules. Regarding the effects of faults in the interconnection logic, the common bus is most vulnerable and the multibus/multiported connection is perhaps least vulnerable. Although the crossbar switch can be vulnerable to single-point failures, the effect of failures can be minimized by segmenting the switch and then by realizing each segment independently. On the other hand, a fault on a bus in a multibus/multiported interconnection is easily overcome by routing data between the affected processor–memory pair through other available processor–memory paths.

The reliability and fault tolerance of multistage networks in the context of Benes networks has been studied by Opferman, Tsao, and Wu in [OPFE71]. These Benes networks consist of 2^n inputs/outputs and $(2n - 1)$ stages. Each stage consists of 2^{n-1} switches, where each switch can be set in two states: the through (T) state, and the cross (X) state. The fault model used by the authors is concerned primarily with failures affecting control of the switches. It is assumed that a switch can fail in two ways; the fault results in setting the switch permanently in one of the two states the (T or X state). These faults are correspondingly formed stuck-at-T (s-a-T), or stuck-at-(s-a-X) faults, as shown in Fig. 7.3.2. Using this model, the authors proposed testing these networks by using two *test permutations* (specified pattern of input/output connections). These test permutations satisfy the property that they are realizable only through a unique combination of switch settings. The testing is performed by applying the appropriate control inputs to set the switches, in order to realize the test permutations. Then any deviation in switch setting caused by faults is observed by determining the input/output connections actually realized.

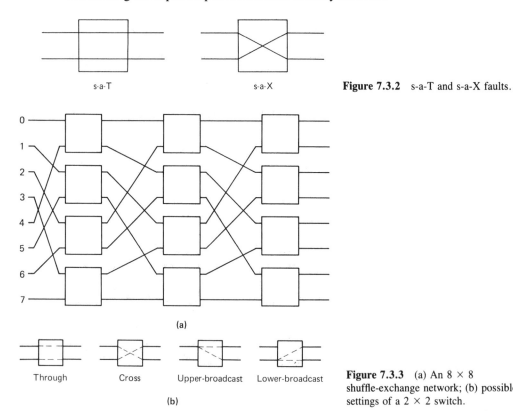

Figure 7.3.2   s-a-T and s-a-X faults.

(a)

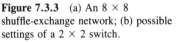

Through   Cross   Upper-broadcast   Lower-broadcast

(b)

Figure 7.3.3   (a) An 8 × 8 shuffle-exchange network; (b) possible settings of a 2 × 2 switch.

Fault diagnosis in shuffle-exchange-based networks has been the focus of more recent research. These shuffle-exchange networks are blocking networks and consist of $N = 2^n$ inputs/outputs connected through n stages of 2^{n-1} (2×2) switches. The interconnection between any two adjacent stages, and between the network inputs and the first stage, correspond to the perfect-shuffle permutation.

The perfect shuffle permutation routes data from position j, whose binary representation is $j_{n-1}, \ldots, j_1, j_0$, to position k, whose binary representation is $j_{n-2}, \ldots, j_1, j_0, j_{n-1}$. Figure 7.3.3a illustrates an 8×8 shuffle-exchange network. Here each switch is capable of assuming four possible settings: through (T), cross (X), upper broadcast (ub), and lower broadcast (lb), as shown in Fig. 7.3.3b. Thus these networks can produce many one-to-one and one-to-many interconnections, although not all (e.g., the interconnections $0 \rightarrow 0$ and $4 \rightarrow 2$ in Fig. 7.3.3a are not possible simultaneously).

The testing and diagnosis of these shuffle-exchange networks have been studied in [FALV81a]. Here it is assumed that a switch may get stuck at any one of its states or at a combination of different states.

Thus it is seen that there are altogether nine possible faults that correspond to the nine possible distinct combinations, enumerated in Fig. 7.3.4a.

1. Stuck-at-X (s-a-X)   Fig. 7.3.4a
2. Stuck-at-T (s-a-T)   Fig. 7.3.4b
3. Stuck-at-ub (s-a-ub)   Fig. 7.3.4c
4. Stuck-at-lb (s-a-lb)   Fig. 7.3.4d
5. Stuck-at-T and X (s-a-T/X)   Fig. 7.3.4e
6. Stuck-at-T and ub (s-a-T/ub)   Fig. 7.3.4f
7. Stuck-at-T and lb (s-a-T/lb)   Fig. 7.3.4g
8. Stuck-at-X and ub (s-a-X/ub)   Fig. 7.3.4h
9. Stuck-at-X and lb (s-a-X/lb)   Fig. 7.3.4i

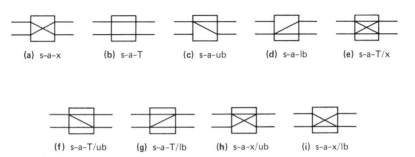

(a) s-a-x   (b) s-a-T   (c) s-a-ub   (d) s-a-lb   (e) s-a-T/x

(f) s-a-T/ub   (g) s-a-T/lb   (h) s-a-x/ub   (i) s-a-x/lb

Figure 7.3.4 Possible faults in a 2×2 switch.

The fault model described in Fig. 7.3.4a is developed on the basis that any test set designed to detect all the faults above in a 2×2 switch will detect most of the single- and multiple-line stuck-at faults.

The following observations are used in formulating the test sets.

Assertion 1: A 2×2 switch can be tested for all the faults above by applying (01) or (10) combinations to the switch inputs and by observing the outputs of the switch by setting it in the two states T and X.

Assertion 2: A $(0,0)$ $[(1,1)]$ input to a 2×2 switch will always produce $(0,0)$ $[(1,1)]$ at its output, *independent* of the state of the switch and also *independent* of whether any of the foregoing faults in the switch exist.

The fault diagnosis technique developed in [FALV81a] assumes the following as the replacement module in accordance with the current technology: The set of switches in a single stage, or in a group of adjacent stages will be assumed to form the smallest unit of replacement.

The fault diagnosis procedure developed here is based on two possible strategies:

1. Diagnosis without any repair
2. Diagnosis with repair, where repair constitutes replacing the faulty module with a good module

For fault diagnosis without repair, it is assumed that all the faulty switches are confined to a single stage. On the other hand, for diagnosis with repair it is assumed that any number of switches in any number of stages can be faulty.

Therefore, the extent of fault location depends on the particular fault diagnosis procedure used, as described below.

1. *Fault diagnosis without repair*: All faulty switches are located as long as faulty switches are confined to a single stage.
2. *Fault diagnosis with repair*: All faulty switches are located independent of the number and distribution of the faulty switches.

The following example is presented to better illustrate the material presented later and to introduce a key concept called *stage test*.

Example 3. Consider the 8×8 shuffle-exchange network and the three input combinations t_1, t_2, and t_3 shown in Fig. 7.3.5. It can easily be seen that each input, t_k, applies $(0, 1)$ to all the switches in stage k, and applies $(0, 0)$ or $(1, 1)$ to switches in all other stages—given that the switches in stage k are set to the same state, T or X. It may be further noted that this observation holds independent of whether any faults exist in stages 1 through $(k - 1)$.

For example, consider the input t_2. This input applies $(0, 0)$ or $(1, 1)$ to all the switches in stage 1. Thus, from assertion 2, one can deduce that the outputs of these

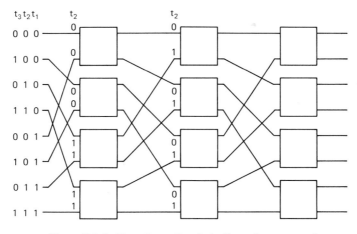

Figure 7.3.5   Tests for an 8 × 8 shuffle-exchange network.

switches in stage 1 will be the same as the inputs—independent of whether or not any faults exist in these switches. Furthermore, it may be seen that the outputs yielded from stage 1 result in the application of the (0, 1) combination to the switches in stage 2, shown in Fig. 7.3.5.

Now, if the switches in stage 2 are exercised through both T and X states with this (0, 1) input, one would have applied all the tests required in assertion 1. It can be seen now that any errors that are produced by the faulty switches in stage 2 during these tests can be propagated easily to the network outputs through stage 3 if the switches in stage 3 are fault-free. The input t_2 is thus capable of detecting all faults in stage 2; thus this is referred to as a stage 2 test. In the following we define, in general, a stage-k test: An input t_k is a stage-k test if it can detect all faults in stage k when stages $k + 1, k + 2, \ldots, n$ between the faulty stage and network outputs are fault-free.

Results are presented in [FALV81a] that compute t_k for various networks. Also presented are results that can be used to determine the exact locations of the faulty switches within the stage. The following procedure was also described that can be used for the two different diagnosis procedures.

Let $T = \{t_k \mid 1 \leq k \leq n\}$ be the set of all of the n-stage tests. The following describes the fault diagnosis procedures that use the test set T for various networks.

Fault diagnosis without repair:

A1:   Let $k = n$.

A2:   Apply t_k to the network. Set all the switches to T state and observe the network outputs. Then change the setting of the switches in stage k, from T, to X and observe the network outputs. If any errors are observed in either case, stage k is diagnosed as faulty; thus, exit. Else, go to A3.

A3:   Let $k = k - 1$ if $k = 0$; then, exit. Else, go to A2.

Fault diagnosis procedure with repair: This procedure is the same as above except that the last sentence in A2 would change to: "If any errors are observed in either case, replace the faulty stage k by a spare stage (spare module containing stage k); then, go to A3."

Other work in the area of fault diagnosis of interconnection networks has been reported in [FENG81] and [OPPE84]. A good survey of this can be found in [AGRA82].

In addition to testing and fault diagnosis, work has also been reported on how to incorporate redundancy in multistage networks so as to achieve a degree of fault tolerance.

Sowrirajan and Reddy [SOWR79] have used the fault model of stuck-at-T and stuck-at-X to design a one-fault-tolerant Benes network. Specifically, they have proposed augmenting the Benes network with the addition of one extra switching element at the output of the network.

Shen and Hayes [SHEN80] have introduced a connectivity property which is used as a criterion for fault tolerance. This property is called the *dynamic full-access property* (DFA). A network with a 2×2 switching element is said to have DFA if any desired input/output can be connected in a finite number of passes through the network. Using the s-a-T and s-a-X fault model, they have analyzed the DFA property of multistage networks. The design of fault-tolerant shuffle-exchange-based networks has also been studied in [FALV81b], [ADAM82], and [LAWR83].

One shortcoming of the shuffle-exchange interconnection networks is that only one path exists from every input, i, to every output, j. Thus two different settings of switching elements will result in two different permutations. Consequently, if a switch does become faulty, many permutations will not be admissible by the network.

For example, the number of distinct permutations that are admitted by a $2^n \times 2^n$ multistage network which consists of n stages, with a 2×2 switch, is

$$2^{n \cdot 2^{n-1}}$$

Now, if one of the switches in the ($2^n \times 2^n$) network becomes stuck-at-T or X state, the number of admissible permutations by the faulty network reduces to

$$2^{n \cdot 2^{n-1} - 1}$$

This, then, results in a severe degradation. Furthermore, several inputs cannot be connected to certain outputs. For example, if the faulty switch is in stage k, $1 \leq k \leq n$, there are some 2^k inputs where each input cannot be connected to certain 2^{n-k} outputs.

Therefore, it was proposed in [FALV81b] that these networks be augmented by adding one additional stage, so that in the event of a single faulty switch, one is still able to realize *all* the permutations using at most two passes through the network. Here a class of interconnection networks, called *two-path interconnection networks*, has been introduced. In these networks, any input can be connected to any output through two disjoint paths. Therefore, if a switch in the networks becomes stuck-at-T or X state, any input can still be connected to any output and all permutations can still be realized by the faulty network in two passes.

The fault-tolerant concept for these networks here is based on the idea of realizing the permutations in two passes. The first pass connects $(N - 2)$ input/output pairs, and the second pass connects the two input/output pair connections that are blocked due to the faulty switch, through alternate paths that do not contain the faulty switch.

The design procedure augments a given interconnection network with the addition of one additional stage to the network. This creates two disjoint paths between any input and any output.

The key concept at work here is: Given source S and destination D, one can easily see that the two paths $S \rightarrow D$ and $S \rightarrow \overline{D}$ $(\overline{S} \rightarrow D)$, where $\overline{S}$ and $\overline{D}$ are the bit-by-bit complement of S and D, are switch disjoint, except for the one switch in the first (last) stage. However, the setting of this switch, for both these connections, differs. Therefore, a source S can be connected to destinations D and $\overline{D}$ through two disjoint paths.

An additional stage has been developed which allows connection of D to $\overline{D}$ $(S$ to $\overline{S})$, and of $\overline{D}$ to D $(\overline{S}$ to $S)$, by using two *different* paths. So this additional stage means that there are two switch-disjoint paths between any source and any destination, except for the first (last) stage. But the state of the switch in these two stages will be different for these two paths. This particular approach is used in [FALV81b] for the designing of various two-path interconnection networks. One such network is described below.

A permutation $p(i, Z(i))$ is said to be an *identity (bit-complement) permutation* if the input i is mapped to the output $Z(i)$, where

$$Z(i) = \begin{cases} i & \text{identity} \\ \overline{i} & \text{bit complement} \end{cases}$$

Consider the network LAMDA (λ) shown in Fig. 7.3.6a. This network consists of $(N/2)$ 2×2 switches. The inputs of this network are connected to the switch inputs through a fixed permutation, η, described below; the outputs of the switches are permuted according to η before they are connected to the network outputs.

Let $i = (i_n, i_{n-1}, \ldots, i_2, i_1)$ be the binary representation of i. Now η is defined as

$$\eta(i_n i_{n-1} \cdots i_2 i_1) = \begin{cases} i_n i_{n-1} \cdots i_2 i_1 & \text{if } i_1 = 0 \\ \overline{i}_n \overline{i}_{n-1} \cdots \overline{i}_2 i_1 & \text{if } i_1 = 1 \end{cases}$$

The following observation may be made about the LAMDA network. This network realizes the identity (bit-complement) permutation when the switches are configured in the T(X) state. Also, an input, v, can be connected to either the output $Z(v) = v$ or to $Z(v) = \overline{v}$, by setting the corresponding switch to the T or X state, respectively.

Using the LAMDA network one can design a two-path network as illustrated in

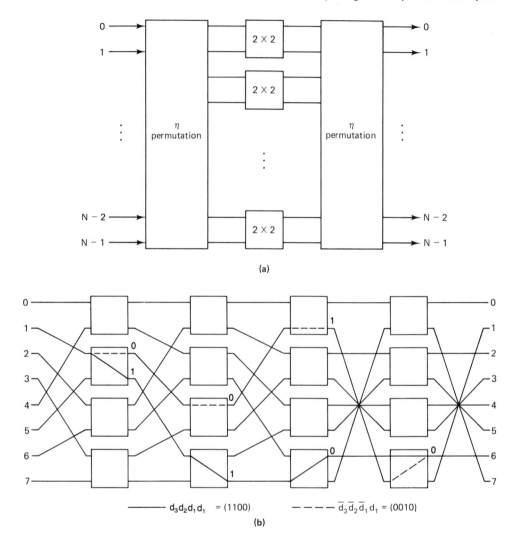

Figure 7.3.6 (a) LAMDA network; (b) an 8 × 8 two-path shuffle-exchange network, $\Omega\lambda$ with connection of $1 \rightarrow 6$ realized in two different paths.

Fig. 7.3.6b for an 8 × 8 shuffle-exchange network. (The tag bits are computed as $d_3 d_2 d_1 d_1$ for the first path, and as $\overline{d_3}\,\overline{d_2}\,\overline{d_1}\, d_1$ for the second path. The switches are set by using the conventional technique of connecting to upper switch output, if the corresponding tag bit is 0, and to the lower, if the corresponding tag bit is 1 as shown.) Other fault-tolerant designs of multistage networks have been reported in [ADAM82] and [LAWR83].

Another important concern in the shared-memory interconnection is the effect of memory module faults. If spare memory modules are available, one can reconfigure the memory by using the spare module to replace the faulty module(s). On the other hand, if no spare modules are available, the system may have to be operated in a degraded mode using the available fault-free modules. Different reconfiguration strategies [LANG79] are available that achieve such graceful degradation. The particular technique that may be chosen would depend on the memory organization.

Basically, there are two different memory organizations with multiple memory modules: noninterleaved and interleaved. In the noninterleaved memory, consecutive logical addresses are mapped into consecutive addresses within each module and then sequentially across the modules. In the interleaved memory, consecutive logical addresses are mapped into consecutive modules. The interleaved memory has the potential for providing a higher bandwidth because it allows simultaneous access to consecutive (logical) addresses. However, as seen below, degradation due to faults can be quite severe in an interleaved memory.

The following discussion assumes that the memory modules are of the same size, $M = 2^m$, and that the number of modules, K, is a power of 2; that is, $K = 2^k$. This assumption is in keeping with most of the common implementations, since it facilitates address mapping. Thus the total address space available is $MK = 2^{(m+k)}$. Let n denote $(m + k)$; so the logical addresses are n bits long.

Given the n-bit logical address, $A = (a_{n-1}, a_{n-2}, \ldots, a_1, a_0)$, it first has to be mapped into a two-component physical address for memory access. One component of this represents the modules; the other, the address within the module. For the noninterleaved memory, the most significant k bits of the address, $(a_{n-1}, \ldots, a_{n-k})$, represent the module number; the remaining bits, $(a_{n-k-1}, \ldots, a_0)$, represent the address within the module. For the interleaved memory, the least significant k bits of A [i.e., $(a_{k-1}, \ldots, a_0)$] represent the module number. The remaining bits, $(a_n, \ldots, a_k)$, represent the address within the module. Thus it may be noted that for the interleaved memory, any set of 2^k consecutive addresses map into 2^k distinct modules. So the number of modules must always be a power of 2. This requirement poses a problem in reconfiguring the memory when memory faults occur. The following discusses various reconfiguration schemes for noninterleaved and interleaved memories.

First, it may be noted that any reconfiguration scheme must strive to utilize the remaining memory space as fully as possible. At the same time, it is desirable to preserve, as much as possible, the simplicity of the address map of the original system.

When a module becomes faulty, the available memory space reduces to $(K - 1)M$. The problem becomes how to reconfigure the memory address map so as to utilize fully the remaining memory space.

In this section we assume that f denotes the faulty module. Also, all expressions that represent module numbers are assumed to be reduced to modulo K.

When the memory module, f, becomes faulty, one has to reassign all the logical addresses, previously assigned to f, to other modules. This can be performed for noninterleaved memories, and for interleaved memories, as follows.

Reassignment for noninterleaved memory is accomplished fairly easily by mapping the logical module number j into physical module number $(j + f + 1)$ modulo K. However, this simple reconfiguration technique cannot be applied to interleaved memory because this would require a $(K - 1)$-way interleaving, which will result in a complex address map since $(K - 1)$ is not a power of 2. An alternative to this is to reduce the memory size by half, to $K/2$ modules, and then to perform $(K/2)$-way interleaving. Since $K/2$ is always a power of 2, the resulting address map can be simple, as seen below.

Let the module f satisfy $f \geq K/2$. Then modules 0 through $(K/2\text{-}1)$ are fault-free. Now one can perform a $(K/2)$-way interleaving by using modules 0 through $(K/2\text{-}1)$. Since the memory size is half of the original, the logical addresses range from 0 through $2^{n-1} - 1$. Hence, $a_{n-1} = 0$ for all addresses, and the module number is given by $(a_{k-2}, \cdots, a_0)$, the least significant $(k - 1)$ bits. The address within the module is represented by the $(n - k)$ bits $(a_{n-2}, a_{n-3}, \ldots, a_{k-1})$.

On the other hand, if $f \leq K/2 - 1$, the modules $K/2$ through $(K - 1)$ are fault-free. These modules can be used to perform $K/2$-way interleaving. With this interleaving, the module number is given by $(1, a_{k-2}, \ldots, a_1, a_0)$. The address within the module is given by $(a_{n-2}, a_{n-3}, \ldots, a_{k-1})$. For example, given an eight-module system, with module 3 faulty, one can use modules 4, 5, 6, and 7 to perform a four-way interleaving. Here the module number is given by $(1, a_1, a_0)$, and the address within the module is given by $(a_{n-2}, \ldots, a_2)$.

The basic shortcoming of the technique just described is that the available memory size reduces drastically to half of the original size—with just a single module failure. Alternative techniques described below require a more complex address map and utilize the memory more fully.

The strategy with these alternative techniques is to partition the set of modules to either fixed- or variable-sized groups [LANG79]. The addresses are then interleaved within each group. Therefore, the number of modules within each group has to be a power of 2, as illustrated in the following example.

Example 4.   Consider an eight-module system with eight cells per module. Thus, in the absence of any faults, the logical addresses can range from 0 through 63 and these can be eight-way interleaved.

Now, assume that the module 4 becomes faulty. One can now partition six of the seven fault-free modules into three groups:

$$group\ 0 = [5, 6]$$

$$group\ 1 = [7, 0]$$

$$group\ 2 = [1, 2]$$

The addresses are then interleaved as shown in Fig. 7.3.7a. Given the 6-bit logical address $A = (a_5, a_4, a_3, a_2, a_1, a_0)$, one can obtain the memory address as follows:

$$\text{module number} = 5 + (a_5, a_4, a_0)\ \text{modulo 8}$$

$$\text{address within the module} = (a_3, a_2, a_1)$$

Any pair of consecutive words can be accessed simultaneously, since the addresses are two-way interleaved. However, in the scheme above, one of the memory modules (the module numbered 3) is unused. This unutilized memory space can be a

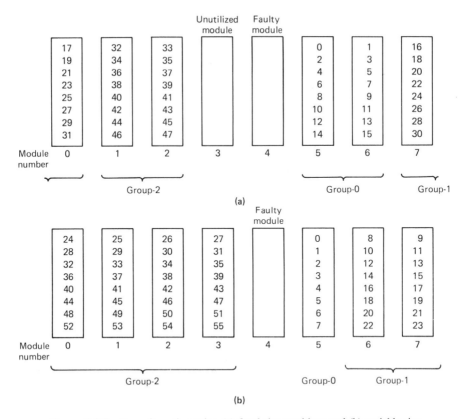

Figure 7.3.7 Reconfiguration using (a) fixed-size partitions and (b) variable-size partitions.

significant factor if each group consists of a large number of memory modules so as to achieve a high degree of interleaving.

Thus, instead of partitioning the modules into a fixed size, one can partition the modules into variable-sized groups to better utilize the memory space as shown below. Let the seven fault-free modules be partitioned into the following three groups:

$$group \ 0 \ = \ [5]$$

$$group \ 1 \ = \ [6, 7]$$

$$group \ 2 \ = \ [0, 1, 2, 3]$$

Then the addresses in group 1 and group 2 can be two-way and four-way interleaved, respectively. This is shown in Fig. 7.3.7(b).

The advantage of variable-sized partitions is that after a fault, all the remaining memory space is fully utilized. However, the variable-sized partitions require a complex address map (Problem 7.6).

Thus there are a broad range of issues related to fault tolerance in shared-memory interconnections—the subject of significant research.

7.4. FAULT-TOLERANT LOOP ARCHITECTURES

The loop or ring network is commonly used for the interconnection of computers that are in close proximity, such as those in local area networks. Some key examples of loop networks include the Newhall loop [FARM69], the Pierce loop [PIER72], and the delay insertion loops [HAFN74, REAM75].

In the *Newhall loop*, shown in Fig. 7.4.1, a single control token is circulated around the loop. The token is used by each node in the loop, in round-robin fashion. That is, control is passed from node to node, using this token. For a node to transmit a message, it must first wait for the arrival of the control token. When this token is received, the node takes possession of the token and then transmits the message. Thus there can be only one message in transit on the loop at any one time. Since the length of the message is not restricted, a node can send all the messages at one time once it has taken possession of the control token.

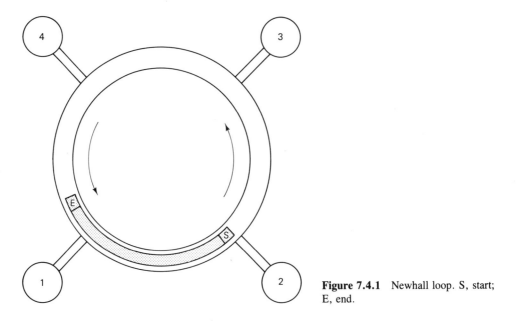

Figure 7.4.1 Newhall loop. S, start; E, end.

The *Pierce loop*, shown in Fig. 7.4.2, uses fixed-size slots for its message transmission. Here the communication space of the loop is segmented to a certain fixed number of slots. A message is also segmented into packets of size that can fit into those slots. The message is then transmitted by the node as packets using available empty slots.

The third type, *delay insertion loops*, [SWAR 82] shown in Fig. 7.4.3, uses shift registers to insert the message into the loop. The maximum length of the message (packet) is limited by the length of the shift register used. All the shift registers may be controlled by a central clock, as shown in Fig. 7.4.3. During each clock cycle, the shift registers are shifted by one bit.

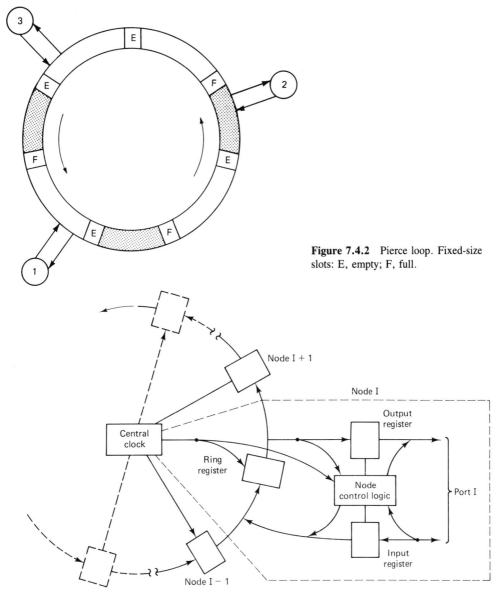

Figure 7.4.2 Pierce loop. Fixed-size slots: E, empty; F, full.

Figure 7.4.3 Delay insertion loop.

Every time a message is inserted into the loop by a transmitter, the communication space (delay required to admit the number of bits in transit) is incremented correspondingly. Similarly, the removal of a message by the receiver shortens the communication space accordingly. So the delay insertion technique utilizes the loop efficiently by dynamically tailoring the available communication space on the loop to the total number of message bits that are in transit.

The three types of loops described above are all unidirectional, as all the links are configured to carry messages in one direction only. This factor of unidirectionality, while eliminating any routing overhead, poses a serious reliability problem. A single link failure disconnects the loop and thus makes the loops highly vulnerable to single-point failures. Several bidirectional, double-loop structures have been proposed that overcome the inherent fault-tolerance problem. Included in the reported fault-tolerant architectures are the multiloop networks of Zafiropulo [ZAFI74], the braided loop interconnection of Hafner, and the daisy chain network of Granov et al. [GRAN80]. This section reviews the underlying fault-tolerance concepts of these networks.

The *double-loop networks* have two or more independent loops where each loop is operated in a unidirectional mode during normal operation, shown in Fig. 7.4.4. (Normally, the two loops in a double-loop structure carry messages in opposite directions when there are no faults in the system.) When faults do occur, the loop is reconfigured so as to maintain complete connectivity. Reconfiguration is achieved by reversing the direction of one or more links and/or by operating one or more links in a bidirectional (duplex or half-duplex) mode.

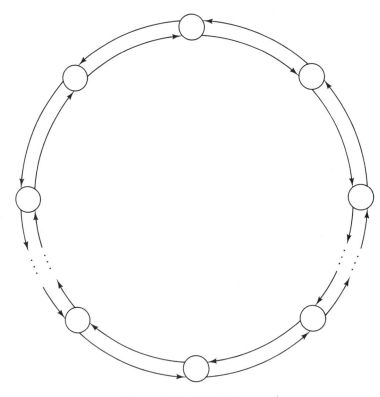

Figure 7.4.4 Double-loop structure.

Topologically, two basic reconfiguration strategies can be employed: the self-heal technique and the bypass technique. The *self-heal technique*, illustrated in Fig. 7.4.5, is useful in disconnecting the faulty node. In this, the loops wrap around those two nodes adjacent to the faulty node, thus effectively isolating the faulty node. On the other hand, the *bypass technique*, given in Fig. 7.4.6, is particularly useful for bypassing faulty links. When a link fault occurs, the loop is reconfigured so as to bypass the faulty link, as discussed below. There are two links between every adjacent node pair. So with a single link fault, there still exists a link that can be used to maintain connection between the node pair affected. By logically assigning the fault-free link to one of the two loops, one can maintain one of the loops. This may require reversing the direction of flow in the link. The selection of the preferred direction in which the flow is to be maintained is a design consideration that may be decided a priori, or dynamically, after the fault occurs. The implementation of this bypass technique is easily accomplished once it has been established which logical loop (clockwise or counterclockwise) is to be maintained. Of course, reversing the direction of flow in a link requires a certain degree of coordination between the two adjacent interface units.

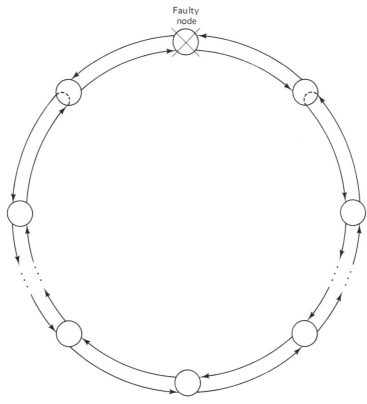

Figure 7.4.5 Self-heal technique.

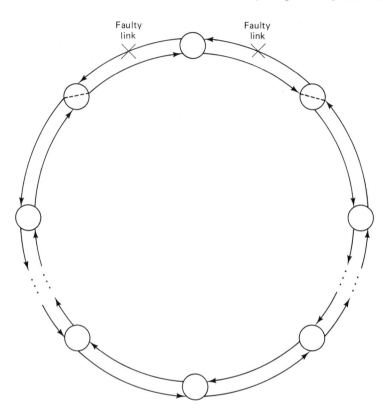

Figure 7.4.6 Bypass technique.

The bypass technique is also useful for multiple link faults, provided that there is at least one operational link present between every pair of adjacent nodes. Other techniques, though, are available (below) that are useful for recovery from the type of double-link fault which disconnects some adjacent pair of nodes.

A detailed implementation of a fault-tolerant double-loop structure has been presented in [WOLF79]. In this, the delay insertion technique is used for message transmission during fault-free operation and both delay insertion and control token types of transmission are used during faulty operation. Central to this design is a *multifunctional loop interface unit*, illustrated in Fig. 7.4.7. This unit incorporates a microprocessor that supports a variety of transmission modes in addition to performing fault detection and loop reconfiguration, as described below.

The loop interface unit transmits certain timing signals on the outgoing links whenever there are no messages being transmitted. Thus at any time, there are either message signals or timing signals on each link. The interface unit also continuously monitors each incoming link; thus a link is assumed to be faulty when neither message nor timing signals are received through the link.

When such a fault is detected on the link, the detecting interface unit initiates the reconfiguration. The reconfiguration is performed in order to maintain the pre-

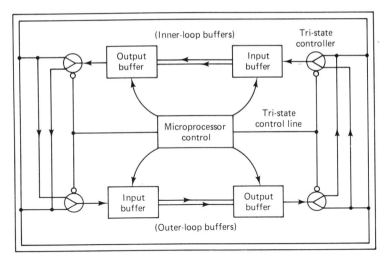

Figure 7.4.7   Fault-tolerant loop interface.

ferred loop. This process may require logically exchanging a link from the outer loop with the corresponding link from the inner loop. It is proposed that this exchange be performed fairly easily, by using tri-state controllers. Before effecting the change, the interface unit informs all the other units about the fault that has been detected.

To facilitate the recording and updating of faulty information, each interface unit is provided with a *master link map* (MLM). The MLM has one bit per link and the bit indicates the status of the link—whether it is operational or faulty. Whenever a fault is detected, a suitable message is generated by the detecting interface unit. The message is broadcast to all the other units—which then update their MLMs. The messages are all acknowledged, so any message that may be lost in the faulty link during this updating process is automatically retransmitted.

In addition to the link failure, provision is made for the loop interface unit to detect faults within itself. When such a fault is detected, the interface unit short-circuits both the inner and outer loops. Thus the faulty interface unit effectively removes itself from the loop. Before disconnecting, the faulty interface unit broadcasts a message to all the other units, informing them of the fault.

An interesting feature of the design is that it is proposed that both the Newhall type and the delay insertion type of transmission be made possible simultaneously, when needed. This allows for operation of the loop, in spite of double-link failures which may completely disconnect two adjacent nodes as follows.

Upon detection of a fault that disconnects the loop, the detecting interface unit generates a Newhall type of control token. The loop is then operated in both delay insertion mode and Newhall mode, simultaneously. This token is then propagated from node to node until it reaches the interface unit on the other side of the double fault. This interface unit then reverses the direction of the token and sends it back. Thus the token travels back and forth between the two nodes that were disconnected by the fault. This back-and-fourth traveling of the token may necessitate time sharing some of the links, in order to support flow in both directions.

For a node to transmit a message, it first checks to see if there is a directed (delay insertion) path to the receiver (by using its MLM), to enable transmission using the delay insertion mode. If it finds that such a path exists, the node transmits the message using the regular delay insertion technique. Otherwise (if no such directed path exists), the node then waits for the Newhall control token (that is circulating) to arrive and then uses this to transmit the message. This use of the token would require temporarily reversing the direction of some of the links. This is illustrated further in the following example.

Example 5. Consider an eight-node double-loop system, shown in Fig. 7.4.8. The multiple-link fault shown has completely disconnected nodes 4 and 5. A Newhall token would therefore be traveling back and forth between nodes 4 and 5, continuously. This would require periodically reversing the direction of some of the links temporarily. (For example, while traveling from node 5 to node 4, the links from nodes 3 to 2 and 2 to 1 have to be reversed.)

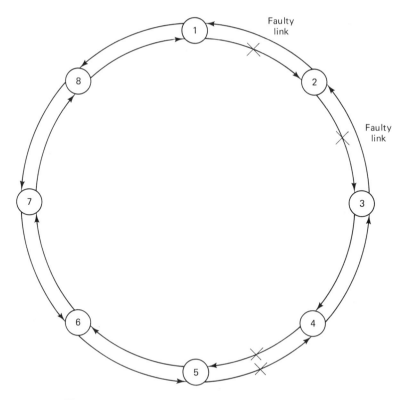

Figure 7.4.8 Eight-node double-loop system in Example 5.

Now if node 1 needs to send a message to node 3, it cannot use the delay insertion technique because there is no directed path since the links from 2 to 3 and 1 to 2 have become faulty. The node must therefore wait for the arrival of the Newhall token to take control of the loop, to send the message to 3. This would obviously require, first, reversal of the link 1 to 2, followed by the link 2 to 3.

As can be seen here, this design is fairly robust and provides a significant degree of fault tolerance.

Basic loop architectures can thus be adapted to provide a measure of fault tolerance. However, although these architectures are fairly versatile, they may not be suitable for very large systems, especially because the internode distance (number of hops required to route the message) can still be too large (i.e., of the order n).

Therefore, certain other loop-based interconnection topologies that address some of these inadequacies of the basic loop interconnection have been proposed. These include the multiloop organizations proposed in [ZAFI74] and the daisy chain structures proposed in [GRAN80].

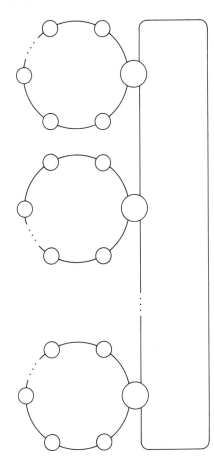

Figure 7.4.9   Two-level multiloop organization.

The *multiloop organization* interconnects the nodes into several loops, which are then interconnected using additional loops in two or more levels. A two-level organization is shown in Fig. 7.4.9. The basic advantage is that the internode distances are reduced. Also, multiple failures that may affect any one group need not be catastrophic. Assuming that all the nodes are equally likely to fail, a two-level approach is shown to be optimal from the point of view of reliability improvement and cost-effectiveness.

The *daisy chain structure* [GRAN80] is an interesting variation of the double-loop network and is based on the braided-loop concept of Hafner [HAFN76]. Here there is one outer loop and two smaller inner loops. A 12-node daisy chain structure is illustrated in Fig. 7.4.10. One of the inner loops connects all the odd nodes, while the other connects all the even nodes. During fault-free operation, the outer and inner loops are configured logically, in opposite directions, reducing the number of hops between nodes. In addition, the loops can be reconfigured to provide fault tolerance. These various adaptations of loop networks remain the subject of research, from the point of view of both fault tolerance and performance.

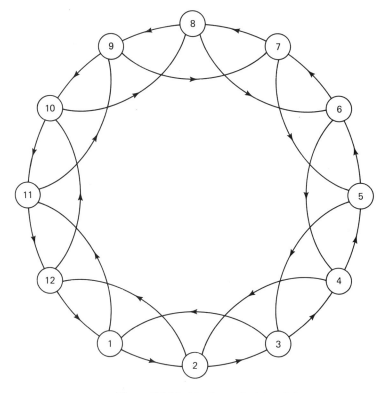

Figure 7.4.10 Twelve-node daisy chain.

7.5. FAULT-TOLERANT TREE NETWORKS

The two logical organizations of multiprocessor systems are referred to as the horizontal and heirarchical organizations. In the *horizontal* system, each processor is autonomous in that there are no "master-slave" relationships (i.e., the processors involved all cooperate to perform the computations). This is not the case in the *hierarchical* system, where, as the name suggests, processors at a lower level are controlled by processors at a higher level.

It is obvious, then, that bus, shared-memory, and loop-type interconnect techniques are most appropriate for the horizontally organized multiprocessors. On the other hand, for hierarchically organized multiprocessors, tree interconnections provide the most natural interconnect architecture. But an inherent shortcoming of the basic tree structure is that of vulnerability to single-point failures. Fortunately, a variety of techniques are now availalbe that address the problem of fault tolerance with the addition of extra links and possibly extra nodes.

Two basic approaches to this problem of fault-tolerant tree design have been pursued by researchers. The first [DESP78] considers augmenting the basic binary tree by adding links so that the tree remains fully connected—in spite of the occurrence of single node or link failures that may occur. The reduced tree can thus provide for degraded performance.

The second approach, proposed by Hayes [HAYE76] and extended by Kwan-Toida [KWAN81a, KWAN81b], involves the design of redundant tree structures by using extra nodes and links. Here the objective is to preserve the original tree structure fully, in spite of faults: by reconfiguring the tree using these extra (standby) nodes and links. This ensures that the overall system performance experiences no degradation because of faults. The chief concern of this design approach is augmenting the original system for fault tolerance while keeping the addition of nodes to a minimum.

The following subsections review the fault-tolerant tree structure designs in detail.

7.5.1. Fault-Tolerant Binary Tree Design with Added Links

Basically, a binary tree is a rooted tree where each nonterminal node is connected to two other nodes in the lower level. Techniques that augment binary trees to enable them to achieve fault tolerance are described in [DESP78] and [HORO81] and are summarized below.

In the following it is assumed that the nodes in the binary tree are numbered 1, 2, 3, . . . , n, where node 1 is the root node. The construction of the tree will be described using the terms *leaf nodes* and *nonleaf nodes*. (Leaf nodes are any terminal nodes that appear at the bottom of the tree; nonleaf nodes, all others.)

The number of levels in the tree is denoted as m, where the root node is assumed to be in level 1, and the nonleaf nodes appear in levels 1 through $(m - 1)$. A common technique used for constructing a binary tree connects each nonleaf node i in level h to two nodes, $2i$ and $(2i + 1)$, in level $(h + 1)$. A full binary tree thus consists of $n = (2^m - 1)$ nodes.

Figure 7.5.1 illustrates a full binary tree with $n = 15$ nodes. Techniques for augmenting basic binary trees by adding links to achieve fault tolerance result in the following types of trees:

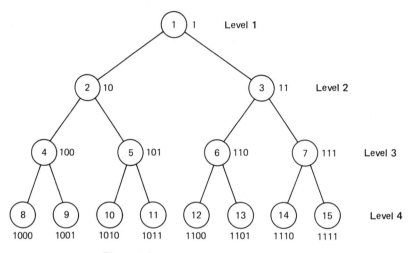

Figure 7.5.1 Full binary tree.

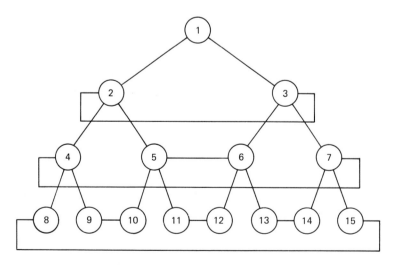

Figure 7.5.2 Half-ringed binary tree.

1. *Half-ringed tree*: This type is constructed by connecting alternate pairs of nodes in every level in a binary tree. Figure 7.5.2 illustrates a half-ringed 15-node binary tree.
2. *Full-ringed binary tree*: This type is constructed by adding links connecting all the adjacent nodes in every level in a binary tree. Figure 7.5.3 illustrates a full-ringed binary tree with 15 nodes.
3. *Leaf-ringed binary tree*: This type is constructed by adding links connecting all the adjacent leaf nodes in a binary tree. Figure 7.5.4 illustrates a 15-node leaf-ringed binary tree.

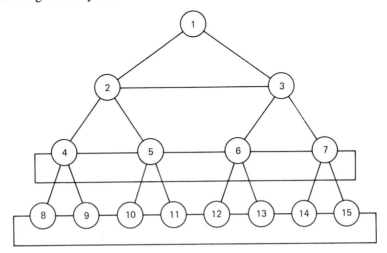

Figure 7.5.3   Full-ringed binary tree.

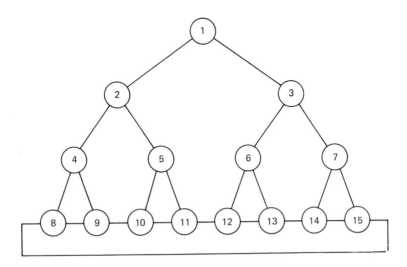

Figure 7.5.4   Leaf-ringed binary tree.

The interconnection complexity of these three types of trees is given in Table 7.5.1.

TABLE 7.5.1 COMPLEXITY OF BINARY TREES

	Total number of links	Maximum number of connections per node
Binary tree	$n - 1$	3
Half-ringed binary tree	$3(n - 1)/2$	4
Full-ringed binary tree	$2n - 3$	5
Leaf-ringed binary tree	$(3n - 1)/2$	3

Discussed below is a routing strategy that can be used for all the trees listed above when there are no faults. In describing this algorithm, it is assumed that the addresses of level h nodes are represented by h-bit binary numbers, as illustrated in Fig. 7.5.1 for a 15-node binary tree.

Let d denote the address of the destination node, which is assumed to be in level p of the tree. Thus let $d = (d_{p-1}, d_{p-2}, \ldots, d_0)$ represent the p-bit binary number that represents d. When a message arrives at a node, y, the following steps are performed in routing. Let y be a level-q node and thus let $y = (y_{q-1}, y_{q-2}, \ldots, y_0)$ represent the q-bit address for y.

Path 7.5.1.

Step 1: If $y = d$, the message is accepted by y. Else, step 2 is performed.
Step 2:
  (a) If $p > q$ and if $d_{p-1}, \ldots, d_{p-q} = y_{q-1}, \ldots, y_0$, the message is forwarded to

$$\begin{cases} 2y & \text{if } d_{p-q-1} = 0 \\ 2y + 1 & \text{if } d_{p-q-1} = 1 \end{cases}$$

  (b) If $p \leq q$ or if $d_{p-1}, \ldots, d_{p-q} \neq y_{q-1}, \ldots, y_0$, the message is forwarded upward to node $[y/2]$.

Thus in step 2, the destination address is checked to see if the node is in the right or left subtree of y. If the destination node belongs to one of the subtrees, the message is forwarded to the appropriate node directly below node y. Otherwise, the message is forwarded to the node directly above y.

For example, given that the source node is equal to 9 and that the destination node is equal to 3, the message will be routed through the path $9 \rightarrow 4 \rightarrow 2 \rightarrow 1 \rightarrow 3$. Furthermore, it is easily seen that the maximum number of hops in any path is limited to, at most, $2\lceil \log n \rceil$.

Fault-tolerance. The fault model assumed here as well as in the subsequent sections is a general model of node and link faults where a node or link is assumed to become totally disabled. Thus this model is an abstraction of many typical failures which can affect data links, interface hardware, the processing element–host computer, and the like. The following describes the fault tolerance of the system by considering first the case of node faults and then link faults.

These interconnections are fault tolerant in that they remain fully connected despite the occurrence of any single node or link failures. Also, simple detours can be constructed that bypass a single faulty node or link in half-ring or full-ring trees. This is illustrated in detail below, with consideration of full-ring trees. In this it is assumed that the node t is faulty (the case of the faulty link can be formulated analogously).

First, it may be observed that if t is a leaf node, the fault does not pose any problem. This is due to the fact that according to the routing algorithm presented above, the leaf nodes do not appear as intermediate nodes in any path. Thus we need only be concerned with the case when t is a nonleaf node.

Case I: Let $t = 1$, the root node.

The effect of a fault in the root node is that the path between 2 and 3 via node 1 is severed. But since a direct link between 2 and 3 does exist, the fault has no real impact in the routing of the message between other pairs of nodes in the tree.

Case II: Let $t > 1$, node other than the root node.

First, it may be seen that in the routing paths admitted in Path 7.5.1, the pairs of nodes that may appear adjacent to t are $(\lfloor t/2 \rfloor, 2t)$, $(\lfloor t/2 \rfloor, 2t + 1)$, and $(2t, 2t + 1)$. Thus detours are needed between each pair of these nodes that bypass node t. Figure 7.5.5 describes such detour paths. In these paths, the node numbers are to be interpreted as modulo-2^h expressions, where h denotes the level of the node.

For example, in a 15-node, full-ring tree, if $t = 5$, one can travel from node $2t = 10$ to $(t - 1)/2 = 2$, by using the following detour:

$$10 \rightarrow 11 \rightarrow 12 \rightarrow 6 \rightarrow 3 \rightarrow 2$$

Recently, a more complex message routing algorithm was proposed [HORO81] that achieves fault tolerance in leaf-ringed trees. This procedure is based on the graph traversal technique. An attractive feature of this proposed procedure is that it can be used in the presence of both single and multiple faults. Also, if because of faults, no path should exist between the source and the destination, the message is returned back to the source. The algorithm, though, does require a considerable amount of overhead for implementation. This algorithm is described in detail below.

In a leaf-ringed tree, there are exactly three neighbors for each node except for the root. The leaf nodes also have three neighbors. For the purpose of this algorithm, these are identified as the left, right, and parent nodes. The left and right neighbors of the nonleaf nodes appear at the level immediately below the node. In the case of leaf nodes, the left and right neighbors appear in the same level, as shown in Fig. 7.5.4.

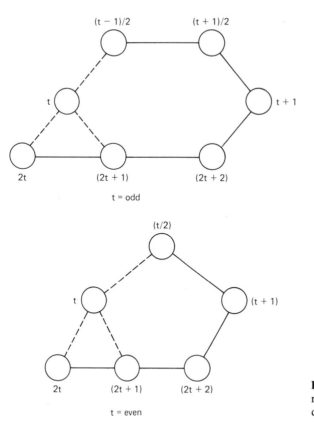

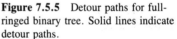

Figure 7.5.5 Detour paths for full-ringed binary tree. Solid lines indicate detour paths.

The parent node is that node in the level immediately above, which is connected to the node.

Let s and d denote the source and destination nodes, respectively.

Let x represent the current node in the message path.

Let w represent the node preceding x in the path (w is undefined at the start of the algorithm). Thus w is a neighbor of x.

Let ST represent a stack where the entries are quadruples of the following type:

$$K = (k, P, L, R)$$

Here k denotes a node number and P, L, and R are Boolean variables. These Boolean variables assume logical true (T) or false (F) values. A value of T in P, L, R in K signifies that the corresponding neighbor of k has already been visited by the message, or is faulty. Such a stack is appended to each message and is initially empty at the source. Each node in the path may modify the stack by pushing or popping elements. So the stack size varies as the message travels from node to node.

Path 7.5.2.   When a message arrives at a node x, the following steps are performed. To begin with, it is checked if $x = d$; then obviously the message has just reached the destination and if so, it is removed. Else if $x = s$, it is checked to see if the message has returned to the source, being unable to find a path to the destination. This would be indicated if an entry $S = (s, P, L, R)$ already exists in the stack where $P = L = R = T$ (true). (It may be noted that a direction marked as T implies that the direction need not be taken because the corresponding adjacent node is either faulty or has already been visited.)

If neither of the above is true, the message has to be forwarded to the next node in the path. The selection of a particular neighbor of x is done by using the following steps.

Step 1: Check if an element $X = (x, P, L, R)$ is already in ST. If there is no such quadruple, push (x, F, F, F) onto stack ST.

Step 2: Next, check if ST contains elements that correspond to any of the neighbor(s) of x other than w (w is that neighbor from where the message was sent to x the *first* time, that is, the node index in the tuple immediately below the top of the stack). If any such quadruple(s) exists in the stack, mark the corresponding component of X as T. [For example, if there already exists a quadruple $U = (u, P, L, R)$ in ST, where u is the parent neighbor of x, set the P component of X as T. This will reflect the fact that the message has previously traveled through u.] Also, check to determine if any of the neighbors of x are faulty. If there are faulty neighbor(s), mark the corresponding component(s) of X as T.

Step 3: Check the relationship of the node w that preceded x with the node x. Branch according to the following:

$$\text{If } w = \begin{cases} \text{left of } x & \text{go to step 4} \\ \text{right of } x & \text{go to step 5} \\ \text{parent of } x & \text{go to step 6} \\ \text{undefined} & \text{go to step 7} \end{cases}$$

//When w is undefined, the message is just starting out at the source and thus there is no preceding node.//

Step 4: //w = left of x.// Select the next node to which the message is to be forwarded, in the following manner:

If the destination node, d, is in the right subtree of x and $R = F$, set $R = T$ and forward the message to the right of x.

//The subtree inclusion test can easily be performed by using the test described in the earlier algorithm, Path 7.5.1, for routing in basic binary trees.//

Else if P = F, then set P = T and forward the message to the parent of x.

Else if R = F, then set R = T and forward the message to the right of x.

Else pop(x) (delete the top element of the stack) and forward the message to the left. //Here the message backtracks to w, the preceding node, as a last resort.//

Step 5: //w = right of x.//

If d is in the left subtree of x and L = F, set L = T and forward the message to the left.

Else if P = F, set P = T and forward the message to the parent.

Else if L = F, set L = T and forward the message to the left.

Else pop(x) and forward the message to the right of x (the message backtracks).

Step 6: //w = parent of x.//

If d is in the left subtree of x and L = F, set L = T and forward the message to the left of x.

Else if d is in the right subtree of x and R = F, set R = T and forward the message to the right of x.

Else if L = F, set L = T and forward the message to the left of x.

Else if R = F, set R = T and forward the message to the right of x.

Else pop(x) and forward the message to the parent of x (the message backtracks).

Step 7: //w = undefined.//

If d is in the left subtree of x and L = F, set L = T and forward the message to the left of x.

Else if d is in the right subtree of x and R = F, set R = T and forward the message to the right of x.

Else if P = F, set P = T and forward the message to the parent of x.

Else if L = F, set L = T and forward the message to the left of x.

Else set R = T and forward the message to the right of x.

The following example illustrates the algorithm in detail.

Example 6.   Consider the leaf-ringed tree of 31 nodes shown in Fig. 7.5.6. Let the faulty nodes be 13, 26, and 15, as shown. Consider routing a message from the source node, $s = 12$, to the destination node, $d = 30$. The message will follow the path

$$12 \rightarrow 6 \rightarrow 3 \rightarrow 7 \rightarrow 14 \rightarrow 28 \rightarrow 27 \rightarrow 28 \rightarrow 29 \rightarrow 30$$

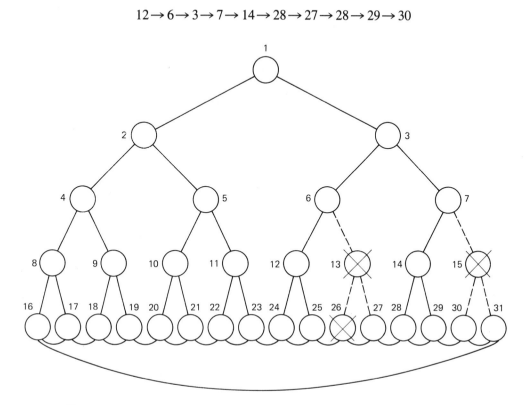

Figure 7.5.6 A 31-node leaf-ringed tree with faults. Dashed lines indicate a disabled link to faulty node.

Table 7.5.2 describes in detail the execution of the algorithm at various steps as the message winds through the path from node to node.

Thus, in the algorithm above, the message always strives to travel on a new link. A message backtracks on a link only as a last resort. There are two possible routing outcomes: a message is either successfully delivered to the destination, or it is returned to the source if no path exists between the source and the destination. (Thus the possibility of a message being lost is eliminated.)

As has been stated, the algorithm above requires a large amount of overhead for implementation and can therefore be slow. Specifically, in addition to the large amount of computations $O(n^2)$ that have to be performed at each node in the path of the message, the path length itself can be as large as $O(n)$. In the worst case, the message may wander around $O(n)$ nodes; hence path length = stack depth = $O(n)$.

TABLE 7.5.2 ROUTING STEPS

X	W	Routing step	Stack operation	Stack contents just before leaving X
12	—	7	PUSH (12, F, F, F)	(12, T, F, F)
6	12	4	PUSH (6, F, F, F)	(6, T, F, T) (12, T, F, F)
3	6	4	PUSH (3, F, F, F)	(3, F, F, T) (6, T, F, T) (12, T, F, F)
7	3	6	PUSH (7, F, F, F)	(7, F, T, T) (3, F, F, T) (6, T, F, T) (12, T, F, F)
14	7	6	PUSH (14, F, F, F)	(14, F, T, F) (7, F, T, T) (3, F, F, T) (6, T, F, T) (12, T, F, F)
28	14	6	PUSH (28, F, F, F)	(28, F, T, F) (14, F, T, F) (7, F, T, T) (3, F, F, T) (6, T, F, T) (12, T, F, F)
27	28	5	PUSH (27, F, F, F) POP (27, T, T, F)	(28, F, T, F) (14, F, T, F) (7, F, T, T) (3, F, F, T) (6, T, F, T) (12, T, F, F)
28	14	6		(28, F, T, T) (14, F, T, F) (7, F, T, T) (3, F, F, T) (6, T, F, T) (12, T, F, F)
29	28	4	PUSH (29, F, F, F)	(29, T, F, T) (28, F, T, F) (14, F, T, F) (7, F, T, T) (3, F, F, T) (6, T, F, T) (12, T, F, F)
30	29	—	—	—

Each node, when it receives a message, will have to look through the entire stack; hence it performs $O(n)$ operations. Hence the entire algorithm from source to destination will require $O(n) \cdot O(n) = O(n^2)$ [i.e., the $O(n^2)$ total number of operations is distributed among $O(n)$ nodes]. However, the algorithm is robust and is guaranteed to find a path if any exist.

7.5.2. Fault-Tolerant Binary Tree Design with Added Nodes and Links

In [HAYE76], a different approach to the design of fault-tolerant tree structures has been proposed. In this approach, both extra nodes and extra links are used for the construction of the fault-tolerant trees. In the event of a fault, reconfiguration to an alternate tree structure—similar to the original one—is performed. Thus, at least theoretically, no degradation will be caused by the fault.

The following describes the construction of a redundant binary tree structure based on the techniques described in [HAYE76]. This approach can be applied to certain other tree structures as well [KWAN81a, KWAN81b].

It will be assumed that the binary tree is a full tree with $(2^m - 1)$ nodes. The technique uses m extra (redundant) nodes and $(2^{m+1} + 2m - 5)$ extra links. These extra nodes and links are connected to the original tree by means of the following procedure. Each node in the resulting binary tree requires at most five connections per node. The following procedure describes the construction of the redundant binary tree.

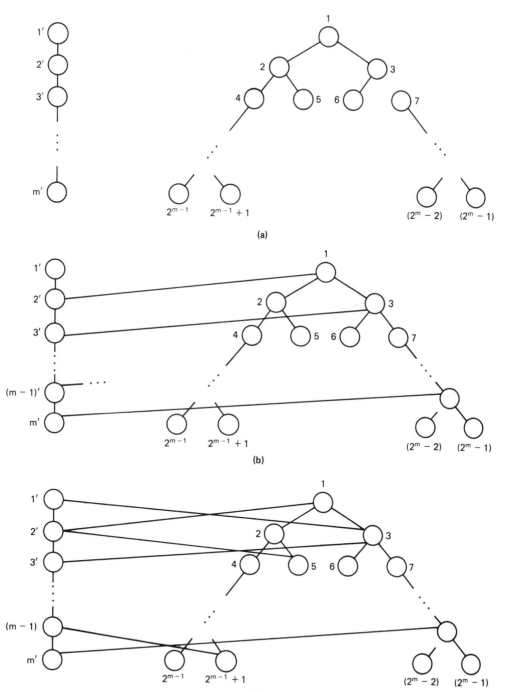

Figure 7.5.7   (a) A connection in step 3; (b) connections in step 4; (c) connections in step 5.

Procedure 7.5.1

Step 1: Construct a full binary tree with $(2^m - 1)$ nodes, where the nodes are numbered as usual, $1, 2, \ldots, (2^m - 1)$.

Step 2: Add m spare nodes, $1', 2', \ldots, m'$, to the binary tree. Node i' may be placed in level i, adjacent to the binary tree.

Step 3: Connect the spare node, i' to $(i + 1)'$ for all i, $1 \leq i \leq (m - 1)$, as shown in Fig. 7.5.7a.

Step 4: For all i, $2 \leq i \leq m$, connect the spare node, i', to the node $2^{i-1} - 1$ in the binary tree, as shown in Fig. 7.5.7b.

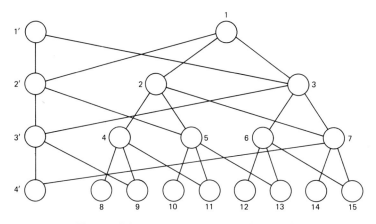

Figure 7.5.8　Redundant binary tree for 15 nodes.

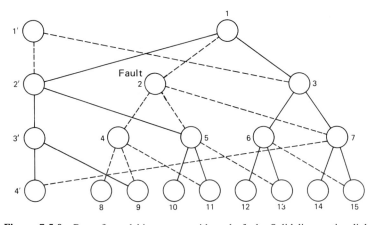

Figure 7.5.9　Reconfigured binary tree with node fault. Solid line: active link; dashed line: inactive link.

Step 5: For all i, $1 \leq i \leq (m - 1)$, connect the spare node, i', to the node $(2^i + 1)$ in the binary tree, as shown in Fig. 7.5.7c.

Step 6: For all h, $2 \leq h \leq m - 1$, and all j, $0 \leq j \leq (2^{h-1} - 2)$, connect node $(2^{h-1} + j)$ in level h to node $2^h + 2j + 3$ in level $(h + 1)$.

Figure 7.5.8 illustrates the redundant binary tree that results from modifying a tree with 15 nodes.

The total number of extra links required can be deduced as being equal to $(2^{m-1} + 2m - 3)$, using the following observations. Step 3, step 4, and step 5 each require $(m - 1)$ extra links. Step 6 requires altogether $(2^{m-1} - m)$ extra links. Also, the number of connections per node is, at most, equal to five.

These binary trees described are single-fault tolerant in that when a single node/link failure occurs, the tree can be reconfigured (using the extra nodes and links). The resulting new structure is a full binary tree which is structurally isomorphic to the original one. As an illustration, if node 2 in Fig. 7.5.8 fails, the structure can be reconfigured as a new binary tree with 15 nodes, as seen in Fig. 7.5.9. Several reconfiguration algorithms are available in [KWAN81b].

7.6. DYNAMICALLY RECONFIGURABLE FAULT-TOLERANT NETWORKS

As in 7.5, the class of interconnection structures of interest here is the so-called message-passing direct link networks [SEIT85]. Their advantage is that no switching network is employed between processors and storage. In addition, these networks are potentially simpler and more economical than shared-storage networks. The differences between this approach and the traditional shared memory approach is best illustrated by Fig. 7.6.1 by Seitz [SEIT85]. In the context of such direct link networks, two types of distinct interconnection configurations that have broad practical significance are the linear array and the tree interconnections. These are useful for the horizontal and the hierarchical architectures, respectively. Different applications are best executed in different types of architectures as shown in Table 7.6.1. For example, pipelined computation is best executed in a linear array configuration. Additionally, a linear array of processing elements can efficiently execute computations such as matrix-vector multiplication, LU decomposition, convolutions, and finite impulse filters [MEAD79]. On the other hand, divide-and-conquer computations are best executed by a binary tree configuration and there are a wide variety of applications that use binary tree configurations. Thus networks that can (logically) provide for *both* array and tree configurations, dynamically as required, are of practical importance. Such networks can be used to realize multiple, logically distinct architectures using the same physical interconnection. The advantage of such a design is that the logical

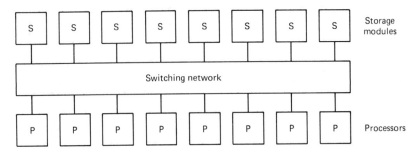

(a) Most multiprocessors are structured with a switching network, either a crossbar connection of buses or a multistage routing network, between the processors and storage. The switching network introduces a latency in the communication between processors and storage, and does not scale well to large sizes. Communication between processes running concurrently in different processors occurs through shared variables and common access to one large address space.

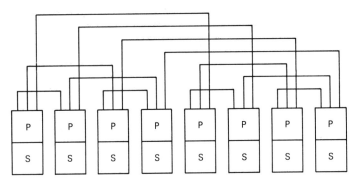

(b) Message-passing multicomputer systems retain a physically close and fast connection between processors and their associated storage. The concurrent computers (nodes) can send messages through a network of communication channels. The network shown here is a three-dimensional cube, which is a small version of the communication plan used in six dimensions in the 64-node Cosmic Cube.

Note: Actual machines need not follow one model or the other absolutely: Various hybrids are possible.

Figure 7.6.1 A comparison of shared-storage multiprocessors and message-passing machines [SEIT85].

TABLE 7.6.1 APPLICATIONS FOR DIFFERENT TYPES OF ARCHITECTURES

Linear Array	Tree structures
Pipeline computing	Search algorithm
Pattern matching	Evaluation of arithmetic expressions
Odd-even transposition sorting	Binary addition
Real-time finite impulse response filtering	Finding maximum and minimum
Recurrence evaluation	Linear recurrences
Priority queue	
Fourier transforms	

configuration can be dynamically changed to best fit the application in hand. Certain fault-tolerant network architectures have been proposed recently [PRAD85b, CHUN83, ROSE83] in this framework of dynamically reconfigurable architectures.

In [CHUN83] and [ROSE83], a VLSI-based bus network is proposed that provides linear array and binary tree configurations. The network topology proposed here has several interesting features and merits consideration in its own right. The proposed network is called DIOGENES network and has the following features: Here the processors are fabricated in a (logical, if not physical) line, with "bundles" of uncommitted interconnection wires and controlling switches available along the line of processors. Processors found fault-free upon testing are then connected together to obtain the desired topology. An important advantage of this approach is that all fault-free processors can be utilized. However, the DIOGENES methodology is best suited to relatively small arrays of large processors where the interconnect and switch complexity is small as compared to the processor size. This is because the designs are only fault-tolerant with respect to processor failures; interconnect failures can be catastrophic. The probability of an interconnect failure must, therefore, be kept very small. Also, interprocessor connections for commonly employed topologies such as binary trees and square grids can get very long for large arrays, resulting in significantly degraded performance.

In [PRAD85b], the design of dynamically reconfigurable architectures is studied in the context of closely coupled homogeneous systems. This network is discussed here in detail and will be referred to simply as a DFT (dynamically reconfigurable fault-tolerant) network.

It should be added here that another network that possesses some of the dynamic reconfigurability properties is the mesh connectioned network (see Section 7.9). In comparing the DFT networks with the mesh connection, it may be noted that achieving fault-tolerant dynamic reconfigurability is relatively more difficult in mesh connection; in addition, mesh connections are not easily extensible.

The following defines the toplogy of DFT network. Here it is assumed that the network has n nodes, numbered 0, 1, 2, . . . , $(n - 1)$. All the links between nodes are assumed to be bidirectional.

DFT topology.   A pair of nodes i, j, $i \neq j$, are connected if they satisfy the relationship $i = (j + 1)$ or $i = 2j$.

Figures 7.6.2 and 7.6.3 illustrate DFT topologies for $n = 11$ and $n = 12$ nodes, respectively. The complexity of these topologies is described in Table 7.6.2. It can be seen that the maximum number of I/O ports that is required per node is limited to four or five, depending on whether n is odd or even. Also, the total number of links is less than $2n$. So the interconnection complexity may be considered to be on a par with other topologies, such as the double-loop and full-ringed tree, discussed earlier.

The significant aspect of DFT architecture is its dynamic reconfigurability with fault tolerance, as discussed below. Also, the network is both extensible and par-

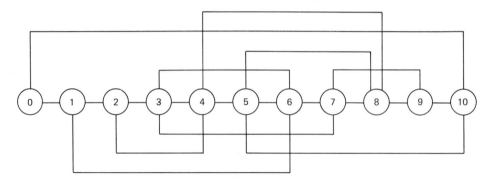

Figure 7.6.2 An 11-node DFT network.

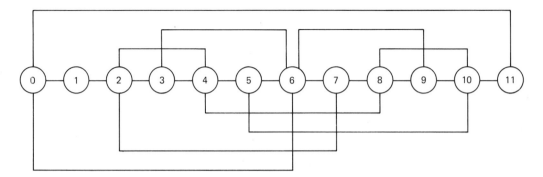

Figure 7.6.3 DFT topology for $n = 12$ nodes.

titionable where the basic characteristic of dynamic reconfigurability with fault tolerance is not altered.

Finally, these DFT architectures also admit algorithmic routing, which is implemented by using only certain local information that is included in the message. Also,

TABLE 7.6.2 INTERCONNECTION COMPLEXITY OF DFT

	n = odd	n = even
Number of links	$(2n - 3)$	$\begin{cases} (2n - 4) & \text{if 3 divides } n \\ (2n - 3) & \text{otherwise} \end{cases}$
Nodes with:		
2 connections	0	1, $(n - 1)$
3 connections	1, 2, $(n - 1)$, $(n - 2)$	0, and all other odd nodes
4 connections	All other nodes	2, $(n - 2)$ and $(n/3)$, $(2n/3)$ if 3 divides n
5 connections	None	All other even nodes

importantly, the maximum number of hops that is required for a message to be transmitted from one node to another is limited to $(2 \log n - 1)$. (Hereafter $\log n$ denotes $\log_2 n$, where x is the smallest integer greater than or equal to x.) A key fault-tolerant aspect of this routing procedure is that it is easily adaptable to node/link failures. Especially, the number of hops that is required for a message to be transmitted from one node to another may be increased only slightly when faults occur in the system.

7.6.1. Dynamic Reconfigurability with Fault Tolerance

Two types of distinct interconnection configurations that have broad practical significance are the linear array, and the tree interconnections, which respectively correspond to the horizontal and the hierarchical architectures. Different applications are best executed in different types of architectures as described in Table 7.6.1.

For example, pipe-lined computation is best executed in a linear array configuration, whereas divide and conquer computation is best executed by a binary tree configuration. The DFT networks can realize both of these structures and thus can be used for providing different applications for different problem environments. As seen below, changing one interconnection to another can be accomplished without altering the physical structure, therein providing for dynamic reconfigurability. Finally and most importantly, the network is still capable of realizing these configurations efficiently in spite of faults.

Any linear array configuration is easily realized by using the embedded interconnection that connects all the nodes in a cycle. Also, this embedded interconnection provides the capability of configuring the network as a linear array of $(n - 1)$ or n nodes in the presence of a single faulty node or link, as shown in Fig. 7.6.4.

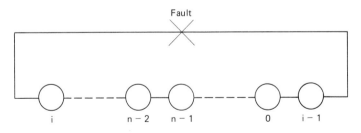

Figure 7.6.4   Horizontal configuration in the presence of fault.

The network can also be configured as a binary tree, as described below. First, it may be noted that every node i is connected to nodes $2i$ modulo n and $(2i + 1)$

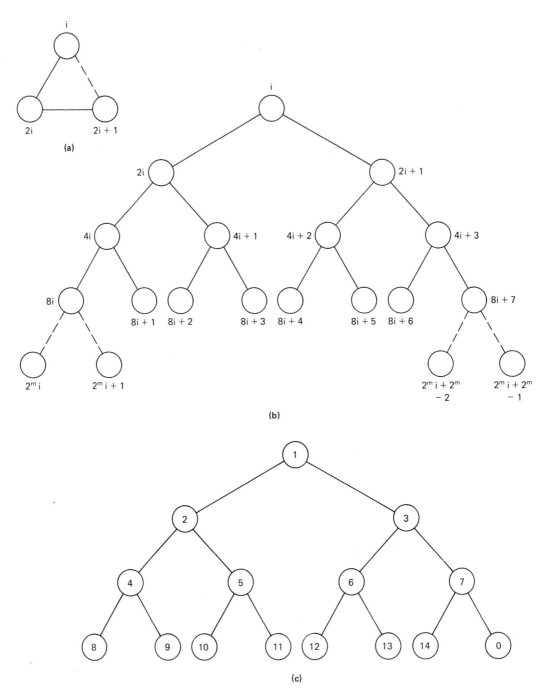

Figure 7.6.5 (a) Node i connected to 2i and (2i + 1); (b) Logically hierarchical configuration; (c) Binary tree logical configuration of DFT⟨15⟩.

modulo n, as shown in Fig. 7.6.5a. Here the dashed link connecting i to $(2i + 1)$ represents the logical link via node $2i$. Thus one can configure the network logically as a binary tree of n nodes, starting with any node i as the root node shown in Fig. 7.6.5b. For example, given DFT$\langle 15 \rangle$, one can configure this as a logical binary tree starting with node 1 as the root node, illustrated in Fig. 7.6.5c.

Now, in evaluating the effect of a fault on the binary tree reconfigurability, the location of the faulty node determines the extent of the damage. The maximum damage occurs when the root node, itself, is faulty; this will separate the tree into two smaller trees of almost equal size. On the other hand, a fault on a leaf node results in minimal impact. If a leaf node becomes faulty in a tree configuration of DFT, one may easily prune the tree by switching out the faulty node. The reduced tree will have $(n - 1)$ or $(n - 2)$ nodes, depending on whether or not the faulty leaf node is connected to another leaf node, as shown in Fig. 7.6.6. The following describes how given any faulty node f, that there always exists at least one binary tree configuration of DFT, where f appears either as a leaf node or as a node to which only a single leaf node is connected below it. In effect, the network can always admit a binary tree configuration of at least $(n - 2)$ nodes, in spite of any single faulty node. Thus at most two nodes may be lost due to a fault and therefore the degradation can be limited.

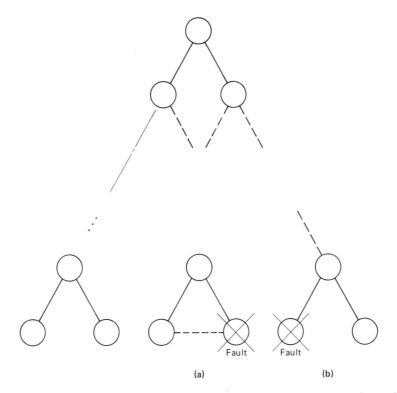

Figure 7.6.6   Faulty leaf node not connected to any other node in (a) and connected to another leaf node in (b).

Let BIT(h) represent the binary tree constructed as follows:

Let tr $(h, 1)$ represent a one-level binary tree with root node h and with leaf nodes $2h$ and $(2h + 1)$, where $h \neq 2h$ and $h \neq (2h + 1)$. If $h = 2h$ ($h = 2h + 1$), there will be only one leaf node $2h + 1$ ($2h$), for tr(h, 1).

Let tr (h, m) represent an m-level binary tree, constructed recursively from tr $(h, m - 1)$ as follows. First, replace each leaf node i in tr $(h, m - 1)$ with the respective tr $(i, 1)$. Then delete those leaf nodes of tr (h, m) that have already appeared somewhere in tr $(h, m - 1)$.

Let tr $(h, \log n)$ be denoted as BIT(h). The tree shown in Fig. 7.6.5c represents BIT(1) in DFT⟨15⟩.

The following observations can be made, in general:

1. Nodes in BIT(h) are all distinct.
2. BIT(h) is a binary tree with h as the root node and contains all the n nodes 0, 1, 2, . . . , $(n - 1)$.
3. For $n =$ even, given any node f, there exists at least one node h for which f appears as a leaf node of BIT(h).
4. For $n =$ odd, given any node $f, f \neq (n - 1)/2$, there exists at least one node h for which f appears as a leaf node of BIT(h). The node $(n - 1)/2$ appears in BIT(0) connected to a single leaf node $(n - 1)$.

Thus, in spite of any single fault, the network can operate both as a binary tree and a linear array of slightly reduced capacity of $(n - 2)$ nodes. For example, given that node 2 becomes faulty, one can reconfigure DFT⟨15⟩ as shown in Fig. 7.6.7 with loss of only node 2. This provides for graceful degradation of the dynamic reconfigurability feature.

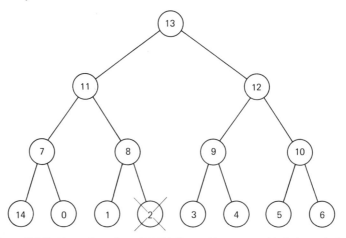

Figure 7.6.7   Reconfiguration of DFT⟨15⟩ as a binary tree with faulty node 2.

7.6.2. Message Routing

One obvious way to perform message routing will be to use those paths delineated by one of the embedded binary trees BIT (h). Such a path connecting any source s to destination d would be short and require at most $2 \log n - 1$ hops. Additionally, an algorithm can be implemented using these paths and will be similar to that formulated for regular binary trees. Such an algorithm, though, suffers from two shortcomings: (1) like binary tree routing, the nodes closer to the root node may become a bottleneck to message traffic among nodes farther away from the root node; and (2) any such algorithm may not be easily adaptable to faults. The following therefore describes a different routing algorithm. This not only provides short paths of length at most $2 \log n - 1$, but also provides for more uniform message traffic and adaptability to faults. The message-routing strategy discussed here is implemented by using a small number of tag bits, carried by the message. These tag bits are generated at the node where the message originated. The message is routed by the nodes in the path by simple interpretation of these tag bits. This eliminates any need for expensive routing tables, directories, and so on, at each node.

To describe the routing algorithm, the following notations will be used:

Let the source node at which the message originated be s.

Let the destination node, where the message is delivered, be d.

Let $\log n$ denote $\lceil \log_2 n \rceil$, where $\lceil x \rceil$ denotes the smallest integer greater than or equal to x.

Let all expressions that represent node numbers be reduced to modulo n.

The path construction technique described below provides the basic framework used for routing.

Path   7.6.1.

Step 1:   Let $m = 1$.
Step 2:   If $[(d - s2^{m-1}) \bmod n] \leq (2^m - 1)$, then set $p = (d - s2^{m-1}) \bmod n$ and $u = 0$; else, if $[(s2^{m-1} - d) \bmod n] \leq (2^m - 1)$, set $p = (s2^{m-1} - d) \bmod n$ and $u = 1$; else $m = m + 1$ and repeat step 2.

//Step 2 computes the least m for which either $(d - s2^{m-1}) \bmod n$ or $(s2^{m-1} - d) \bmod n$ is less than or equal to $(2^m - 1)$. Obviously, there always exists such an m, where $m \leq \log n$.//

Let $p = (p_{m-1}, p_{m-2}, ..., p_0)$, in binary (it may be noted that p is an $m - $ bit number).

//For example, given $s = 3$, $d = 9$ and $s = 6$, $d = 10$, one computes $p = 3 = (1, 1)$, $u = 0$ and $p = (1, 0)$, $u = 1$ respectively, where $n = 11$.//

//The following steps construct the path from s to d by using a pointer, x. The value of x during each iteration represents successive node numbers in the path.//

Step 3: Let $x = s$ and $h = (m - 1)$.

Step 4: Repeat the following while $h \geq 1$:
  (a) If $p_h = 0$, let the new value of $x = 2x$, and let $h = (h - 1)$.
  (b) If $p_h = 1$, let $x = (x + 1 - 2u)$, and let $p_h = 0$; go to step 4(a).

Step 5: If $p_0 = 0$, then stop. If $p_0 = 1$, let $x = (x + 1 - 2u)$ and stop.

//Thus, if $u = 0$, then $x = x + 1$; else $x = x - 1$.//

For example, given $x = 2$, $d = 9$ with $n = 11$, the successive values of x are computed as 3, 4, 8, and 9. Thus the path constructed from 3 to 9 is $3 \to 4 \to 8 \to 9$. This path uses the connection $i \to (i + 1)$ and $i \to 2i$. On the other hand, given $s = 6$ and $d = 10$, the path constructed is $6 \to 5 \to 10$, which used the connection $i \to (i - 1)$ and $i \to 2i$. One possible implementation of the routing algorithm that uses Path 7.6.1 is discussed next.

A message may be formatted as shown in Fig. 7.6.8a. Here a set of routing tag bits, R, is provided in addition to the usual source/destination addresses and parity check bit. The width of this tag field, R, is $\log n$ bits; let $R = \log n$. In addition, a one bit tag field, U, is provided.

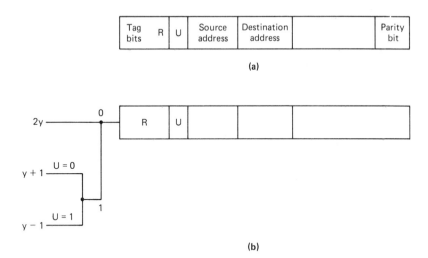

Figure 7.6.8 (a) Message format; (b) routing using tag bit from R.

The source node computes p and initializes R, the tag field, as $R = (p_{m-1}, p_{m-2}, \ldots, p_0, 0, 0, \ldots, 0)$. Thus initially R is equal to left-justified p. Also, at the source, U is initialized to u. So $R = (1, 1, 0, 0)$ and $U = 0$, given that $s = 3$, $d = 9$, and $n = 11$.

When a message arrives at a node, y, the following steps are to be carried out by the interface unit at y.

Step 1:   If R is equal to all 0, the message is removed; otherwise, step 2 is performed.

Step 2:
(a) If $R_{r-1} = 0$, then set $R_{q-1} = R_{q-2}$ for $q = r, r - 1, \ldots, 1$ (left shift R by one bit) and forward the message to $2y$.
(b) If $R_{r-1} = 1$, set $R_{r-1} = 0$ (change the most significant bit to 0) and forward the message to

$$\begin{cases} y + 1 & \text{if } U = 0 \\ y - 1 & \text{if } U = 1 \end{cases}$$

//The most significant bit of R determines the next node in the path, as shown in Fig. 7.6.8(b). The steps in this procedure thus correspond directly to the steps given in Path 7.6.1.//

Example 7.   Let $s = 3$, $d = 9$, and $n = 11$. Hence the message is routed to 9 via 4 and 8. The tag field, R, assumes the following different values enroute to 9. Here $U = 0$.

Node	\multicolumn{2}{c}{Tag Field R}	
	At arrival	At departure
3	1 1 0 0	0 1 0 0
4	0 1 0 0	1 0 0 0
8	1 0 0 0	0 0 0 0
9	0 0 0 0	

Consequently, it can be seen that the very first time that R assumes all 0s on arrival is when the message reaches the destination node. So the routing field, R, is self-contained—that is, the nodes do not have to check the destination field at any time during the routing. This factor makes the implementation of a check-and-forward scheme easier. Also, it can be deduced from the above-described procedure that the maximum number of hops any message may go through is limited to $2 \log n - 1$, which corresponds to the case when R is initially all 1; that is $R = (1, 1, \ldots, 1)$. Furthermore, it can be seen that the maximum number of hops is less than $2 \log n - 1$, when n is not a power of 2.

Next we discuss one possible strategy that may be used for error checking at each node using single parity check. Assume a message format where a single parity bit, P, is provided for checking R and the rest of the message shown in Fig. 7.6.9. The only portion of the message that undergoes any change during the routing is the tag field R. The leading bit of the tag field R is changed to 0 when it arrives at a node with

Faulty

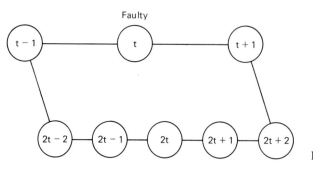

Figure 7.6.9   Detour around t.

the leading bit equal to 1. This changes the parity, and thus the check bit P may be recomputed at certain nodes. The updating of this parity bit P can be performed very easily, by modifying step 2(b) as follows:

If $R_{r-1} = 1$, set $R_{r-1} = 0$ and $P = \bar{P}$, complement the parity bit P, and forward the message to

$$\begin{cases} (y + 1) & \text{if } U = 0 \\ (y - 1) & \text{if } U = 1 \end{cases}$$

Fault tolerance.   The following describes how the routing procedure earlier described is easily adaptable to faults requiring only a small increase in path lengths.

It may be noted that the effect of a link failure, in reality, can be no worse than the effect of a node failure. This follows from the observation that a link fault affects a communication path which is only a subset of the paths affected by a fault in one of the two nodes connected by the link.

The following describes the construction of detours around a faulty node or link which can be effectively used to bypass the fault.

Faulty node.   First, the following may be observed regarding the message path which was followed in the routing procedure Path 7.6.1 when $u = 0$ (the case $u = 1$ can be considered similarly). Given any node t there are in the path, at most, two possible nodes that can be the immediate predecessors of t in any path (when $u = 0$). These are precisely $(t - 1)$ if $t = $ odd, and $(t - 1)$, $(t/2)$ if $t = $ even. Also, there are two possible immediate successors of t in any path $(u = 0)$ and these are $(t + 1)$ and $2t$. Therefore, faults in node t can, at the very worst, disable the paths through t from $(t - 1)$ and $t/2$ to $(t + 1)$ and $2t$. Hence, what are needed are alternative paths from $(t - 1)$ and $t/2$ to $(t + 1)$ and $2t$. These can be used as detours in the event of a fault in t and are constructed easily, as seen below:

Case I: Let t satisfy $3 \le t \le (n - 3)$.

$(t - 1) \rightarrow (2t - 2) \rightarrow (2t - 1) \rightarrow 2t \rightarrow (2t + 1) \rightarrow (2t + 2) \rightarrow t + 1$

$(t/2) \rightarrow (t/2 + 1) \rightarrow (t + 2) \rightarrow (t + 1) \rightarrow (2t + 2) \rightarrow (2t + 1) \rightarrow 2t$

These short paths from $t/2$ and $(t - 1)$ to $2t$ and $(t + 1)$ do not pass through t and are of, at most, length 6, as illustrated in Fig. 7.6.9.

As an example, when $t = 4$, one can find the following paths from $(t/2) = 2$ and $(t - 1) = 3$ to nodes $(t + 1) = 5$ and $2t = 8$, without going through node 4:

$$3 \to 6 \to 7 \to 8 \to 9 \to 10 \to 5$$

$$2 \to 3 \to 6 \to 5 \to 10 \to 9 \to 8$$

Case II: $t = 0, 1, 2, (n - 1), (n - 2)$, the remaining nodes.

Consider the case of $t = 2$. For $t = 2$, one has $(t - 1) = (t/2) = 1$, $(t + 1) = 3$, and $2t = 4$. The paths shown below from 1 to 3 and 1 to 4 do not pass through the node $t = 2$.

n even: $1 \to 0 \to n/2 \to (n/2 + 1) \to (n/2 + 2) \to 4 \to 3$

n odd: $1 \to (n + 1)/2 \to ((n + 1)/2 + 1) \to 3 \to 4$

Detours for other values of t can be constructed similarly.

It may be noted that these detours will result in an increase in the path lengths of certain paths; the increase is, however, small—only four extra hops. Consequently, the maximum number of hops in any path is limited to $2 \log n + 3$, in spite of any single node failure.

Also, the implementation of the path reconfiguration scheme above requires only, at most, six nodes in the detour to perform some local routing changes (once the fault has been detected). The remaining nodes can still use the original routing procedure. Thus the advantage of using detours is that as far as routing is concerned, the global impact of failure may be minimal.

Faulty link.   Analogous techniques that bypass a faulty link are easily formulated. First, it may be observed that in the routing procedure described earlier, given any node t, the message is forwarded to either $(t + 1)$ or $2t$ in any path when $u = 0$ (the case $u = 1$ can be considered similarly). Thus the two links that are used by t for forwarding the message are $t \to (t + 1)$ and $t \to 2t$. So a failure in one of these links can prevent a message from being forwarded from t to one of its successors. The faulty link is, however, easily bypassed, as seen below.

First, consider the case when link $t \to 2t$ is faulty. The following describes a path from t to $2t$ without the use of the link $t \to 2t$:

$$t \to (t + 1) \to (2t + 2) \to (2t + 1) \to 2t$$

In the event of a fault on the other link, $t \to (t + 1)$, the following path can be used from t to $(t + 1)$:

Case I: $t \neq 0$.

$$t \to 2t \to (2t + 1) \to (2t + 2) \to (t + 1)$$

Case II: $t = 0$.

n even: $0 \rightarrow (n/2) \rightarrow (n/2 + 1) \rightarrow 2 \rightarrow 1$

n odd: $0 \rightarrow (n - 1) \rightarrow (n - 1)/2 \rightarrow (n - 1)/2 + 1 \rightarrow 1$

These detours in the path may increase the path length by three extra hops for some paths. Thus the maximum path length between any source–destination pair is limited to 2 log n + 2, in spite of a single link fault. As a result, both single node failures and link failures are easily tolerated.

Other aspects of these networks such as extensibility, partitionability, and fault-diagnosability have been discussed in [PRAD81, PRAD82b, PRAD 85b]. Also, a variation of this network which provides some of the same dynamic reconfigurability properties is described in [SCHL74, PRAD82a, PRAD85b]. In this, each node i is connected to nodes $2i$ mod n and $(2i + 1)$ mod n, as described in Fig. 7.6.10 for a 12-node system. The latter interconnection is obtained as a generalization of shift and replace (DeBruijn) graphs [DEBR46, SCHL74] and is the subject of further study [PRAD85b, ESFA85].

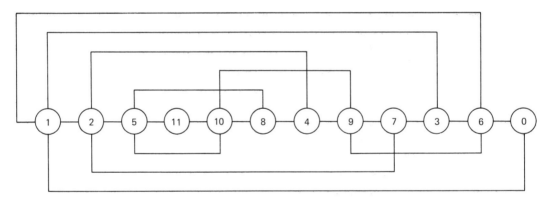

Figure 7.6.10   Generalized shift-and-replace graph.

7.7. FAULT TOLERANCE IN BINARY CUBE INTERCONNECTION

The binary cube interconnection architecture has received considerable attention recently and is highly fault tolerant [ARMS81, KUHL80a, KUHL80b]. One example of a proposed design that incorporates binary n-cube interconnection is the Cosmic Cube system [SEIT85], in which a large number of microprocessors are interconnected to form a homogeneous parallel system. The number of nodes, n, in a binary cube interconnection is always a power of 2; thus, let $n = 2^m$. Nodes 0 through $(n - 1)$ can be represented as m-bit binary numbers.

7.7.1. Binary Cube Interconnection

A pair of nodes, i and j, are connected if the binary numbers representing i and j differ in only one bit position. Figure 7.7.1 illustrates a four-dimensional binary cube with 16 (2^4) nodes. In general, each node has $m = \log n$ links connected to it, and the system has a total of $(mn)/2$ links.

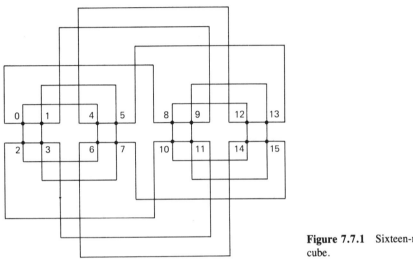

Figure 7.7.1   Sixteen-node binary n-cube.

The key features of the binary cube are as follows:

1. The maximum internode distance is only $m = \log n$.
2. The routing is relatively simple.
3. The system is highly fault tolerant since there are m node-disjoint paths between every pair of nodes.

The maximum internode distance and the ease of routing are apparent from the following observations. Given a node, i, one can travel to any node, j, in one hop if j differs from i in one bit position. Thus, given a source and a destination node, s and d, respectively, one can travel from s to d in k hops, where k represents the number of bit positions in which s and d differ. This path is constructed starting with node s and then successively complementing one bit per hop in the k positions in which s and d differ.) When a node, x, receives a message, it can execute the following simple steps to route the message.

The node first checks the destination address, d, in the message. If $d = x$, the message has reached its destination and is thus removed. If $d \neq x$, the message is forwarded by x to one of the adjacent nodes, which differs from x in one of the bit positions in which x and d also differ. The path taken by a message corresponds to a shortest path, although not a unique one. For example, in Fig. 7.7.1, in traveling from 3 to 0, the message may travel the path $3 \rightarrow 2 \rightarrow 0$ or $3 \rightarrow 1 \rightarrow 0$.

7.7.2. Fault Tolerance

Recently, several researchers [KUHL80b, ARMS81] have demonstrated the fault-tolerance properties of these binary cube networks. It has been shown that it is possible to send a message from any node to any other node, in spite of failures in any $(m - 1)$ components (a *component* is a node or link). It is shown that there exist m node-disjoint paths between every pair of nodes.

The concept of Hamming distance is useful in describing these paths. The Hamming distance between binary numbers i and j will be denoted as $d_H(i, j)$ and will represent the number of positions in which i and j differ.

Let s and d represent the source and destination nodes, respectively. Let $s = (s_{m-1}, \ldots, s_1, s_0)$ and $d = (d_{m-1}, \ldots, d_1, d_0)$ in binary.

Example 8. Let $s = (1001)$ and $d = (0110)$ in binary. Here s and d are bit-by-bit complements of each other, and thus $d_H(s, d) = 4$. There exist four paths between s and d which are node disjoint:

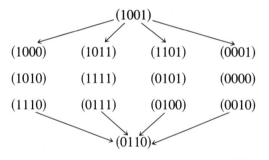

Next, consider a case when s is not a complement of d. Let $s = (1001)$ and $d = (1010)$. Here, $d_H(s, d) = 2$.

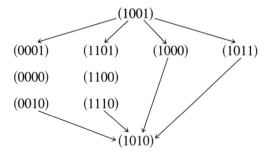

These four paths are all disjoint and of length at most 4. The disjoint paths between s and d are described by considering two different cases:

Case I: Let $d_H(s, d) = m$. Thus s and d are bit-by-bit complements of each other.

Let $\bar{g}$ denote the complement of g. The following m paths are described using a binary representation of node numbers.

path 0: $s = (s_{m-1}, \ldots, s_1, s_0) \rightarrow (s_{m-1}, \ldots, s_1, \bar{s}_0) \rightarrow (s_{m-1}, \ldots, \bar{s}_1, \bar{s}_0)$

$\rightarrow \cdots \rightarrow (s_{m-1}, \bar{s}_{m-2}, \ldots, \bar{s}_0) \rightarrow (\bar{s}_{m-1}, \bar{s}_{m-2}, \ldots, \bar{s}_0) = d$

path 1: $s = (s_{m-1}, \ldots, s_1, s_0) \rightarrow (s_{m-1}, \ldots, \bar{s}_1, s_0) \rightarrow (s_{m-2}, \ldots, \bar{s}_2, \bar{s}_1, s_0)$

$\rightarrow (\bar{s}_{m-1}, \bar{s}_{m-2}, \ldots, \bar{s}_1, s_0) \rightarrow (\bar{s}_{m-1}, \bar{s}_{m-2}, \ldots, \bar{s}_0) = d$

path h: $s = (s_{m-1}, \ldots, s_1, s_0) \rightarrow (s_{m-1}, \ldots, \bar{s}_h, \ldots, s_0)$

$\rightarrow (s_{m-1}, \ldots, \bar{s}_{h+1}, \bar{s}_h, \ldots, s_0) \rightarrow (\bar{s}_{m-1}, \ldots, \bar{s}_h, \ldots, s_0)$

$\rightarrow (\bar{s}_{m-1}, \ldots, \bar{s}_h, \ldots, s_1, \bar{s}_0) \rightarrow \cdots$

$\rightarrow (\bar{s}_{m-1}, \ldots, \bar{s}_h, s_{h-1}, \bar{s}_{h-2}, \ldots, \bar{s}_0) \rightarrow (\bar{s}_{m-1}, \ldots, \bar{s}_1, \bar{s}_0) = d$

path (m − 1): $s = (s_{m-1}, \ldots, s_1, s_0) \rightarrow (\bar{s}_{m-1}, s_{m-2}, \ldots, s_0)$

$\rightarrow (\bar{s}_{m-1}, s_{m-2}, \ldots, s_1, \bar{s}_0) \rightarrow \cdots \rightarrow (\bar{s}_{m-1}, s_{m-2}, \bar{s}_{m-3}, \ldots, \bar{s}_0)$

$\rightarrow (\bar{s}_{m-1}, \bar{s}_{m-2}, \ldots, \bar{s}_0) = d$

The following argument establishes the node disjointness of the paths above. It may be seen that a node, x, reached in p hops from s in any of the paths above satisfies the Hamming distance relationship $d(x, s) = p$. Consequently, any two nodes, x and y, that are reached in p and q hops, respectively, will always be distinct if $p \neq q$. Thus to show that the paths above are disjoint, one needs to simply establish that any two nodes x and y that are reached in two different paths satisfy $x \neq y$ if $d(x, s) = d(y, s)$.

Let $x \in$ path h and $y \in$ path e, where both x and y are reached in some p hops. Then it can be seen that $x \neq y$, from the binary representation of x and y, which can be deduced as

$$x = (s_{m-1}, \ldots, \bar{s}_{h+p-1}, \bar{s}_{h+p-2}, \ldots, \bar{s}_h, s_{h-1}, \ldots, s_0)$$

$$y = (s_{m-1}, \ldots, \bar{s}_{e+p-1}, \bar{s}_{e+p-2}, \ldots, \bar{s}_e, s_{e-1}, \ldots, s_0)$$

Since $h \neq e$, one has $x \neq y$. Thus, when s is a bit-by-bit complement of d, there exist m node-disjoint paths requiring m hops.

The other case is when s is not a bit-by-bit complement of d.

Case II: Let $d_H(s, d) = f < m$. Thus s and d differ in some f positions where f is less than m.

Without any loss of generality, one can assume for the purpose of path construction that

$$s = (00 \cdots 0 \quad s_{f-1}s_{f-2} \cdots s_0)$$

$$d = (00 \cdots 0 \quad d_{f-1}d_{f-2} \cdots d_0) \qquad \text{where } d_i = \bar{s}_i, \quad 0 \leq i \leq f - 1$$

Because $s_i = \bar{d}_i$, $i = 0, 1, \ldots, f - 1$, first the technique described in case 1 can be used to construct f node-disjoint paths between s and d. These paths will all have length f, and the nodes in the path all have 0s in the leftmost $(m - f)$ positions. Let these paths be denoted as path 0, path 1,..., path $(f - 1)$. Now, an additional $(m - f)$ node-disjoint paths may be constructed, as shown:

path f: $s = (0, 0, \ldots, 0, s_{f-1}, \ldots, s_1, s_0) \rightarrow (0, 0, \ldots, 0, 1, s_{f-1}, \ldots, s_1, s_0)$

$\qquad \rightarrow (0, 0, \ldots, 0, 1, s_{f-1}, \ldots, s_1, \bar{s}_0) \rightarrow (0, \ldots, 0, 1, s_{f-1}, \ldots, \bar{s}_1, \bar{s}_0)$

$\qquad \rightarrow (0, 0, \ldots, 0, 1, \bar{s}_{f-1}, \bar{s}_{f-2}, \ldots, \bar{s}_1, \bar{s}_0)$

$\qquad \rightarrow (0, \ldots, 0, 0, \bar{s}_{f-1}, \ldots, \bar{s}_1, \bar{s}_0) = d$

path h: $h = (f + 1), \ldots, (m - 1)$ is constructed similar to path f with the leftmost $(m - f)$ bits being equal to

$$(m - 1) \cdots h \cdots f$$

$$0 \quad \cdots \quad 010 \cdots 0$$

These paths are disjoint because two nodes in two different paths have different bit combinations in the leftmost $(m - f)$ positions. The paths above are of length $(f + 2)$. Also, these are disjoint from the f paths described earlier from s to d (constructed using the techniques given in Case 1). Thus, given any two nodes, s and d, there always exist m node-disjoint paths of length at most $(m + 1)$ between them.

The fact that these disjoint paths exist guarantees that one can reach any node from any other node, using a path of length up to $(m + 1)$, in spite of the presence of faults affecting at most $(m - 1)$ components.

A problem that yet has to be resolved is the routing of the message given the identity of $(m - 1)$ faulty nodes. Of course, one trivial solution would be to generate the m disjoint paths at the source and then select one particular path. This, however, would require that the messages carry certain tag bits, in addition to the destination addresses.

One basic shortcoming of binary cube interconnection is that the number of connections per node grows with the number of nodes. Therefore, the larger the system, the larger the number of connections. This may not be practical for systems that are to be built by using simple computing elements which are restricted in terms of the number of I/O ports available. Therefore, other fault-tolerant networks have been proposed which require a fixed number of connections per node—independent of the number of nodes. One class of these networks is discussed next.

7.8 FAULT-TOLERANT GRAPH NETWORKS

This section describes a class of fault-tolerant networks that have been developed based on certain graph structures [PRAD83b, PRAD85a, PRAD 86]. These networks combine some of the attractive features of the networks previously described and will be referred to here as FG (fault-tolerant graph) networks. Two different versions of these networks have been proposed: a link-based architecture and a bus-based architecture.

There are a number of reasons why it may not be desirable to connect each processor to all buses:

1. A processor may not have the hardware capabilities to allow its attachment to more than a certain number of buses.
2. For reasons of reliability, the buses may be in physically different locations; hence a processor may not be located next to every bus.

Thus, [PRAD84, PRAD85a, PRAD 86] have recently proposed alternate multi-processor multibus configurations. Here, each bus is connected to a small subset of processors. These architectures are novel and possess certain advantages over traditional multiple bus systems where all processors are connected to all buses. Figure 7.8.1 illustrates an example of such an architecture that interconnects eight processors

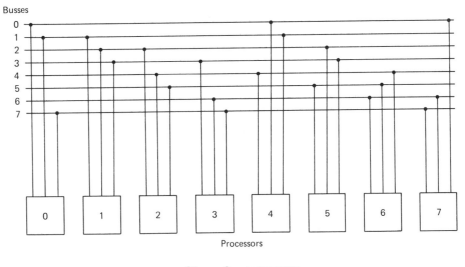

8-bus   8-processor system

Figure 7.8.1   Multibus/multiprocessor network.

using eight buses. In this, each processor is connected to exactly three buses and each bus is connected to three processors. Some of the key features of this design are:

1. Data may be transferred from one processor to another using, at most, two bus transfers.

2. Any processor or bus can fail and still data can be transferred from any processor to any other by using, at most, three bus transfers.

3. There is no bottleneck in the system since each bus supports only a small subset of processors.

4. The multiple bus system is fault-tolerant since the network admits both faulty buses as well as faulty processors.

5. Modifications may be easier to perform on a multiple bus system. For example, the addition of a processor merely requires its attachment to a small subset of buses.

6. Also it may be noted that the above buses may be logical buses; e.g. two adjacent logical buses may be supported on one physical bus.

The following elaborates the networks presented in [PRAD85a].

First, given a graph structure, one can formulate a link network and a bus network based on the graph structure as described below. Let $G = \langle V, E \rangle$ be an undirected graph where V is a set of n vertices represented as 0 through $(n - 1)$. The set E represents the edges denoted as (i, j), where i and j are two neighboring nodes connected by (i, j) in G. Let LA and BA be defined as two mappings of G into a link network and a bus network, as described below:

Let $LA(G) = \langle PE, C \rangle$, where PE is a set of processing elements, represented as PE(0), PE(1), . . . , PE $(n - 1)$, which corresponds to the set of vertices in G. Let C be the set of bidirectional communication links. There is a communication link, $C(i, j)$, in C which connects PE(i) with PE(j) iff $(i, j) \in E$.

Let $BA(G) = \langle B, PE \rangle$ where B represents a set of buses defined as BUS(0), BUS(1), . . . , BUS($n - 1$), corresponding to n vertices. The set PE represents the set of processing elements defined as PE(i, j) $\in$ PE iff $(i, j) \in E$. The processing element PE (i, j) is connected to buses BUS(i) and BUS(j) as shown in Fig. 7.8.2. Thus the link architecture is obtained by using the interpretation that vertices denote processing elements and edges denote communication links. On the other hand, the bus architecture is obtained by using the interpretation that buses are shown in the graph as vertices and computing elements as edges. Thus the number of processing elements in BA(G) is equal to the number of edges in G. Each processing element is connected to two buses and each bus is connected to a subset of the processing elements. [The number of processing elements connected to BUS(i) is equal to the degree of node i in G.] This differs from the conventional multibus design, where all processing elements are connected to all buses. Since each bus is connected to a subset of processing elements, an inter-PE transfer may require several interbus transfers.

However, if bus load is equated to the number of connections per bus, the BA(G) network has a much smaller bus load compared to that of an equivalent design which uses conventional shared buses. Therefore, a BA(G)-type bus network may have certain advantages over the shared bus design when there are large numbers of processing elements to be connected. Also, it may be noted that one of the advantages

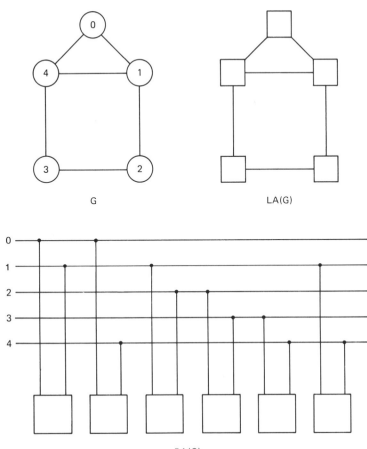

Figure 7.8.2 Link and bus architecture.

of a BA(G) network over an LA(G) network is that it can easily be extended by adding more PEs to buses as required.

Various relationships between G and the corresponding LA(G) and BA(G) are described in Table 7.8.1. In describing the FG networks below, first the underlying graph structure, FG, is defined.

Also, it may be noted that in the link architecture, LA(G), transmitting data from one PE to another PE may require one or more hops through other PEs in the path. Similarly, in the bus architecture, BA(G), direct transfer is possible only when both of the processing elements are connected to the same bus [i.e., PE(x, y) can transfer to PE(u, v) if $x = u$ or v or $y = u$ or v]. In other cases, a transfer would require one or more interbus transfers through the connecting PEs. However, the difference between the bus architecture and the link architecture, insofar as formulating a routing path between a source and a destination PE is concerned, is that in the bus architecture

TABLE 7.8.1 CERTAIN EQUIVALENCES BETWEEN BA(G)
AND LA(G) NETWORKS

LA(G) link network	Equivalence in BA(G) bus network
Number of processors	Number of buses
Number of links	Number of processors
Number of connections/processors	Number of connections/bus
Interprocessor transfer	Interbus transfer
Number of processor–processor transfers in a message path	Number of bus–bus transfers in a message path
Processor fault	Bus fault
Link fault	Processor fault

various choices exist depending on the various combinations of source and destination buses. For example, given PE(x, y) as the source and PE(u, v) as the destination, PE(x, y) can initiate the transmission on bus x or y, and PE(u, v) can receive it from bus u or v.

However, topologically, there are certain equivalences between paths in LA(G) and BA(FG). Given a PE-to-PE path in the link architecture, there is an equivalent BUS-to-BUS path in the bus architecture. If an inter-PE transfer constitutes a single hop, both of these paths will have the same number of hops. On the other hand, given a PE to PE path in BA(G), there is an equivalent link to the link path in LA(G).

7.8.1 FG Network Design

The number of nodes in the graphs defined below is assumed to be equal to r^m. As seen later, the chosen values of r and m will signify the number of connections per PE (or BUS), the routing distance between PEs, and the degree of fault tolerance.

Here the nodes are assumed to be numbered 0 through $(n - 1)$. Each node i has a m-tuple representation in radix r; this will be denoted as $(i_{m-1}, \ldots, i_1, i_0)$.

Given i, j, $0 \leq i, j \leq (n - 1)$, the following defines certain relationships denoted as g and h. It is assumed that $i = (i_{m-1}, \ldots, i_1, i_0)$ and $j = (j_{m-1}, \ldots, j_1, j_0)$ in radix r.

Let $i = g(j)$ if $i_p = j_{p+1}$ for all p, $0 \leq p \leq (m - 2)$ and $i_{m-1} = j_0$. Thus j is an end-around shift of i.

Let $i = h(j)$ if $i_p = j_p$ for all p, $1 \leq p \leq (m - 1)$ *and* $i_0 \neq j_0$. Thus $i = h(j)$ implies that $j = h(i)$ (i and j differ only in the last digit).

These graphs are constructed using a two-step approach. First, a skeletal graph, SG, is constructed, which is then augmented to obtain the fault-tolerant graph, FG. The skeletal graph, denoted as SG(r, m), is obtained by connecting every pair of nodes i and j that satisfy the relationship $i = g(j)$ or $i = h(j)$.

Let k denote $(r^m - 1)/(r - 1)$ and hence $k = (1, 1, \ldots, 1)$ in radix r.

$FG(r, m)$ design, $m = 2$

$r = even$. Construct a SG$(r, 2)$ graph for the specific r; then augment the graph by adding $r/2$ links, defined as $(0, k), (2k, 3k), \ldots, ((r - 2)k, (r - 1)k$.

$r = odd$. Construct a SG$(r, 2)$ graph for the specific r; then augment it by adding an extra node, n, which is then connected to nodes $0, k, 2k, \ldots, (r - 1)k$ by adding r additional links: $(n, 0), (n, k), \ldots, (n, (r - 1)k)$.

[The resulting graph when $r = $ odd has $(n + 1)$ nodes. This extra node can be used as a spare and as shown later is useful for routing when faults occur in the system.]

$FG(r, m)$ design, $m \geqq 3$.   Let

$$\text{Let } q = \begin{cases} (r^m - 1)/(r^2 - 1) & \text{for } m = \text{even} \\ (r^{m+1} - 1)/(r^2 - 1) & \text{for } m = \text{odd} \end{cases}$$

Thus, in radix r,

$$q = \begin{cases} (0, 1, 0, 1, \ldots, 0, 1) & \text{for } m = \text{even} \\ (1, 0, 1, 0, \ldots, 1, 0, 1) & \text{for } m = \text{odd} \end{cases}$$

$r = 2$. Construct a SG$(2, m)$ graph for the given m; then add links:

$$\begin{cases} (0, k), (k, k - q), \text{ and } (q, 0) & \text{if } m = \text{even} \\ (0, k), (k, k - q), (q, 0) \text{ and } (k - q, q) & \text{if } m = \text{odd} \end{cases}$$

$FG(2, 4)$ graph is illustrated in Fig. 7.8.3.

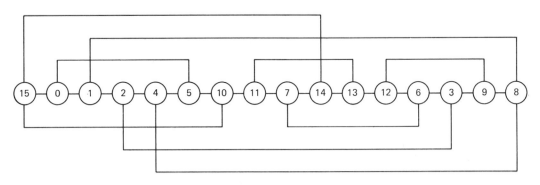

Figure 7.8.3 FG(2, 4) network.

$r \geqq 3$. Construct a SG(r, m) graph for the given r, m. Add r links, as defined below: $(0, k), (k, 2k), \ldots, ((r - 2)k, (r - 1)k), ((r - 1)k, 0)$. If $m = $ even, add additional $(r^2 - r)/2$ links defined by the following expression for all $a, b, a \neq b$ and $0 \leqq a, b \leqq (r - 1)$:

$$(arq + bq, (r - 1 - a)rq + (r - 1 - b)q)$$

FG(3, 3) graph is illustrated in Fig. 7.8.4.

The following basic property of FG(r, m) networks for $r \geq 3$ can easily be proven:

$$FG(r, m) \text{ is a regular network of degree } \begin{cases} r & \text{if } m = 2 \\ (r + 1) & \text{if } m \geq 3 \end{cases}$$

Also, FG$(2, m)$ networks are regular of degree 3 for all even m.

The LA(FG) and BA(FG) networks derived from FG will have the following characteristics. Each PE in LA(FG) will have the same number of links connected to it—either r or $(r + 1)$. Analogously, each bus in BA(FG) will be connected to the same number of PEs—either r or $(r + 1)$. Thus, from the point of view of I/0 ports and interconnections, these networks can be considered regular.

Below, the routing in these networks is described in the context of the link network LA(FG). The formulations below can be adapted for the bus architecture, BA(FG), as well.

Consider the following path from the source PE(s) to the destination PE(d). Let $s = (s_{m-1}, \ldots, s_1, s_0)$ and $d = (d_{m-1}, \ldots, d_1, d_0)$ in radix r.

$$(s_{m-1}, \cdots \cdots \cdots, s_1 s_0)$$
$$(s_{m-1}, \cdots \cdots \cdots, s_1, d_{m-1})$$
$$(s_{m-2}, \cdots, s_1, d_{m-1}, s_{m-1})$$
$$(s_{m-2}, \cdots, s_1, d_{m-1}, d_{m-2})$$
$$\vdots$$
$$(s_1, d_{m-1}, d_{m-2}, \cdots \cdots, s_2)$$
$$(s_1, d_{m-1}, d_{m-2}, \cdots \cdots, d_1)$$
$$(d_{m-1}, \cdots \cdots \cdots, d_1, s_1)$$
$$(d_{m-1}, \cdots \cdots \cdots, d_1, d_0)$$

The path above will be denoted as pt(s, d). This can be used to formulate a simple message routing procedure that routes the message from node to node using only the destination address information.

A message-routing algorithm suitable for LA(FG(r, m)) is described next. It is assumed that each message carries m tag bits. These m bits, denoted as T, are initialized at the source PE as equal to d, the destination address. The destination address d is carried by the message separately.

Although the routing algorithms given below are for LA(FG) networks, they can be used for the bus network BA(FG) as well with some modifications. Each PE(x) in LA(FG) corresponds to a node x in FG, and vice versa. Also, every path from PE(x) to PE(y) in LA(FG) has a corresponding path from node x to y in FG, and vice versa.

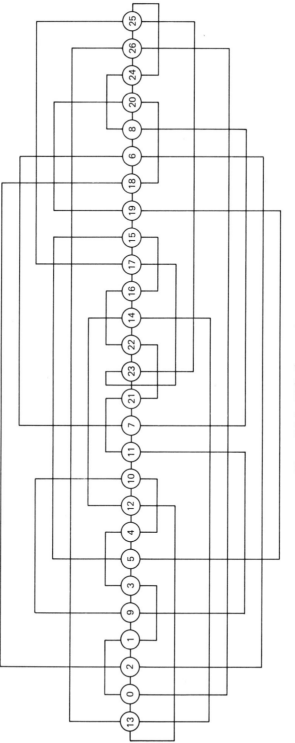

Figure 7.8.4 FG(3, 3) network.

Therefore, all the paths and routing actions for LA(FG) will be described by using the graph FG. The remainder of the section will use node x to denote PE(x).

When a message arrives at node x, the following steps are executed to determine the next node in the path. Here x_0 denotes the least significant bit of the binary number x.

> *Step 1:* If $x = d$, the message has reached the destination and is accepted. Otherwise, the message is forwarded to a neighbor of x by using the following steps.
>
> *Step 2:* Compare x_0 (the least significant bit of x) with the leading bit of T. If they are equal, go to step 3; else, forward the message to the neighbor of x, given as $(x_{m-1}, \ldots, x_1, \bar{x}_0)$ in binary.
>
> *Step 3:* Shift the tag field T left by one bit as shown in the example below.

Now, if $x = 0$ or $x = (n - 1)$, go to step 2; else, forward the message to the neighbor y of x, given as $(x_{m-2}, \ldots, x_1, x_0, x_{m-1})$ in binary.

The following example illustrates the routing steps further.

Example 9. Consider the 16-node FG(2, 4) network. Let $s = 8$ and $d = 11$. The following table describes the path and the corresponding tag bits at different nodes:

	Node							
x	8	9	3	2	4	5	10	11
Binary (x)	1000	1001	0011	0010	0100	0101	1010	1011
T at arrival		1011	0110	0110	1100	1100	1000	1000
T at departure	1011	0110	0110	1100	1100	1000	1000	—

It can easily be seen that the steps above route the message according to the path pt(s, d), described earlier. The routing procedure discussed above is algorithmic and uses only local information contained in the message.

7.8.2. Fault Tolerance

In considering the fault tolerance of LA(FG) and BA(FG), the following may be noted regarding the effects of various faults from the point of view of communciation and routing, as described in Table 7.8.1. The effect of a faulty PE in the link architecture is equivalent to the effect of a faulty BUS in the corresponding bus architecture. Similarly, a faulty PE in the bus architecture has an effect on the routing equivalent to that of a faulty link in the link architecture. The following discusses fault tolerance in the context of link architecture and can be extended fairly easily to bus architecture.

First, LA(FG(2, m)) networks are considered, followed by LA(FG(r, m)) networks $r \geqq 3$. Routing techniques are presented which admit faults. Although not discussed here, these networks also admit certain detour techniques of routing [PRAD85a] in the event of faults. The detour technique of routing provides for transparency of faults with respect to the global routing strategy. This permits the routing to degrade proportionately to the number of faults: thus, graceful degradation.

Fault tolerance of FG(2, *m*) networks.   An algorithm is described below that routes messages from one node to another despite any single faulty PE or link.

Given a binary number x, let the weight of x, (wt(x)), represent the number of 1s in x. Let pt(i, j) represent the path pt$(s = i, d = j)$. The following is easily established:

Any node x, $x \neq i$, in the path pt$(i, 0)$ or pt$(0, i)$ satisfies the following relationship:

$$\text{wt}(x) \leqq \text{wt}(i) \qquad \text{if } i_0 = 0$$

$$\text{wt}(x) < \text{wt}(i) \qquad \text{if } i_0 = 1$$

Any node x, $x \neq i$, in the path pt$(i, n - 1)$ or pt$(n - 1, i)$ satisfies the following relationship:

$$\text{wt}(x) \geqq \text{wt}(i) \qquad \text{if } i_0 = 1$$

$$\text{wt}(x) > \text{wt}(i) \qquad \text{if } i_0 = 0$$

The algorithm discussed below is based on the foregoing observations and is useful for routing messages when a node becomes faulty. This also establishes an upper bound on the maximum path length in the presence of a fault. The algorithm given is shown to be easily implementable.

Let f denote the faulty PE, PE(f).

Let s denote the source PE, PE(s).

Let d denote the destination PE, PE(d).

Routing with a faulty PE.   The following describes different paths from s to d in FG which correspond to different cases of f.

1. wt$(f) >$ wt(s) and wt$(f) >$ wt(d).

$$s \rightarrow \cdots \text{pt}(s, 0) \cdots \rightarrow 0 \cdots \rightarrow \text{pt}(0, d) \cdots \rightarrow d$$

2. wt$(f) <$ wt(s) and wt$(f) <$ wt(d).

$$s \rightarrow \cdots \text{pt}(s, n - 1) \cdots \rightarrow (n - 1) \rightarrow \cdots \text{pt}(n - 1, d) \cdots \rightarrow d$$

3. wt$(f) >$ wt(s) and wt$(f) <$ wt(d).

$$s \rightarrow \cdots \text{pt}(s, 0) \cdots \rightarrow 0 \rightarrow (n - 1) \rightarrow \cdots \text{pt}(n - 1, d) \cdots \rightarrow d$$

4. $\text{wt}(f) < \text{wt}(s)$ and $\text{wt}(f) > \text{wt}(d)$.

$$s \to \cdots \text{pt}(s, n-1) \cdots \to (n-1) \to 0 \to \cdots \text{pt}(0, d) \cdots \to d$$

5. $\text{wt}(f) = \text{wt}(s)$ and $\text{wt}(f) > \text{wt}(d)$.

$$\text{If } s_0 = \begin{cases} 1 & \text{path as case (1)} \\ 0 & \text{path as case (4)} \end{cases}$$

6. $\text{wt}(f) = \text{wt}(s)$ and $\text{wt}(f) < \text{wt}(d)$.

$$\text{If } s_0 = \begin{cases} 1 & \text{path as case (3)} \\ 0 & \text{path as case (2)} \end{cases}$$

7. $\text{wt}(f) = \text{wt}(d)$ and $\text{wt}(f) > \text{wt}(s)$.

$$\text{If } d_0 = \begin{cases} 1 & \text{path as case (1)} \\ 0 & \text{path as case (3)} \end{cases}$$

8. $\text{wt}(f) = \text{wt}(d)$ and $\text{wt}(f) \leqq \text{wt}(s)$.

$$\text{If } d_0 = \begin{cases} 1 & \text{path as case (4)} \\ 0 & \text{path as case (2)} \end{cases}$$

9. $\text{wt}(f) = \text{wt}(s) = \text{wt}(d)$.

$$\text{If } \begin{cases} s_0 = 0, d_0 = 0 & \text{path as case (2)} \\ s_0 = 0, d_0 = 1 & \text{path as case (4)} \\ s_0 = 1, d_0 = 0 & \text{path as case (3)} \\ s_0 = 1, d_0 = 1 & \text{path as case (1)} \end{cases}$$

For example in the event of a fault in node g in Example 9 the message will be routed as: $8 \to 1 \to 0 \to 15 \to 14 \to 11$.

The following is an immediate consequence of the routing steps above. The maximum path length in above routing is $(4m - 1)$.

It has been shown that in the presence of any two faults, a message can be routed from any node, s, to any node, d, in FG(2, m), using at most $(4m + 2)$ hops [PRAD85a]. Thus a second fault may cause a small increase in the path length: $(4m + 2)$ versus $(4m - 1)$.

The FG(r, m) networks in general have been shown to tolerate upto $(r - 1)$ faults [PRAD85a]. Also these networks admit certain detours around faulty components.

These FG networks combine some of the advantages of other networks described earlier. Specifically, Table 7.8.2 compares various different networks, including generalized hypercube [BHUY84], cube-connected cycles [PREP81], shift and replace graphs [SCHL74, PRAD82a, PRAD84, HAKI84], and leaf-ringed binary tree networks, described earlier.

TABLE 7.8.2   DIFFERENT INTERCONNECTION NETWORKS

Network	Number of nodes	Number of connections/node	Routing distance	Fault tolerance
Leaf-ringed binary tree	$2^m - 1$	3	$2m - 1$	2
Cube-connected cycles	$3 \cdot 2^m$	3	$2m$	2
Binary cube	2^m	m	m	$m - 1$
Generalized hypercube	$\prod_{i=1}^{m} x_i$	$\sum_{i=1}^{m} x_i$	m	$\sum_{i=1}^{m} x_i - 1$
SR network	r^m	$2r$	m	$2r - 3$
FG network	r^m	r or $(r + 1)$	$2m - 1$	$(r - 1)$ or r

7.9. FAULT TOLERANCE IN VLSI-BASED SYSTEMS

Two VLSI-based areas in which important innovations are likely to occur are in the single-chip/multiprocessing cell architectures, and in the wafer-scale integrated (WSI) architectures. The former does make it possible to build a high-speed processor on a single chip, designed by interconnecting a large number of simple processing cells. The latter has the potential for a major breakthrough—with its ability to realize a complete multiprocessing system on a single wafer. This will eliminate the expensive steps required to dice the wafer into individual chips and bond their pads to external pins. In addition, internal connections between chips on the same wafer are more reliable and have a smaller propagation delay than external connections. These architectures already have captured the imagination of several computer manufacturers as well as researchers. For example, the Triology System and McDonnell Douglas have already reported progress in redundant wafer-scale systems design [PLET83, HSIA81].

The motivation for incorporating fault tolerance (redundancy) is twofold: yield enhancement and reliability improvement [KORE 85]. *Yield enhancement* is achieved by incorporating redundancy on the chip or wafer so that when a defect is detected during production testing, the defective element can be switched with a spare on the same chip or wafer. This type of restructuring is thus done once at the production site before it is shipped to the field. Yield enhancement is achieved because defective circuits can be accepted for use. For example, given a multiprocessing cell chip where any single defective cell can be replaced by a spare, the resulting yield is equal to the sum of the yield with zero cell defects and the yield with single cell defects.

Reliability improvement is achieved by replacing—in the field—a faulty element with a spare element on the same chip or wafer. The requirements of restructuring for reliability improvement differ from those for yield enhancement in the following ways. In the field, the chip or wafer may not be directly accessible as it is at the production site before assembly. If multiple spare elements are used, the restructuring technology used should allow for more-than-once restructuring capability. Therefore, the type of restructing capability used can be termed static or dynamic, depending on whether it can be performed only once (*static*) or as many times as may be required (*dynamic*).

Static restructurability has two possible applications: aside from yield enhancement, this allows the array to be structured differently for different applications. For example, given a rectangular array interconnection, one can embed a binary tree fairly easily. Thus the same array can then be marketed to different users as different processors—by suitably restructuring it after manufacturing. Dynamic restructurability, on the other hand, provides for dynamically reconfigurable architectures in the field as required. Thus both achieving yield enhancement and providing architectural flexibility are of significant industrial importance.

Various programmable link technologies are now available which allow for restructurability. Included among these are irreversible links (formed using laser technology) and dynamically programmable links (formed using latches). Laser and e-beam technology allow altering existing links by selectively burning fuses, using pulses. Because these types of alterations are irreversible, they are termed static. Dynamic restructurability can be obtained with programmable links, using latches or dynamic memory cells, as shown in Fig. 7.9.1. By reprogramming the latches, these links can be altered an unlimited number of times. However, it should be noted that use of latches or dynamic storage cells does require extra circuitry as well as extra input lines. Also, the dynamic links are volatile; therefore, a loss of power to the circuit will require a reprogramming of all the connections.

Both forms of restructurability have proven to increase substantially the yield of high-density chips. This has been done in practice for memory chips and logic circuits [LINC81, PLET83, ARNO83, HSIA81] and has been proven theoretically for processor array chips [KORE84, KORE86]. Such a chip contains redundant processors which can be substituted for defective ones. This substitution can be either physical substitution: for example, using laser programming [LINC81, SMIT81, MINA81] (or any other static restructuring technique) or logical substitution, which implies dynamic restructuring.

Thus the emerging VLSI technology provides a new framework for development of fault-tolerant techniques. Recent research has focused on the following areas:

1. Formulation of various fault-tolerance concepts related to VLSI processor arrays and development of design techniques for fault tolerance
2. Development of analytical models and quantitative relationships between redunancy, degree of fault tolerance, and yield enhancement

Mesh-connected arrays of processing cells is an ideal architecture for single-chip implementation and have been demonstrated to execute matrix-type manipulations concurrently at a high speed [KUNG80]. Therefore, much research has recently been focused on developing specialized concurrent algorithms for different applications to

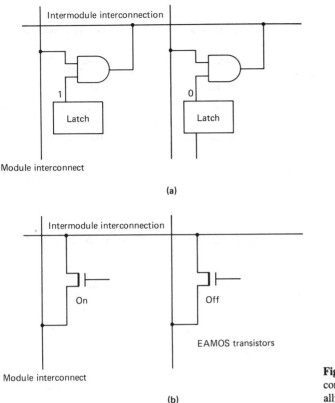

Figure 7.9.1   (a) Programmable interconnections using latches; (b) dynamically restructurable links.

be executed on these arrays. Typical examples of mesh connection include triangular, rectangular, and hexagonal arrays, as shown in Fig. 7.9.2.

Fault tolerance may be introduced into the architecture of such an array by adding extra cells, links, or buses. However, it has been observed [LINC81] (in the MIT Lincoln Laboratory Project) that the probability of interconnect failure is much lower than the probability of cell failure because of their relative fabrication complexities. Therefore, the most appropriate levels at which redundancy can be incorporated is at the processing cell itself and at the network level using redundant cells.

At the processing cell level, one might incorporate fault tolerance into the internal architecture of the cell by employing techniques such as self-checking and fault masking in such a way as to increase the reliability and computational availability of the entire array. At the network level, redundant cells may be added to achieve fault tolerance. Thus one of the first questions that arises is how the array can be augmented with redundant cells so as to achieve a desired level of fault tolerance.

A Taxonomy for Processor Architectures

Broadly, there are two types of interconnection architectures that are of interest to VLSI processor array implementation. The first type is the nearest neighbor inter-

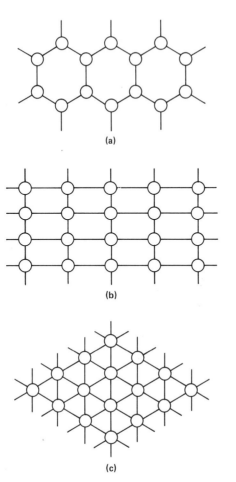

(a)

(b)

(c)

Figure 7.9.2 Mesh connected arrays: (a) triangular array; (b) rectangular array; (c) hexagonal array.

connection which includes various mesh interconnections, illustrated in Fig. 7.9.2. The second type we refer to here as algebraic graph networks which includes networks such as binary n-cube, cube-connected cycles [PREP81], shuffle-exchange graph, shift-and-replace graph networks [SAMA84, SAMA85a], and group graph networks [AKER84]. Examples of the latter are illustrated in Fig. 7.9.3. Like the mesh connection networks, these admit efficient execution of certain algorithms. Also, the algebraic structure of some of these networks can be exploited so as to realize asymptotically optimum VLSI-layouts [LEIG81].

In order to represent uniformly different types of such architectures using different types of processing nodes (processors with internal switches and processors with external switches) and different types of switches (switches used for routing and switches used for fault-detection and reconfiguration), we present the following taxonomy. Generally, there are two types of system nodes: nodes capable of only computation, and nodes capable of both computing and switching for routing. In addition, there are two types of switches: conventional switches capable of only

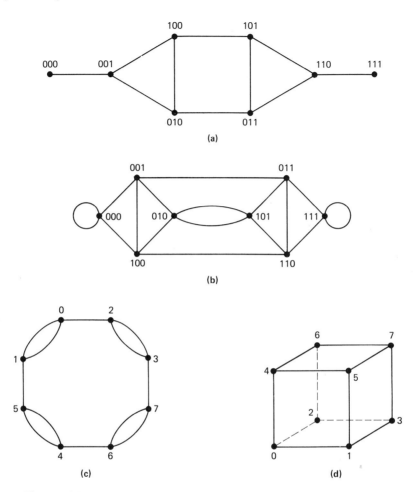

Figure 7.9.3   Algebraic graph networks: (a) shuffle-exchange graph; (b) shift-and-replace graph; (c) cube-connected cycles; (d) cube network.

establishing connections, and fault-detecting switches that perform the function of both fault-detection and reconfiguration. The advantage, generally, in using external switches is that the computational space can be distinct from the communication space which, therefore, provides greater flexibility for emulation of a variety of communication geometries. The disadvantage of external switches, though, is that they require additional hardware support and occupy extra VLSI area.

Different types of architectures are illustrated in Fig. 7.9.4. First, Fig. 7.9.4a illustrates an architecture where the PE's perform internally all the switching necessary to establish connections. Figure 7.9.4b represents an architecture where all the connections are established by using external switches. Such differences are best illustrated by using the following 5-tuple representation of networks. Let $N = \langle P, S, E_p, E_s, E_{p-s} \rangle$ denote the network, where P represents the set of PE's, S denotes the

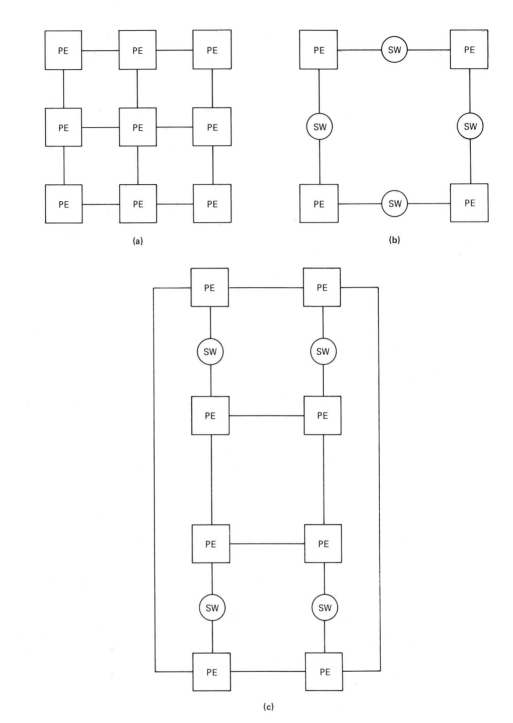

Figure 7.9.4 (a) Type 1 architecture using internal switches; (b) type 2 architecture using external switches. (c) type 3 architecture; (d) type 4 architecture. PE: processing element; SW: switch.

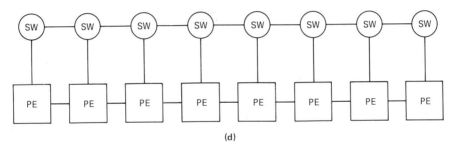

(d)

Figure 7.9.4   (cont.)

set of switches, E_p denotes the set of direct processor-processor links, E_s denotes the set of direct switch-switch links, and E_{p-s} denotes the set of processor-switch links. Different architectures can be conveniently categorized into the following four types, as shown below, where Φ represents the null set:

$$\text{Type 1: } \langle P, S = \Phi, E_p, E_s = E_{p-s} = \Phi \rangle$$

This denotes the type of architecture shown in Fig. 7.9.4(a). Here, the array contains only processing nodes with switches built-in as an integral part of the processor. The mesh connection considered in [KORE81] is an example of such an architecture.

$$\text{Type 2: } \langle P, S, E_p = \Phi, E_s, E_{p-s} \rangle$$

This denotes the type of architecture shown in Fig. 7.9.4(b) where all of the configuration and communication functions are performed by switches that are external to the processor. The CHIP architecture proposed by Snyder [SNYD82] is an example of this type.

$$\text{Type 3: } \langle P, S, E_p, E_s = \Phi, E_{p-s} \rangle$$

Figure 7.9.4(c) delineates such an architecture. Here, in addition to the external switches, each processor has an internal switch which sets up the connections between processors. The external switches are used to provide the function of fault-detection through disagreement detection and subsequent switching-out of the faulty processor, thus disconnecting it from the network.

$$\text{Type 4: } \langle P, S, E_p, E_s, E_{p-s} \rangle$$

This denotes a type of architecture where all of the different types of links are used. An example of such an architecture is illustrated in Fig. 7.9.4(d). Here, a linear array of PE's is provided with external switch connections which can be configured in four ways, as shown in Fig. 7.9.5(a). The switches in such an architecture have dual purpose. First, they can be used to provide multiple logical configurations such as binary tree in addition to the linear array; thus, an application that requires both linear array and binary tree can use this architecture as shown in Fig. 7.9.5(b). Secondly, the switches can be used to bypass the faulty elements as shown in Fig. 7.9.5(c).

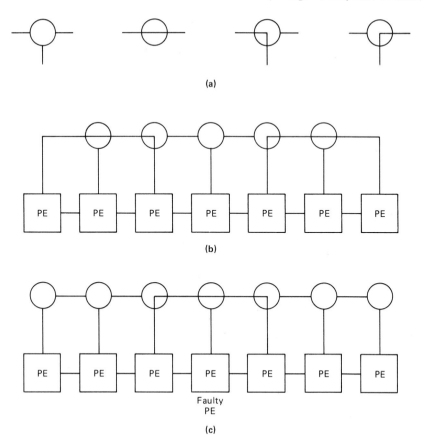

Figure 7.9.5 (a) Different switch configurations; (b) linear array and binary tree configuration; (c) bypassing faulty PE.

Thus, these different categorizations encompass all of the different possible architectures that can be conceived. The above taxonomy provides a convenient framework for both the analysis of different architectures as well as for the conceptualization of new architectures.

There are two basic ways one can introduce fault-tolerance into these arrays. The first approach would be to provide redundancy at each node so that the node can be reconfigured internally in the event of a fault. For example, consider a 9-node mesh connection shown in Fig. 7.9.6. If we assume that the interconnects are highly reliable, one way to design this array so that it will be fault-tolerant is to use two self-checking processors at each node, as shown in Fig. 7.9.7. The function of the external switch is to determine, in the event of a fault, which one of the two checkers is indicating errors and then switch out the appropriate module.

However, if the interconnects cannot be assumed to be reliable, one has then to provide redundancy by designing an array larger than the maximum size required for

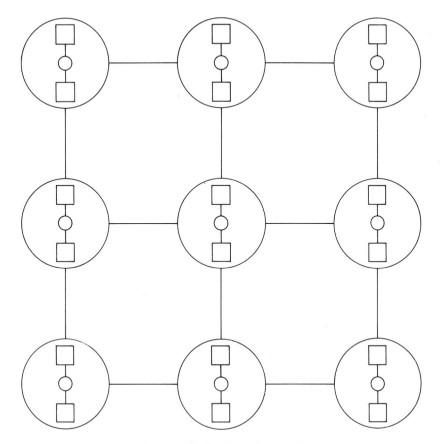

Figure 7.9.6   9-node mesh connection.

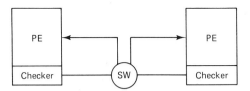

Figure 7.9.7   Fault-tolerant node.

the applications. For example, consider the 4 × 4 array shown in Fig. 7.9.8 which is designed to support various applications including the binary tree configuration shown in Fig. 7.9.9(a). The mapping of the binary tree onto the array, is depicted in Fig. 7.9.9(b). In this figure, the mapped nodes of the binary tree are shown, along with the inactive components which are shown using dashed lines. Consider now that the active node 6 becomes faulty. It can be easily seen that the network can no longer admit the binary tree configuration shown in Fig. 7.9.9(a). However, should it be possible to execute the same application on a reduced binary tree (perhaps with a

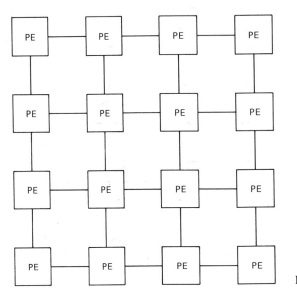

Figure 7.9.8   4 × 4 mesh connection.

degraded performance) such as the one shown in Fig. 7.9.10, the application can still
be supported by the faulty array, as demonstrated below.

There are two different ways this can be achieved. First, the original 4 × 4 array
can be restructured into a smaller 3 × 3 array as shown in Fig. 7.9.11. This would
require giving up the use of some processing nodes by turning them into connecting
nodes. Then, any application that can be executed on a 3 × 3 array can be executed
on this new (logical) 3 × 3 array. The second approach would be to directly map the
application configuration onto the faulty physical array. However, the latter approach
can be computationally complex [FUSS82]. Thus, depending on whether or not such
reduction is possible, the network may or may not be fault-tolerant with respect to this
application.

Several important concepts emerge from the above discussion [NANY 83].
First, a node or link can assume several distinct states. The following shows various
possible states of the node:

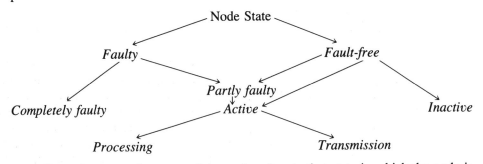

Here, the processing state of the node refers to that state in which the node is
assigned to perform some useful computational task.

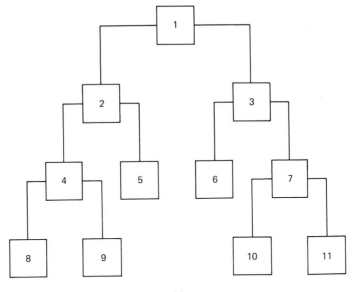

(a)

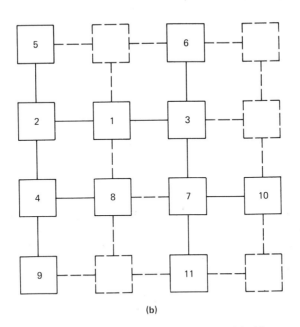

(b)

Figure 7.9.9   (a) Binary tree configuration; (b) mapping of the binary tree onto the mesh.

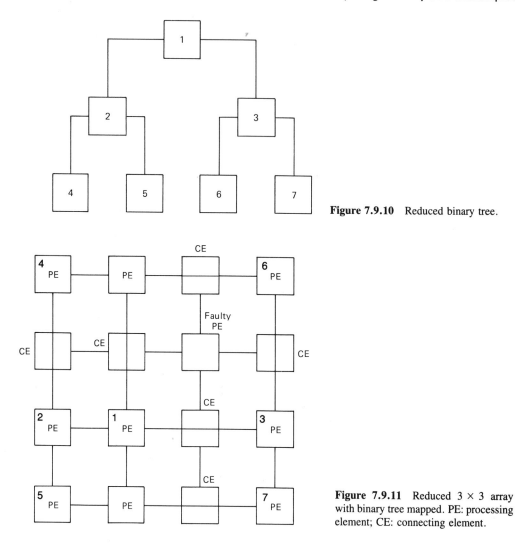

Figure 7.9.10   Reduced binary tree.

Figure 7.9.11   Reduced 3 × 3 array with binary tree mapped. PE: processing element; CE: connecting element.

On the other hand, a node in the transmission state is assigned to perform only switching, so as to establish a path. Thus, a node in this state does not perform any computations except those which may be required for routing, etc. For a link, though, this distinction does not apply. Accordingly, there are fewer states for a link, as shown below:

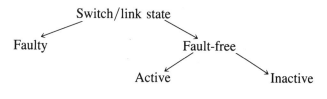

Second, the various reconfiguration processes can be conceptualized through an abstraction of layers, [NANY83] as formulated below:

1. Let the *physical* layer represent the topology that describes the interconnection structure, together with the status of the nodes and links in the physical array. A node/link in the physical layer can be either in the fault-free or faulty state.
2. Let an *application* layer represent that topology which is required to support a given application. Thus, in this layer, all the nodes are processing nodes; the links, active links.
3. Let the *logical* layer represent the topology that realizes a given application layer on a given physical layer. Thus a node in this layer is either in the processing state or in the transmission state. All the links in the logical layer are in the active state.

For a given configuration, the layers above are related topologically, as shown in Fig. 7.9.12. The nodes in the application layer are a subset of the nodes in the corresponding logical layer and these are a subset of the nodes in the physical layer.

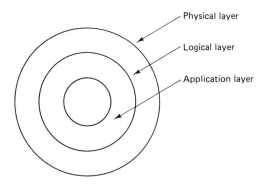

Physical layer

Logical layer

Application layer

Figure 7.9.12   Topological relationships.

One of the problems that has been the focus of recent research is how a particular application can be realized in a given physical array with faults. Stated differently, this problem relates to how to embed a given application layer on a faulty physical layer. In [KORE81], a restructuring algorithm is presented that can realize a linear array in a faulty rectangular array; also in [FUSS82], the problem of realizing a binary tree in a faulty array is discussed.

These discussions are also applicable to the second type of networks, the algebraic networks. Consider the shift-and-replace graph networks proposed recently in [SAMA84] as a candidate for VLSI processor networks. Such an 8-node network is shown in Fig. 7.9.13(a). This network is capable of emulating various useful logical structures such as the linear array, binary tree, shuffle and the shuffle-exchange communication structures, as shown in Fig. 7.9.13(b). More importantly, this algebraic network can emulate structures such as the linear array and binary tree in spite of a fault. Consider the link connecting nodes 1 and 2 becoming faulty. In this case,

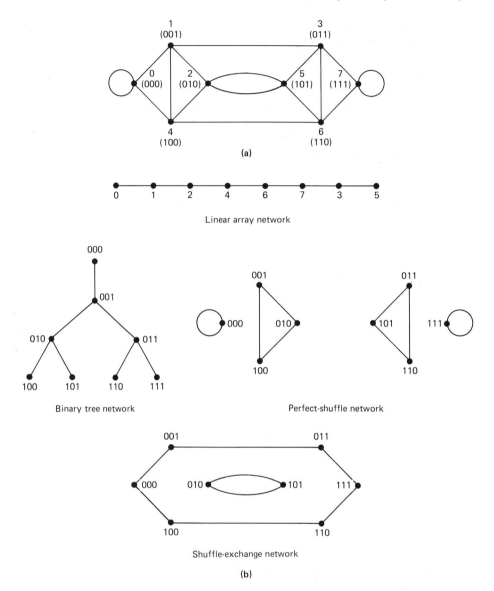

Figure 7.9.13 (a) Shift-and-replace graph; (b) emulating logical structures on a shift-and-replace graph.

the networks can still be restructured both as a linear array and as a binary tree, as shown in Fig. 7.9.14. Similarly, the network is also capable of emulating these structures in spite of any single node failures.

It may also be noted that networks such as the binary n-cube and the cube-connected cycles provide some interesting fault-tolerant reconfiguration capabilities. Consider a 4-cube of 16 nodes, shown in Fig. 7.7.1. In the event of a fault, one can

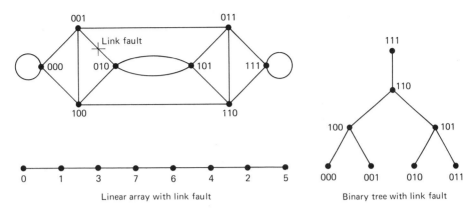

Figure 7.9.14 Emulations in the presence of a faulty link.

degrade this to a 3-cube of eight nodes, shown in Fig. 7.9.15(a). However, this would require giving up the use of seven good nodes. Alternatively, one can partition the 4-cube into four subnetworks of 2-cubes. Assuming that the problem can be divided into subproblems that can be executed on 2-cubes, one can use three of these, as shown in Fig. 7.9.15(b). This would necessitate giving up the use of only three good nodes. It is obvious that the fault-tolerance of algebraic networks can be studied in the context of VLSI processor arrays.

Other relevant considerations include which strategies are best suited for fault detection and reconfiguration [KORE81].

Test and reconfiguration procedures can be performed internally or externally. Internal implementation would require providing the additional capability for the processing cells to test their neighbors and perform appropriate reconfiguration. Such a localized testing and reconfiguration strategy may simplify, if not eliminate, the problem of formulating algorithms for determining the location of faulty cells. This would, of course, require additional hardware/software support for the processing cells.

Conversely, external testing and reconfiguration requires the use of a reliable external processor which can periodically test and observe the status of the processing cells. This approach, although it does simplify the design of the processing cells, suffers from the following shortcomings:

1. It may not be possible to apply tests to all the processing cells from an external source because of pin limitations and also the large number of cells. Additionally, being able to observe the test results may not always be possible because of the presence of faulty cells.

2. The reliability of the system reduces to the reliability of the external source that has been assigned to perform testing and reconfiguration.

In general, testing may have to interrupt all the computations in the array. Since it is assumed that the testing is done periodically, it is desirable that the number of tests

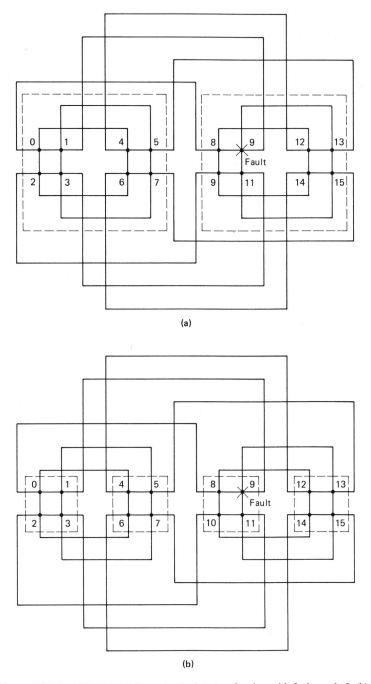

Figure 7.9.15 (a) Partioned binary 4-cube into two 3-cubes with faulty node 9; (b) partitioned binary 4-cube into four 2-cubes with faulty node 9.

and the testing time should be minimized when there are no faults. The testing time should be proportionate to the number of faults; thus a fault-free array would require a minimum number of tests with the number of tests increasing with the number of faults. In [MEYE85], a possible diagnosis strategy was suggested that makes the testing very simple in the absence of any fault; the testing becomes progressively more time-consuming with the number of faults. Since there are usually no faults present, the performance penalty due to interruption for testing can be minimal. This is illustrated further below.

In Fig. 7.9.16, possible testing graphs for a 5 * 5 end-around mesh (the boundary nodes are also adjacent) are shown. The darkened boxes represent nodes already diagnosed as being faulty. The edges with arrows indicate those communication edges included in the testing graph. The arrows point from the tester to the tested unit. Algorithm SELF2 [KUHL80a] would require a graph with 75 directed edges to diagnose up to three faults. The strategy presented in [MEYE85] never employs more than 25 periodic tests.

Figure 7.9.16(a) indicates a possible initial testing graph. Since the end-around mesh is node-symmetric, the first fault may always be viewed as occurring in the

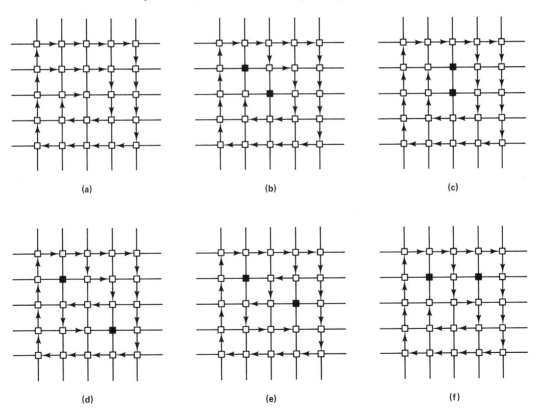

Figure 7.9.16   Various testing graphs for 5 * 5 end-around mesh.

center node; and the same testing graph may then be used after the first fault is diagnosed. There must exist two adjacent fault-free rows (also columns) after no more than two faults have occurred. This ensures that the graph may be viewed with the faults restricted to the interior, i.e., with the border intact.

Figures 7.9.16(b) through (f) illustrate five possible cases for the fault locations. In each instance, the interior is shown to include a Hamiltonian path. As proved in [MEYE85], at least one fault amongst the nodes in the loop along the border may be diagnosed. (If all are fault-free, the first faulty node along the path through the interior may be diagnosed.)

Let $[\alpha, \beta]$ denote the closed interval from α to β. Let the nodes in the mesh be represented by pairs $\langle a, b \rangle$ where $a, b \in [1, 5]$ with a indicating the row and b indicating the column. Let the first fault, without loss of generality, be at node $\langle 3, 3 \rangle$. By symmetry we need only to consider the second fault occurring at (1) $\langle 2, 4 \rangle$, (2) $\langle 2, 3 \rangle$, (3) $\langle 1, 5 \rangle$, (4) $\langle 1, 4 \rangle$, or (5) $\langle 1, 3 \rangle$. These possibilities (1) through (5) correspond to the illustrations in Figs. 7.9.16(b) through (f), respectively. Consequently, Fig. 7.9.16 gives testing graphs for all unique fault patterns in this case. Precise necessary and sufficient conditions for such a dynamic testing of general systems are given in [MEYE85].

Another area of study that is receiving considerable attention is the problem of trade-off of redundancy and yield in the context of VLSI processor arrays. Particularly, what has been studied in [MANG82a, MANG82b, STAD80, KORE84, GREE83, and LEIG82] is the formulation of models for evaluating yield enhancement in terms of area and delay overheads that may be required for restructuring from defects. Recently a model for evaluating the effective use of redundancy for both yield and performance enhancements has been studied in [KORE85].

In [MANG82], a yield model was developed based on the assumptions that the interconnections are perfectly reliable and that any spare module can replace any faulty module. The relationship of the modules and interconnection complexities was also studied and their main conclusions were as follows.

There is an optimum amount of redundancy for yield enhancement, given the chip size and the defect density. This optimum amount of redundancy (which maximizes the yield) increases gradually with the increasing defect density, while the maximum yield decreases.

A different study carried out more recently by Koren and Breuer [KORE84] examines the trade-off between redundancy and fault tolerance from the point of view of self-testing. It is assumed that each processing element can be made self-testing and when a fault is detected, the array is reconfigured by using redundant PEs. It is further assumed that each processing element can be made self-testing, either via duplication or by means of other self-checking techniques. The duplication technique is assumed to require twice the silicon area of a simplex processing element. Self-checking design, on the other hand, is assumed to require less silicon area than duplication. Under these assumptions it is shown that the yield may increase with the number of defective cells tolerated—up to a certain point—and then the yield may decrease with the increase in number of defective cells tolerated. Also, self-testing through duplication may actually produce a lower yield than the simplex design; therefore, other methods of self-testing should be employed.

Most recently, researchers have formulated certain models that quantify performance penalties that may result when restructuring is carried out to achieve higher yield. One such model, derived in [GREE84], is described below to illustrate some of the fundamental trade-offs. The framework used here is wafer-scale integration. Here it is assumed that the wafer consists of an array of identical elements, some of which may be defective. After testing, the nondefective elements are connected so as to realize a specified configuration. It is assumed here that only the processing elements can be defective, and that the interconnections are free of defects (because the interconnections require a small number of processing steps). Also assumed is that additional connecting tracks are available on the wafer which can be used to bypass the defective elements in connecting the active elements. This bypassing may result in an increase in the length of the interconnections. Also, these redundant elements and additional connecting tracks provided in the wafer require extra silicon area, a fact that may also affect the connection lengths. Therefore, the performance of the defective wafer circuit, after restructuring, will be inferior to a wafer circuit that is free from any defects. This loss of performance may or may not be acceptable. Therefore, in developing a model for evaluating this performance yield trade-off, various parameters that may be useful include the following: the total number of processing elements on the wafer, the minimum number of active elements required for realizing the desired configuration, the maximum allowable performance penalty due to restructuring, and the minimum acceptable yield. These trade-off relationships are illustrated below by using the following example [GREE84].

Consider a linear array of k processing elements to be realized on a wafer, by interconnecting k elements in a chain, on the wafer. If one assumes that the defects are independent and that the probability of a processing element being defective is p, the probability that all of the k elements are defect-free is $(1 - p)^k$. Thus, if the wafer has no redundancy, the yield will be equal to the probability that there are no defects, which is equal to $(1 - p)^k$. Thus, independent of p, since $p \geqq 0$ the yield approaches 0 as k increases. Consequently, for an arbitrarily large k, the yield is bound to be too low to be acceptable.

An alternative will be to provide redundant elements and redundant connecting tracks so that one or more defects can be tolerated. Thus, if e defects are tolerated, the yield will be equal to the sum of the probability that there are $0, 1, \ldots, e$ defects. So, given N processing elements on the wafer where $N \geqq k$, and given one additional connecting track that will allow bypassing the defective elements as shown in Fig. 7.9.17, one can tolerate up to $(N - k)$ defects.

However, the by-product of bypassing defective elements to make connections is that the restructured connections will be longer than the original ones. This increase in length may result in additional delays. However, the maximum allowable interconnection lengths may have to be limited by performance considerations. Thus the question that arises, given the allowable limit on the length of the connections, is: What relationship holds between N, k and the yield?

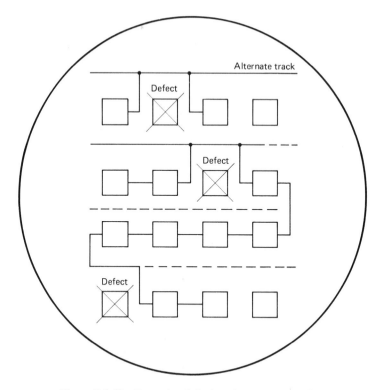

Figure 7.9.17 Bypassing defective elements on a wafer.

First, it may be noted that given the distance between two adjacent elements constituting the unit distance, the distance between two elements separated by t elements is $(t + 1)$. So, given the maximum allowable distance as d, one can allow a chain of at most $(d - 1)$ successive elements to be defective in the linear array configuration. The yield, then, is equal to the probability that one can form a linear array by connecting k active elements where no two elements are separated by a string of d or more defective elements. The probability that some $(d - 1)$ adjacent elements are defective is less than $(1 - p^d)$. Since there are altogether k active elements in the configuration, the probability that there will be fewer than d defective elements adjacent to all the k active elements is less than $(1 - p^d)^k$. Since there are altogether N elements on the wafer, there are, at most, N places where the chains of linear array can be started. So the probability that one can successfully find k active elements to be connected, starting with one of the N elements, is less than $N(1 - p^d)^k \leq Ne^{-kp^d}$. For a fixed d, then, this implies that as k increases, N has to increase exponentially with k; otherwise, the yield will reduce to 0 asymptotically ($k \rightarrow \infty$). Obviously, if N grows exponentially with k, this will result in a very poor utilization of silicon area on the wafer for active use. Thus d cannot remain fixed as the number of elements on the wafer grows; d has to increase with k and N. However, it can be shown that d needs to grow only as $\log N$ in order to achieve good yield, given that k grows as N (i.e.,

k/N is fixed). This is based on the observation that the probability that log N contiguous cells are defective is of the order $1/N$.

This illustrates two basic facts: Given a fixed speed/performance requirement, one cannot allow arbitrarily large numbers of elements on a wafer without significantly reducing the total yield (including restructured defective circuits). Conversely, given a fixed yield requirement, the allowable speed/performance degradation due to restructuring may have to be increased with the number of elements on the wafer.

Related work has been reported in [HUAN82], [KUHN83], and [KUNG84]. Each of these discusses various means of achieving fault tolerance in systolic computations by using processor arrays. In [HUAN82], the problem of matrix multiplication using mesh-connected systolic arrays is considered. Given two matrices, A and B, which are to be multiplied, it is proposed that an additional checksum column and row be added. It is shown that these checksums allow one to detect and correct all single errors in the multiplication. Thus a fault in a single processor is tolerated. A mapping technique is discussed in [KUHN83] that proposes dynamically altering computational assignments to processors in a systolic array so as to achieve fault tolerance. Such an approach is based on the observation that in various systolic algorithms, the processors may alternate between the active and idle states during different cycles. The idea proposed in [KUHN83] is to use the idle processors during a cycle when the computation normally assigned to a processor cannot be performed because of a fault.

Algorithmic specific solutions like [HUAN82] and [KUHN82] are efficient for special purpose dedicated architectures but can tolerate a single fault. Kuhn's IFT approach [KUHN82] requires massive redundancy and it can be shown that for any algorithm where IFT is applicable, there exists an equivalent algorithm that uses a fraction of the number of processors proportional to the number of faults tolerated. In a recent paper [FORT84] an approach for a gracefully degrading array processor is proposed where both the algorithm and the processor array is reconfigured. The objective there is to be able to use a more general class of arrays for a more general class of algorithms.

Finally, Kung and Lam [KUNG84] propose the restructuring of a systolic array using registers in the data path in the event of fault. The basic idea here is to use the systolic arrays as pipelined processors, using the registers to bypass faulty processors. The effect of this will be to introduce additional stages in the pipeline itself. The registers will be used as dummy stages, simply to store data in the pipeline. The addition of extra stages, though, increases the latency of the pipeline but will not affect its throughput provided that a sufficiently large string of data is used. Also, the concept of a systolic ring is proposed that performs fault-tolerant computations related to triangular systems and LU decomposition with graceful degradation.

7.10. SUMMARY

The multiprocessor communication networks described here provide a broad overview of various issues and techniques related to the design of closely integrated fault-tolerant multiprocessor networks. An underlying problem that is receiving considerable attention is the area of the testing and diagnosis of multiprocessor systems [KUHL80a, KIME84, MEYE 85]. With the feasibility of multiprocessing cell chips, the observability and controllability problems have become even more complex to tackle. Therefore, it is expected that future research will focus on these and related issues, such as self-testing and reconfiguration. Also, it can be expected that the design of fault-tolerant, dynamically reconfigurable networks is likely to remain a vital research area. This is true particularly because of their potential commercial importance, since this will allow the semiconductor industry to manufacture "universal" chips with high yield that are user programmable to suit the application in hand.

Other important problems of fault tolerance in multiprocessors are the problem of achieving interactive consistency [PEAS80] in spite of faults, and the problem of load balancing [PRAD81b] in the event of faults. Interactive consistency refers to attaining agreement among all the (fault-free) processors as to the value of those certain variables which are to be shared by all the processors. Each variable is assumed to be private for some processor in that the processor has direct access to that variable. Also, each processor must rely on indirect information in order to ascertain the value of the private variables of other processors. A typical example of such a variable is the value of sensor data that may be read by different processors in a real-time control environment. Because each of the processors may have direct access to only certain sensors, it is therefore important that all the processors assume the same value for each variable. In the absence of faults, this can easily be achieved, by message exchange and by averaging.

However, this problem becomes quite complex when faults are present; in this event, one has to take into account the possibility that a faulty processor may be transmitting the wrong data or no data at all. Simple majority voting by the fault-free processors of the received values of the variables from all the processors is not sufficient to guarantee interactive consistency. It has been shown that, generally, one needs $(3m + 1)$ processors exchanging data in order to achieve interactive consistency when the possibility of m processors being faulty exists. Distributed algorithms are also proposed in [PEAS80] that can be used to achieve interactive consistency in the presence of faults.

Load balancing in the fault-tolerant environment refers to the problem of reassigning the work load evenly among the fault-free processors when one or more processors fail. In [PRAD81b] a graph-theoretic solution to this load-balancing problem is presented.

REFERENCES AND BIBLIOGRAPHY

[ABBO81] Abbott, R., et al., "Equipping a Line of Memories with Spare Cells," *Electronics,* pp. 127–130, July 1981.

[ABRA83] Abraham, J. A., and T. C. Chou, "Load Balancing in Distributed System under Failures," *IEEE Trans. Comput.,* pp. 799–808, Sept. 1983.

[ADAM82] Adams, G. B., and H. J. Siegel, "The Extra Stage Cube: A Fault-Tolerant Interconnection Network for Supersystems," *IEEE Trans Comput.*, vol. C-31, May 1982.

[AGRA82] Agrawal, D. P., "Testing and Fault-Tolerance of Multistage Interconnection Networks," *Computer*, vol. 15, no. 4, pp. 41–53, Apr. 1982.

[AKER84] Akers, S. B. and B. Krishnamurthy, "Group Graphs as Interconnection Networks," *Dig., 14th Annu. Int. Symp. Fault-Tolerant Comput.*, Orlando, Fla., June 1984.

[ARMS81] Armstrong, J. R. and F. G. Gray, "Fault Diagnosis in Boolean n-Cube Array of Microprocessors," *IEEE Trans. Comput.*, pp. 590–596, Aug. 1981.

[ARNO83] Arnold, W., "Redundant Chips Promise High Yields, Low Price," *Electronic Business*, pp. 142–144, February 1983.

[AUBU78] Aubusson, R., and I. Catt, "Wafer-Scale Integration—A Fault Tolerant Procedure," *IEEE J. Solid State Circuits*, vol. SC-13, no. 3, pp. 339–344, June 1978.

[BHUY84] Bhuyan, L. N., and D. P. Agrawal, "Generalized Hypercube and Hyperbus Structures for a Computer Network," *IEEE Transactions on Computers*, C-33, pp. 323–333, April 1984.

[BROA57] Broadbent, S., and J. Hammersley, "Percolation Processes, I," *Proc. Camb. Philos. Soc.*, vol. 53, PP. 629–641, 1957.

[BROO83] Broomell, G., and J. R. Heath, "Classification Categories and Historical Development of Circuit Switching Topologies," *ACM Computing Surveys*, vol. 15, no. 2, June 1983.

[CANT71] Cantor, D. G., "On Nonblocking Switching Networks," *Networks*, vol. 1, no. 4, pp. 367–377, 1971.

[CART71] Carter, W. C., et al., "A Theory of Design of Fault-Tolerant Computers Using Standby Sparing," *Dig., First Annu. Int. Symp. Fault-Tolerant Comput.*, Pasadena, Calif., pp. 83–86, Mar. 1971.

[CART77] Carter, W. C., et al., "Cost Effectiveness of Self-Checking Computer Design," *7th Annu. Int. Symp. Fault-Tolerant Comput.*, Los Angeles, pp. 117–123, June 28–30, 1977.

[CENK79] Cenker, R. P., et al., "A Fault-Tolerant 64K Dynamic Random-Access Memory," *IEEE Trans. Electron Devices*, vol. ED-26, pp. 853–860, June 1979.

[CHUN83] Chung, F. R. K., F. T. Leighton, and A. L. Rosenberg, "DIOGENES: A Methodology for Designing Fault-Tolerant VLSI Processor Arrays," *Dig., 13th Annu. Int. Symp. Fault-Tolerant Comput.*, Milan, Italy, June 1983.

[CLIF80] Cliff, R. A., "Acceptable Testing of VLSI Components Which Contain Error Correctors," *IEEE Trans. Comput.*, vol. C-29, pp. 125–134, Feb. 1980.

[CLOS53] Clos, C., "A Study of Non-blocking Switching Networks," *Bell Syst. Tech. J.*, vol. 32, no. 2, pp. 406–426, Mar. 1953.

[DAVI78] Davies, D., and J. Wakerly, "Synchronization and Matching in Redundant Systems," *IEEE Trans. Comput.*, vol. C-27, no. 6, pp. 531–539, June 1978.

[DEBR46] deBruijn, N. G., "A Combinatorial Problem," *K. Ned. Adad. Wet. Proc.*, vol. 49, pt. 20, pp. 758–764, 1946.

[DESP78] Despain, A., and D. Patterson, "X-Tree: A Tree Structured Multiprocessor Computer Architecture," *Proc. 5th Annu. Symp. Comput. Archit.*, pp. 144–151, Apr. 1978.

[ESFA85] Esfahanian, A. and S. L. Hakimi, "Fault-Tolerant Routing in De Bruijn Communication Networks," *IEEE Transactions on Computers*, vol. C-34, no. 9, pp. 777–788, Sept. 1985.

[FALA81a] Falavarajani, K. M., and D. K. Pradhan, "Fault-Diagnosis of Parallel Processor Interconnection Networks," *Dig., 11th Annu. Int. Symp. Fault-Tolerant Comput.,* Portland, Me., pp. 209–212, June 24–26, 1981.

[FALA81b] Falavarajani, K., "Fault-Diagnosis and Fault-Tolerant Design of Parallel Processor Interconnection Networks," *Ph.D. dissertation,* School of Engineering, Oakland University, Rochester, Mich., 1981.

[FALA81c] Falavarajani, K., and D. K. Pradhan, "Fault-Tolerant Design of SIMD Networks," Tech. Rep., School of Engineering, Oakland University, Rochester, Mich., June 1981.

[FARM69] Farmer, W. D., and E. E. Newhall, "An Experimental Distributed Switching System to Handle Bursty Computer Traffic," *Proc. ACM Symposium Problems Optimization Data Comm. Systems,* Pine Mountain, Georgia, October 1969, pp. 1–34.

[FENG81] Feng, R. Y., and C. L. Wu, "Fault Diagnosis for a Class of Multistage Interconnection Networks," *IEEE Transactions on Computers,* vol. C-30, no. 10, pp. 743–758, October 1981.

[FITZ80] Fitzgerald, B. F., and E. P. Thoma, "Circuit Implementation of Fusible Redundant Addresses of RAMs for Productivity Enhancement," *IBM J. Res. Dev.,* vol. 24, no. 3, pp. 291–298, May 1980.

[FORT80] Fortes, J. A. B., and C. S. Raghavendra, "Dynamically Reconfigurable Fault-Tolerant Array Processors," *Proc. FTCS-14,* Orlando, Florida, pp. 386–392, June 1984.

[FUSS82] Fussell, D., and P. Varman, "Fault Tolerant Wafer-Scale Architecture for VLSI," *9th Annu. Symp. Comput. Archit.,* pp. 190–198, 1982.

[GOLD79] Goldberg, et al., "Formal Techniques for Fault-Tolerance in Distributed Data Processing (DDP)," Final Report, SRI Project 7242, Apr. 1979.

[GORD84] Gordon, D., I. Koren, and G. M. Silberman, "Embedding Tree Structures in Fault-Tolerant VLSI Hexagonal Arrays," *IEEE Trans. Comput.,* vol. C-33, no. 1, pp. 104–108, Jan. 1984.

[GRAN80] Granov, L., L. Kleinrock, and M. Gerla, "A Highly Reliable Distributed Loop Network Architecture," *Dig., 10th Annu. Int. Symp. Fault-Tolerant Comput.,* Oct. 1980.

[GREE84] Greene, J. W., and A. El Gamal, "Configuration of VLSI Arrays in the Presence of Defects," *JACM,* vol. 31, no. 4, pp. 694–717, Oct. 1984.

[HAFN76] Hafner, E. R., and Z. Nenadal, "Enhancing the Availability of a Loop System by Meshing," *Proc. 1976 Int. Zurich Semin. Digit. Commun.,* Zurich, Mar. 1976.

[HAKI69] Hakimi, S. L., "An Algorithm for the Construction of the Least Vulnerable Communication Network or the Graph with the Maximum Connectivity," *IEEE Trans. Circuit Theory,* vol. CT-16, pp. 229–230, May 1969.

[HAM78] Ham, W., "Yield-Area Analysis: Part I-A Diagnostic Tool for Fundamental Integrated-Circuit Process Problems," *RCA Rev.,* vol. 39, pp. 231–249, June 1978.

[HARA62] Harary, F., "The Maximum Connectivity of a Graph," *Proc. Natl. Acad. Sci. USA,* vol. 48, pp. 1142–1146, July 1962.

[HAYE76] Hayes, J. P., "A Graph Model for Fault-Tolerant Computing Systems," *IEEE Trans. Comput.,* vol. 25, no. 9, pp. 875–884, Sept. 1976.

[HEDL82] Hedlund, K., and L. Synder, "Wafer Scale Integration of Configurable, Highly Parallel (CHIP) Processors," Extended Abstract, *Proc. Int. Conf. Parallel Process., IEEE,* pp. 262–264, 1982.

[HOPK78] Hopkins, et al., "FTMP—A Highly Reliable Fault-Tolerant Multiprocessor for Aircraft," *Proc. IEEE,* pp. 1221–1239, Oct. 1978.

[HORO81] Horowitz, E. and A. Zorat, "The Binary Trees as an Interconnection Network: Applications to Multiprocessor Systems, and VLSI," *IEEE Trans. Comput.,* vol. C-30, no. 4, pp. 247–253, Apr. 1981.

[HSIA80] Hsia, Y., G. Chang, and F. Erwin, "Adaptive Wafer Scale Integration," *Jap. J. Appl. Phys.,* vol. 19, Suppl. 19-1, pp. 193–202, 1980.

[HSIA81] Hsia, Y., and R. Fedorak, "Impact of MNOS/AWSI Technology on Reprogrammable Arrays," *Symp. Rec., Semi-Custom Integrated Circuit Technol. Symp.,* Washington, D. C., May 1981.

[HUAN82] Huang, K., and J. Abraham, "Low-Cost Schemes for Fault-Tolerance in Matrix Operation with Processor Arrays," *Dig., 12th Annu. Int. Symp. Fault-Tolerant Comput.,* Los Angeles, June 1982.

[IEEE85] "IEEE 802.4, Token-Passing Bus Access Method," IEEE Press, New York, 1985.

[KATS78] Katsuki, D., et al., "Pluribus—An Operational Fault-Tolerant Multiprocessor," *Proc. IEEE,* vol. 66, no. 10, pp. 1146–1159, Oct. 1978.

[KIM78] Kim, C., and W. Ham, "Yield-Area Analysis: Part II-Effects of Photomask Alignment Errors on Zero Yield Loci," *RCA Rev.,* vol. 39, pp. 565–576, Dec. 1978.

[KORE81] Koren, I., "A Reconfigurable and Fault-Tolerant VLSI Multiprocessor Array," *Proc. 8th Annu. Symp. Comput. Archit.,* Minneapolis, Minn., pp. 425–442, May 1981.

[KORE84] Koren, I., and M. Breuer, "On Area and Yield Considerations for Fault-Tolerant VLSI Processor Arrays," *IEEE Trans. Comput.,* vol. C-33, no. 1, pp. 21–27, Jan. 1984.

[KORE85] Koren, I., and D. K. Pradhan, "Introducing Redundancy into VLSI Designs for Yield and Performance Enhancement," *Proc. of the 15th Annual Symposium on Fault-Tolerant Computing,* June 1985, pp. 330–335.

[KORE86] Koren, I., and D. K. Pradhan, "Yield and Performance Enhancement Through Redundancy in VLSI and WSI Multi-processor Systems", *Proceedings of IEEE,* Special Issue on Fault-Tolerant VLSI, May 1986.

[KUHL80a] Kuhl, J., and S. Reddy, "Distributed Fault-Tolerance for Large Multiprocessor Systems," *Proc. 7th Annu. Symp. Comput. Archit.,* pp. 23–30, May 1980.

[KUHL80b] Kuhl, J., "Fault Diagnosis in Computing Networks," Ph. D. dissertation, Department of Electrical and Computer Engineering, University of Iowa, Aug. 1980.

[KUHN83] Kuhn, L., "Experimental Study of Laser Formed Connections for LSI Wafer Personalization," *IEEE Journal of Solid-State Circuits,* vol. SC-10, pp. 219–228, Aug. 1975.

[KUHN83] Kuhn, R. H., "Interstitial Fault Tolerance—A Technique for Making Systolic Arrays Fault Tolerant," *Proc. 16th Annu. Int. Conf. Syst.,* Jan. 1983, pp. 215–224.

[KUNG80] Kung, H. T., and C. E. Leiserson, "Algorithms for VLSI Processor Arrays," in *Introduction to VLSI Systems* by C. Mead and L. Conway, Addison-Wesley, Section 8.3, 1980.

[KUNG82] Kung, H. T., "Why Systolic Arrays?" *Computer,* vol. 15, no. 1, January 1982.

[KUNG84] Kung, H. T., and M. S. Lam, "Fault-Tolerance and Two-Level Pipelining in VLSI Systolic Arrays," *Proc. 1984 Conf. Adv. Res. VLSI,* MIT, Cambridge, Mass., Jan. 23–25, 1984.

[KWAN81a] Kwan, C. L., and S. Toida, "Optimal Fault-Tolerant Realizations of Some Classes of Hierarchical Tree Systems," *Dig., 11th Annu. Int. Symp. Fault-Tolerant Comput.,* Portland, Me., pp. 176–178, June 24–26, 1981.

[KWAN81b] Kwan, C. L., Ph.D., dissertation, Department of System Design, University of Waterloo, Waterloo, Ontario, 1981.

[LANG79] Lang, T., Unpublished notes, UCLA, Los Angeles, Apr. 1979.

[LAWR83] Lawrie, D. H., and K. Padmanabhan, "A Class of Redundant Path Multistage Interconnection Networks," *IEEE Transactions on Computers,* vol. C-32, no. 12, pp. 1099–1108, December 1983.

[LEIG81] Leighton, F. T., and G. L. Miller, "Optimal Layouts for Small Shuffle-Exchange Graphs", *Proceedings of the VLSI 81 International Conference*, Edinburgh, U.K., August 1981.

[LEIG82] Leighton, F. T., and C. Leiserson, "Wafer Scale Integration of Systolic Arrays," (Extended Abstract), *23rd Annu. Symp. Found. Comput. Sci.,* pp. 297–311, Nov. 1982.

[LEUN80] Leung, C. K. C., and J. B. Denis, "Design of Fault-Tolerant Packet Communication Architecture," *Dig., 10th Annu. Int. Symp. Fault-Tolerant Comput.,* Kyoto, Japan, Oct. 1980.

[LEVI68] Levitt, K. N., M. W. Green, and J. Goldberg, "A Study of the Data Communication Problems in a Self-Repairable Multiprocessor," *Proc. 1968 Spring Joint Comput. Conf.,* pp. 515–527, 1968.

[LINC81] Lincoln Laboratories, "Semiannual Technical Summary: Restructurable VLSI Program," ESD-TR-81-153, Oct. 1981.

[LIU78] Liu, M. T., "Distributed Loop Computer Networks," *Adv. Comput.,* vol. 17, pp. 163–221, 1978.

[LOSQ78] Losq, J., "Fault-Tolerant Communication Networks for Computer Networks," Technical Note 127, Computer Systems Lab., Stanford University, Stanford, Calif., Mar. 1978.

[MALE83] Malek, M., and E. Opper, "Multiple Fault Diagnosis of SW-Banyan Networks," *Proc. of FTCS-13,* Milan, Italy, June 1983.

[MANG82a] Mangir, T., Use of On-Chip Redundancy for Fault-Tolerant VLSI Design," Computer Science Dept., UCLA Rep. CSD-820201, Feb. 1982.

[MANG82b] Mangir, T., and A. Avizienis, "Effects of Interconnect Requirements on VLSI Circuit Yield Improvement by Means of Redundancy," *IEEE Trans. Comput.,* June 1982.

[MANN77] Manning, F., "An Approach to Highly Integrated Computer-Maintained Cellular Arrays," *IEEE Trans. Comput.,* vol. C-26, no. 6, pp. 536–552, June 1977.

[MANN80] Manner, R., "A General Purpose Multi-Micro-System with High Fault-Tolerance and Unlimited System Capacity," *Euromicro J.,* vol. 6, pp. 388–390, 1980.

[MANO80] Mano, T., et al., "A Fault Tolerant 256K RAM Fabricated with Molybdenum-Polysilicon Technology," *IEEE Journal of Solid-State Circuits,* vol. SC-15, no. 10, pp. 685–872, Oct. 1980.

[MASS72] Masson, G. M., and B. W. Jordan, "Generalized Multi-stage Connection Networks," *Networks,* vol. 2, pp. 191–209, Fall 1972.

[MCMI82] McMilen, R. J., and H. J. Siegel, "Performance and Fault-Tolerance Improvements in the Inverse Augmented Data Manipulator Network," *Proc. 9th Annu. Symp. Comput. Archit.,* vol. 10, no. 3, Apr. 1982.

[MEYE85] Meyer, F. J., and D. K. Pradhan, "Dynamic Testing Strategy for Distributed Systems," *Proc. of the 15th Annual Symposium on Fault-Tolerant Computing,* June 1985, pp. 84–90.

[MILI78] "Military Standard Aircraft Internal Time Division Command/Response Multiplex Data Bus," MIL-STD-1553b, Sept. 1978.

[MINA81] Minato, O., et al., "HI-CMOS II 4K Static RAM," *Dig., IEEE Solid-State Circuits Conf.,* pp. 14–15, 1981.

[NANY83] Nanya, T., and D. K. Pradhan, "Design of Fault-Tolerance VLSI Processor Arrays," Tech. Rep., School of Engineering, Oakland University, Rochester, Mich., Jan. 1983.

[OPFE71] Opferman, D. C., and N. T. Tsao-Wu, "On a Class of Rearrangeable Switching Networks; Part I: Control Algorithms; Part II: Enumeration Studies and Fault-Diagnosis," *Bell System Tech. J.,* pp. 1579–1618, May–June 1971.

[OPPE84] Opper, E., and M. Malek, "Fault Diagnosis in Banyan Networks," submitted to *IEEE Trans. Comput.*

[PARH79] Parhami, B., "Interconnection Redundancy for Reliability Enhancement in Fault-Tolerant Digital Systems," *Digit. Process.,* vol. 5, pp. 199–211, 1979.

[PEAS80] Pease, M., R. Shostak, and L. Lamport, "Reaching Agreements in the Presence of Faults," *J. Assoc. Comput. Mach.,* vol. 27, no. 2, pp. 228–234, Apr. 1980.

[PIER72] Pierce, J. R., "How Far Can Data Loops Go?" *IEEE Transactions on Computers,* vol. COM-20, pp. 527–530, June 1972.

[PLET83] Pletzer, D. L., "Wafer Scale Integration—The Limits of VLSI?" *VLSI Design,* pp. 43–47, September 1983.

[PRAD81a] Pradhan, D. K., "Interconnection Topologies for Fault-Tolerant Parallel and Distributed Architectures," *Proc. 10th Int. Conf. Parallel Process.,* pp. 238–242, Aug. 1981.

[PRAD81b] Pradhan, D. K., and K. Matsui, "A Graph Theoretic Solution to Load Leveling and Fault-Recovery in Distributed Systems," *Proc. Symp. Reliab. Distributed Softw. Database Syst.,* Pittsburgh, Pa., pp. 89–94, July 1981.

[PRAD82a] Pradhan, D. K., and S. M. Reddy, "A Fault-Tolerant Communication Architecture for Distributed Systems," *IEEE Trans. Comput.* vol. C-31, no. 9, Sept. 1982.

[PRAD82b] Pradhan, D. K., "On a Class of Fault-Tolerant Multiprocessor Network Architectures," *Proc. of 3rd Int. Conference on Distributed Processing,* pp. 302–311, Miami, Fl., Oct. 1982.

[PRAD83a] Pradhan D. K., "Partitionability and Diagnosability of a Class of Multiprocessor Network Architectures," *Proc. Int. Conf. Distrib. Process.,* Miami, Fl., Oct. 1983.

[PRAD83b] Pradhan, D. K., "Fault-Tolerant Architectures for Multiprocessors and VLSI Systems," *Dig., 13th Annu. Int. Symp. Fault-Tolerant Comput.,* Milan, Italy, pp. 436–441, June 1983.

[PRAD84] Pradhan, D. K., H. Zhang, and M. Schlumberger, "Fault-Tolerant Multi-bus Multiprocessor Architectures," *Dig., 14th Annu. Int. Symp. Fault-Tolerant Comput.,* Orlando, Fl., June 1984.

[PRAD85a] Pradhan, D. K., "Fault-Tolerant Link and Bus Multiprocessor Architectures," *IEEE Transactions on Computers,* vol. C-34, no. 1, pp. 34–45, Jan. 1985.

[PRAD85b] Pradhan, D. K., "Dynamically Restructurable Fault-Tolerant Processor Network

Architecture," *IEEE Transactions on Computers,* vol. C-34, no. 5, pp. 434–447, May 1985.

[PRAD 86] Correction to "Fault-Tolerant Multiprocessor Link and Bus Architectures," *IEEE Transactions on Computers,* p. 94, vol. C-35, no. 1, Jan. 1986.

[PREP81] Preparata, F. P., and J. Vuillemin, "The Cube-Connected Cycles: A Versatile Network for Parallel Computation," *CACM,* vol. 24, no. 5, pp. 300–309, May 1981.

[REAM75] Reames, C. C., and M. T. Liu, "A Loop Network for Simultaneous Transmission of Variable Length Messages," *Proc. Ann. Symposium on Computer Architectures,* pp. 7–12, January 1975.

[REDD80] Reddy, S. M., D. K. Pradhan, and J. Kuhl, "Directed Graphs with Minimal Diameter and Maximal Connectivity," Tech. Rep., School of Engineering, Oakland University, Rochester, Mich., Aug. 1980.

[RENN80] Rennels, D., "Distributed Fault-Tolerant Computer Systems," *IEEE Comput.,* vol. 13, no. 3, pp. 55–65, Mar. 1980.

[ROSE83] Rosenberg, A., "The Diogenes Approach to Testable Fault-Tolerant Networks of Processors," *IEEE Trans. Comput.,* vol. C-32, pp. 902-910, Oct. 1983.

[ROTH67] Roth, J. P., et al., "Phase II of an Architectural Study for a Self-Repairing Computer," IBM Rest. Rep., SAMSO-TR-67-106, T. J. Watson Rest. Cent., 1967 (also available as NT1S Doc. Ad-825460).

[SAMA84] Samatham, M. R., and D. K. Pradhan, "A Multiprocessor Network Suitable for Single-Chip VLSI Implementation," *Proc. of the 11th Annual Symposium on Computer Architecture,* pp. 328–337, May 1984.

[SAMA85] Samatham, M. R., and D. K. Pradhan, "The De Bruijn Multiprocessor Network: A Versatile Sorting Network", *IEEE Proceedings of the 12th International Symposium on Computer Architecture,* Boston, Mass, pp. 360–367, June 1985.

[SCHL74] Schlumberger, M., "DeBruijn Communication Networks," Ph.D. dissertation, Stanford University, Stanford, Calif., 1974.

[SEDM80] Sedmak, R. M., and H. L. Liebergot, "Fault-Tolerance of a General Purpose Computer Implemented by Very Large Scale Integration," *IEEE Trans. Comput.,* vol. 29, pp. 492–500, June 1980.

[SEIT85] Seitz, C. L., "The Cosmic Cube", *CACM,* vol. 28, pp. 22–33, Jan. 1985. Copyright 1985, Association for Computing Machinery, Inc., reprinted by permission.

[SEQU83] Sequin, C. H., and R. M. Fujimoto, "X-Tree and Y-Component," in *VLSI Architectures,* B. Randell and P. C. Treleaven, eds., pp. 299–326, Prentice-Hall, Englewood Cliffs, NJ, 1983.

[SHEN80] Shen, J. P. and J. P. Hayes "Fault-tolerance of a Class of Connecting Networks," *Proc. 7th Int. Symp. Comput. Archit.,* La Baule, France, pp. 61–71, May 1980.

[SIEW78] Siewiorek, D., et al., "A Case Study of Cm., mp., Cm., and C. Vmp: Part I and Part II," *Proc. IEEE,* pp. 1160–1220, Oct. 1978.

[SMIT81] Smith, R., et al., "Laser Programmable Redundancy and Yield Improvement in a 64K DRAM," *IEEE J. Solid-State Circuits,* vol. SC-16, pp. 506–513, Oct. 1981.

[SOWR80] Sowrirajan, S., and S. M. Reddy, "A Design of Fault-Tolerant Full Connection Networks," *Proc. 1980 Conf. Int. Sci. Sys.,* Mar. 16–18, pp. 536–54, 1980.

[STAP79] Stapper, C. H., "LSI Yield Modeling and Process Monitoring," *IBM J.Res. Dev.,* vol. 20, pp. 228–234, 1976.

[STAP80] Stapper, C. H., A. N. McLaren, and M. Dreckmann, "Yield Model for Productivity Optimization of VLSI Memory Chips with Redundancy and Partially Good Product," *IBM J. Res. Dev.*, vol. 24, no. 3, pp. 398–409, May 1980

[STON71] Stone, H. S., "Parallel Processing with Perfect Shuffle," *IEEE Trans. Comput.*, vol. C-20, pp. 153–161, Feb. 1971.

[STON82] Stone, H., *Microcomputer Interfacing*, Addison-Wesley, Reading, Mass., 1982.

[SULL77] Sullivan, H., T. R. Bashkow, and D. Klappholz, "A Large Scale Homogeneous Fully Distributed Parallel Machine," *Proc. 4th Annu. Symp. Comput. Archit.*, pp. 105–124, Mar. 1977.

[SWAR82] Swartzlander, E. and B. Gilbert, *Super Systems: Technology and Architecture*, vol. C-31, no. 5, May 1982.

[THUR81] Thurber, K. J., "Hardware Interconnection Technology," *Distributed Systems Architecture and Implementation*, Lecture Notes in Computer Science, Springer-Verlag, New York, 1981.

[TOY78] Toy, W. N., "Fault-Tolerant Design of Local ESS Processors," *Proc. IEEE*, pp. 1126–1145, Oct. 1978.

[WILK72] Wilkov, R. S., "Analysis and Design of Reliable Computer Networks," *IEEE Trans. Commun.*, vol. COM-10, pp. 660–678, June 1972.

[WOLF79] Wolf, J. J., et al., "Design of a Distrubuted Fault-Tolerant Loop Network," *Dig., 9th Annu. Int. Symp. Fault-Tolerant Comput.*, Madison, Wis., pp. 17–24, June 20–22, 1979.

[ZAFI74] Zafiropulo, P., "Performance Evaluation of Reliability Improvement Techniques for Single-Loop Communications Systems," *IEEE Trans. Commun.*, vol. 22–26, pp. 742–51, June 1974.

PROBLEMS

7.1. Security considerations in networks have become an important issue; it has been suggested that these be integrated with fault-tolerant considerations to develop robust designs. Discuss how this can be achieved in the context of shared bus designs.

7.2. Suggest possible modifications of FTMP bus structures so that they can tolerate multiple failures.

7.3. Consider the loop network design shown in Fig. P7.3 (how are the internode links routed through a central switch). Examine the possible advantages and disadvantages of such a design from the point of view of fault tolerance.

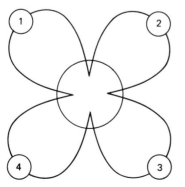

Figure P7.3 Loop through a central switch.

7.4. The test set presented in Fig. 7.3.5 detects various faults in the data paths of the shuffle-exchange network. Discuss what specific types of data path faults are detected by the test set. Show that this test set together with its complement are sufficient to detect all switch-setting and data path faults.

7.5. Consider an 8×8 shuffle-exchange network. This network can be augmented with the network shown in Fig. 7.3.6 so that a path always exists between any input and any output, in spite of a s-a-T or s-a-X fault in any switch. Instead of this additional stage, if one augments the network by adding one or more additional shuffle-exchange stages, is it possible to achieve some sort of fault tolerance? Examine how many such additional stages may be necessary to achieve single fault tolerance.

7.6. In Example 4, derive an expression for determining the physical address from the logical address for interleaved memory when partitioned into variable-sized partitions.

7.7. Design a 15-node leaf-ringed tree. Assume that nodes 2, 3, 7, and 11 are faulty. Using the algorithm Path 7.5.2, determine the various nodes through which a message may be routed, starting with node 14 enroute to node 1.

7.8. Construct a 31-node single-fault-tolerant redundant binary tree using Procedure 7.5.1. Reconfigure the tree in the event of a fault in node 7.

7.9. Construct a DFT$\langle 15 \rangle$ and embed a 15-node binary tree, starting with root node 7. By assigning multiple logical addresses to each physical node, it is possible to configure DFT$\langle 15 \rangle$ into any arbitrarily large binary tree. Discuss how this is possible and then show how to embed a 31-node binary tree in DFT$\langle 15 \rangle$, starting with node 1 as the root node.

7.10. Modify routing algorithm Path 7.6.1 to include links defined by the relationships $i \rightarrow i/2$ and $i \rightarrow i/2 + n/2$, in addition to $i \rightarrow 2i$, $i \rightarrow i + 1$, and $i \rightarrow i - 1$.

7.11. Formulate a routing algorithm for a cube network that performs algorithmic routing in the event of faults.

7.12. Construct a BA$\langle FG \rangle$ network where $r = 3$ and $m = 2$. The network will have 15 processors. Now, combine groups of three processors to form clusters of processors in such a way that a failure of any single cluster will not be catastrophic—in that the surviving processors can still communicate with each other. Can a general technique be formulated to form such clusters in any arbitrary network?

7.13. Develop a routing algorithm for FG$(2, m)$ networks that can tolerate any double node failures.

7.14. Compare rectangular mesh connection with hexagonal mesh connection from the point of view of fault tolerance.

Chapter 8

SYSTEM DIAGNOSIS

Charles R. Kime

8.1. INTRODUCTION

The detection and location of faults play a significant role in the implementation of fault-tolerant systems. Even in those computer systems that are not labeled as fault tolerant, software or self-test capability is provided to do fault detection and, perhaps, fault location. Previous chapters have treated a number of areas closely tied to fault detection and location tasks, including test generation, design for testability, simulation, and the design of self-checking circuits. The application of software-based tests and the operation of checking circuits provide test results that are used for fault diagnosis. Simulation is another means of obtaining information that is useful in interpreting test results and relating them to the faults present. This chapter is concerned with *system diagnosis,* which is precisely this interpretation of test results for the purpose of locating faults.

System diagnosis is a very important component of the maintenance strategy for conventional (i.e., non-fault-tolerant) systems. The maintenance function is a very costly one because it is frequently performed away from a centralized, cost-effective facility and is personnel intensive. Thus design for maintainability, including use of testability features and effective system diagnosis tools, is vital to cost containment. In addition, customer satisfaction is frequently tied to minimizing the downtime of the system, which in turn requires rapid fault detection and location.

In fault-tolerant systems, diagnosis is an important tool. Regardless of the fault-tolerance principles that serve as a basis for the system design, it is important to detect and ultimately identify faulty units and take the necessary actions to restore the system to a fault-free condition. Because of the critical computational environments of many such systems, diagnosis is frequently implemented in hardware in order to minimize the time required for corrective action. Distributed systems, in which computational tasks are performed by multiple processors, are ideal for the implementation of fault tolerance due to the redundant hardware available. In a distributed system, diagnosis permits faults to be located so that the system can be configured around faulty units for continued operation in a degraded mode. Distributed systems also provide an environment in which software tests and diagnostics are part of the normal computational load.

In this chapter, system diagnosis is viewed principally in terms of models of faults, tests, and fault-test relationships. Initially, models for fault-test relationships that are quite general will be introduced. These can be applied at any level from logic gates to geographically distributed networks. Then, directed graph models which are useful primarily at the system level are presented. These models provide the basis for a sound, theoretical treatment of diagnosis and serve as a foundation for results relating to a priori analysis of system diagnosability. These results help to quantify the ability of a test set to locate the faults in a system. Such results are useful in numerous design decisions relating to diagnosis, including test design and modification, addition of tests, placement of hardware test points, and location of checkers. Diagnosis algorithms, which are used to locate faults on the basis of test data as input, are covered. Consideration is given to performing diagnosis algorithms in a distributed system and the diagnosability analysis for such algorithms. Finally, system diagnosis approaches that use probabilistic techniques are treated briefly.

8.2. FAULTS, TESTS, AND FAULT–TEST RELATIONSHIPS

The concept of treating the fault diagnosis problem via carefully formulated modeling approaches became firmly established in the early-to-mid-1960s [BRUL60, JOHN60, POAG63, CHAN65, KAUT68]. Because hardware was composed of discrete and small-scale integrated circuits, diagnosis of faults to the individual gate or line level was of particular interest. Thus much of the modeling dealt with stuck-at faults in combinational networks. During the 1960s, the number of gates per printed circuit board or circuit package increased, thereby creating larger field-replaceable units (FRUs). Also, due to the proliferation of smaller systems and to increased maintenance costs, a philosophy of repair resulted involving only replacement of FRUs on-site, with the more detailed diagnosis and repair of the FRUs performed at centralized points. Thus diagnosis to the subsystem level became an important element in the overall diagnosis picture. Efforts were made to design system diagnosis procedures systematically and to analyze test data systematically [HACK65, FORB65, AGNE65, CHAN67]. These efforts motivated the early theoretical work in system diagnosis [RAMA67, PREP67, KIME70]. Another factor motivating such approaches was the movement to fault-tolerance techniques employing redundancy at higher levels. For example, in fault-tolerant systems employing dynamic redundancy, the switchable units are at present at the level of processors, memories, or complete computers rather than registers and ALUs.

The various fault diagnosis models were developed over a period of 10 to 15 years for hardware at a variety of levels. These models often appear to be unrelated to each other and thus do not provide a common underlying foundation for modeling diagnosis. In contrast, the model initially presented here is broad enough to encompass past diagnostic modeling efforts and many of the approaches used in contemporary diagnosis practice as well. To attain this breadth of modeling power, it is essential that terminology be developed in a general, perhaps somewhat unconventional way. On this basis, it is appropriate to discuss the concepts of "fault" and "test," both of which are treated from a hierarchical viewpoint [KIME79].

At the most basic level, a physical phenomenon occurs in the system hardware which we will refer to as a *failure*. For example, an open circuit may occur in an output transistor in a NOR gate. This open circuit may manifest itself as a logical *fault* at the line or device level. For example, if the open circuit is in a driver transistor in NMOS logic, the fault is a stuck-at-0 fault on the corresponding gate input. This fault is at the lowest level in the fault hierarchy. At the next higher level, we can define a faulty NOR gate. Suppose that the faulty NOR gate is in an arithmetic-logic unit (ALU) in a microprocessor integrated circuit. Then the ALU is faulty, giving a fault at a higher level. Further, the microprocessor is also faulty at the next level in the hierarchy. Suppose that the microprocessor is a part on a printed circuit board constituting a microcomputer. Then the microcomputer is faulty, yielding an added level. The microcomputer, in turn, could be part of a local network, yielding a final level. The hierarchy just described is illustrated in Fig. 8.2.1.

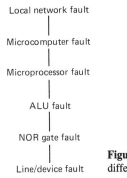

Local network fault

Microcomputer fault

Microprocessor fault

ALU fault

NOR gate fault

Line/device fault

Figure 8.2.1 Interpretation of a fault at different levels in a fault hierarchy.

Note that at each level in the hierarchy a fault is said to be *present* if one or more faults from a particular set at lower levels in the hierarchy are present; otherwise, the fault is *absent*. For example, an ALU fault is present if one or more of the gates making up the ALU or connections between the gates is faulty. In much of the literature, the term *faulty unit* is employed at higher levels in the hierarchy; the terms fault and faulty unit will be considered synonymous here. Also, much of the work tends to deal with only one level of the hierarchy and does not consider higher or lower levels. It has been demonstrated, however, that consideration of multiple hierarchical fault levels can be useful in diagnosis [KIME79, MCPH79].

The importance of the hierarchical view of faults will become apparent in the discussion of testing but can be very simply illustrated here with regard to the goals of a diagnosis. At the highest level in the hierarchy in Fig. 8.2.1, suppose that the goal of diagnosis is to identify a faulty microcomputer in the local network so that it can be configured out of the network, which will continue to operate. Once the microcomputer board is removed from the network, the new diagnosis goal is to locate the faulty physical component on the board. When the level of the faulty component is reached, it is unnecessary to perform further diagnosis because no lower level of repair is possible. The lower levels in the hierarchy are still important, however, because the accomplishment of the series of diagnostic goals depends on the *detection* of a fault at the lowest level, such as a stuck-at-1 fault on the output of a gate.

Most of the discussion to follow will be based on a single level in the hierarchy. Thus the notation will treat just a single level. A potential fault will be denoted by f_i and the set of potential faults under consideration by $\mathcal{F}$. Thus $\mathcal{F} = \{f_1, \ldots, f_n\}$, assuming that n potential faults are under consideration. For simplicity, the word "potential" will be omitted and we will simply refer to fault f_i, which may be either present or absent. Since multiple faults may occur, we define a *fault pattern* F^j as a subset of $\mathcal{F}$ consisting of faults that are present in the system. The set of all fault patterns to be considered is $F = \{F^0, \ldots, F^{m-1}\}$. In addition, a vector notation may be used to describe a fault pattern. The vector can, in general, be written $F^j = (f_1, \ldots, f_n)$, where f_i takes on value 1 if fault f_i is present and value 0 if fault f_i is absent. $F^1 = (0, 0, 1, 1)$ is a fault pattern for $n = 4$ in which f_1 and f_2 are absent and f_3 and f_4 are present. For most of the discussion, faults will be assumed to be solid and determinate and no new faults are assumed to occur during the testing and diagnosis process.

As a vehicle for illustration of faults and other concepts, an example is introduced in Fig. 8.2.2. Faults are modeled at the third level in the hierarchy of Fig. 8.2.1. This subsystem consists of duplicated 8-bit ALUs which have their outputs compared by a self-checking equality comparator. The source of the data for the ALUs is a pair of 8-bit registers A and B. Register C provides control signals for the ALUs. Register A, B, and C can also be configured as counters to perform an exhaustive test on the ALUs. The equality comparator which is used for concurrent fault detection during normal operation is used here to compare outputs of the ALUs under the applied test.

The fault model for the subsystem consists of a fault set $\mathcal{F} = \{f_1, f_2, f_3, f_4, f_5, f_6\}$, where fault f_i is present if the unit in the subsystem corresponding to f_i is faulty. In this particular case, the emphasis is on field testing at frequent enough intervals so that single faults can be assumed. The fault pattern set is thus $F = \{F^0, F^1, F^2, F^3, F^4, F^5, F^6\}$ in which $F^0 = \emptyset$, $F^1 = \{f_1\}$, $F^2 = \{f_2\}$, and so on.

A *test,* in a general sense, can be thought of as the application of some sequence of input patterns and the observation of one or more outputs for one or more time frames. Depending on the entity under test and the particular testing approach employed, this general test concept can take a variety of forms. A test for a particular

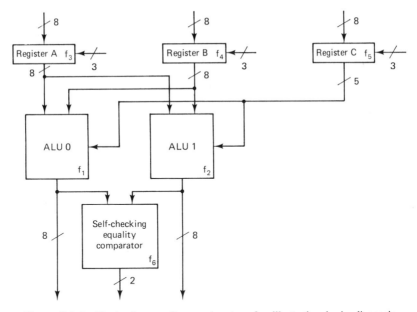

Figure 8.2.2 Block diagram for a subsystem for illustrating basic diagnosis concepts.

stuck-at fault in a combinational network might simply consist of the application of a single input pattern to the network and the observation of a single output line. A test for an entire combinational network could consist of the application of all input combinations while observing all output lines. In both cases, the observed outputs are typically compared to correct (or possibly, expected erroneous) values to detect faults (or possibly, attempt to locate them) within the network. Clearly, at higher levels, the input sequence application and output observation processes are incorporated into programs or microprograms. In addition, tests can also be performed by hardware at a variety of levels by use of concepts such as self-checking circuits.

Tests can be considered from a hierarchical view just as faults were [KIME79]. The levels in the test hierarchy, to some degree, coincide with those of the fault hierarchy. There are four basic concepts to be discussed relative to the test and fault hierarchies.

First, tests can be generated in relation to any level of the fault hierarchy. For example, if a microprocessor is to be tested, one possible approach is to test carefully for each single stuck-at-1 and stuck-at-0 fault in the microprocessor logic. Another approach is to write a program to test the instruction set, addressing modes, and so on, of the microprocessor. The first approach is related to the very lowest level of the fault hierarchy in Fig. 8.2.1 and constitutes the lowest level in a corresponding test hierarchy. The second approach corresponds to the fourth level in the hierarchy, the microprocessor level, and the test generated constitutes a higher level in the test hierarchy. Ultimately, both approaches must, to be effective, detect a significant portion of the faults potentially present at the lowest level in the hierarchy.

This same example illustrates two additional concepts. One approach to producing a microprocessor test is to combine a large collection of tests for stuck-at-1 and stuck-at-0 faults within the microprocessor. Thus the second concept involves producing a test at a higher level in the hierarchy by combining tests generated at a lower level. A third concept is the handling of the test results of combined tests. A simple possibility is to OR together the lower-level pass–fail test results to obtain a high-level result. This assumes that the outcome of a failing test is represented by a 1 and that of a passing test is represented by a 0, an assumption that will be employed throughout the remainder of this chapter. These test outcomes are generated, for example, by comparing a stored correct response to the actual hardware response.

The final concept associated with the testing hierarchy is closely tied to the diagnostic goal. Suppose that in the example used to develop Fig. 8.2.1, the goal is to locate faults within a microcomputer. In such a framework, it would seem logical to concentrate at the microcomputer test level in the test hierarchy. Thus the diagnosis would be attempted based on pass–fail test results on microcomputers. Depending on the system structure and testing methods, this may be a poor approach. Better fault location can result from testing at a lower level in the testing hierarchy, such as at the microprocessor, ROM, and RAM level. The added test result detail at this level can help to more clearly separate faulty microcomputers for a variety of lower-level faults that can occur. This detail can be lost via the function used to combine test results in moving up the hierarchy or does not exist if the test is generated at the microcomputer level. Thus care must be exercised in relating the testing level to the diagnostic goals.

An alternative approach to the consideration of fault and test hierarchies uses the concept of an error at the levels of the hierarchy above the line or device fault. Errors are the effects of faults as observed at definable system interfaces, notably at the boundaries of subsystems at various levels in the hierarchy. This approach is particulary prevalent in those systems in which extensive concurrent error checking based on coding and duplication approaches is employed. Although it is a very useful viewpoint for such approaches, it has not been employed here because the error concept is absent in most of the system theoretic diagnosis literature.

To a large degree, the following discussion of diagnosis will not deal significantly with the test hierarchy. The hierarchy is, however, an important concept in the overall diagnosis process.

The notation and terminology associated with tests closely parallel that given for faults. A test will be denoted by t_i, and the set of tests under consideration will be denoted by $\mathcal{T}$. Thus, assuming that p tests are under consideration, $\mathcal{T} = \{t_1, \ldots, t_p\}$. The results of the tests in the set $\mathcal{T}$ are of interest. A *test pattern* T^j is defined as a subset of $\mathcal{T}$ consisting of the set of all tests that failed on application of test set $\mathcal{T}$. The set of all test patterns that are expected to occur is $T = \{T^0, \ldots, T^{q-1}\}$. In addition, a vector notation may be used to describe test patterns. The vector can be written as $T^j = \{t_1, \ldots, t_p\}$ in which t_i takes on value 1 if test t_i fails and value 0 if test t_i passes. Thus $T^1 = (1, 0, 1, 0, 0)$ represents test results in which t_1 and t_3 fail and t_2, t_4, and t_5 pass.

To illustrate tests, the example in Fig. 8.2.2 will be used. In this case, tests on the six faults previously defined will be considered. First, note that the ALUs are duplicates and that their outputs are compared by a self-checking equality comparator. The comparator has two binary outputs that are equal if the inputs to the comparator are unequal or if one of a certain class of faults occurs in the comparator and are unequal, otherwise. This overall structure is self-checking during normal operation. This testing, which takes place concurrent with normal operation, will not be specifically considered, however. Instead, it is assumed that the registers are configured to perform an exhaustive test of the ALUs which uses the comparator to detect a fault. In addition, the test checks the comparator. If, during the application of the test inputs, for equality checker output becomes equal, the test fails and $t_1 = 1$. If, throughout the application of the inputs, the equality checker outputs remain opposite, the test t_1 passes and $t_1 = 0$.

The remaining tests to be considered are software tests applied by hardware external to the subsystem. Typically, such tests might be executed by micro-diagnostics [BART70, JOHN71]. Let t_2 be such a test on ALU0 and t_3, a test on ALU1. Test t_4 is for registers A and B, and test t_5 for register C. These four tests each might consist of a sequence of inputs accompanied by stored responses that test all combinational logic in the respective units for single stuck-at-1 and stuck-at-0 faults. In addition, for latches or flip-flops, the ability to load a 1 and a 0 into the structure and to store a 1 and a 0 in the structure is tested. The results of these four tests are determined by comparing the actual outputs of ALU0 and/or ALU1 with the correct outputs. The test set defined for the subsystem in Fig. 8.2.2 consists of these five tests and is $\mathcal{T} = \{t_1, t_2, t_3, t_4, t_5\}$.

Up to this point, the fault set $\mathcal{F}$ and test set $\mathcal{T}$ have been defined. In addition, subsets, called *fault patterns* and *test patterns*, respectively, of these sets have been defined and represented by vectors. At this point, fault patterns and test patterns are to be related to each other. This will be done by use of a *fault pattern–test pattern event space*, which will specify in some fashion the test pattern(s) that can occur for each of the fault patterns under consideration. The first step in forming such a space is to define the fault pattern set F. The definition of this set depends on the definition of the fault set $\mathcal{F}$, and other factors, such as failure rates and the time since the system was last tested. Once F is defined, test pattern(s) that occur for each fault pattern present must be determined.

The process of manual generation of test patterns can be illustrated by the example in Fig. 8.2.2. Suppose that F is restricted to consist of the good subsystem plus subsystems containing exactly one of the faults. Then $F = \{F^0, F^1, F^2, F^3, F^4, F^5, F^6\}$, as defined previously. The vector representation for these fault patterns is

$$
\begin{array}{ll}
F^0 & 000000 \\
F^1 & 100000 \\
F^2 & 010000 \\
F^3 & 001000
\end{array}
$$

$$F^4 \quad 000100$$

$$F^5 \quad 000010$$

$$F^6 \quad 000001$$

To determine the associated test patterns, we will examine the behavior of each test for each fault pattern. This information can be used to formulate the event space shown in Table 8.2.1. For fault pattern F^0, all tests are assumed to pass, so the associated test pattern is 00000. For the remaining fault patterns, it is easiest to examine each test individually or selected combinations of tests.

TABLE 8.2.1   FAULT TABLE FOR THE SUBSYSTEM IN FIG. 8.2.2

Row	Fault pattern	Fault in pattern	Test pattern (vector form)				
			t_1	t_2	t_3	t_4	t_5
1	F^0	None	0	0	0	0	0
2	F^1	f_1	1	1	0	0	0
3			1	1	0	1	0
4	F^2	f_2	1	0	1	0	0
5			1	0	1	0	1
6	F^3	f_3	0	0	0	1	0
7			0	0	0	1	1
8			0	1	1	1	0
9			0	1	1	1	1
10	F^4	f_4	0	0	0	1	0
11			0	0	0	1	1
12			0	1	1	1	0
13			0	1	1	1	1
14	F^5	f_5	0	0	0	0	1
15			0	0	0	1	1
16			0	1	1	0	1
17			0	1	1	1	1
18	F^6	f_6	1	0	0	0	0

Test t_1 is for F^1, F^2, and F^6 and will fail when these patterns are present. If no pathological failures, such as "stuck in the threshold region," occur on the register outputs for F^3, F^4, or F^5 present, all that can occur is the application of wrong inputs to both ALUs. Because the test result t_1 is based on an equality check, these faults can, at worst, cause test t_1 to falsely pass. Under the single-fault assumption this is, however, impossible.

Test t_2 is on f^1 and will fail for F^1 present. It is a software test that uses the registers but does not use ALU1 (F^2) or the equality comparator (F^6). In this case, F^2 and F^6 could affect the test result only via faults at a lower level in the fault hierarchy that reverse-propagate from inputs, such as shorts. It is assumed that such fault types are not included; thus F^2 and F^6 do not affect the test result, and t_2 passes for F^2 or F^6 present. Since F^3, F^4, and F^5 cause wrong inputs to be applied to ALU0, they can cause test t_2 to fail. There may, however, be some register faults that will not affect this test, so t_2 may also pass. On this basis, the result of t_2 in the presence of these three fault patterns is unpredictable.

Test t_3, by symmetry with test t_2, fails for F^2, passes for F^1 and F^6, and has an unknown result for F^3, F^4, and F^5. It is assumed, however, that the results of tests t_2 and t_3 are identical in the presence of F^3, F^4, and F^5, since these are the same tests on identical components. Thus, for these fault patterns t_2 and t_3 will both fail or t_2 and t_3 will both pass.

Test t_4 is for F^3 and F^4 and so will fail if either of these fault patterns is present. A faulty ALU that is used to pass the register response to the outputs may cause this test to fail. Thus since ALU0 is used for test t_4, the test result is unpredictable for F^1. Also, failure to control ALU0 properly during t_4 can cause t_4 to fail, so the test result is unknown for F^5. A similar argument can be applied to test t_5, which fails for F^5 present, is unknown for F^2, F^3, and F^4 present, and passes for F^1 and F^6 present.

The information has now been assembled for completing the event space. For fault pattern F^1, t_1 and t_2 fail, t_3 and t_5 pass, and t_4 has an unpredictable result. Thus the two test patterns 11000 and 11010 are associated with F^1. These two vectors combined with the vector for F^1 appear in the event space. In Table 8.2.1, for simplicity, the fault patterns have not been shown as vectors, but the associated test pattern vectors have been listed. Thus, for F^1, 11000 and 11010 appear in rows 2 and 3 in Table 8.2.1. The test results for F^2 can similarly be derived as 10100 and 10101, which appear in rows 4 and 5 of Table 8.2.1.

For fault pattern F^3, test t_1 passes, test t_4 fails, and test t_2, t_3, and t_5 have unknown results; test t_2 and t_3, however, have the same results. This produces four test patterns, 00010, 00011, 01110, and 01111. Identical results occur for fault pattern F^4. This gives the test pattern entries for rows 6 through 13 of Table 8.2.1.

F^5 causes t_1 to pass, t_5 to fail, and unknown results for tests t_2 through t_4, with the results of t_2 and t_3 identical. The resulting test patterns for F^5 in rows 14 through 17 of Table 8.2.1 are 00001, 00011, 01101, and 01111. Finally, F^6 fails test t_1 and causes all other tests to pass. This yields 10000 as the final entry in Table 8.2.1.

Table 8.2.1 can be used to perform diagnosis by assembling the actual test results into a test pattern which is also called a *syndrome*. The syndrome is then compared with each of the tabulated test patterns. For each of the cases in which a match occurs, the fault pattern corresponding to the test pattern may be present. For example, if the syndrome is 01101, the only fault pattern that is indicated as present is F^5, indicating that register C is faulty. If 01111 occurs, however, the fault patterns indicated as possibly present are F^3, F^4, or F^5. In this case, it cannot be determined from the test results which of the registers (A, B, or C) is faulty.

Description of the event space in this form is rather bulky and not very convenient to use. Thus we would like to explore other possibilities. To reduce the bulk of the table, the vector array can be compressed by use of cubical complexes [DIET78]. A compressed version of Table 8.2.1 is shown as Table 8.2.2. An x

TABLE 8.2.2   CONDENSED FAULT TABLE FOR THE SUBSYSTEM IN FIG. 8.2.2

Fault pattern	Fault in pattern	Test pattern (vector form)				
		t_1	t_2	t_3	t_4	t_5
F^0	None	0	0	0	0	0
F^1	f_1	1	1	0	x	0
F^2	f_2	1	0	1	0	x
F^3	f_3	0	0	0	1	x
		0	1	1	1	x
F^4	f_4	0	0	0	1	x
		0	1	1	1	x
F^5	f_5	0	0	0	x	1
		0	1	1	x	1
F^6	f_6	1	0	0	0	0

represents the occurrence of either a 0 or a 1. A vector containing j x's represents 2^j different vectors.

A representation that can be derived from either of the tables or directly from the test behavior is the Boolean expression [KIME79, PREP68, ADHA77]. A Boolean expression is written which has value 1 if it is evaluated for a fault pattern–test pattern combination in the event space and value 0, otherwise. This can easily be done from a tabular representation by using canonical or standard forms. For example, from Table 8.2.1,

$$\begin{aligned} S = {} & \bar{f_1}\bar{f_2}\bar{f_3}\bar{f_4}\bar{f_5}\bar{f_6} \;\; \bar{t_1}\bar{t_2}\bar{t_3}\bar{t_4}\bar{t_5} \quad &\text{(row 1)} \\ & + f_1\bar{f_2}\bar{f_3}\bar{f_4}\bar{f_5}\bar{f_6} \;\; t_1\bar{t_2}\bar{t_3}\bar{t_4}\bar{t_5} \quad &\text{(row 2)} \\ & + f_1\bar{f_2}\bar{f_3}\bar{f_4}\bar{f_5}\bar{f_6} \;\; t_1t_2\bar{t_3}t_4\bar{t_5} \quad &\text{(row 3)} \\ & + \cdots \quad & \text{(8.2.1)} \end{aligned}$$

This is quite tedious and does not result in any direct simplification of the representation. If, however, advantage is taken of the fact that certain fault and test patterns are don't cares and of factoring possibilities, simplified expressions can result. It is important, however, when don't cares are used, that the resulting expressions not be employed later in situations in which these patterns are expected to occur. Using the information in Table 8.2.2 and assuming that all multiple-fault patterns correspond to don't cares, judicious factoring produces the following expression results:

$$\begin{aligned} S' = {} & (\bar{f_1}\bar{f_2}\bar{f_3}\bar{f_4}\bar{f_5}\bar{f_6}\bar{t_1} + f_6 t_1)\bar{t_2}\bar{t_3}\bar{t_4}\bar{t_5} \\ & + f_1 t_1 t_2 \bar{t_3}\bar{t_5} + f_2 t_1 \bar{t_2} t_3 \bar{t_4} \\ & + [(f_3 + f_4)t_4 + f_5 t_5](\bar{t_2}\bar{t_3} + t_2 t_3)\bar{t_1} \quad (8.2.2) \end{aligned}$$

Another possibility is to write an expression based on test behavior as described earlier:

$$S'' = [t_1(f_1 + f_2 + f_6) + \bar{t}_1\bar{f}_1\bar{f}_2\bar{f}_6][t_2\bar{t}_3 f_1 + \bar{t}_2 t_3 f_2 + (t_2 t_3 + \bar{t}_2\bar{t}_3)(f_3 + f_4 + f_5)$$

$$+ \bar{t}_2\bar{t}_3(\bar{f}_1\bar{f}_2 + f_6)][t_4(f_3 + f_4) + \bar{t}_4\bar{f}_3\bar{f}_4 + f_1 + f_5][t_5 f_5 + \bar{t}_5\bar{f}_5 + f_2 + f_3 + f_4]$$

$$(8.2.3)$$

Note that each of these expressions may describe a slightly different event space due to the don't cares employed. In order to see how an expression might be used in diagnosis, suppose that the test result is $t_1 = 0$, $t_2 = 1$, $t_3 = 1$, $t_4 = 1$, and $t_5 = 1$. Evaluating S' or S'' for these values results in

$$f_3 + f_4 + f_5$$

Any one of these three faults may be present; this is in agreement with the earlier result from Table 8.2.1 for this same test pattern. Note that no more than one fault was assumed to be present and that all multiple faults were assumed to be don't cares in obtaining the expressions given. In general, this is not the case. It is interesting to note that by considering all possible test patterns, it can be determined from the tabular or Boolean expression representation how good the tests are for locating faults. For the example, consideration of the potential faults identified for each of the distinct test patterns indicates that all faults are located exactly except for f_3, f_4, and f_5, which are not always distinguished.

It should be noted that the tabular and Boolean expression representations covered thus far are quite general and can, in theory, represent any fault pattern–test pattern event space; the directed graph (digraph) representations to appear in the next section do not share this generality. They do, however, share some problems involved in the formulation of the event space that are characteristic of real diagnosis problems. These include test completeness, test invalidation, and test result information loss. All of these problems can be related back to the fault hierarchy, which will serve as a basis for the discussion.

A test is said to be *complete* for a set of faults if it fails for exactly one fault from the set present and passes for all faults absent. But, in order to be complete for a fault, a test must detect all underlying faults in the hierarchy that manifest themselves in the fault under consideration. As a specific illustration, suppose that the register A fault in the example in Fig. 8.2.2 is considered. Suppose that the test for register A was obtained by combining all tests for single stuck-at faults in the logic of register A. Now, suppose that instead of a stuck-at fault, a bridging fault occurs between two bits of the register A output so that the 0 value dominates. There is a good possibility that the test will not detect the fault in this form. Thus, if bridging faults are assumed to occur at a lower hierarchical level and the test was not designed to detect them, it is likely to be incomplete. As another illustration, suppose that a functional test is generated that detects only 80% of all stuck-at faults in a microprocessor. If all stuck-at faults are included in a lower level of the hierarchy, this test is quite incomplete. In general, test completeness, although assumed in the modeling process through Section 8.6, is difficult to achieve absolutely in reality.

A second problem that arises is test invalidation. A complete test is defined to be *valid* if it always fails when one or more of the faults for which the test is complete is present and always passes when all faults for which the test is complete are absent; otherwise, it is *invalid* for one or more faults present. Ideally, the result of a test on one or more faults is not influenced by the presence or absence of other faults. Unfortunately, this is usually not the case in reality. In the example of Fig. 8.2.2, test t_5 on f_5 might also fail due to faults f_2, f_3, or f_4, which, if they occur, may cause the test t_5 to be performed incorrectly. Thus t_5 is invalid for F^2, F^3, or F^4 present. It is evident from this that the test result which occurs when one of these faults is present is highly dependent on how the fault occurs (i.e., what fault or faults in lower levels of the hierarchy are present). The presence of a particular stuck-at fault may affect the test, whereas another stuck-at fault may not affect it. This invalidation process plays a significant role in the digraph models to be introduced.

A final problem relates to the trade-off between model complexity and information loss. Suppose that two tests t_i and t_j have the same result (00 or 11) for fault pattern F^1 and different results (01 or 10) for fault pattern F^2. Suppose that the modeler, due either to constraints on the model or to ignorance of this information, was unable to account for it and modeled the test results as xx for both F^1 and F^2 (i.e., assumed 00, 01, 10, or 11 could result for either fault). Further, suppose that the information ignored was the only way to distinguish the two faults. Then valuable test result information has been lost in the modeling process.

These three problems can all be dealt with via a complex probabilistic model. In the deterministic modeling done thus far, the completeness problem has been ignored and the other two dealt with to some degree. In the digraph models, there will be, in many cases, test result information loss; these models emphasize treatment of invalidation.

8.3. DIGRAPH REPRESENTATIONS

Digraphs have been applied to system diagnosis in two distinct but related ways. One of these deals with fault-test relationships and the other with the interconnection structure or information flow of the system being diagnosed. The earliest work dealing with graph approaches to system diagnosis was that in Forbes et al. [FORB65] and Agnew et al. [AGNE65]. In 1967, Preparata, Metze, and Chien [PREP67] published the first solidly based work on fault-test relation digraphs. Ramamoorthy [RAMA67] published early work dealing with a model for interconnection structure and information flow. This model, which was used in the LAMP system [CHAN74] and considerably refined by Poisel [POIS77], will not be treated here, and actual interconnection structures will be modeled only for distributed systems. This is not intended to diminish the importance of structural results; structure, in fact, is an important mechanism for yielding system-level diagnosability. Thus structural models are very useful for formulating the fault-test relationship graphs [POIS77].

A recently proposed modification of earlier graph models [HOLT81a] is to be used here as the primary model representation because of its generality and its usefulness for visualizing concepts. It will be related, however, to more traditional system-theoretic graph models [PREP67, KIME70, KIME79]. The model is a bipartite digraph with a node for each fault and a node for each test. An arc exists from test node t_j to fault node f_i if test t_j is a complete test for fault f_i. An arc exists from node f_k to node t_j if the presence of fault f_k invalidates test t_j. In the absence of additional assumptions, the presence of such an arc implies that t_j may sometimes pass when it otherwise should fail, or vice versa. Since the direction of this arc can be inferred from the outgoing arcs of t_j, the arrowhead is deleted for simplicity. The general structure of the digraph is illustrated in Fig. 8.3.1. This digraph representation is illustrated in Fig. 8.3.2a for the diagnosis of the subsystem in Fig. 8.2.2. From Fig. 8.3.2a, note that t_1 is a complete test for faults f_1, f_2, and f_6 and is not invalidated by any faults. Test t_4 is a complete test for f_3 and f_4 and is invalidated by f_1 and f_5. Note that the testing structure would be evident even if the labels were deleted. Figure 8.3.2b is the corresponding representation obtained by using the more traditional labeled nonbipartite digraph based on references [KIME70, RUSS75a]. The test nodes are replaced by test labels on arcs. An arc exists from node f_k to node f_i if there exists one or more complete tests for fault f_i that are invalidated by f_k. The arc is labeled with all such tests. If there exists a test t_j on fault f_i that is not invalidated by any fault, the label t_j is written next to the node for fault f_i. In this representation, the test labels are frequently essential to fully represent the testing structure.

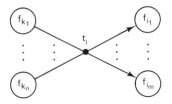

Figure 8.3.1   General structure of the preferred digraph representation.

Next, certain restrictions are detailed on the modeling power of graph-theoretic models. These restrictions can be illustrated most easily by relating the graph models back to the more general tabular and Boolean expression models. First, consider the situation in the example system with f_3 alone present. From Fig. 8.3.2a we can see that test t_4 is complete for f_3 and thus t_4 will fail. Tests t_2, t_3, and t_5 are, from Fig. 8.3.2a, invalidated by the presence of f_3. Thus the results of these tests are unknown in the presence of f_3. Note that the correlation of the results of tests t_2 and t_3 given previously is not represented by the graph. In general, the graph-theoretic models do not represent correlation between results of invalid tests. For the example, the possible test results predicted for f_3 from the digraph model are obtained as follows. Since f_3 is present, test t_4 will fail and tests t_2, t_3, and t_5 will be invalid and may either pass or fail. In vector terms, the test patterns can be represented by 0xx1x. The result for test t_1 is 0 since

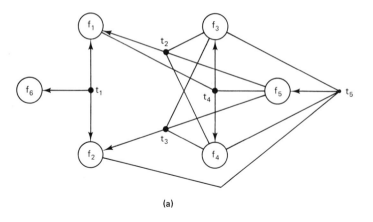

(a)

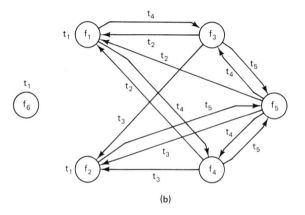

(b)

Figure 8.3.2 Digraph models for the testing of the subsystem in Fig. 8.2.2.

it is unaffected by the presence of f_3. In detail, the possible test patterns predicted are 00010, 00011, 00110, 00111, 01010, 01011, 01110, and 01111. The four additional test patterns predicted due to lack of correlation information are 00110, 00111, 01010, and 01011. These results will not actually occur, so the graph model is inaccurate in this sense. Note that the technique just used for determining possible test patterns for a fault or fault patterns from the graph model can be used, if desired, to generate a tabular model corresponding to the graph.

The fact that correlation of results of invalid tests is not represented is only one of the limitations of the graph models. In general, by use of a Boolean expression representation as a basis, it is possible to characterize the form of representation for the graph models. If it is assumed (1) that a test which is complete for a set of faults fails not only for each fault in the set singly present but for any allowable subset of faults in the set present, and (2) that a test if invalidated may either incorrectly pass or incorrectly fail, then the Boolean expression for a graph model takes the general form:

$$\prod_{i=1}^{p} \left[t_i \left(\sum_{f_j \in A} f_j \right) + \bar{t}_i \left(\prod_{f_j \in A} \bar{f}_j \right) + \sum_{f_k \in B} f_k \right] \qquad (8.3.1)$$

in which:

1. Π represents AND.
2. Σ represents OR.
3. A is the set of all faults f_j corresponding to nodes in the graph having an arc from node t_i to node f_j.
4. B is the set of all faults f_k corresponding to nodes in the graph having an arc from node f_k to node t_i.

Thus, given a graph, it is possible to write a Boolean expression corresponding to the graph. More important, however, is the fact that any system that is to be accurately modeled by a graph under the assumptions given must have a Boolean expression (with possible use of don't cares) that can be placed in this form. Different assumptions from those used here would yield different Boolean expression forms.

Other restrictions on graph models relate specifically to the occurrence of multiple faults. In the example system model, test t_1 is complete for $f_1, f_2,$ and f_6 and is not invalidated by any faults. If, however, both ALUs fail in an identical fashion, test t_1 will pass. Thus, although the test is complete for faults $f_1, f_2,$ and f_6 occurring singly, it is not valid for f_1 and f_2 occurring in combination in a particular way. In effect, f_1 invalidates the test on f_2, and vice versa. Thus, representing invalidation of a test on multiple faults poses a problem. First, the test may be complete and valid for all combinations of the tested faults, in which case there is no problem. Second, a constraint may be attached to the graph model which specifies a subset of the set of fault patterns for which it is known to be valid. For example, the model in Fig. 8.3.2 is constrained to hold for at most single faults present. Third, tests can be restricted to be defined as complete only for a single fault. Thus in Fig. 8.3.2, t_1 would be replaced by t_1, t_1', and t_1'' and invalidation arcs would be added.

Another situation relating to multiple faults can be illustrated by the system in Fig. 8.3.3. Test t_4 is performed on subsystem 4 by using the voted output of subsystems 1, 2, and 3 as input. In this example, t_4 is valid with certainty if at most one of the subsystems 1, 2, or 3 is faulty. It is invalid if two or more of 1, 2, or 3 are faulty. Such a system in which invalidation is determined by the presence of sets of faults rather than individual faults is said to be *semimorphic*. If invalidation is based on the presence of individual faults, the system is *morphic*. To be fully represented by a graph model, the system must be morphic. Since the system in Fig. 8.3.3 is morphic for at most one fault present, it can be represented by a graph, but any results obtained apply only to this restricted fault pattern case. Semimorphic system results are given in [RUSS75a] and [RUSS75b].

One final restriction that may be placed on some graph models is an assumption with regard to the symmetry of test invalidation. Invalidation of a test is *symmetric* if the presence of an invalidating fault can cause the test to fail incorrectly in at least one

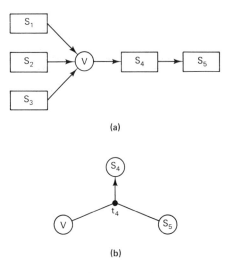

(a)

(b)

Figure 8.3.3 Illustration of a semi-morphic system.

test pattern and to pass incorrectly in at least one test pattern. Invalidation of a test is *asymmetric* if the presence of an invalidating fault can cause the test to fail incorrectly but never to pass incorrectly. Earlier models used symmetric invalidation exclusively with asymmetric invalidation primarily attributed to Barsi et al. [BARS76]. Asymmetric invalidation implies that a test on a fault that is present always fails. If asymmetric invalidation holds for a particular system, diagnosability is frequently better than with symmetric invalidation and diagnosis algorithms are easier to formulate. Thus it is frequently of value to design systems so that the asymmetric invalidation property has a high probability of holding. The assumption is not too difficult to justify in many instances. For example, suppose that a unit is tested by applying inputs via one or more units and analyzing the responses via one or more units. Further, suppose that the unit under test as well as one or more of the other units involved in the test are faulty. The only way that the test can pass is if the faults in the units used to execute the test perfectly cancel the erroneous behavior of the faulty unit under test. This is not impossible, but is not very likely to occur. Holt and Smith [HOLT81a] discuss in more detail the validity of the asymmetric invalidation restriction.

A scheme for classifying graphs is useful for subsequent discussions. The approach to be followed is to define a general graph type and then classify specialized graphs by restricting graph properties in one of four dimensions. These dimensions are: (1) number of faults invalidating a test, (2) number of faults that a test is complete for, (3) symmetry of invalidation, and (4) allowance of hardcore tests (i.e., tests that are not invalidated). The graphical structures that characterize the general case and the restricted case for each dimension are shown in Table 8.3.1. For dimension (1), the restriction on invalidation is single, denoted SI, meaning that each test is invalidated by at most one fault. For dimension (2), the restriction on completeness is single, denoted SC, meaning that each test is complete for exactly one fault. For dimension (3), the restriction is asymmetric invalidation denoted by A. For dimension (4), the

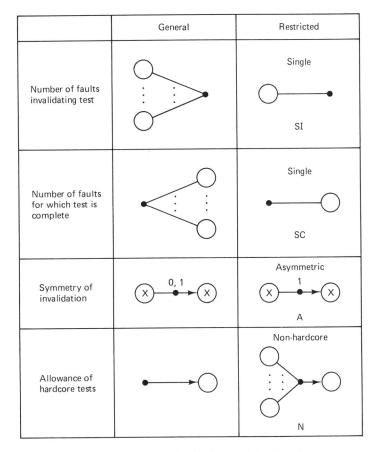

	General	Restricted
Number of faults invalidating test		Single SI
Number of faults for which test is complete		Single SC
Symmetry of invalidation	0, 1	Asymmetric 1 A
Allowance of hardcore tests		Non-hardcore N

Table 8.3.1   Characterization for graph classification.

restriction, denoted N, permits only nonhardcore tests (i.e., insists that every test have at least one invalidating fault).

In order to classify a graph, the abbreviations denoting the applicable restrictions are concatenated in the order of the four dimensions. As an illustration of the classification scheme, Fig. 8.3.4a shows a graph in which each test is invalidated by a single fault and is complete for a single fault. In addition, there are no hardcore tests and symmetric invalidation is assumed to apply. Thus this is an SISCN graph. This is precisely the classification of the most general form of the Preparata, Metze, and Chien model [PREP67]. Thus we will refer to this model as the SISCN model, although elsewhere it is also referred to as the PMC model. Note that for this model it is possible for a graph to be drawn in which each arc corresponds to a test. Thus the test nodes and test labeling are unnecessary, as shown in Fig. 8.3.4b.

The model proposed by Russell and Kime [RUSS75a], an example of which is shown in Fig. 8.3.4c is, in general, an SC model (i.e., the only restriction applying is that each test be complete for only one fault). The graph proposed by Kime

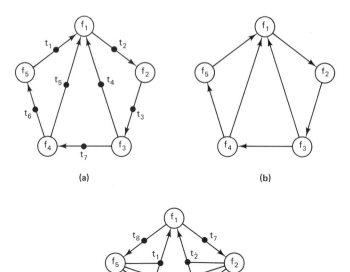

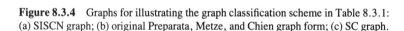

Figure 8.3.4 Graphs for illustrating the graph classification scheme in Table 8.3.1: (a) SISCN graph; (b) original Preparata, Metze, and Chien graph form; (c) SC graph.

[KIME70] is an N model and the graph studied by Maheshwari and Hakimi [MAHE76] is unrestricted. The use of the non-SC models have been limited because of the complexity plus the problems of test completeness on multiple faults discussed earlier. It is interesting to note, however, that under the asymmetric invalidation assumption (i.e., within an A model), if a test fails in the presence of a single fault, it will also fail when additional faults are present (i.e., for the other faults present for which the test is complete). Thus the asymmetric invalidation assumption guarantees that a test is complete for any subset of faults that it is complete for individually, removing the major difficulty with non-SC modeling discussed earlier.

8.4. DIAGNOSABILITY ANALYSIS

Much of the theory developed for the graph models has concentrated on a priori analysis of a system model to determine the effectiveness of a test set in diagnosing faults. These results are useful in predicting whether or not the goals that have been set for system diagnosis have, in fact, been met. In addition, the results can be used as an analysis tool in a design–analysis cycle for evaluation of changes in the diagnosis procedure. Such changes include additional tests, added hardware test points, or special data paths for use in diagnosis.

A very basic measure of effectiveness is diagnostic resolution as defined in [KIME70]. Let $R' = \{R^i \mid R^i \subseteq F$ and there exists a test pattern which occurs for all fault patterns in $R^i\}$. Then the *diagnostic resolution* $R = \{R^i \mid R^i \in R'$ and there exists no $R^j \in R'$ such that $R^i \subset R^j\}$. Less formally, R is the collection of maximal sets of fault patterns for which a common test pattern occurs. For example, for the system model in Fig. 8.4.1 with F^0 corresponding to the good system, $F^i = \{f_i\}$ for $i = 1, 2, 3$, and no more than one fault present:

$$R = \{\{F^0\}, \{F^1, F^3\}, \{F^2, F^3\}\}$$

This indicates, since F^0 does not appear in a set with any other fault pattern, that all faults are detectable. In addition, since F^1 and F^3 appear together in a set, f_1 faulty is not distinguishable in some cases from f_3 faulty. Similarly, f_2 faulty and f_3 faulty are, in some cases, not distinguishable. If the diagnostic resolution goal is to locate all faults exactly, R indicates that this goal is not met. R is particularly useful for evaluating goals stated in the following form: "Locate all single faults to within two field-replaceable units."

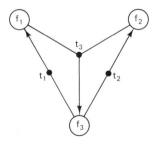

Figure 8.4.1 Digraph example for illustrating diagnostic resolution.

Unfortunately, R may be large and cumbersome. Thus, for simplicity, diagnostic resolution has been parameterized by a single parameter. In particular, diagnostic measures based on t, the maximum number of faults to be present simultaneously, have been defined as follows:

1. A system is *t-fault detectable* if some test in $\mathcal{T}$ will definitely fail provided that the number of faults present is at least one but does not exceed t.

2. A system is *t-fault diagnosable with repair (sequentially t-fault diagnosable)* if there exists a sequence of applications of test set $\mathcal{T}$ and repairs of identified faults in $\mathcal{F}$ that allows all faults to be identified provided that the number of faults originally present does not exceed t.

3. A system is *t-fault diagnosable without repair (one-step t-fault diagnosable)* if one application of test set $\mathcal{T}$ is sufficient to identify precisely which faults are present provided that the number of faults present does not exceed t.

A desirable value for parameter t is specified based on numerous considerations. Most prominent is the likelihood of multiple faults in terms of their probability of occurrence. This depends, in turn, on whether or not fault occurrences are statistically independent and the length of time since the system was last tested.

With these definitions, the diagnostic resolution for a particular measure has been abstracted to the single parameter t. For example, the system modeled by Fig. 8.4.1 is one-fault detectable and zero-fault diagnosable (with or without) repair.

The most basic of the diagnosability results for the SISCN model [PREP67] will be presented first to serve as an introduction to diagnosability analysis. The simple digraph model in Fig. 8.4.2 will be used for illustration. Since the approach used in [PREP67] is oriented to consideration of potentially faulty units, that terminology will be used here. Also, for the SISCN model, the size of the fault set, n, is a significant parameter. The first result relates n and the number of tests on each unit to the parameter t.

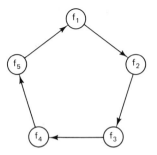

Figure 8.4.2 Digraph for illustration of SISCN diagnosability results.

For a morphic system that is t-fault diagnosable without repair,

1. $n \geq 2t + 1$, and
2. the number of tests on each unit is $\geq t$.

In order to prove condition 1, assume a system in which there are $\leq 2t$ units and each unit tests all other units. We want to show that for such a system two distinct faulty unit patterns of t or fewer faulty units exist which cannot be distinguished. In order to do this, divide the units into two sets P_1 and P_2, each consisting of t or fewer units, as shown in Fig. 8.4.3a. Assume that all units in set P_1 are faulty and that all units in P_2 are good. Then the test results shown in Fig. 8.4.3a are possible. Specifically, all tests by good units on good units pass and all tests on faulty units by good units fail. Due to invalidation, all tests by faulty units can arbitrarily pass or fail. Thus it is possible for all tests by faulty units on good units to fail and for all tests by faulty units on faulty units to pass. Careful examination of Fig. 8.4.3a indicates that exactly the same test results could occur for all units in $P2$ faulty and all units in $P1$ good. Thus the same test results can occur for two distinct faulty unit patterns and the system is not diagnosable without repair for $n \leq 2t$. Further, it can be noted that the two faulty unit patterns have no faulty unit in common so that no faulty unit can be identified for repair in order to do diagnosis with repair. Thus, for a system to be t-fault diagnosable with repair, the condition $n \geq 2t + 1$ must also hold.

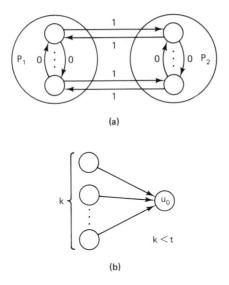

(a)

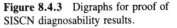

(b)

Figure 8.4.3 Digraphs for proof of SISCN diagnosability results.

To prove condition (2), assume that a unit u_0 has $k < t$ tests on it as shown in Fig. 8.4.3b. Further, suppose that all the k units performing the tests are faulty. Then all tests on u_0 could potentially pass due to invalidation by faulty units. But since $k < t$, u_0 could be either good or faulty. Since the condition of u_0 cannot be determined under such circumstances from the test results, t-fault diagnosis without repair is not generally possible with $k < t$ tests on each unit. From a pragmatic view, this indicates that t-fault diagnosis with repair is likely to be more attractive in terms of number of tests required for all but the smallest values of t.

The results just proved can be illustrated by the system represented by Fig. 8.4.2. Since $n = 5$, the system is at most two-fault diagnosable with or without repair. Since there is just one test per unit, however, the system is at most one-fault diagnosable without repair.

The most significant of the t-fault diagnosis with repair results in [PREP67] deals with single-loop systems (i.e., SISCN systems in which there is exactly one test on each unit and one test performed by each unit). A single loop system is t-fault diagnosable with repair if and only if n, the size of the loop, satisfies

$$n \geq \left\lfloor \left(\frac{t+2}{2}\right)^2 \right\rfloor + 1$$

in which $\lfloor X \rfloor$ is the largest integer $\leq X$. The reader is referred to [PREP67] and [PREP68] for the relatively complex proof of this result. Also, a somewhat more basic proof of sufficiency of the condition on n is given for the more general SC model later in this section. Applying this result to the digraph in Fig. 8.4.2 indicates that the represented system is two-fault diagnosable with repair.

With this background, more general diagnostic analysis results for SC graphs [RUSS75a, RUSS75b] will now be considered. To illustrate these results, the system having the block diagram in Fig. 8.4.4 will be used. The system consists of two

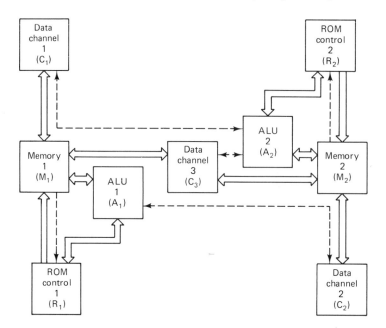

Figure 8.4.4 Block diagram for example computer system. Double arrows: major data and control paths; dashed lines: special diagnostic paths.

computers (made up of a channel Ci, and read-only memory Ri, memory Mi, and an ALU Ai) and an extra channel $C3$. Testing is organized as follows. A channel operating alone has sufficient intelligence to test a memory. The channel and memory acting together test a ROM control. The channel, memory, and ROM control test an ALU. These basic tests constitute tests t_2, t_3, t_4, t_6, t_7, and t_8 in Fig. 8.4.5a. The channels are tested by an ALU, ROM control combination but from the alternative computer giving tests t_1 and t_5. Test t_9 is on the extra channel $C3$ and tests t_{10} and t_{11} are added to Fig. 8.4.5a to achieve the desired diagnostic resolution. Figure 8.4.5b gives additional tests that are used to further enhance resolution for the diagnosis-without-repair case.

Detectability and diagnosability with repair for morphic systems will be dealt with initially since they have a common theoretical basis, the closed fault pattern. A fault pattern F^k is *closed* if in the presence of F^k, no valid test exists on a fault in F^k (i.e., F^k invalidates all tests on its elements). The size of the smallest closed fault pattern in F is the *system closure index* denoted by $c(S)$. $c(S)$ is by convention ∞ if there are no closed fault patterns.

A system S is t-fault detectable if and only if $c(S) \geq t + 1$ [for $t = n$, if and only if $c(S) = \infty$]. The detection result is immediate since $c(S)$ is the size of the smallest potentially undetectable fault pattern; that is, since all tests on a closed fault pattern are invalid, they could all pass with the fault pattern present.

The diagnosis-with-repair result is more complex [RUSS75a].

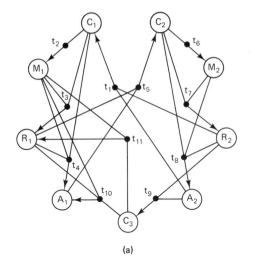

(a)

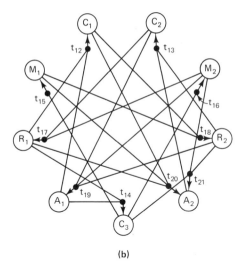

(b)

Figure 8.4.5 Diagnostic graph for system in Fig. 8.4.4.

1. If a system S is t-fault diagnosable with repair, then $c(S) \geq 2t + 1$.
2. A system is t-fault diagnosable with repair if $c(S) \geq \lfloor ((t + 2)/2)^2 \rfloor + 1$.

$\lfloor X \rfloor$ denotes the largest integer less than or equal to X. The first condition is necessary and the second is sufficient for a system to be t-fault diagnosable with repair. The two conditions coincide for $t = 1, 2,$ and 3 and the condition $c(S) \geq 2t + 1$ is the more general form of the condition $n \geq 2t + 1$ which was given earlier for the SISCN model.

These results will now be justified. If $c(S) \leq 2t$, one can postulate a fault pattern of size less than or equal to $2t$ but ≥ 2 that is closed (i.e., has no valid tests on it).

This fault pattern can be split into two nonempty disjoint fault patterns. Since every test on the union of these two patterns is invalid, every test on the two patterns must be invalid for one pattern or the other present. Thus there is no test which is valid for both of the patterns present, so there is no test that can distinguish them. Since the two fault patterns have no common fault and cannot be distinguished, no repair action can be taken. Thus the system is not t-fault diagnosable with repair, so that $c(S)$ must be $\geq 2t + 1$.

The condition $c(S) \geq \lfloor ((t + 2)/2)^2 \rfloor + 1$ is a more general form of the condition given for the single-loop case of the SISCN model. The approach used to obtain sufficiency of this condition for t-fault diagnosability with repair will be outlined here. To show that t-fault diagnosis with repair can be performed, it needs to be shown that any set of fault patterns containing t or fewer faults that potentially cannot be distinguished from each other at all have a common fault so that a repair can still be made. The first question to be considered is: How can we identify a set of fault patterns that potentially cannot be distinguished at all from each other? Suppose that the fault pattern composed of the union of a set of fault patterns is of some size k and is *not* a closed fault pattern and that the intersection of the fault patterns is empty. Then there exists at least one test on some fault that is valid regardless of which of the component fault patterns in the set is present. But this test will be certain to guarantee that at least one of the component fault patterns is distinguishable from the others. Thus this proves that the set of potentially indistinguishable fault patterns must have the fault pattern which is their set union closed. Thus we need only be concerned about having a common fault in sets of fault patterns that have as their union a closed fault pattern. The next question to be raised is: What is the maximum size of the union of a set of t-fault patterns which have no fault common to all patterns in the set and have a fault common to all patterns in any subset of the set? With this knowledge, $c(S)$ one larger than this size guarantees that all sets of fault patterns having no faults common to all patterns are not indistinguishable sets (i.e., guarantees that all indistinguishable sets of fault patterns have a common element). This question can be answered by construction. Assume that the set under consideration has r t-fault patterns in it. To satisfy the conditions in the question posed, there must be some r faults of which $r - 1$ are present in each pattern. Such a structure is shown for faults f_1 through f_3 in Table 8.4.1 for $r = 3$ and $t = 4$. This leaves $t - r + 1$ additional faults outside this structure in each pattern. These $t - r - 1$ faults can each be present in exactly one pattern, as shown for $t - r + 1 = 2$ in Table 8.4.1, in order to maximize the size of the set union. Thus the size of the set union is $r + (t - r + 1)r$. This expression is maximized for $r = (t + 2)/2$. Additional work which will not be detailed here is necessary because r is not an integer for t odd. The resulting set union size is $\lfloor ((t + 2)/2)^2 \rfloor$. By adding 1 to ensure that the described set union is not closed, the sufficient condition for t-fault diagnosability with repair $c(S) \geq \lfloor ((t + 2)/2)^2 \rfloor + 1$ is obtained. Note that in Table 8.4.1, $r = (4 + 2)/2 = 3$ and the size of the set union is 9. Thus $c(S) \geq 10$ guarantees four-fault diagnosability with repair. It is interesting to note that the condition $c(S) \geq \lfloor ((t + 2)/2)^2 \rfloor + 1$ is also necessary for those systems in which

TABLE 8.4.1 EXAMPLE FOR STRUCTURE WITH $r = 3$ AND $t = 4$ FOR PROOF OF DIAGNOSABILITY WITH REPAIR RESULT FOR SC MODEL

	f_1	f_2	f_3	f_4	f_5	f_6	f_7	f_8	f_9
F^1	0	1	1	1	1	0	0	0	0
F^2	1	0	1	0	0	1	1	0	0
F^3	1	1	0	0	0	0	0	1	1

each fault has one and only one test on it [RUSS75a]. The SISCN model single-loop system is a member of this class.

The results as justified can be illustrated by the system model in Fig. 8.4.5a. $\{C1, R1, A1, M1\}$ is not a closed fault pattern since test t_1 on $C1$ is valid in its presence. $\{C1, M1, R1, C2, R2\}$ is, however, a closed fault pattern and is, in fact, a smallest one, and thus for this system, $c(S) = 5$. By the results given, the system is four-fault detectable and two-fault diagnosable with repair.

In order to consider diagnosability without repair for morphic systems, additional terminology is required. A fault pattern F^j is *masked* by a fault pattern F^k if every complete test in $\mathcal{T}$ for each fault in F^j is invalid in the presence of F^k. A fault in F^j is *exposed* if it is not masked by F^j. The *exposure index* of a fault pattern F^j denoted $e(F^j)$ is the number of faults exposed in it. The *system exposure index* of order k, denoted $e_k(S)$, is the minimum of the exposure indices of all fault patterns containing k faults and is defined for $1 \le k \le n$. These concepts can be illustrated by the system model in Fig. 8.4.5 (including the added tests in Fig. 8.4.5b). Consider the fault pattern $F^j = \{C1, A1, A2\}$. Fault $C1$ is not exposed in F^j since both t_1 and t_{12} are invalidated. Fault $A1$ is exposed in F^j since t_{10} is valid. Also, fault $A2$ is exposed in F^j since t_{21} is valid. Thus two of the three faults in F^j are exposed and $e(F^j) = 2$. A linear zero–one programming algorithm is given in [RUSS73] for evaluating system exposure indices. For the system S modeled in Fig. 8.4.5, $e_1(S) = 1$, $e_2(S) = 2$, $e_3(S) = 2$, $e_4(S) = 1$, $e_5(S) = e_6(S) = e_7(S) = e_8(S) = e_9(S) = 0$.

The conditions for t-fault diagnosability without repair can now be stated in terms of system exposure indices. A system S represented by an SC graph model is t-fault diagnosable without repair if and only if $e_k(S) \ge \min(k, 2t + 1 - k)$ for $k = 1, \ldots, \min(2t, n)$ [RUSS75b]. The basis for this result is as follows. For diagnosability without repair, every pair of distinct fault patterns must be distinguished. To accomplish this, there must be a sufficient number of exposed faults in the set union of the pair of fault patterns to guarantee that at least one exposed fault is not in the intersection. This ensures that a fault exists which is in one of the fault patterns and not in the other and that a test for the fault exists that is valid for both patterns present. This guarantees that one can always distinguish the two fault patterns from each other. In the result, k is the size of the union of the fault patterns and the exposure condition ensures that not all exposed faults are in the intersection of the fault patterns.

For the system model in Fig. 8.4.5, the conditions are satisfied by the exposure indices for $t = 2$. Thus the system is two-fault diagnosable without repair. It is interesting to note that the original system represented by Fig. 8.4.5a is only one-fault diagnosable without repair but is two-fault diagnosable with repair. This indicates that the same level of diagnosability is significantly more difficult to accomplish without repair than it is with repair.

It is interesting to compare the SISCN model [PREP67] with the SC model just discussed. First, the SISCN model does not permit tests which are not invalidated (i.e., hardcore tests), whereas the SC model does. This assumption, together with the simplification produced by the SI assumption, constrains graphs to have a structure consisting of maximal strongly connected subgraphs with acyclic structures either interconnecting them or outgoing from them. With a maximal strongly connected subgraph with no incoming arcs, the closure is simply the size of the subgraph. Thus the closure index $c(S)$ for the overall system graph in the SISCN model is simply the size of the smallest maximal strongly connected subgraph with no incoming arcs. In much of the work based on the SISCN model, the system graph itself is assumed to be strongly connected. As a consequence, the number of fault nodes in the system graph, n, is an important parameter in diagnosability results since it is the closure index $c(S)$ for the graph. The necessary and sufficient conditions for t-fault diagnosability without repair for the SISCN model are given by Hakimi and Amin [HAKI74] and can be shown to be a special case of the conditions on the exposure parameters given earlier. Perhaps more interesting in this work [HAKI74] is a special set of conditions for t-fault diagnosability without repair that applies to SISCN system models in which no two units test each other. Such a system is t-fault diagnosable without repair if and only if each unit is tested by at least t other units. With this result, diagnosability is comparatively easy to check.

A factor which results in a trade-off between diagnostic resolution and graph complexity is the use of the asymmetric invalidation assumption which first appeared as a SISCNA model in Barsi et al. [BARS76]. It was extended to the most general modeling case by Holt and Smith [HOLT81a], yielding the A model. The asymmetric invalidation assumption provides a number of immediate advantages. First, fault detection is guaranteed since no complete test on a faulty unit can be invalidated such that it passes. Further, self-test is permitted and a test complete for multiple faults is guaranteed to fail regardless of the subset of tested faults present. Thus the extension to the model involving only the asymmetric restriction is straightforward.

We will now present a portion of the diagnosability results from Holt and Smith. Note that the results in Barsi et al. [BARS76] are special cases of these more general results. A fault *affects* a test if it is either completely tested by or invalidates the test. A subset F^m of $\mathcal{F}$ is said to *mask* fault f_i if all tests on f_i are affected by some fault in F^m other than f_i. Note that this new definition of mask is needed because the SC restriction no longer applies and the result of a test on a fault can be affected by the other faults for which the test is complete. The *masking index* $m(f_i)$ is the size of the smallest set of faults that masks f_i. The *system masking index* $m(S)$ is the minimum of the masking indices for the faults in $\mathcal{F}$. Based on this index, a system is t-fault diagnosable without repair if $m(S) \geq t + 1$. If a system is t-fault diagnosable without repair, then $m(S) \geq t$ [HOLT81a]. Thus there is a difference of just one in $m(S)$ that separates the sufficient condition for t-fault diagnosability without repair from the necessary one. Necessary and sufficient conditions which are more complex appear in [HOLT81a].

In order to consider diagnosability with repair, additional terminology is necessary. A fault pattern F^b that affects all tests on elements in a fault pattern F^c is a *blanking pattern* for F^c. A subset of $\mathscr{F}$, F^c, is *t-unreadable* if there exist fault patterns $F^i, \ldots, F^k \varepsilon F(t)$ which are subsets of F^c and are blanking patterns for F^c such that $F^i \cap \cdots \cap F^k = \emptyset$. Otherwise, a subset F^c is *t-readable*. Based on this definition, a system is t-fault diagnosable with repair if all its closed subsets are t-readable. A number of diagnosability conditions for handling special cases are also given in [HOLT81a] since this general condition is potentially difficult to evaluate.

The concept of t-fault diagnosability is, practically speaking, too stringent for some applications. When diagnosis is being performed for manual repair, it is frequently adequate to locate a fault at worst within two or three potential candidates. As a result, modified measures of diagnosability in which the repair of good units is permitted have been defined.

Friedman [FRIE75] and Karunanithi and Friedman [KARU79] define an alternative diagnosis measure and provide diagnosability conditions as well as diagnosis algorithms for the SISCN model of Preparata, Metze, and Chien. Diagnosability results in terms of potentially faulty units will be summarized briefly here. A system is *k-step t/s-diagnosable* if, by no more than k applications of the tests in $\mathscr{T}$, any set of $f \leq t$ faulty units can be diagnosed and repaired by replacing at most s units. It is assumed that $s \geq t$ and $s < n$. Two special classes of the SISCN model are treated: single-loop systems and $D_{\delta,A}$ systems. A system is a $D_{\delta,A}$-*design* if there exists a test arc from unit u_i ($i = 0, \ldots, n - 1$) to unit u_j for $(j - i) \bmod n = \delta m \bmod n$ with δ an integer less than n and $m = 1, \ldots, A \leq t$. A $D_{1,2}$ design is given in Fig. 8.4.6.

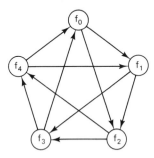

Figure 8.4.6 SISCN model for a $D_{1,2}$ design.

For single-loop systems it is shown that sufficient conditions for an optimal (in the sense of a minimal number of units and test arcs for a given value of t) one-step t/s-diagnosable system are identical to those for a t-diagnosable with repair system, namely, $n \geq \lfloor ((t + 2)/2)^2 \rfloor + 1$. In this case, the maximum number of units replaced in a diagnosis is $n - 2$. For one-step diagnosis of $D_{\delta,A}$ systems, the necessary and sufficient conditions for an optimal system are $n = 2t + 1$ and $A = \lfloor t/2 \rfloor + 1$. In this case, the maximum number of units replaced is about $3t/2$.

For sequential diagnosis of single-loop systems, three diagnosis approaches are given together with a tabulation of the bounds on diagnosability in terms of the maximum number of units replaced. For $D_{\delta,A}$ designs with $A > t/2$, it is shown that an optimum design has $n \geq 2t + 1$ and that diagnosis requires exactly two steps.

Kavianpour and Friedman [KAVI78] consider a special class of one-step t/s-diagnosis in which $s = t$. This condition guarantees that exact diagnosis occurs for t faulty units present but may not occur for $f < t$ faulty units. The advantage of this approach over basic t-fault diagnosability is a reduction in the number of test arcs required. A paper by Chwa and Hakimi [CHWA81] also considers this type of diagnosability.

An additional diagnosability measure is defined by Mallela and Masson [MALL78] for the SISCN model. In contrast to our assumptions thus far, this measure is for intermittently faulty units. A system is t_i-*fault diagnosable* if for no more than t_i units intermittently faulty, a fault-free unit will never be diagnosed as faulty and the diagnosis at any time is at worst *incomplete* (but never *incorrect*). Correct but incomplete means that the identified faulty units are indeed faulty, but there may be additional intermittently faulty units not identified even though t_i or fewer intermittently faulty units are present. It is shown that the necessary and sufficient conditions for the "with repair" and "without repair" cases are identical and as a consequence the measure need not distinguish these cases.

Necessary and sufficient conditions for t_i-fault diagnosability are defined and are related to t-fault diagnosability without repair conditions. For any system that is t-fault diagnosable without repair and where no two units test each other, $\lfloor(2t + 1)/3\rfloor^* \leq t_i \leq t - 1$, where $\lfloor X \rfloor^*$ denotes the largest integer less than X. In the event that some pair of units tests each other, the upper bound on t_i becomes t. This is illustrated by the system in Fig. 8.4.6 for which $t = 2$. Since no units test each other, $1 \leq t_i \leq 2$. A procedure is given in [MALL78] for determining the exact value of t_i. For the example system, $t_i = 1$ (i.e., the system can be diagnosed for at most one intermittently faulty unit present). This work has also been extended to a hybrid fault case in which the measure is t_h/t_{h_i}—*diagnosability without repair*, where t_h is the maximum number of (permanently or intermittently) faulty units and t_{h_i} is the maximum number of intermittently faulty units for which the system is diagnosable without repair [MALL80].

This concludes the discussion of a priori analysis of diagnosability. Next, concern will shift to the actual analysis of test results in order to determine the faults that are present.

8.5. DIAGNOSIS ALGORITHMS

Regardless of the model employed for diagnosis and the diagnostic resolution potentially available, it is necessary to have an effective means to determine the fault or faults present by analyzing the test results. Such means will be referred to here as *diagnosis algorithms* (sometimes referred to as *syndrome decoding*). To some degree, the algorithm used depends on the model representation employed. Initially, an algorithm operating on a tabular data base will be discussed. Then a tree-structured approach and bootstrap approaches will be introduced. Algorithms for use with graph models are considered, and simple algorithms that allow repair or replacement of good units are treated.

It is possible to use Table 8.2.1 or 8.2.2 as a basis for a straightforward *table-look-up diagnosis*. For example, suppose that the test results obtained for t_1 through t_5 are 01110 (such a test result vector is frequently referred to as a *syndrome*). By comparing this test pattern to Table 8.2.1, a match is found for fault patterns F^3 and F^4. Thus one of the two faults f_3 and f_4 is present, recalling that single faults were assumed. The same result is obtained by comparison to Table 8.2.2 by noting that an x matches to either a 0 or a 1. Another tabular data base is the fault dictionary, which lists each possible test pattern together with the associated fault patterns. Such a fault dictionary derived from Table 8.2.1 is shown in Table 8.5.1. In this case, one can rapidly access the test pattern and determine the corresponding fault patterns. For larger fault dictionaries, data compression techniques such as hash coding can be used on the test results to produce a concise representation of results for large numbers of tests. Fault dictionary approaches are discussed in Chang et al. [CHAN70].

TABLE 8.5.1   FAULT DICTIONARY FOR TESTING OF SUBSYSTEM IN FIG. 8.2.2

Test pattern					Fault patterns	Faults
t_1	t_2	t_3	t_4	t_5		
0	0	0	0	0	F^0	—
0	0	0	0	1	F^5	f_5
0	0	0	1	0	F^3, F^4	f_3 or f_4
0	0	0	1	1	F^3, F^4, F^5	$f_3, f_4,$ or f_5
0	1	1	0	1	F^5	f_5
0	1	1	1	0	F^3, F^4	f_3 or f_4
0	1	1	1	1	F^3, F^4, F^5	$f_3, f_4,$ or f_5
1	0	0	0	0	F^6	f_6
1	0	1	0	0	F^2	f_2
1	0	1	0	1	F^2	f_2
1	1	0	0	0	F^1	f_1
1	1	0	1	0	F^1	f_1

Diagnosis algorithms can also be designed which employ a *tree* as the data structure. Such a structure may be used to examine test results in a fixed order or may be adaptive and examine test results in an order that depends upon the prior results examined. Figure 8.5.1 is a tree structure derived in a straightforward manner from Table 8.5.1. By using a more carefully selected ordering and adaptive examination of the test results, an alternative tree shown in Fig. 8.5.2 can be derived. This tree is considerably simpler than that in Fig. 8.5.1. In addition, it is interesting to note that for many fault pattern occurrences, only a subset of the test results needs to be

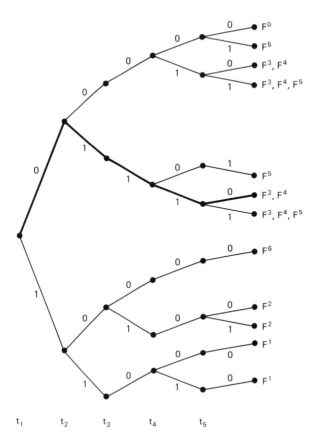

Figure 8.5.1 Diagnosis tree derived from Table 8.5.1.

t_1 t_2 t_3 t_4 t_5

examined. This suggests that the tree could be used not only for analysis but for directing the testing process on an adaptive basis as well. Thus the tree is used to determine at each step which test to run next. Trees can also be derived by the expansion of a Boolean expression about the test variables. For example, to develop the tree in Fig. 8.5.2, we would begin by expanding S, S', or S'' about the variables t_5 and $\bar{t}_5$. The coefficient of t_5 would then be expanded about t_1 and the coefficient of $\bar{t}_5$ about t_4. The decision as to the variable about which to make the expansion can be based on a heuristic criterion. One approach is to select the test for which the maximum amount of information is to be gained about fault patterns not yet distinguished from each other. This type of approach is treated in [CHAN65], [KAUT68], and [KIME69].

Once a tree has been obtained and stored as a data structure, the diagnosis algorithm consists of simply tracing the tree to a leaf node on the basis of the test results. Suppose that the tree in Fig. 8.5.1 is used and that the test result is 01110. Then the trace obtained is shown in Fig. 8.5.1 as a bold path, with the result that f_3 or f_4 is present.

As demonstrated earlier, the Boolean expression itself can also be used as a data base for a diagnosis algorithm. The algorithm, if all test results are available, simply

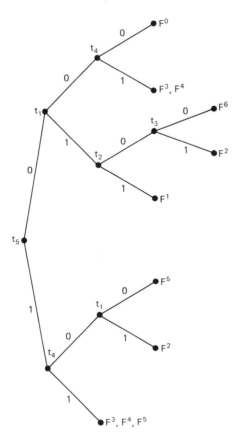

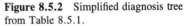

Figure 8.5.2 Simplified diagnosis tree from Table 8.5.1.

consists of evaluating the expression. A Boolean expression, just as a tree, can be used to direct the testing process. If a Boolean expression has been evaluated for some subset of the test variables, the test variables left in the residual expression not common to all terms indicate tests that give additional useful information in completing the diagnosis. Factoring within the residual expression may also be used to indicate which among the subset of remaining useful tests should be executed first. As an illustration of this, suppose that S' [Eq. (8.2.2)] has been evaluated for $t_5 = 1$ and $t_3 = 1$. The expression obtained is

$$S'(t_5 = 1, t_3 = 1) = f_2 t_1 \bar{t}_2 \bar{t}_4 + ((f_3 + f_4)t_4 + f_5)\bar{t}_1 t_2 \tag{8.5.1}$$

Thus additional information is available from t_1, t_2, or t_4. Obtaining the result $t_1 = 1$, S' becomes

$$S'(t_5 = 1, t_3 = 1, t_1 = 1) = f_2 \bar{t}_2 \bar{t}_4 \tag{8.5.2}$$

Thus the fault present is f_2. Tests t_2 and t_4 provide no additional information.

The diagnosis algorithms considered thus far are based on tabular, tree, and expression models. There is also interest in diagnosis algorithms for graph models.

The previous results for tables, trees, and expressions can be applied to graph models by transforming the graph to one of these other representations. It is also possible, however, to formulate algorithms based directly on diagnostic graph information. Since distributed diagnosis will be considered in a subsequent section, the algorithms considered here are restricted to those executable by a central observer which obtains all test results and performs an analysis to determine necessary corrective actions to be performed. This central observer must be highly reliable general-purpose or special-purpose hardware since its failure precludes handling of other faults.

The *bootstrap* approach is frequently used as a basis for practical diagnosis algorithms. In this approach, hardware is assumed to have been tested (and repaired, if necessary) before it is used in testing other hardware. If this assumption can be met, a simple diagnosis algorithm results. A bootstrap algorithm is based on an acyclic diagnostic graph. The algorithm executes first those tests with no incoming invalidation arcs and then proceeds to perform tests that are invalidated only by faults that have been tested (and repaired, if necessary). If a test on a potential fault fails, that fault is known to be present and is repaired. This process is repeated until all faults have been diagnosed.

An example of bootstrap diagnosis can be based on the description of the IBM System/360 Model 50 diagnosis as given by Hackl and Shirk [HACK65]. The system has the following components: (1) main storage, (2) read-only memory control, (3) arithmetic processor, (4) local storage, and (5) channel. These correspond to nodes f_1 through f_5, respectively, in the diagnostic graph in Fig. 8.5.3. In addition, a certain amount of manually checked hardcore is distributed about the system. The diagnosis begins with the loading of tests into main storage via special hardcore controls. During load, a storage malfunction will cause the load control to "hang up." Thus test t_1 is performed on main storage by hardcore and thus is not invalidated. If the tests have been successfully loaded into main storage, the main storage is used as a source for data and control to test the ROM control. As a result, test t_2 on the ROM control can be invalidated by a main storage fault. Thus test t_2 in Fig. 8.5.3 has an arc from f_1. Test t_3 on the arithmetic processor uses both the main storage and ROM control, and tests t_4 and t_5 on the local storage and channel use main storage, ROM control, and the arithmetic processor. The definition of these tests gives the additional arcs in Fig. 8.5.3. The order of testing for a bootstrap algorithm for this system is t_1, t_2, t_3, t_4, and t_5 (or t_5 and t_4). It is interesting to note that for an acyclic SC graph, the closure $c(S) = \infty$. Thus this example system is, in theory, diagnosable with repair for any number of faulty units present. It should be noted that the bootstrap algorithm is given in terms of a certain order of performing tests. For alternative algorithms, it is not always necessary to tie test order to the diagnosis algorithm. For a bootstrap algorithm, however, an advantage is obtained by doing so since each test needs to be performed only once in performing an entire diagnosis with repair.

An algorithm for an SISCN model by Meyer and Masson [MEYE78] deals with one-step t-fault diagnosis of $D_{1,t}$ designs under symmetric invalidation. This algorithm is of particular interest because of its simplicity and the fact that it can be converted easily to an algorithm for distributed diagnosis.

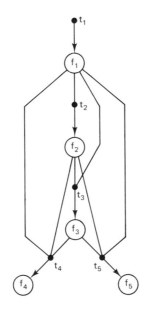

Figure 8.5.3 Example of bootstrap diagnosis.

For each potentially faulty unit subscript $i = 0, \ldots, n - 1$, a table B_i is constructed which represents the conclusion of unit i regarding the faulty or nonfaulty state of all units in the system. The table B_i is constructed by assuming that unit i is good, and, based on this assumption, inferring the condition of the units in the system. First i is recorded as good. In ascending order modulo n from i, units that fail a test are recorded as faulty until a test passes. This unit is recorded as good. Results from the unit on which the test passes are then used in the same way as u_i results were used. This iterative process terminates when either t faulty units have been found or the next test result to be recorded is on unit i. Upon termination, all units with unspecified entries in B_i are labeled as good. After formation of the tables, a diagnosis is obtained by indicating that unit j is faulty if it is labeled as faulty in greater than t of the B_i tables; otherwise, unit j is good. Note that the formation of the B_i tables is based on a bootstrap-like analysis which terminates at faulty units.

This algorithm is illustrated by Table 8.5.2 for the system graph in Fig. 8.5.4b, which is a two-fault diagnosable $D_{1,2}$ design. Note that tabular entries for faulty units may be arbitrary, but all good units obtain a correct picture of the system fault state. In this case, the faulty units 0 and 2 obtain an incorrect view of system state. Since there are at least $t + 1$ good units out of $2t + 1$ units, any unit identified as faulty by $t + 1$ units must be faulty. In this case, unit 0 is identified by three units as faulty and unit 2 is identified by four units as faulty.

In contrast to the highly structured graph employed by Meyer and Masson, Smith [SMIT79] gives universal diagnosis algorithms not tied to any particular diagnosis data structure. The actual graph structure is not used, but analysis is performed for selected graph classes. Clearly, in most instances one would be likely to use more structure in developing algorithms, but these results provide some important bounding

TABLE 8.5.2 B_i TABLES FOR MEYER AND MASSON
ALGORITHM FOR DIAGNOSIS OF SYNDROME IN FIG. 8.5.4b

		j				
		0	1	2	3	4
i	0	0	1	1	0	1
	1	1	0	1	0	0
	2	0	0	0	1	1
	3	1	0	1	0	0
	4	1	0	1	0	0

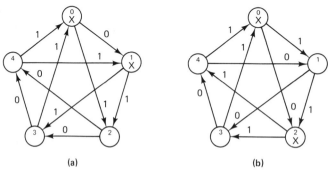

(a)   (b)

Figure 8.5.4 Example digraph for illustrating diagnosis algorithm.

points for evaluating more complex algorithms. They are valid for either symmetric
or asymmetric invalidation. The algorithms are for diagnosis with repair, but do not
specify a maximum number of faulty units, t. Thus a new definition is employed. A
system is *f/s-diagnosable* if, for f faulty units initially present, at most s units need
to be repaired to restore the system to a fault-free state. Also, an *aggregate syndrome*,
which we will denote as σ^a, is used where σ_i^a for $i = 0, \ldots, n - 1$ is the total
number of tests on unit i that fail for an application of the test set.

The two algorithms given are based on the following scheme:

Step: Perform the tests in $\mathcal{T}$ and compute σ^a. Let $F = \{$units $\mid \sigma_j^a \neq 0$ and the
unit has not been replaced$\}$. If $F = \emptyset$, the system is assumed correct, so exit; else
replace all units in F', a nonempty subset of F, and go to STEP.

Specific algorithms are obtained by specifying F'.

Algorithm 1: $F' = F$ (replace all units that fail a test).
Algorithm 2: $F' = $ units in F for which σ_i^a is maximum (replace all units that fail
a maximum number of tests).

It is shown that these algorithms will always result in a fault-free system provided that at each step at least one fault (if any are present) is always detectable. In addition, it is shown that for single-loop systems $f/2f$ diagnosability results for algorithm 1. This compares favorably with the results for more complex algorithms given in [KARU79]. For $D_{1,A}$ systems, $f/2f$ diagnosis results for algorithm 2.

Application of algorithm 1 to the system represented by Fig. 8.5.4b results in the replacement of all units. If algorithm 2 is used, unit 0 is replaced on the first step and unit 2 is replaced on the second step. For the system represented by Fig. 8.5.4a and algorithm 2, units 0 and 2 are replaced on the first step and unit 1 is replaced on the second step. Thus, in this case, one good unit is replaced.

A hierarchical approach to dealing with algorithm complexity versus diagnosability is given in Holt and Smith [HOLT81a] for systems using the A model. It is shown that by obeying certain constraints on the diagnostic graph, simpler algorithms are effective, whereas for arbitrary graph structures, diagnosis is difficult for some fault patterns.

8.6. DISTRIBUTED DIAGNOSIS

Up to this point, in examining both diagnosability analyses and diagnosis algorithms, we have not dealt with the issues of how test result information is communicated. Frequently, it is proposed that the test information is reliably communicated to highly reliable *central observer* hardware for analysis and control of subsequent corrective action (if necessary). This communication and analysis hardware is *diagnostic hard-core* in the sense that it must be fault-free for the diagnosis to be carried out correctly in all cases. The use of a distributed system provides the opportunity, and in some cases the necessity, for use of a *distributed observer* approach in which no global observation is employed. This permits elimination of the central observer while presenting added complexity in performing diagnosability analyses.

The environment for distributed diagnosis by use of a distributed observer will be assumed to be a distributed system in which computational tasks are performed by multiple processors. It will be assumed that communication between processors is via messages transmitted over links, where links are buses or serial lines. These links will be used in executing tests, for communication of test results, and for communication of fault information. Thus, in a complete model it is necessary to treat the execution of tests, communication of test results, analysis of test results, and communication of fault information to fully model the diagnosis. It will be assumed here that each test result is generated at a point called a *test origin* and is communicated with other test results to an "intelligent" unit called an *analyzer* to determine potential faults present. This fault information is then communicated to one or more *controllers* that are responsible for corrective action [HOLT81b]. Much of the work discussed here will deal with only a portion of the steps. To keep the different approaches clear, models, diagnosability results, and diagnosis algorithms for each approach are treated as a unit.

As indicated earlier, the diagnosis algorithm given by Meyer and Masson [MEYE78] is useful for distributed diagnosis in a SISCN model. Suppose that, for the system representation in Fig. 8.5.4b, each unit is an analyzer. Then each unit i will build its own B_i table, which will be its diagnosis of the system. Note that in Table 8.5.2, all good units obtain a correct diagnosis of the system, whereas faulty units obtain an incorrect one. This is, in general, the case for this algorithm; that is, a correct diagnosis of the system is obtained in a good analyzer provided that no more than t faulty units are present. This algorithm does not deal, however, with communication problems.

Another algorithm that uses the SISCN model is given by Kuhl and Reddy [KUHL80a]. Each node represents a processing element referred to as a PE (processing element). In addition, an undirected interconnection graph is defined for inter-processing-element communication. Tests are assumed to be executed via these communication paths and it is assumed that there can be arcs in the diagnostic graph only between units that are directly connected in the interconnection graph. Test invalidation in this model includes alteration and destruction of messages by PEs as well as the usual invalidation by the PE performing the test. Thus the effect of faulty PEs on test result communication is explicitly considered.

Kuhl and Reddy define a distributed multiprocessor system as *t-fault self-diagnosable* if each fault-free PE can correctly identify all faulty and fault-free PEs in the system provided that no more than t PEs are faulty. This indicates that each PE is considered as an analyzer and develops its own view of the system condition.

A system with a diagnostic graph D and which employs the algorithm SELF described next is t- fault self-diagnosable if and only if the connectivity of D is at least t. In fact, this condition is necessary for t-fault self-diagnosability regardless of the algorithm used.

In the algorithm SELF, each PE computes a fault vector containing its conclusions about the condition of all PEs. Initially, all tests indicated by the diagnostic graph are performed. A PE then labels itself as good and all other PEs as unknown in the fault vector. It then examines the results of tests it has performed on other PEs and records these results in the fault vector. In addition, PE_i prepares a message containing these results for broadcast to all other PEs that test PE_i. From each message that PE_i receives from a PE that it tested and found to be good, it enters any new test results on other PEs into the fault vector and passes the new information on to the PEs that test PE_i. This information is not passed back to the PE it came from or to PEs tested by PE_i and found to be faulty. This process iterates at PE_i until either the fault vector is fully specified or it contains an indication of t faulty PEs. In the latter case, the remaining unspecified entries in the fault vector are filled with fault-free PE indications because it is assumed that at most t faults are present.

As an illustration of the algorithm SELF, suppose that its execution in PE_2 in Fig. 8.5.4a is considered. Initially, PE_2 establishes a fault vector $xx0xx$, where 0 indicates good, 1 indicates faulty, and x indicates unknown. Based on the results of the tests PE_2 performs, it labels PE_3 and PE_4 as good, giving $xx000$. Based on results passed to it by PE_3 it labels PE_0 as faulty, yielding $1x000$. Finally, based on results passed to PE$_2$ by PE$_4$, PE$_1$ is labeled as faulty, yielding 11000 and completing the process.

A modeling approach by Nair [NAIR78] employs the SC diagnostic graph. A distributed fault detection and location strategy called "roving diagnosis" is presented in which one or more executives "roves" through all nodes in the system searching for faulty units. The strategy is based on a roving graph, a subgraph of the diagnostic graph chosen so that it forms a partial ordering of all system nodes. A test of the system begins with tests by "initial nodes" of the partial ordering, and proceeds through the ordering with each unit being tested before being allowed to perform any tests on other units. If the initial nodes are good, then the test ordering guarantees that only good nodes will perform tests. Thus the problem of test invalidation is avoided. The number of faulty units that can be diagnosed is found to be equal to the minimum number of faulty units required to invalidate all tests on a unit of the roving graph.

The roving approach depends heavily on diagnosis of the initial nodes. Either tests performed by hardcore must be arranged or a cooperative initial diagnosis must be established whereby each initial node is tested by a set of others which cooperate to form a diagnosis. Methods for arriving at this cooperative decision and communicating it to the initial nodes are not considered in detail.

It is interesting to note the relationship of the fault location algorithms by Meyer and Masson, Kuhl and Reddy, and Nair to the bootstrap approach discussed earlier. All of these algorithms employ either the concept of testing a unit before it is used to test other units or diagnosing its condition before it is used to originate or communicate test results. This is similar to the basis for bootstrap diagnosis except that two of these algorithms are for diagnosis without repair, whereas the bootstrap algorithm is for the diagnosis with repair. The acyclic graph involved in the Meyer and Masson algorithm and the Kuhl and Reddy algorithm is defined by the passage of information in assembling the B_i table or fault vector. Such an acyclic graph is shown in Fig. 8.6.1a for the diagnosis at PE$_2$ for the situation in Fig. 8.5.4a and the Kuhl and Reddy algorithm. The graph in Fig. 8.6.1b is a roving graph with f_0 as an assumed good initial node for the diagnosis of the system represented in Fig. 8.4.6.

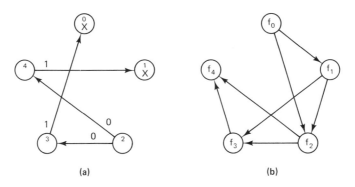

(a)   (b)

Figure 8.6.1   Bootstrap graphs for distributed diagnosis algorithm.

A straightforward diagnostic modeling approach for distributed systems can be based on the SC diagnostic graph model by simply including the hardware used for communication of test results as added sources of test invalidation. Because the communication requirements may differ for each analyzer, a diagnostic graph per analyzer may be required. Only good analyzers are assumed to obtain a correct diagnosis; thus if an analyzer is faulty, it must be prevented from directing controllers to take incorrect repair or reconfiguration actions. This diagnostic modeling approach permits the modeling of "nonintelligent" units such as communication links and their role in testing.

This approach is considered by examining the model of an example system consisting of three processing elements interconnected by two shared buses (links). The block diagram is shown in Fig. 8.6.2. To maximize the use of the system under faulty conditions, it is necessary to employ a model that explicitly includes ports which represent the hardware that interfaces processors to buses. Suppose that we attempt to model only potentially faulty processors and links and that port A1 (which is not modeled separately) becomes faulty. Processor A can still be good and be reached via link 2; thus the faulty port cannot be modeled as faulty processor A without a loss of good hardware. Similarly, link 1 can still be good with regard to communication between processors B and C; thus the faulty port cannot be modeled as a faulty link 1 without a loss of good hardware. To prevent this loss of hardware, the ports need to be modeled as separate potentially faulty units. Note that if a link between two processors is dedicated rather than shared, this would not be necessary. In general, the structure model in Fig. 8.6.2 is a processor, link, port (PLP) model [KIME80]. This model can be extended to other entities, such as switches and memories, if appropriate.

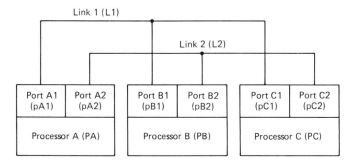

Figure 8.6.2 Example system for illustrating distributed diagnosis.

In order to model the diagnosis of the system in Fig. 8.6.2, a set of tests $\mathcal{T}$ needs to be defined. This can be most easily done for a regularly structured system by defining one or more test templates, as in Fig. 8.6.3. A template indicates how a particular unit type is tested. An actual test is defined by specifying the actual unit identifiers for tested and invalidating units. In Fig. 8.6.3, the dashed lines in the templates indicate differences in invalidation depending on the particular processor

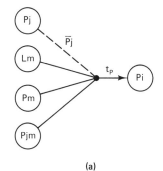

(a)

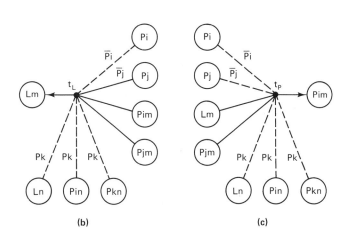

(b)   (c)

Figure 8.6.3 Testing templates for distributed diagnosis: (a) processor test; (b) link test; (c) port test.

considered as the analyzer. We will assume that each processor is an analyzer developing its own view of the system. Thus the effects on the test template graph are as follows. First, for the diagnosis for which a processor P is the analyzer, P is assumed to be good and cannot invalidate any tests. Second, the communication requirements (i.e., units used for communication) depend on which processor is the analyzer for a particular diagnosis. The simple Boolean expressions on the dashed arcs in Fig. 8.6.3 are complemented and noncomplemented variables which are 1 if the corresponding processor is the analyzer and 0, otherwise. If the Boolean expression is 1, the invalidation arc is present; otherwise, it is absent. Note that $i \neq j \neq k$.

The structure of each of the templates is to be discussed briefly. It is assumed that a processor is tested as in Fig. 8.6.3a by another processor via a link and the two ports at the end of the link. Thus the processor test on Pi can be invalidated by the testing processor Pj, the link Lm, or the connecting ports pim or pjm. If the testing processor Pj is the analyzer, it is assumed good and does not invalidate the test. Thus, for $Pj = 1$, $\overline{Pj} = 0$ and the arc from Pj to tp is absent. If another processor Pk is the analyzer, Lm can be used to communicate the result from Pj to Pk, since it is not under test. Thus there are no added units used for communication of test results that invalidate *tp* in this case.

A link is tested as in Fig. 8.6.3b by two processors passing test messages through the link and connecting ports. Thus the test of link *Lm* is invalidated by processors *Pi* and *Pj* and ports *pim* and *pjm*. The processor that is the analyzer does not invalidate the tests by the earlier assumption. If the third processor *Pk* is not involved in the test and is the analyzer for the diagnosis, a result must be communicated to it via the alternative link *Ln* and ports *pin* (or *pjn*) and *pkn*. In this case communication via *pin* is arbitrarily selected. This test result communication invalidation is reflected in Fig. 8.6.3b and is activated for *Pk* = 1.

A port is tested as in Fig. 8.6.3c by two processors passing messages through it via the attached link and another port. Thus the test on port *pim* is invalidated by processors *Pi* and *Pj*, link *Lm*, and port *pjm*. If either processor is the analyzer, it cannot invalidate the test. If the third processor *Pk* is the analyzer, an alternate link is used for test result communication, producing additional invalidation for *Pk* = 1 as shown in Fig. 8.6.3c. The alternate link is used to prevent any direct effect on the test result by the port under test if it is faulty.

These templates can serve as a basis for 18 tests which are carefully chosen to maximize faulty unit resolution. Two tests are run on each processor using alternate link and port sets. Three tests are run on each link using alternate pairs of processors and corresponding ports. A single test is run on each port. Due to its complexity, the overall diagnostic graph is not shown. Figure 8.6.4 shows a small portion of the tests with processor *PA* as analyzer. The tabular representation of the diagnosis with *PA* as analyzer is shown in Table 8.6.1. Since *PA* is assumed good, the results of tests 1 and 2 would not ordinarily be examined by *PA* but are shown for completeness. Analysis of this table indicates that all faulty units are distinguished except for ports *B* 1 and *B* 2. By symmetry for processor *PB* as analyzer, faulty ports *C* 1 and *C* 2 are not distinguished, and for processor *PC* as analyzer, faulty ports *A* 1 and *A* 2 are not distinguished. A modification of the test origins and communication of results for tests 13 through 18 will permit these faulty unit pairs to be distinguished, resulting in a one-fault diagnosable system.

This particular approach has disadvantages, particularly for larger systems. Multiple diagnostic graphs are required. In addition, there is no convenient way to represent alternative communication paths for test results. As a consequence, an alternative approach which deals separately with the communication issue and uses the A model has been proposed by Holt [HOLT81b]. In addition, the treatment of multiple faulty units emphasizes diagnosis with repair for repairable systems. Thus the goal of a diagnosis is to correctly determine the exact location of one or more faulty units and to correctly convey this information to a fault-free controller.

The model employs a diagnostic graph and a communication graph. A set of analyzers and a set of controllers is specifically identified. The diagnostic graph is the bipartite graph illustrated in Fig. 8.3.2a with one addition. The unit (or units) at which the test result for t_j appears is denoted in the graph by a solid block drawn at the f_i end of the arc (f_i, t_j). A diagnostic graph for the partial set of tests shown in Fig. 8.6.4

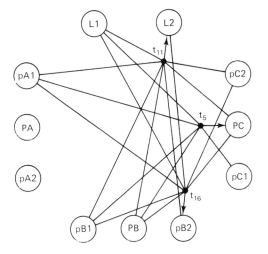

Figure 8.6.4 Representative tests on the system in Fig. 8.6.2 with processor A as the analyzer.

TABLE 8.6.1 TABULAR REPRESENTATION FOR THE DIAGNOSIS OF THE SYSTEM IN FIG. 8.6.2 WITH PA AS ANALYZER AND NO MORE THAN ONE UNIT FAULTY

	1	2	3	4	5	6	7	8	9	10	11	12	13	14	15	16	17	18
∅	0	0	0	0	0	0	0	0	0	0	0	0	0	0	0	0	0	0
PA	1	1	0	0	0	0	0	0	0	0	0	0	0	0	0	0	0	0
PB	0	0	1	1	x	x	x	x	0	x	x	0	x	x	x	x	0	0
PC	x	x	0	0	1	1	0	x	x	0	x	x	0	0	x	x	x	x
L1	x	0	x	0	x	0	1	1	1	0	x	0	x	0	x	x	x	0
L2	0	x	0	x	0	x	0	x	0	1	1	1	0	x	x	x	0	x
pA1	x	0	x	0	x	0	x	0	x	0	x	0	1	0	0	x	x	0
pA2	0	x	0	x	0	x	0	x	0	x	0	x	0	1	x	0	0	x
pB1	0	0	x	0	x	0	x	x	0	0	x	0	x	0	1	x	0	0
pB2	0	0	0	x	0	x	0	x	0	x	x	0	0	x	x	1	0	0
pC1	x	0	0	0	x	0	0	x	x	0	0	0	0	0	x	0	1	0
pC2	0	x	0	0	0	x	0	0	0	0	x	x	0	0	0	x	0	1

is presented in Fig. 8.6.5a. Note that communication invalidation is no longer shown since it is handled via the communication graph $\mathcal{M}$. The nodes in $\mathcal{M}$ correspond to the elements in $\mathcal{F}$ and either a directed or undirected edge may be used to represent the flow of information between units. A directed edge from f_i to f_j indicates that messages may pass directly from f_i to f_j. An undirected edge represents bilateral passage of messages. The communication graph for the system in Fig. 8.6.2 is given in Fig. 8.6.5b.

Based on these graphical models, conditions for t-self diagnosability and diagnosis algorithms for repairable systems are derived. It is important to note that in this case the definition of t-fault self-diagnosable includes the effects of faults on communication of test results, analysis of test results, and communication of fault information to the controller.

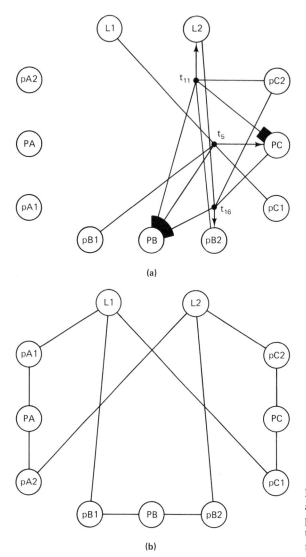

(a)

(b)

Figure 8.6.5 Model for distributed diagnosis of the system in Fig. 8.6.2: (a) partial diagnostic graph for the set of the tests shown in Fig. 8.6.4; (b) communication graph.

8.7. PROBABILISTIC TREATMENTS

Some of the earliest work [BRUL60, JOHN60] in system diagnosis involved the use of probabilistic concepts. To a large extent, deterministic approaches to both definition of diagnosis algorithms and diagnosability analysis have been predominant. Interest in probabilistic approaches, however, again appeared in the mid-1970s. The use of probability in diagnosability analysis potentially provides more accurate results. Its use in the definition of diagnosis algorithms permits optimization of such algorithms to a greater degree than possible with deterministic methods alone. The discussion here will be limited to probabilistic approaches associated with digraph representations.

Maheshwari and Hakimi [MAHE76, MAHE78] assign a probability of failure $\Pr(f_i)$ to each unit in a SISCN model. Unit failures are assumed to be statistically independent. On this basis, a new measure of diagnosability without repair is defined. A system is *p-t-diagnosable* if for any test pattern there exists at most one associated fault pattern F^i such that $\Pr(F^i) > t$, where t is a value between 0 and 1. This measure is more general than t-fault diagnosability for those cases in which fault pattern F^i and F^j exist such that $\Pr(F^j) > \Pr(F^i)$ and the size of F^j is greater than that of F^i. (Note that the claim in [MAHE76] that the deterministic models assume that unit faults are equiprobable is not true.) Necessary and sufficient conditions for p-t diagnosability without repair are derived. The conditions for p-t diagnosability with repair are given in [FUJI78].

In Blount [BLOU77], sets of probabilities are associated with both faults and tests in the SISCN model. This permits the modeling of such effects as incomplete testing of units and self-testing of units. Results include an approach for determination of the probability that a correct diagnosis is done and an algorithm for developing an optimum diagnosis strategy for a given test set. In treating this work, the notation in [BLOU77] is modified to fit that used in preceding sections of this chapter.

A set of probabilities called test parameters is associated with each test. For clarity, the result of the test t_k which is on unit j and invalidated by unit i faulty will be denoted by t_k^{ij}. Interunit test parameters are defined as follows:

$$p_{ij} = \Pr(t_k^{ij} = 0 \,|\, (f_i, f_j) = (0, 0))$$

$$r_{ij} = \Pr(t_k^{ij} = 1 \,|\, (f_i, f_j) = (0, 1))$$

$$q_{ij} = \Pr(t_k^{ij} = 0 \,|\, (f_i, f_j) = (1, 0))$$

$$s_{ij} = \Pr(t_k^{ij} = 1 \,|\, (f_i, f_j) = (1, 1))$$

Since self-test of a unit is permitted, intraunit test parameters are defined:

$$p_{ii} = \Pr(t_k^{ii} = 0 \,|\, f_i = 0)$$

$$s_{ii} = \Pr(t_k^{ii} = 1 \,|\, f_i = 1)$$

The relationship of the parameters to actual system testing is of interest. p_{ij} is usually equal to 1 unless unmodeled faults can interfere with the test result. For r_{ij}, the unit under test is faulty and the testing unit is good. Unless unmodeled faults are permitted, r_{ij} is the fault coverage provided by t_k^{ij}. If this fault coverage is less than 1, recall that t_k^{ij} is said to be *incomplete*. The fault coverage parameter is usually evaluated and thus readily available. Parameter q_{ij} is the likelihood that t_k^{ij} will fail with the unit under test good and the testing unit faulty. To determine this parameter, an estimate of the portion of faults at a lower hierarchical level that will fail the test is needed unless extensive simulation is done. The parameter s_{ij} deals with the situation in which both units are faulty. This parameter is often close to 1 provided that the fault coverage is high and an incomplete test is regarded as a failed one. A more detailed evaluation of s_{ij} is likely to require extensive simulation of the unit pair.

These parameters can be employed to provide a probabilistic relationship between fault patterns and test patterns. Specifically, a set of probabilities Z can be defined over the set of all possible fault pattern–test pattern combinations:

$$Z = \{\Pr(T^r \mid F^q) \quad \text{such that} \quad (F^q, T^r)$$
$$\text{is in the fault pattern–test pattern event space}\}$$

If the kth component of T^r is denoted t_k^r, then under the assumption that test outcomes are statistically independent,

$$\Pr(T^r \mid F^q) = \prod_{k=1}^{p} \Pr(t_k^{ij} = t_k^r \mid F^q)$$

The evaluation of $\Pr(t_k^{ij} = t_k^r \mid F^q)$ is straightforward since F^q specifies which faulty units are present. Unfortunately, the statistical independence assumption on test results often does not hold. In such a case, this procedure for evaluating Z cannot be applied directly.

By use of the information in the set Z, a procedure for calculating the probability of a correct diagnosis without repair can be given. In a diagnosis without repair (one-step diagnosis) algorithm each test pattern is associated with either a single fault pattern or a special element called NOSDP (non-one-step diagnosable pattern) in the fault pattern space. The set of test patterns associated with fault pattern F^q is called the *diagnostic set of F^q*. The set of test patterns associated with NOSDP is the *nondiagnostic set*. Within this framework, a fault pattern F^q will be correctly diagnosed only if a test pattern which is in its diagnostic set occurs whenever F^q is present. The probability of correct diagnosis of F^q:

$$D(F^q) = \sum_{\substack{\text{over all } T^r \\ \text{in the diagnostic} \\ \text{set of } F^q}} \Pr(T^r \mid F^q)$$

With $\Pr(F^q)$, the probability of the presence of F^q at the time of diagnosis, the probability of correct system diagnosis is

$$D(S) = \sum_{\substack{\text{over all} \\ F^q \text{ in } F}} D(F^q) \Pr(F^q)$$

Because the correct diagnosis of the good system fault pattern F^0 tends to dominate $D(S)$, a normalized measure of diagnosability that excludes the good system diagnosis is useful. The probability of correct system diagnosis given that the system is faulty is

$$ND(S) = \frac{\Sigma D(F^q) \Pr(F^q)}{\Sigma \Pr(F^q)}$$

where $\Pr(F^0)$ is set to zero in both summations.

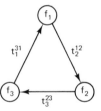

Figure 8.7.1 Digraph for probabilistic diagnosis example.

The use of these measures can be illustrated by the diagnosis of the simple system represented by the digraph in Fig. 8.7.1. Suppose that $\Pr(f_i) = 0.001$ for $i = 1$, 2, and 3, and $p_{ij} = 1$, $r_{ij} = 0.90$, $q_{ij} = 0.15$, and $s_{ij} = 0.85$ for the (i, j) subscript pairs on the tests in Fig. 8.7.1. The test patterns are associated with fault patterns as follows:

TEST PATTERNS			FAULT PATTERNS		
t_1^{31}	t_2^{12}	t_3^{23}	f_1	f_2	f_3
0	0	0	0	0	0
0	0	1	0	0	1
0	1	0	0	1	0
0	1	1	0	1	0
1	0	0	1	0	0
1	0	1	0	0	1
1	1	0	1	0	0
1	1	1	NOSDP		

To illustrate the calculations of $\Pr(T^r \mid F^q)$, $\Pr(001 \mid 001)$ and $\Pr(101 \mid 001)$ are considered with statistically independent test results assumed.

$$\Pr(001 \mid 001) = \Pr(t_1^{31} = 0 \mid (f_3, f_1) = (1, 0))$$
$$\cdot \Pr(t_2^{12} = 0 \mid (f_1, f_2) = (0, 0))$$
$$\cdot \Pr(t_3^{23} = 1 \mid (f_2, f_3) = (0, 1))$$
$$= q_{31} \cdot p_{12} \cdot r_{23} = (0.15)(1)(0.90) = 0.135$$
$$\Pr(101 \mid 001) = \Pr(t_1^{31} = 1 \mid (f_3, f_1) = (1, 0)$$
$$\cdot \Pr(t_2^{12} = 0 \mid (f_1, f_2) = (0, 0))$$
$$\cdot \Pr(t_3^{23} = 1 \mid (f_2, f_3) = (0, 1))$$
$$= (1 - q_{31}) \cdot P_{12} \cdot r_{23} = (0.85)(1)(0.90) = 0.765$$

The probabilities of the remaining test pattern–fault pattern pair can be calculated similarly.

The probability of a good system being present at the time of diagnosis is $(1 - 0.001)^3 = 0.997$ and the probability of a single fault pattern is $(1 - 0.001)^2$ $(0.001) = 0.000998$. These values can be used to calculate $D(S) = 0.99969$ and $ND(S) = 0.90$. It is interesting to note that, for this example, the values of q_{ij}, although used in the calculation, have no effect on the result. This property is exploited in a general approach in [HWAN82] for evaluating $D(S)$ and $ND(S)$ for systems which are t-fault diagnosable with repair and for which limited statistical data are available.

Further work in [BLOU77] includes an algorithm for assigning test patterns to fault patterns in order to maximize $D(S)$. A subsequent paper [BLOU78] includes probabilistic modeling of the decision step of the diagnosis process. An interesting probabilistic model that differs somewhat from those presented here was used in the development of diagnostics for the IBM 3081 processor [BOSS82].

8.8. ADDITIONAL WORK

There are a number of important areas of investigation, particularly relative to the graph models, that have not been treated in detail. Each will be summarized briefly and references will be provided.

A significant effort has been devoted to the development of optimum graph structures for a given level of diagnosability where optimality has been defined in terms of the number of nodes and number of testing links in an SISCN model [PREP67, CIOM79]. The results are restricted to cases in which the SISCN model is valid and in which the flexibility of determining the testing links is not highly constrained by the interconnection structure of the system.

The issue of the occurrence of faults during the testing process is addressed by Kuhl and Reddy [KUHL80b] for the SISCN model. This work is based on the notion that, in large systems, testing is likely to be distributed over time (e.g., as in roving diagnosis). In addition, they have provided means for handling communication link faults in the context of an SISCN model graph [KUHL81].

Two topics related to distributed system diagnosis are the concurrency of diagnosis with processing which has been investigated by Saheban and Friedman [SAHE78, SAHE79] and diagnosis in the presence of known unrepaired faults as considered by McPherson [MCPH81]. Issues of actual application of distributed diagnosis are treated in [CIOM81]

Additional work of interest includes that in [BUTL81] on the use of binary erasures, corresponding to tests for which results are missing; that in [ARMS81] on diagnosis in Boolean n-cube arrays of processors; and that in [PRAD81, PRAD82], which deals with interconnection structures for distributed processors, including an algorithm for distributed diagnosis. A survey paper by Freidman and Simoncimi [FRIE80] provides additional references and discussion.

ACKNOWLEDGMENT

The helpful comments of James E. Smith and John A. McPherson are gratefully acknowledged.

REFERENCES

[ADHA77] Adham, M., and A. Friedman, "Digital System Fault Diagnosis," *J. Des. Autom. Fault-Tolerant Comput.*, vol. 1, no. 2, pp. 115–132, Feb. 1977.

[AGNE65] Agnew, P., D. Rutherford, R. Suhocki, C. Yen, and D. Muller, "An Architectural Study for a Self-Repairing Computer," USAF Space Systems Div., Final Tech. Rep. SSD-TR-64-159, Nov. 1965.

[ARMS81] Armstrong, J., and F. Gray, "Fault Diagnosis in a Boolean n-cube Array of Microprocessors," *IEEE Trans. Comput.*, vol. C-30, no. 8, pp. 587–590, Aug. 1981.

[BARS76] Barsi, F., F. Grandoni, and P. Maestrini, "A Theory of Diagnosability of Digital Systems," *IEEE Trans. Comput.*, vol. C-25, no. 6, pp. 585–593, June 1976.

[BART70] Bartow, N., and R. McGuire, "System/360 Model 85 Microdiagnostics," *1970 Spring Joint Comput. Conf., AFIPS Conf. Proc.*, p. 36, 1970.

[BLOU77] Blount, M., "Probabilistic Treatment of Diagnosis in Digital Systems," *Dig., 7th Annu. Int. Symp. Fault-Tolerant Comput.*, Los Angeles, pp. 72–77, June 28–30, 1977.

[BLOU78] Blount, M., "Modeling of Diagnosis in Fail-Softly Computer Systems," *Dig., 8th Annu. Int. Symp. Fault-Tolerant Comput.*, Toulouse, France, pp. 53–58, June 21–23, 1978.

[BOSS82] Bossen, D., and M. Hsiao, "Model for Transient and Permanent Error-Detection and Fault-Isolation Coverage," *IBM J. Res. Dev.*, vol. 26, no. 1, pp. 67–77, Jan. 1982.

[BRUL60] Brule, J., R. Johnson, and E. Kletsky, "Diagnosis of Equipment Failures," *IRE Trans. Reliab. Quality Control*, vol. RQC-9, no. 4, pp. 23–34, Apr. 1960.

[BUTL81] Butler, J., "Properties of Three-Valued System Diagnosis," *Proc. 11th Int. Symp. Multiple-Valued Logic*, pp. 85–89, 1981.

[CHAN65] Chang, H., "An Algorithm for Selecting an Optimum Set of Diagnostic Tests," *IEEE Trans. Electron. Comput.*, vol. EC-14, no. 10, pp. 706–711, Oct. 1965.

[CHAN67] Chang, H., and W. Thomis, "Methods of Interpreting Diagnostic Data for Locating Faults in Digital Machines," *Bell. Syst. Tech. J.*, vol. 43, no. 2, pp. 289–317, Feb. 1967.

[CHAN70] Chang, H., E. Manning, and G. Metze, *Fault Diagnosis of Digital Systems*, Wiley, New York, 1970.

[CHAN74] Chang, H., and G. Heimbigner, "LAMP: Controllability, Observability, and Maintenance Engineering Technique (COMET)," *Bell Syst. Tech. J.*, vol. 53, no. 8, pp. 1505–1534, Oct. 1974.

[CHWA81] Chwa, K., and S. Hakimi, "On Fault Identification in Diagnosable Systems," *IEEE Trans. Comput.*, vol. C-30, no. 6, pp. 414–422, June 1981.

[CIOM79] Ciompi, P., and L. Simoncini, "Analysis and Optimal Design of Self-Diagnosable Systems with Repair," *IEEE Trans. Comput.*, vol. C-28, no. 5, pp. 362–365, May 1979.

[CIOM81] Ciompi, P., F. Grandoni, and L. Simoncini, "Distributed Diagnosis in Multi-processor System: The Mu Team Approach," *Dig. 11th Annu. Int. Symp. Fault-Tolerant Comput.*, Portland, Me., pp. 25–29, June 24–26, 1981.

[DIET78] Dietmeyer, D., *Logic Design of Digital Systems,* 2nd ed., Allyn and Bacon, Boston, 1978.

[FORB65] Forbes, R., D. Rutherford, C. Stieglitz, and L. Tung, "A Self-Diagnosable Computer," *1965 Fall Joint Comput. Conf., AFIPS Proc.*, vol. 27, pp. 1073–1086.

[FRIE75] Friedman, A., "A New Measure of Digital System Diagnosis," *Dig. 5th Annu. Int. Symp. Fault-Tolerant Comput.*, Paris, pp. 167–170, June 18–20, 1975.

[FRIE80] Friedman, A., and L. Simoncini, "System-Level Fault Diagnosis," *Computer,* vol. 13, no. 3, pp. 47–53, March 1980.

[FUJI78] Fujiwara, H., and K. Kinoshita, "Connection Assignments for Probabilistically Diagnosable Systems," *IEEE Trans. Comput.*, vol. C-27, no. 3, pp. 280–283, Mar. 1978.

[HACK65] Hackl, F., and R. Shirk, "An Integrated Approach to Automated Computer Maintenance," *1965 IEEE Conf. Record Switching Theory Logical Des.*, pp. 289–302, 1965.

[HAKI74] Hakimi, S., and A. Amin, "Characterization of Connection Assignment of Diagnosable Systems," *IEEE Trans. Comput.*, vol. C-23, no. 1, pp. 86–88, Jan. 1974.

[HOLT81a] Holt, C., and J. Smith, "Diagnosis of Systems with Asymmetric Invalidation," *IEEE Trans. Comput.*, vol. C-30, no. 9, pp. 679–690, Sept. 1981.

[HOLT81b] Holt, C., "Diagnosis and Self-Diagnosis of Digital Systems," Ph. D. thesis, Dept. of Electrical and Computer Engineering, University of Wisconsin-Madison, 1981.

[HWAN82] Hwang, I., and C. Kime, "On a Diagnostic Confidence Measure for a Class of Digital Systems," *Proc. 20th Allerton Conf. Commun. Control Comput.*, pp. 241–250, 1982.

[JOHN60] Johnson, R., "An Information Theory Approach to Diagnosis," *Proc. 6th Natl. Symp. Reliab. Quality Control,* pp. 102–107, 1960.

[JOHN71] Johnson, A., "The Microdiagnostics for the IBM System 360 Model 30," *IEEE Trans. Comput.*, vol. C-20, no. 7, pp. 798–803, July 1971.

[KARU79] Karunanithi, S., and A. Friedman, "Analysis of Digital Systems Using a New Measure of System Diagnosis," *IEEE Trans. Comput.*, vol. C-28, no. 2, pp. 121–133, Feb. 1979.

[KAUT68] Kautz, W., "Fault Testing and Diagnosis in Combinational Digital Circuits," *IEEE Trans. Comput.*, vol. C-17, no. 4, pp. 352–366, Apr. 1968.

[KAVI78] Kavianpour, A., and A. Friedman, "Efficient Design of Easily Diagnosable Systems," *Proc. 3rd USA–Japan Comput. Conf.*, pp. 14-1 to 14-17, 1978.

[KIME69] Kime, C., and M. Ellenbecker, "The Generalized Fault Table and Its Use in Diagnostic Test Selection," *Proc. Natl. Electron. Conf.*, vol. 25, pp. 663–667, 1969.

[KIME70] Kime, C. "An Analysis Model for Digital System Diagnosis," *IEEE Trans. Comput.*, vol. C-19, no. 11, pp. 1063–1073, Nov. 1970.

[KIME79] Kime, C., "An Abstract Model for Digital System Fault Diagnosis," *IEEE Trans. Comput.*, vol. C-28, no. 10, pp. 754–766, Oct. 1979.

[KIME80] Kime, C., C. Holt, J. McPherson, and J. Smith, "Fault Diagnosis of Distributed Systems," *Proc. Comput. Softw. Appl. Conf.*, pp. 355–364, 1980.

[KUHL80a] Kuhl, J., and S. Reddy, "Distributed Fault-Tolerance for Large Multi-processor Systems," *Proc. 7th Int. Symp. Comput. Archit.*, pp. 23–30, 1980.

[KUHL80b] Kuhl, J., and S. Reddy, "Some Extensions to the Theory of System Level Fault Diagnosis," *Dig., 10th Annu. Int. Symp. Fault-Tolerant Comput.*, Kyoto, Japan, pp. 291–296, Oct. 1–3, 1980.

[KUHL81] Kuhl, J., and S. Reddy, "Fault-Diagnosis in Fully Distributed Systems," *Dig., 11th Annu. Int. Symp. Fault-Tolerant Comput.*, Portland, Me., pp. 100–105, June 24–26, 1981.

[MAHE76] Maheshwari, S., and S. Hakimi, "On Models for Diagnosable Systems and Probabilistic Fault Diagnosis," *IEEE Trans. Comput.*, vol. C-25, no. 3, pp. 228–236, Mar. 1976.

[MAHE78] Maheshwari, S., and S. Hakimi, "Corrections and Comments on 'On Models for Diagnosable Systems and Probabilistic Fault Diagnosis'," *IEEE Trans. Comput.*, vol. C-27, no. 3, pp. 287–288, Mar. 1978.

[MALL78] Mallela, S., and G. Masson, "Diagnosable Systems for Intermittent Faults," *IEEE Trans. Comput.*, vol. C-27, no. 6, pp. 560–566, June 1978.

[MALL80] Mallela, S., and G. Masson, "Diagnosis without Repair for Hybrid Fault Situations," *IEEE Trans. Comput.*, vol. C-29, no. 6, pp. 461–470, June 1980.

[MCPH79] McPherson, J., and C. Kime, "A Two-Level Diagnostic Model for Digital Systems," *IEEE Trans. Comput.*, vol. C-28, no. 1, pp. 16–27, Jan. 1979.

[MCPH81] McPherson, J., "Fault-Tolerant Process Maintenance," Ph.D. thesis, Dept. of Electrical and Computer Engineering, University of Wisconsin-Madison, 1981.

[MEYE78] Meyer, G., and G. Masson, "An Efficient Fault Diagnosis Algorithm for Symmetric Multiple Processor Architecture," *IEEE Trans. Comput.*, vol. C-27, no. 11, pp. 1059–1063, Nov. 1978.

[NAIR78] Nair, R., "Diagnosis, Self-Diagnosis, and Roving Diagnosis in Distributed Digital Systems," Rep. R-823, Coordinated Sci. Lab., University of Illinois-Urbana, 1978.

[POAG63] Poage, J., "Derivation of Optimal Tests to Detect Faults in Combinational Circuits," *Proc. Symp. Math. Theory Automata*, pp. 483–528, 1963.

[POIS77] Poisel, R., and C. Kime, "A System Interconnection Model for Diagnosability Analysis," *Dig., 7th Annu. Int. Symp. Fault-Tolerant Comput.*, Los Angeles, pp. 59–64, June 28–30, 1977.

[PRAD81] Pradhan, D., and S. Reddy, "A Fault-Tolerant Communication Architecture for Distributed Systems," *Dig., 11th Annu. Int. Symp. Fault-Tolerant Comput.*, Portland, Me., pp. 214–220, June 24–26, 1981.

[PRAD82] Pradhan, D., and S. Reddy, "A Fault-Tolerant Communication Architecture for Distributed Systems," *IEEE Trans. Comput.*, vol. C-31, no. 9, pp. 863–870, Sept. 1982.

[PREP67] Preparata, F., G. Metze, and R. Chien, "On the Connection Assignment Problem of Diagnosable Systems," *IEEE Trans. Comput.*, vol. EC-16, no. 6, pp. 848–854, Dec. 1976.

[PREP68] Preparata, F., "Some Results on Sequentially Diagnosable Systems," *Proc. Hawaii Int. Conf. Syst. Sci.*, pp. 622–626, 1968.

[RAMA67] Ramamoorthy, C., "A Structural Theory of Machine Diagnosis," *1967 Spring Joint Comput. Conf., AFIPS Proc.*, vol. 30, pp. 743–756, 1967.

[RUSS73] Russell, J., "On the Diagnosability of Digital Systems," Ph.D. thesis, Dept. of Electrical and Computer Engineering, University of Wisconsin-Madison, 1973.

[RUSS75a] Russell, J., and C. Kime, "System Fault Diagnosis: Closure and Diagnosability with Repair," *IEEE Trans. Comput.*, vol. C-24, no. 11, pp. 1078–1089, Nov. 1975.

[RUSS75b] Russell, J., and C. Kime, "System Fault Diagnosis: Masking, Exposure, and Diagnosability without Repair," *IEEE Trans. Comput.*, vol. C-24, no. 12, pp. 1155–1161, Dec. 1975.

[SAHE78] Saheban, F., and A. Friedman, "Diagnostic and Computational Reconfiguration in Multiprocessor Systems," *Proc. ACM Annu. Conf.*, pp. 68–78, 1978.

[SAHE79] Saheban, F., L. Simoncini, and A. Friedman, "Concurrent Computation and Diagnosis in Multiprocessor Systems," *Dig., 9th Annu. Int. Symp. Fault-Tolerant Comput.*, Madison, Wis., pp. 149–156, June 20–22, 1979.

[SMIT79] Smith, J., "Universal System Diagnosis Algorithms," *IEEE Trans. Comput.*, vol. C-28, no. 5, pp. 374–378, May 1979.

PROBLEMS

8.1. A combinational network is given.
   (a) Define a stuck-at-1, stuck-at-0 fault set for the network.
   (b) By combining the faults in part (a) into sets, define a set of faults at a gate level in the hierarchy.
   (c) Assuming that the dashed lines are component boundaries, define sets of gate-level faults from part (b) that correspond to component-level faults.

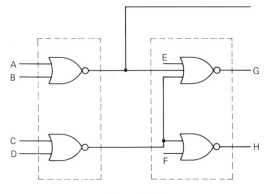

Figure P8.1

8.2. **(a)** Find a small, complete test set for the faults in Problem 8.1(a) assuming only single faults.
   (b) By forming sets of the tests generated in part (a), define a set of component tests for the component-level faults in Problem 8.1(c).

8.3. **(a)** Form a fault table similar to Table 8.2.1 for the fault set in Problem 8.1(a) and the test set in Problem 8.2(a).

(**b**) Form a fault table similar to Table 8.2.1 for the fault set in Problem 8.1(c) and the test set in Problem 8.2(b).

(**c**) Compare the two tables with respect to the capability for locating component level faults. Is there any information lost that is essential to locating faults? Would the use of a larger or different test set cause a reduction in the information lost?

8.4. (**a**) Find a simplified Boolean expression for the fault table in Problem 8.3(a).

(**b**) Find a simplified Boolean expression for the fault table in Problem 8.3(b).

(**c**) Is a digraph representation possible for either of the expressions in part (a) or (b)? If so, construct it.

8.5. A block diagram of a subsystem is shown. The following tests are defined:

t_{11}: a complete test on unit 1 using units 3 and 5

t_{12}: a complete test on unit 1 using units 4 and 5

t_2: a complete test on unit 2 using units 4 and 5

t_3: a complete test on unit 3 using unit 1

t_4: a complete test on unit 4 using units 1, 2, and 5

t_5: a complete test on unit 5 using unit 4

(**a**) Find a Boolean expression for diagnosis assuming single faulty units.

(**b**) Find a digraph for diagnosis assuming single faulty units.

(**c**) Is the system one-fault diagnosable? If not, how could observation test points be added to the system to make it one-fault diagnosable?

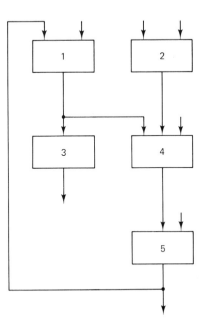

Figure P8.5

8.6. A subsystem block diagram is shown.

(a) Assuming that in order to test a block: (1) all inputs must be controlled and (2) all outputs must be propagated to subsystem outputs, define a minimum size set of tests in terms of the units involved to provide one-fault diagnosability.

(b) Construct a digraph representation for the diagnosis and find the closure $c(S)$.

(c) Indicate how the subsystem could be modified by adding an observation test point to make it four-fault diagnosable with repair and draw the corresponding digraph.

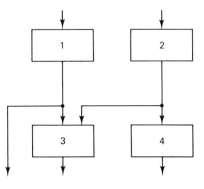

Figure P8.6

8.7. A basic triplicated system with a voter-disagreement detection structure is shown. Assume that the voter disagreement detection hardware is, relatively speaking, reliable enough so that it can be considered diagnostic hardcore.

(a) Assuming that no more than one of the triplicated units is faulty, draw a diagnostic graph for the system. How did you define the tests? What assumptions did you make with regard to applied inputs?

(b) Assuming that the voter-disagreement detection structure is not hardcore and that any number of the triplicated units can fail, write a Boolean expression for the diagnosis of the system. Is it possible to draw a digraph representing this situation? Why or why not?

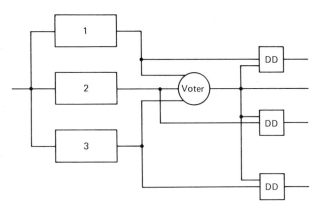

Figure P8.7

8.8. A portion of a self-checking register file is shown in the block diagram below. Each of the checkers in the system is self-checking with a hardcore EXOR to combine the output lines. Assume that the lowest-level fault patterns considered are only those that are detected by the checkers for the respective units (including faults within the checkers themselves). Assume that only one unit in the system is faulty at any given time where a checker is also defined as system unit.

(a) Write an expression in terms of

$$t_1, \ldots, t_5, f_1, \ldots, f_{10}$$

for the portion of the system shown. Carefully state assumptions made.

(b) Determine the resolution R from your expression.

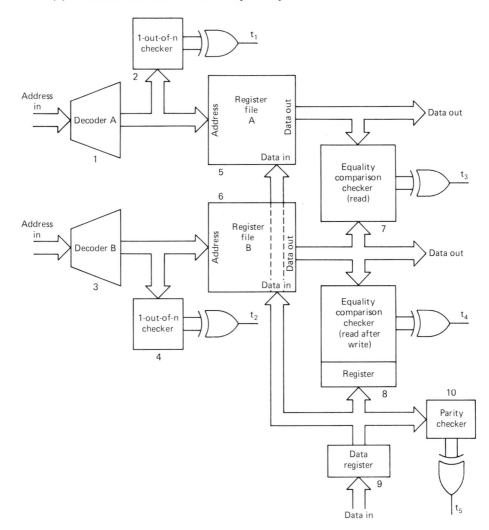

Figure P8.8

8.9. The microdiagnostic tests for a large processor are executed in the following order:

1. Maintenance processor
2. Microinstruction register
3. Processing hardware—part 1
4. Register file
5. Processing hardware—part 2
6. Memory address and data registers
7. Hamming error-detection and error-correction hardware
8. Memory output bus

It is assumed that test i uses the parts tested by tests 1 through $i - 1$.

(**a**) Formulate a graph-theoretic model for the diagnosis process. State assumptions and discuss validity.

(**b**) Evaluate the model to determine diagnosability with repair.

8.10. (**a**) Find the closure for the SC digraph model given and indicate t-diagnosability with repair. Can any tests be deleted without changing the value of t?

(**b**) Repeat part (a) assuming that each edge of the graph represents a *different* test, [i.e., each test is performed by one and only one unit (SISC model)].

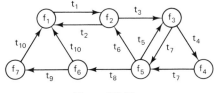

Figure P8.10

8.11. (**a**) Find the t-diagnosability without repair for the digraph given with and without the asymmetric assumption and compare.

(**b**) Could any tests be deleted in either of the cases in part (a) without affecting the diagnosability?

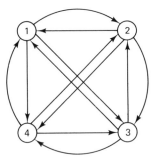

Figure P8.11

8.12. **(a)** For the given SISC digraph determine the t-fault diagnosability without repair and the one-step t/s diagnosability and compare.

(b) What is an approximate value of s?

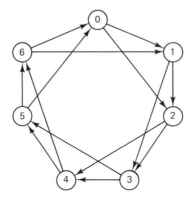

Figure P8.12

8.13. Find a diagnosis tree for the diagnosis in
(a) Problem 8.5.
(b) Problem 8.6(b).

8.14. Find a diagnosis tree for the diagnosis of the system in
(a) Problem 8.8.
(b) Problem 8.9.

8.15. Execute the Meyer and Mason diagnosis algorithm for the digraph given in Problem 8.12 with units 2 and 4 faulty.

8.16 Execute Smith's algorithm 2 for the same digraph and set of faulty units as in Problem 8.15. Assume that all invalid tests fail. Compare the result with that obtained in Problem 8.15.

8.17. An interconnection diagram for a 16-processing-element system is shown on page 632.
(a) For what value of t is it self-diagnosable?
(b) Execute the algorithm SELF in processor 0 with processors 1, 3, 4, and 10 faulty.

8.18. A block diagram for a distributed system is shown on page 632.
(a) Develop a set of realistic testing templates similar to those given for the system in Fig. 8.6.2.
(b) Use the testing templates to define a set of tests and form a fault table for the view of the diagnosis from processor A.
(c) Analyze the fault table to determine how well the system is diagnosed.

8.19. Draw the communication graph for the diagnosis of the system having the block diagram given in Problem 8.18. Make realistic assumptions.

8.20. Evaluate $D(S)$ and $\text{ND}(S)$ for the system having the SISCN model given in Fig. 8.4.6. Assume that unit faults and test results are all statistically independent. Unit failure probabilities are 0.01 and the other parameters are as follows for all (i, j) pairs in the digraph: $p_{ij} = 1$, $r_{ij} = 0.95$, $q_{ij} = 0.50$, $s_{ij} = 0.90$. Note that it will be necessary to define the diagnostic set for each fault pattern.

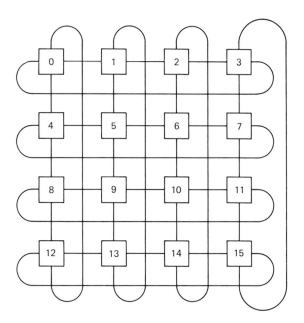

Figure P8.17

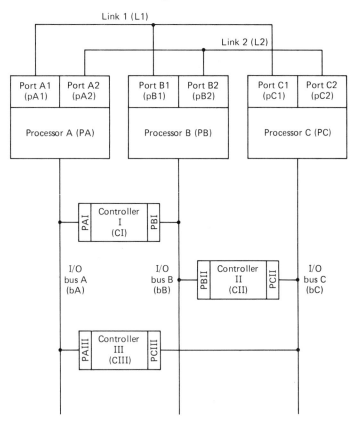

Figure P8.18

Chapter 9

COMPUTER-AIDED RELIABILITY ESTIMATION

J. J. STIFFLER

9.1. INTRODUCTION

Fault-tolerant systems, capable of functioning properly even after sustaining certain component failures, are being used in an increasing variety of applications. Some of these applications are highly critical for safety or economic reasons and place a correspondingly high demand on system reliability. Since the reliability of such systems frequently cannot be determined adequately by conventional testing and simulation methods, various reliability modeling techniques have been developed to help assess the reliability levels actually achieved. Several of these techniques are discussed in the literature [CONN77, LAND78, NG77, BJUR76]. This chapter describes another, more recently developed technique.

CARE III (computer-aided reliability estimation, version three) is a computer program designed to help estimate the reliability of complex, redundant systems. Although the program can model a wide variety of redundant structures, it was developed specifically for fault-tolerant avionics systems—systems distinguished by the need for extremely reliable performance since a system failure could well result in the loss of human life.

It is usually relatively easy to design enough redundancy into a system to reduce to acceptably small levels the probability that it fails due to inadequate resources. The dominant cause of failure in ultrareliable systems thus tends to be due not to the exhaustion of resources but rather to the failure to detect and isolate a malfunctioning element before it has caused the system to take an erroneous action. Such failures are called *coverage* failures [BOUR69]. CARE III differs from its predecessors in, among other things, the attention given to coverage failure mechanisms.

The first CARE program [MATH72] developed at the Jet Propulsion Laboratory provided an aid for estimating the reliability of systems consisting of a combination of any of several standard configurations (e.g., standby-replacement configurations, triple-modular redundant configurations, etc.). CARE II [STIF75] was subsequently developed by Raytheon, under contract to the NASA Langley Research Center. It substantially generalized the class of redundant configurations that could be accommodated, and included a coverage model to determine the various coverage probabilities as a function of the applicable fault recovery mechanisms (detection delay, diagnostic scheduling interval, isolation and recovery delay, etc.).

CARE III further generalizes the class of system structures that can be modeled and greatly expands the coverage model to take into account such effects as intermittent and transient faults, latent faults, and error propagation. To accomplish this, it was necessary to depart from the approaches taken in previous reliability modeling efforts. The nature of, and the reasons for, this departure are explained in the following section.

9.2. BACKGROUND

Reliability models tend to fall into one of two classes: combinatorial or Markov. *Combinatorial models* attempt to categorize the set of operational states (or, conversely, the number of nonoperational states) of a system in terms of the functional states of its components in such a way that the probabilities of each of these states can be determined by combinatorial means. *Markov models* concentrate on the rate at which transitions take place between different system states and then use this information to determine the probabilities that the system is in each of these states at any given time. These two approaches, and the CARE III departure, are best illustrated by an example.

Consider a simple, redundant structure consisting of four identical elements, the (binary) outputs of which are passed through a majority voter. If the outputs of at least three of these units are correct, the voter output is likewise correct. Further, if any one unit is determined to be faulty, its outputs are subsequently ignored by the voter, so that a second failure can also be tolerated without producing an incorrect output. First, assume that the voter is perfect both in its ability to produce an output determined by the majority of its inputs and in its ability to identify and to ignore without further delay the outputs of the first faulty element.

The combinatorial method for assessing the reliability of such a structure is entirely straightforward: the probability that the output is correct is simply the probability that at most two of the four elements have failed. If any single element has a probability $P(t)$ of surviving until time t, the probability $R(t)$ that the voter outputs are still correct at time t is therefore

$$R(t) = \sum_{i=0}^{2} \binom{4}{i} [P(t)]^{4-i} [1 - P(t)]^i$$

$$= 6P^2(t) - 8P^3(t) + 3P^4(t)$$

(9.2.1)

The Markov model of the structure in question is equally straightforward. In general, a structure can be represented by a Markov model if it is possible to characterize it in terms of states (the various states defined, for example, by the number of component failures and other relevant parameters) and transition rates between states, with the proviso that the transition rate $r_{ij}(t)$ between state S_i and state S_j is, for all i and j, a function only of i and j and, possibly, the time t measured from the entry into some known initial state (see Fig. 9.2.1). Thus, if the system is known to be in state S_i at time τ, the probability $S_i(t)$ that it has not left that state by time $t \geq \tau$ is given by the solution to the differential equation

$$-S_i'(t) = \sum_{j} r_{ij}(t) S_i(t) \qquad t \geq \tau$$

with the initial condition $S_i(\tau) = 1$.

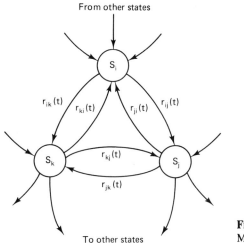

From other states

To other states

Figure 9.2.1 General structure of a Markov model.

If the transition rates $r_{ij}(t)$ are all independent of t, the Markov model is said to be (time) homogeneous. In this case, the differential equation is readily solved, yielding

$$S_i(t) = e^{-\lambda(t-\tau)} \qquad t \geq \tau$$

with $\lambda = \Sigma_j \, r_{ij}$. The holding time in each state, in this case, is exponentially distributed.

Consequently, if in the structure of concern here the probability $P(t)$ that any single element survives until time t is exponentially distributed [$P(t) = e^{-\lambda t}$], and if state S_i refers to the state of the system characterized by i component failures, then the distribution of the holding time in state i is just $e^{-(4-i)\lambda t}$, with 4 the number of initially operational elements and λ the hazard rate of each element. The transition rate $r_{ij}(t)$ is then simply

$$r_{ij}(t) = \frac{P_i'(t)}{P_i(t)} = \begin{cases} (4-i)\lambda & j = i + 1 \\ 0 & j \neq i + 1 \end{cases}$$

and the Markov model is as shown in Fig. 9.2.2. The three states, labeled 0, 1, and 2, correspond to the number of failed elements; the state labeled F denotes the failed state (more than two failed elements).

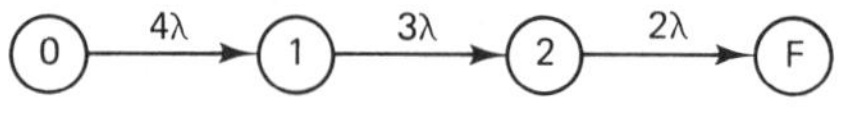

Figure 9.2.2 Markov model of a two-out-of-four structure.

The reliability of the structure is also easy to determine from its Markov model: Let $P_i(t)$ be the probability that the system is in state i at time t. Then

$$P_0'(t) = -4\lambda P_0(t)$$
$$P_1'(t) = 4\lambda P_0(t) - 3\lambda P_1(t)$$
$$P_2'(t) = 3\lambda P_1(t) - 2\lambda P_2(t) \qquad (9.2.2)$$
$$P_F'(t) = 2\lambda P_2(t)$$

This set of linear, first-order differential equations can be solved by conventional methods to yield

$$P_0(t) = e^{-4\lambda t}$$
$$P_1(t) = 4e^{-3\lambda t}(1 - e^{-\lambda t})$$
$$P_2(t) = 6e^{-2\lambda t}(1 - e^{-\lambda t})^2 \qquad (9.2.3)$$
$$P_F(t) = 1 - P_0(t) - P_1(t) - P_2(t)$$

so that

$$R(t) = 1 - P_F(t) = 6e^{-2\lambda t} - 8e^{-3\lambda t} + 3e^{-4\lambda t} \qquad (9.2.4)$$

as before.

The analysis so far has assumed perfect coverage. In particular, it has been assumed that the first faulty element is correctly identified with probability 1. Suppose, instead, that it is correctly identified with probability C; that is, with probability $1 - C$ the outputs of the first failed element are not ignored by the voter. Then with probability $1 - C$, a second failure will cause the voter to accept two erroneous inputs and hence to produce an unreliable output. The system reliability can be determined combinatorially by observing that the system will function properly if at time t it has sustained no more than one element failure or, with probability C, if it has sustained exactly two element failures. Thus

$$R(t) = \sum_{i=0}^{1} \binom{4}{i}[P(t)]^{4-i}[1 - P(t)]^i + \binom{4}{2}C[P(t)]^2[1 - P(t)]^2$$

$$= R^*(t) - 6(1 - C)[P(t)]^2[1 - P(t)]^2 \tag{9.2.5}$$

with $R^*(t)$ the perfect-coverage reliability as given in Eq. (9.2.1).

The Markov model of Fig. 9.2.2 needs only to be modified as shown in Fig. 9.2.3 to account for this imperfect coverage effect. An analysis virtually identical to that of the previous Markov model establishes that

$$P_0(t) = e^{-4\lambda t}$$

$$P_1(t) = 4e^{-3\lambda t}(1 - e^{-\lambda t})$$

$$P_2(t) = 6Ce^{-2\lambda t}(1 - e^{-\lambda t})^2 \tag{9.2.6}$$

$$P_F(t) = 1 - P_0(t) - P_1(t) - P_2(t)$$

so that, again, the combinatorial model and the Markov model yield identical results.

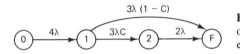

Figure 9.2.3 Markov model of a two-out-of-four structure with imperfect coverage.

The procedures for extending both the combinatorial and the Markov methodologies to more complex structures are generally straightforward. One of the major limitations to both approaches, however, is already evident in the simple example just considered. This limitation stems from the fact that it is rarely satisfactory to treat the coverage probability as a constant parameter. And since, as already observed, coverage failures are typically the dominant source of system failure in highly reliable systems, it is particularly important that coverage be accurately modeled.

Suppose, for example, that in the structure just considered, the reason coverage failures can occur is that a certain amount of time, say τ seconds, is needed to detect that an element has failed and to take the appropriate action to eliminate its output from subsequent voter inputs. Should a second failure occur during that interval, the voter is again presented with two potentially erroneous inputs and its output is consequently unreliable. The probability of a coverage failure, then, is the probability that two element failures occur within a τ-second interval. Unfortunately, this is not a constant probability.

To handle this case combinatorially, observe that the probability that the system has failed by time t is equal to the probability that it has sustained either more than two failures, or exactly two failures within τ seconds of each other. Thus

$$1 - R(t) = \sum_{i=3}^{4} \binom{4}{i}[P(t)]^{4-i}[1 - P(t)]^i$$

$$+ 4 \cdot 3P^2(t) \int_0^t \int_{\eta_1}^{\min[\eta_1+\tau,\, t]} P'(\eta_1)P'(\eta_2)\, d\eta_2\, d\eta_1 \tag{9.2.7}$$

If, as assumed earlier, $P(t) = e^{-\lambda t}$, this expression is easily evaluated, yielding

$$R(t) = \begin{cases} 4P^3(t) - 3P^4(t) & t < \tau \\ R^*(t) - 6P^2(t)[(1 - e^{-\lambda\tau}) - P^2(t)(e^{\lambda\tau} - 1)] & t \geq \tau \end{cases} \qquad (9.2.8)$$

with $R^*(t)$ as defined previously. The actual coverage probability [see Eq. (9.2.5) and (9.2.8)] in this case is

$$C = C(t) = \begin{cases} 0 & t < \tau \\ 1 - \dfrac{(1 - e^{-\lambda\tau}) - P^2(t)(e^{\lambda\tau} - 1)}{[1 - P(t)]^2} & t \geq \tau \end{cases} \qquad (9.2.9)$$

and is indeed a function of time.

The Markov method of modeling redundant structures can also be extended to include more complex coverage situations by using the method of stages [COX68]. The state diagram shown in Fig. 9.2.4a illustrates the principle. This diagram is characterized by the differential equation

$$P'_{A_1}(t) = -(n/\tau)P_{A_1}(t)$$

$$P'_{A_i}(t) = (n/\tau)(P_{A_{i-1}}(t) - P_{A_i}(t)) \qquad 1 < i \leq n$$

These are easily solved to yield, when $P_{A_1}(0) = 1$,

$$P_{A_i}(t) = \frac{(nt/\tau)^{i-1}}{(i - 1)!} e^{-nt/\tau} \qquad 1 \leq i \leq n$$

Thus the expected delay E(t) from entry into state A_1 to exit from state A_n is

$$E(t) = \int_0^\infty \sum_{i=1}^n P_{A_i}(t) \, dt = \tau$$

and the variance of that delay is

$$\text{Var}(t) = 2 \int_0^\infty \sum_{i=1}^n t P_{A_i}(t) \, dt - E^2(t) = \tau^2/n$$

For large n, then, the series of states shown in Fig. 9.2.4a provides a good approximation to a constant τ-second delay. The same series of states embedded in the Markov model of a two-out-of-four structure (Fig. 9.2.4b) represents, approximately, the constant-coverage-delay model under consideration here.

This method of stages can be generalized by introducing other combinations of pseudostates and selecting appropriate interstage transition rates. The advantage of this technique is that it provides an approximate method for handling nonexponentially distributed holding times without abandoning homogeneous Markov models. The disadvantage is that good approximations often entail a substantial increase in the

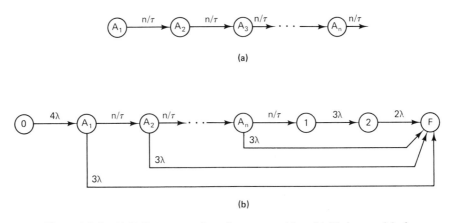

(a)

(b)

Figure 9.2.4   (a) Stall representation of a constant delay; (b) Markov model of a two-out-of-four structure with constant coverage delay.

number of required states, a number that can be enormous for the reliability models of interest here even without the addition of pseudostates.

It is possible to avoid adding pseudostates and still retain some advantages of the Markov method by generalizing the notion of a Markov process. Consider the state diagram shown in Fig. 9.2.5. This diagram is similar to that of Fig. 9.2.4b except that the n pseudostates in the latter diagram have been collapsed into a single state here. The cost of doing this is to introduce a transition rate* $\delta(\eta)/d(\eta)$ which is now a function of the time η from the entry into state A. If η were a measure of the time from entry into the initial state of the model, the model would describe an inhomogeneous Markov process. As it is, however, the process is not even Markov; the probability of a transition from state A to state 1 is a function not only of the two states but of the time spent in state A as well. Such processes are called semi-Markov [FELL64].

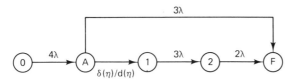

Figure 9.2.5   Semi-Markov model of a two-out-of-four structure with imperfect coverage.

Semi-Markov processes, although less analytically tractable than Markov processes, can nevertheless be represented in terms of linear integral equations and the state-occupation probabilities can often be obtained without undue difficulty. The state-occupation probabilities $P_i(t)$ of the process of Fig. 9.2.5, in particular, satisfy the following set of equations:

---

*The function $\delta(\eta)$ here represents the probability density of a transition from state A to state 1 exactly η time units after a transition into state A, under the condition that no other transitions were possible, and $d(\eta)$ is the probability that no such transition has yet taken place by time η. Thus the rate of such transitions, under the condition just described, is given by the ratio $\delta(\eta)/d(\eta)$.

$$P_0(t) = e^{-4\lambda t}$$

$$P_A(t) = 4\lambda \int_0^t e^{-\lambda(t-\eta)} d(\eta) \, d\eta \, e^{-3\lambda t}$$

$$P_1(t) = 4 \int_0^t (1 - e^{-\lambda(t-\eta)}) \, \delta(\eta) \, d\eta \, e^{-3\lambda t} \qquad (9.2.10)$$

$$P_2(t) = 3\lambda \int_0^t P_1(\eta) e^{-2\lambda(t-\eta)} \, d\eta$$

[The probability $P_A(t)$, for example is just the product of the probability density of a failure at time $t - \eta$, the probability $d(\eta)$ that a transition from state A to state 1 has not taken place in the intervening time η, and the probability $e^{-3\lambda t}$ that no other failure has occurred by time t. Entirely similar arguments can be used to establish the other equations.] In the present example, $\delta(\eta) = \delta_d(\eta - \tau)$ with $\delta_d(t)$ the Dirac delta function and τ the (fixed) coverage delay. Consequently,

$$d(\eta) = 1 - \int_0^\eta \delta(\eta') \, d\eta' = \begin{cases} 1 & \eta < \tau \\ 0 & \eta \geq \tau \end{cases}$$

and

$$P_A(t) = \begin{cases} 4e^{-3\lambda t}(1 - e^{-\lambda t}) & t < \tau \\ 4e^{-3\lambda t}(e^{-\lambda(t-\tau)} - e^{-\lambda t}) & t \geq \tau \end{cases}$$

$$P_1(t) = \begin{cases} 0 & t < \tau \\ 4e^{-3\lambda t}(1 - e^{-\lambda(t-\tau)}) & t \geq \tau \end{cases} \qquad (9.2.11)$$

$$P_2(t) = \begin{cases} 0 & t < \tau \\ 6e^{-\lambda(2t + \tau)} (1 - e^{-\lambda(t-\tau)})^2 & t \geq \tau \end{cases}$$

Since

$$R(t) = P_0(t) + P_A(t) + P_1(t) + P_2(t)$$

this analysis yields results identical to the previous combinatorial analysis of the same example [see Eqs. (9.2.8) and (9.2.11)].

As noted earlier, an overwhelming disadvantage of the Markov method of modeling and analyzing the reliability of redundant structures under the conditions of interest here (with the consequent heavy emphasis on coverage) is the extremely large number of states needed to describe the system. This, of course, is exacerbated if the method of stages is used to approximate nonexponential holding-time distributions, but it remains a decisive limitation even if semi-Markov modeling techniques are used.

To gauge the magnitude of the problem, consider a system consisting of n stages.* If the ith of these stages can sustain as many as m_i faults and still be

---

*In Care III terminology, the term "stage" refers to an ensemble of identical, interchangeable units [i.e., to any of the (presumably, but not necessarily) redundant entities which, in combination, comprise a fault-tolerant system]. This term should not be confused with the "method of stages" described earlier.

operational, and if the number of distinguishable states (e.g., active, benign, detected, etc.)* that can be occupied by a stage i fault is l_i, the number of possible operational system states is

$$N = \prod_{i=1}^{n} \left[\sum_{j=0}^{m_i} \binom{l_i + j - 1}{j} \right] \qquad (9.2.12)$$

This number can be large even for relatively small parameters l_i, m_i, and n. When $n = 4$ and $l_i = 6$, $m_i = 2$ for all i, for example, $N = 614,656$. Since CARE III actually allows n to be as large as 70 and places no restrictions on m_i, it is clear that conventional Markov-like techniques are not appropriate to the problem at hand.

Unfortunately, the combinatorial approach to reliability analysis suffers from a similar computational explosion. A combinatorial analysis, in effect, entails an itemization of the (mutually exclusive) sequences of events that can lead to a failure and then a determination of the probability of each of these event sequences. Thus the emphasis is on the paths connecting the various possible system states rather than on the states themselves. Obviously, however, the number of such paths increases at least as rapidly as the number of states they interconnect, so a purely combinatorial approach to problems of the complexity of those of concern here does not appear to be very attractive either.

9.3. THE CARE III APPROACH

The motivation for the CARE III approach to reliability analysis is evident from an examination of Eq. (9.2.12). It will be noted, in particular, that the magnitude of N in Eq. (9.2.12) is a very rapidly increasing function of the parameters l_i. (If all l_i were equal to 1 rather than the 6 selected in the earlier example, N would be reduced from 614,656 to 81.) The reason these parameters l_i must, in general, be greater than unity is that the coverage associated with a failure depends on the states of other failed elements in the system. That is, the probability that the system recovers from a failure in element A may well depend on whether or not element B has previously failed, whether its failure has been detected, whether an erroneous output has been produced as a result of that failure, and whether element B is in a failed-active state (capable of producing erroneous outputs) or in a failed-benign state (incapable, at least temporarily, of producing further errors).

The key to reducing l_i without decreasing the ability to include all relevant coverage factors in the reliability model is suggested by the previous analysis of the two-out-of-four structure. Figure 9.2.3 shows a Markov model of that structure with the entire effect of coverage reflected in the state-transition rates. While the coverage probability is shown as a constant in Fig. 9.2.3, it was demonstrated that the effect of more complex coverage situations could be handled by allowing this probability to be a suitable defined function of time [see Eq. (9.2.9)].

---

*The probability of recovering from a fault is in general a function of the amount of time it spends in each of several possible states; see Section 9.3.

The CARE III method, then, is to represent the structure of interest by an inhomogeneous Markov model, with the different states distinguished only by the numbers of faults in each of the various stages comprising the system. The state-transition rates are separately determined using a coverage model to account for fault-state effects. Although combinatorial techniques could have been used [as they were, for example, to derive the results of Eq. (9.2.9)], the coverage model found to be most appropriate for CARE III is one based on semi-Markov techniques similar to those used in analyzing the model of Fig. 9.2.5.

The potential advantage of this approach is apparent. The number of states that have to be accounted for in the reliability model is reduced from that given in Eq. (9.2.12) to a number more manageable:

$$N' = \prod_{i=1}^{n} (m_i + 1) \qquad \text{(see Eq. (9.2.12))}$$

The cost of doing this, of course, is (1) to force the reliability model to be inhomogeneous,* and (2) to necessitate a separate analysis to determine the needed coverage parameters. For reliability assessment problems of the complexity of concern here, however, the advantages of this approach, in terms of computational effort, far outweigh its disadvantages. In effect, the model has been reduced from one having $N = n_1 \times n_2 \times \cdots \times n_l$ states to one having $n_1 + n_2 + \cdots n_l$ states, with n_i denoting the number of relevant states given that i faults have already taken place. (The reduction is in fact more dramatic than this since much of the computational effort needed to determine the transition functions given i faults can also be used to determine these functions given $j \neq i$ faults.)

In order to realize the full advantage of this reliability and coverage model separation, however, it is necessary to introduce some approximations having to do with the probability of occurrence of certain joint events. If A and B represent two events and the probability of an event E is denoted $P(E)$, then, as is well known, the probability that either A or B occurs is

$$P(A + B) = P(A) + P(B) - P(A \cdot B)$$

with $P(A \cdot B)$ the probability that A and B both take place. Now suppose that both A and B represent compound events; that is, A is said to have occurred only if the events $A_1, A_2, \ldots A_n$ have all occurred, and similarly for B. Suppose further that at least one of the B events, say B_i, is independent of all events in the set $\{A_1, A_2, \ldots, A_n\}$. Then

$$P(A \cdot B) = P(B \,|\, A)P(A) \leq P(B_i)P(A)$$

and

$$P(A)[1 - P(B_i)] + P(B) \leq P(A + B) \leq P(A) + P(B)$$

---

*This increased flexibility does have ancillary advantages, however: the hazard rates associated with the various system elements are no longer restricted to be time independent. There are situations in which this added degree of freedom is needed to reflect accurately the physical events actually being modeled.

In the present instance, the events of concern are those that lead to system failure. The probability of any one of these events is therefore not greater than the probability $P_f(t)$ of system failure, a probability that is already small, for all t of interest, for the highly reliable systems for which CARE III was designed. Thus, if two events A and B both lead to system failure, if one of these events depends on a subevent B_i not common to the other, and if the probability of this subevent is also of the order of $P_f(t)$ or less, the error introduced by approximating the probability of either event by the sum of their individual probabilities is of the order of $P_f^2(t)$. Since $P_f(t)$ is almost always less than 10^{-4} for cases of interest here and is typically of the order of 10^{-8} or less (if this were not true, reliability models much simpler than CARE III would suffice), the error introduced by such approximations is truly negligible. Moreover, even if this were not true, such approximations overbound the probability of a system failure and hence provide a conservative reliability estimate in any case. Details as to exactly how these approximations are introduced will become apparent in the ensuing discussion.

9.3.1. The Reliability Model

The CARE III reliability model, then, is a generalization of the model shown in Fig. 9.2.3. The system, as represented by the model, passes through a sequence of states defined by the sequence of faults it sustains and by its success in recovering from them. Such a model is not of much value unless it is possible to determine, as a function of time, the probability that the system is in any particular state, given the transition rates between states. The following paragraphs describe how this can be accomplished.

Let $P_{j|i}(t \mid \tau)$ denote the conditional probability that a system is in state j at time t given that it was in state i at time τ. Similarly, let $P_{l|j,i}(t \mid \eta, \tau)$ denote the conditional probability that a system is in state l at time t given that it was in state j at time η and in state i at time τ. Then, clearly, for any $\tau < \eta < t$,

$$P_{l|i}(t \mid \tau) = \sum_j P_{j|i}(\eta \mid \tau) P_{l|j,i}(t \mid \eta, \tau) \tag{9.3.1}$$

with the sum taken over all the (assumed finite number of) possible intermediate states j. [If, for all $\tau < \eta < t$, $P_{l|j,i}(t \mid \eta, \tau) = P_{l|j}(t \mid \eta)$, then Eq. (9.3.1) reduces to the Chapman–Kolmogorov equation for continuous-time, discrete-state systems.]

It follows from Eq. (9.3.1) that

$$P_{l|i}(t + \Delta t \mid \tau) = P_{l|i}(t \mid \tau) P_{l|l,i}(t + \Delta t \mid t, \tau)$$
$$+ \sum_{j \neq l} P_{j|i}(t \mid \tau) P_{l|j,i}(t + \Delta t \mid t, \tau) \tag{9.3.2}$$

Let

$$\lambda_{l|i}(t \mid \tau) = \lim_{\Delta t \to 0} \frac{1 - P_{l|l,i}(t + \Delta t \mid t, \tau)}{\Delta t}$$

and

$$\lambda_{jl|i}(t \mid \tau) = \lim_{\Delta t \to 0} \frac{P_{l|j,i}(t + \Delta t \mid t, \tau)}{\Delta t}$$

Then, rearranging terms in Eq. (9.3.2), dividing by Δt, and taking the limit as $\Delta t \to 0$ yields

$$\frac{\partial P_{l|i}(t \mid \tau)}{\partial t} = -P_{l|i}(t \mid \tau)\lambda_{l|i}(t \mid \tau) + \sum_{j \neq l} P_{j|i}(t \mid \tau)\lambda_{jl|i}(t \mid \tau) \tag{9.3.3}$$

This set of equations is a form of the Kolmogorov forward equations. It differs from the more conventional form in that the transition parameters $\lambda_{jl|i}(t \mid \tau)$ are also functions of the initial state i of the system at time τ. If the notation indicating the condition that the system be in state i at time τ is suppressed, Eq. (9.3.3) can be expressed in the more convenient form

$$\frac{dP_l(t)}{dt} = -P_l(t)\lambda_l(t) + \sum_{j \neq l} P_j(t)\lambda_{jl}(t) \tag{9.3.4}$$

It must be remembered in the ensuing discussion, however, that the transition parameters may also be functions of the initial conditions.

In the CARE III context, it is necessary to distinguish states both in terms of the number of faults that have been sustained in each stage of the system but also, of course, with regard to whether or not the system is still operational. The general structure is shown in Fig. 9.3.1. Here P_l denotes an operational state with l faults and Q_l a failed state with l faults. (Since distinction is made as to where the faults are located, the index l is actually an n-component vector with n the number of system stages.)

The term $\mu_l(t)$ represents the rate of occurrence, in a system which is still operational after l failures, of events that cause the system to fail even though no new faults have taken place.* The terms $\lambda_{jl}^{(1)}(t)$ and $\lambda_{jl}^{(2)}(t)$ represent the rates of occurrence of faults that take the system from operational state j to, respectively, operational state l and failed state l.

If $P_l(t)$ and $Q_l(t)$ are the probabilities of being in states P_l and Q_l, respectively, at time t, Kolmogorov's equations take the form

$$\frac{dP_l(t)}{dt} = -P_l(t)\lambda_l(t) + \sum_{j \neq l} P_j(t)\lambda_{jl}^{(1)}(t) \tag{9.3.5a}$$

$$\frac{dQ_l(t)}{dt} = P_l(t)\mu_l(t) + \sum_{j \neq l} P_j(t)\lambda_{jl}^{(2)}(t) \tag{9.3.5b}$$

with

$$\lambda_l(t) = \mu_l(t) + \sum_{j \neq l} [\lambda_{lj}^{(1)}(t) + \lambda_{lj}^{(2)}(t)]$$

---

*Such events can be caused, for example, by latent faults becoming active and producing erroneous outputs; this will be elaborated upon shortly.

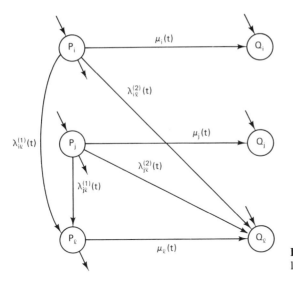

Figure 9.3.1 Segment of CARE III reliability model state diagram.

Since, as has been observed repeatedly in this discussion, the systems of concern here are highly reliable, $\lambda_{jl}^{(1)}(t)$ must in general be much larger than $\lambda_{jl}^{(2)}(t)$ and $\lambda_l(t)$ must be large compared to $\mu_l(t)$. Thus, to a good approximation, Eq. (9.3.6a) can be rewritten in the form

$$\frac{dP_l(t)}{dt} = -P_l(t)\lambda_l^*(t) + \sum_{j \neq l} P_j(t)\lambda_{jl}^*(t) \qquad (9.3.6a)$$

with $\lambda_{jl}^*(t) = \lambda_{jl}^{(1)}(t) + \lambda_{jl}^{(2)}(t)$ and $\lambda_l^*(t) = \sum_{j \neq l} \lambda_{lj}^*(t)$. And, if the solutions to these equations are denoted by $P_l^*(t)$, Eq. (9.3.5b) assumes the approximate form

$$\frac{dQ_l(t)}{dt} = P_l^*(t)\mu_l(t) + \sum_{j \neq l} P_j^*(t)\lambda_{jl}^{(2)}(t) \qquad (9.3.6b)$$

Although the differential equations (9.3.5) could be solved directly, the approximations introduced in replacing $P_l(t)$ by $P_l^*(t)$ are indeed negligible for all cases of interest. It will be observed, in fact, that $P_l^*(t)$ is just the probability that the system would be operating with l failures were the coverage perfect. Thus, replacing $P_l(t)$ in Eq. (9.3.5b) by $P_l^*(t)$ is equivalent to allowing systems that have already suffered from a coverage failure to be counted among those still susceptible to coverage failures. This is, in turn, equivalent to replacing $P(A + B)$ with $P(A) + P(B)$, with A and B both representing highly unlikely coverage failure events. As noted in the introduction to this section, such approximations introduce an error of the order of p^2, with p the, in this case, very small probability of either of these events by itself. The advantage of introducing this approximation is that the probabilities $P_l^*(t)$ can be readily evaluated using straightforward combinatorial techniques, thereby avoiding the need for the more time consuming, and negligibly more accurate, calculation of the probabilities $P_l(t)$ as defined by Eq. (9.3.5a).

9.3.2. The Coverage Model

The purpose of the CARE III coverage model is to determine the transition rates, $\mu_l(t)$ and $\lambda_{jl}^{(2)}(t)$, needed to calculate the failed state probabilities $Q_l(t)$ as defined by the set of equations (9.3.6b). CARE III recognizes three basic causes of coverage failure: (1) An existing latent fault causes the system to take some unacceptable action (an error is propagated); (2) a new fault occurs which, in combination with an existing latent fault, prevents the system from functioning properly; and (3) a pair of existing latent faults for the first time reach a system-disabling state. The transition rates associated with the first and third of these events are collectively represented by the term $\mu_l(t)$ in Eqs. (9.3.6b); the rate of occurrence of the second type of event is represented by the term $\lambda_{jl}^{(2)}(t)$. A fault is said to be latent from the time it first occurs until it is either detected and isolated from the system or, in the case of a transient fault, reaches a benign state. The function of the coverage model is to represent the behavior of each fault during its latency period.

Note that the second and third causes of coverage failure both depend on the existence of a pair of latent faults. It often happens that a fault, while entirely benign itself, can become lethal in combination with some other fault. (A triple-modular redundant configuration consisting of three identical elements feeding a majority voter is an obvious example of this. If any one element malfunctions, its output is ignored by the voter. If a second element fails before the first failure is detected, however, the combination of the two could well produce an erroneous output.) In many reliability analyses, such second-order effects are negligible compared to other causes of failure and consequently are simply ignored. In the highly reliable systems for which CARE III was designed, however, such effects are frequently the dominant cause of system failure.

Obviously, not all pairs of latent faults pose any threat to the system. Two modules, separately protected by independent voters, for example, should create no difficulty even if both are simultaneously in the active, error-producing, state. It is therefore necessary for the user to specify all *critical pairs* of faults, that is, to specify those pairs of modules that could cause the system to fail should the second module malfunction before the first one has been identified as faulty. (This critical-pair specification is easily accomplished using the same input routine used to specify the overall system configuration; see below.)

The coverage model thus actually consists of two coverage models: a single-fault model to trace the various states of a single fault, and a double-fault model to track fault pairs. The single-fault model is shown in Fig. 9.3.2. When a fault first occurs, it is said to be in the active state (state A in Fig. 9.3.2). If the fault is transient or intermittent,* it may jump from the active to the benign state (state B). These transitions take place at a constant rate α; for permanent, nonintermittent faults, of course,

---

*A fault is said to be *transient* if it remains in the active state (and is thus capable of causing the element to malfunction) for some finite time t and then permanently returns to the benign state (in which it can no longer cause the element to malfunction). It is said to be *intermittent* if it randomly oscillates between the active and benign states.

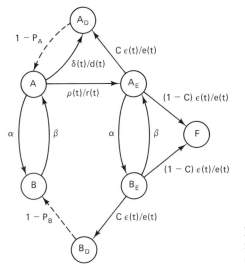

Figure 9.3.2   CARE III single-fault model. t, time from entry into active state; τ, time from entry into error state.

$\alpha = 0$. If the fault is intermittent, the reverse, benign-to-active, transition takes place at some constant rate β; for transient faults, $\alpha \neq 0$ and $\beta = 0$. In the benign state, the fault is incapable of causing any discernible malfunction. Thus it can neither be detected nor can it produce erroneous output. In the active state, however, the fault is both detectable and capable of producing incorrect output. The respective rates $\delta(t)/d(t)$, $\rho(t)/r(t)$ at which these events take place depends on the operating environment and, in particular, on how frequently and how often the faulty element is exercised in a way that causes the defect to manifest itself. Once an erroneous output is produced, the system is said to be in the active-error state (A_E). Again, if the fault is either intermittent or transient, it may jump to the benign state, although now the error is still present so the state is designated the benign-error state (state B_E; the reason for distinguishing between states A_E and B_E will shortly become apparent). When the faulty element is in either of the two error states, the error propagates at some rate $\epsilon(\tau)/e(\tau)$, measured from the time of first entry into state A_E to that instant at which it is either detected (e.g., through a decoder or a voter) or else escapes undetected and results in a system failure (state F). The probabilities of these two alternatives is C and $1 - C$, respectively. If the fault is detected, either through testing or through the detection of an erroneous output, the faulty element enters the active-detected state A_D or benign-detected state B_D, depending on the state of the fault when it was detected. At that time a decision is made as to whether the faulty element is to be retired from the system or whether it can continue to be used. The latter decision might be made, for example, if the fault recovery procedure included a diagnostic routine designed to distinguish between permanent and transient faults. If the fault is detected in the active state, the decision is made with probability P_A that the element must be retired from service; if it is detected in the benign state, the same decision is made with probability P_B. Thus, with probabilities $1 - P_A$ and $1 - P_B$, respectively, the faulty element is returned to service following the detection of the fault. (The dashed lines in Fig. 9.3.2 indicate that the transition takes place immediately with the probability indicated.)

Note that as long as the option is available to diagnose a detected fault as transient, it is possible that this decision is made erroneously. Thus P_B and even P_A may be less than unity even when the fault is, in fact, permanent or intermittent. Similarly, P_B and especially P_A may be greater than zero when the fault is indeed transient. The model assumes that the effect of a decision that the fault is transient is to eliminate the error if an error had already been produced, and to return the faulty element to the error-free active or benign state, depending on its state when the fault was detected. If the fault was transient and detected in the benign state, it either remains in the benign-detected state or returns to the error-free benign state. In either case, since $\beta = 0$, it can never again become active, so it ceases to pose any further threat to the system. If the fault is transient and detected in the active state, or if it is permanent or intermittent and detected in either state, and if it is diagnosed as transient, it remains latent and may have another chance to cause the system to fail.

Even more detailed single-fault models could, of course, be defined. Non-constant active-to-benign and benign-to-active transition rates could be allowed, for example, and distinctions could be made between single and multiple errors. Moreover, such models could easily be incorporated into the CARE III structure. The model selected, however, was felt to be an effective compromise between the desire to allow the user as much flexibility as possible in defining the behavior of a faulty element, and the need to keep the model from becoming so baroque that the user despairs of ever defining all the parameters. At present, the fault detection rate $\delta(t)/d(t)$, the fault generation rate $\rho(t)/r(t)$, and the error propagation rate $\epsilon(t)/e(t)$ are all restricted to assume the form

$$\frac{\phi(t)}{1 - \int_0^t \phi(\eta)d\eta}$$

with

$$\phi(t) = \phi e^{-\phi t} \qquad 0 < t$$

or

$$\phi(t) = \begin{cases} \phi & 0 < t < 1/\phi \\ 0 & \text{otherwise} \end{cases}$$

That is, either the transition rates or the transition density functions are assumed to be constant over some range; the function and, of course, the constant can be independently selected by the user for each of the three transition rates. In addition, the user can define up to five fault types, each with its own set of specifiers $[\alpha, \beta, \delta(t), \rho(t), \epsilon(t), C, P_A, P_B]$, and designate that any or all of these types can afflict each of the system stages, with arbitrary rates of occurrence for each type at each stage.

It might be supposed that the double faults could be modeled by simply combining two single-fault models and then determining if, and when, the two independent fault states form some lethal combination. The problem with this approach is that the two-fault states may independently form a lethal combination repeatedly and the same system failure thereby counted multiply. (Since a second entry into a state is not necessarily a small-probability event given that the first entrance took place, the argument used previously—that the probability of both events is of the order of the square of the probability of either of them—is not applicable here.) It is therefore necessary to introduce a separate double-fault model. The model selected is shown in Fig. 9.3.3. This model is applicable if a second fault occurs when the first fault is in the benign (error-free) state. (If this is not the case, the combination of the two faults is treated as lethal upon the occurrence of the second fault; see below.) Thus the occurrence of the second fault places the fault pair in the $A_2 B_1$ state (first fault benign, second fault active). From there, the fault pair can go to the $B_1 B_2$ state (both faults benign) if the second fault becomes benign before the first fault becomes active, to the detected state D if the active fault is detected and diagnosed as permanent, or to the failed state F if the first fault becomes active with the second fault still also in the active state or if the second fault causes an error to be produced or is diagnosed as transient while still active. Since both faults are benign in the $B_1 B_2$ state, the only possible transitions from that state are back to the $A_2 B_1$ state or to the $A_1 B_2$ state (first fault active, second fault benign) with its entirely analogous transitions.

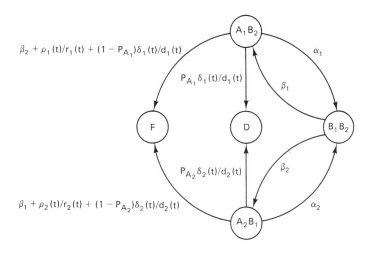

Figure 9.3.3   Double-fault model.

It will be noted that the double-fault model is conservative, relative to the single-fault model, in its definition of a failed state. If both faults are ever simultaneously active, the system fails regardless of whether or not either fault has resulted in an error. Moreover, a system failure results if either fault produces an error even though that error could potentially be detected before it causes any system damage. Obviously, a more elaborate model could have been postulated, one containing additional states to distinguish, among other things, the various possible error conditions. As in the case of the single-fault model, however, a compromise is required between the need to model accurately the important contributors to coverage failures and the desire not to overburden the user with overly fine distinctions. If both faults in a critical pair are active, for example, and one of them produces an error, the probability that that error is detected before it causes system damage is presumably altered, possibly significantly, by the presence of the second fault. Similarly, the coverage parameters may well be affected if both faults produce errors before either error propagates. A more elaborate double-fault model would force the user to examine these issues for every critical-fault pair.

The compromise represented by the double-fault model seems to be a reasonable one for two reasons:

1. The most significant event in determining the probability of a lethal double fault is the existence of the latent first fault at the time of the second. The probability of this event, however, is determined using the single-fault model and hence does not depend on the details of the double-fault model.
2. The conservativism of the double-fault model causes the probability of a double-fault coverage failure to be overbounded.

Thus the double-fault model is consistent with the other CARE III approximations in that it results in a tight overbound on the system unreliability.

The single- and double-fault coverage models are used by the CARE III reliability model as follows. Let $p_f(t - \tau \mid l, t)$ be the probability density of a specific type of element failure at time $t - \tau$, given that l failures have occurred by time t. Then, if $p_{CF}(\tau, f)$ is the probability density of system failures due to the single fault f τ time units after its occurrence, the rate of occurrence of system failures at time t due to this event is just

$$\mu_l^{(1)}(t, f) = \int_0^t p_{CF}(\tau, f) p_f(t - \tau \mid l, t)\, d\tau \qquad (9.3.7)$$

Similarly, if $P_A(\tau, f)$ and $P_B(\tau, f)$ are the probabilities that the fault f is in the active and benign states, respectively, τ time units after its occurrence and if $p_{CF}(\tau, f_1, f_2)$ is the probability density of system failures due to the critical fault pair f_1, f_2 τ time units after the occurrence of the second fault, the rate of system failures at time t due to the first of a critical pair of faults being active when the second takes place is

$$\lambda_{jl}^{(2)}(t, f_1, f_2) = p_{f_2}(t) \int_0^t P_A(\tau, f_1) p_{f_1}(t - \tau \mid l, t)\, d\tau \qquad (9.3.8)$$

with j representing the number of element failures before the fault f_2 and l the number after f_2. (Recall that, in general, j and l are vectors whose components indicate the number of failures in each stage.) The rate of system failures at time t due to a critical fault pair subsequent to the second fault is

$$\mu_l^{(2)}(t, f_1, f_2) = \int_0^t p_{CF}(\tau_2, f_1, f_2)p_{f_2}(t - \tau_2 | l, t)$$

$$\times \int_0^{t-\tau_2} P_B(\tau_1, f_1)p_{f_1}(t - \tau_1 - \tau_2 | l, t) \, d\tau_1 \, d\tau_2 \qquad (9.3.9)$$

The transition rates indicated in Fig. 9.3.1 are thus

$$\mu_l(t) = \sum_{\text{all } f} \mu_l^{(1)}(t, f) + \sum_{\substack{\text{all critical} \\ \text{pairs } f_1, \ f_2}} \mu_l^{(2)}(t, f_1, f_2)$$

$$\lambda_{jl}^{(2)}(t) = \sum_{\substack{\text{all critical} \\ \text{pairs } f_1, \ f_2}} \lambda_{jl}^{(2)}(t, f_1, f_2) \qquad (9.3.10)$$

Note that the function $p_f(t - \tau | l, t)$ is conditioned on the event that the system has suffered exactly l element failures by time t. Actually, the function of interest is subject to the additional condition that the system has also not failed by time t since the transitions of concern are those taking the system from an operating state to a failed state. Without this added condition, the function $p_f(t - \tau | t, l)$ is easily evaluated; with it, it is obviously considerably more difficult. Ignoring this condition, however, is entirely equivalent to replacing $P_l(t)$ with $P_l^*(t)$ as discussed previously and introduces errors of the same order of magnitude. That is, the approximation causes this probability $P_f(t)$ of system failure to be overestimated by an amount of the order of $P_f^2(t)$.

9.3.3. The Integrated Program

As mentioned in an earlier section of this chapter, the system to be modeled is assumed to consist of a number (up to 70) of stages with each stage composed of one or more identical interchangeable elements or modules. The modules in each stage are subject to up to five user-defined categories of faults. A fault is characterized in terms of its rate of occurrence and in terms of its coverage model parameters. Fault occurrence rates are constrained to be of the form $\omega \lambda t^{\omega-1}$ (i.e., fault distributions are constrained to be Weibull) with ω and λ user defined. The user can also specify up to five sets of coverage model parameters $[\alpha, \beta, \rho(t), \epsilon(t), \delta(t), C, P_A, P_B]$; each such set defines a fault type. (For example, it is possible to define a permanent fault type, $\alpha = 0$; a transient type, $\alpha \neq 0$, $\beta = 0$; and an intermittent type, $\alpha \neq 0$, $\beta \neq 0$; each having its own characteristics with regard to detectability, error propagation, etc.) Fault category x_i then refers to a fault that can affect any module in stage x; it is characterized by the parameters λ_{x_i}, ω_{x_i}, and j, with j a fault-type designator.

In addition, the user must specify the number of modules n_x initially available at each stage, the minimum number m_x needed for that stage to function properly, the various combinations of stage failures that constitute a system failure, and the probabilities $b_{xy}(\nu_x, \nu_y)$ that a specific module in stage x forms a critical pair with a specific module in stage y given that ν_x stage-x modules and ν_y stage-y modules are known to have failed and are therefore no longer being used.*

On the basis of this user-supplied information, CARE III then determines the system unreliability using the equation

$$\bar{R}(t) = 1 - R(t) = \sum_{l \in L} Q_l(t) + \sum_{l \in \bar{L}} P_l^*(t) \tag{9.3.11}$$

with L the set of module failure combinations that would leave the system operational in the absence of a coverage failure, $\bar{L}$ the complementary set, $P_l^*(t)$ the probability that the system would be in state l at time t in the absence of a coverage failure, and

$$Q_l(t) = \int_0^t \left[P_l^*(\tau)\mu_l(\tau) + \sum_j P_j^*(\tau)\lambda_{jl}^{(2)}(\tau) \right] d\tau \tag{9.3.12}$$

9.4. AN EXAMPLE

Consider again the four-element, single-stage system described in Section 9.2. As before, the system is assumed to be operational unless either at least three of the four elements have failed or it has experienced a coverage failure. Each of the four elements is subject to faults belonging to a single category characterized by the parameters λ, ω, α, β, $\rho(t)$, $\epsilon(t)$, $\delta(t)$, C, P_A, P_B (see Section 9.3).

This system is an extremely simple example of the class of systems CARE III was designed to model. Nevertheless, it does illustrate some of the features of the CARE III program. Moreover, because it is so simple, it provides a useful vehicle for analyzing the relative effects of the different reliability and coverage parameters.

The reliabilities predicted by CARE III for the system just described are summarized in Table 9.4.1 for various sets of reliability and coverage parameters. In all cases each element is subject to faults at the rate $\lambda = 10^{-5}$ faults per hour, and the reliability is that predicted for time $t = 1$ h. Further, it is assumed that all faults detected while still in the active state are always diagnosed as permanent and that all faults detected in the benign state are always diagnosed as transient ($P_A = 1$, $P_B = 0$).

Thus, if all faults are permanent, then in the absence of a coverage failure, the probability that the system fails to survive until time $t = 1$ h is [See Eq. (9.2.1)]

$$1 - R(t) = 1 - [6e^{-2\lambda t\omega} - 8e^{-3\lambda t\omega} + 3e^{-4\lambda t\omega}] = 4.000 \times 10^{-15}$$

The functions $\delta(t)$, $\rho(t)$, and $\epsilon(t)$ in Table 9.4.1 are all constant-rate functions (see Section 9.3) except for the specifically designated constant-density-function cases; the specified parameter is either the rate or the density, as appropriate.

Several observations can be made concerning the results tabulated in Table 9.4.1:

_____
*These last two tasks are both accomplished with relative ease through a CARE III user interface incorporating a program called FTREE developed by Boeing Aircraft Co. and described in the CARE III User's Manual [BRYA82].

TABLE 9.4.1 SOME CARE III RELIABILITY ESTIMATES

Case	α (sec⁻¹)	β (sec⁻¹)	δ (sec⁻¹)	ρ (sec⁻¹)	ϵ (sec⁻¹)	C	ω	Failure prob. ($\div\ 4 \times 10^{-15}$)
Permanent failures								
1a	0	0	0	1	10	1	1	46.57
1b	0	0	0	10	100	1	1	5.56
1c	0	0	1	10	100	1	1	5.14
1d	0	0	100	10	100	1	1	1.22
1e	0	0	0	1	10	1	1/2	57.75
1f	0	0	0	1	10	1	2	62.05
1g	0	0	1	10	100	$1 - 10^{-9}$	1	14.05
1h	0	0	2	1	10	1	1	16.20
1i	0	0	1[a]	1	10	1	1	17.78
Transient failures								
2a	0.1	0	0	1	10	1	1	0.38
2b	1	0	0	1	10	1	1	0.05
2c	0.1	0	0	10	100	1	1	0.24
2d	1	0	0	10	100	1	1	0.18
2e	10	0	0	10	100	1	1	0.02
Intermittent failures								
3a	1	1	0	1	10	1	1	99.71
3b	1	1	10	1	10	1	1	13.12
3c	1	1	10[a]	1	10	1	1	12.33
3d	1000	1000	0	1	10	1	1	115.69
3e	1000	1000	10	1	10	1	1	9.06
3f	1000	1000	10[a]	1	10	1	1	8.99
3g	1	1000	0	1	10	1	1	46.68
3h	1	1000	10	1	10	1	1	5.15
3i	1	1000	10[a]	1	10	1	1	3.24

[a]Constant-density functions.

653

1. The probability of a system failure can actually decrease as the error generation rate increases (e.g., compare cases 1a and 1b). This is evidently due to the fact that the longer a fault remains hidden, the longer the system is vulnerable to a subsequent fault.

2. The preceding statement holds as well for relatively long-term transients (cases 2a and 2c), but the reverse holds for short-term transients (cases 2b and 2d) since the cost of erroneously identifying a transient failure as permanent offsets the effects of longer latency.

3. Nonconstant hazard rates can exacerbate coverage failure problems by concentrating failure events in time (compare cases 1e and 1f with 1a). (Note that the probability of a noncoverage failure is identical in all three cases.)

4. A nonzero probability $(1 - C)$ that the system fails to recover from a propagated error can be significant, even when this probability is as small as 1 chance in 1 billion (compare cases 1c and 1g).

5. The distributions of the various coverage events can also affect the failure probability. Compare the failure probabilities in cases 1h and 1i. The only difference in the two cases is in the detection distribution $\delta(t)$; even the mean time to detection is the same in the two cases.

6. The failure probability decreases as the detection rate increases, but an improved detection rate is not very valuable when it is small relative to the error generation rate and the coverage of propagated errors is certain (compare cases 1b and 1c).

7. The shorter the transient, the less likely it is to cause a system failure. This is presumably due to two factors: a detected transient fault is less likely to be diagnosed as permanent if it is detected after it reaches the benign state; and, the shorter the time spent in the active state, the less likely the effect of the fault will be present at the time of a subsequent fault.

8. The effect of an intermittent fault depends both on the fraction of time it spends in the active state (compare cases 3b and 3h, for example) and on the rate at which it jumps between the active and benign states (compare cases 3b and 3e).

It is apparent that even in the context of this simple example, both the absolute and the relative magnitudes of the coverage and reliability parameters can significantly affect the system unreliability. Often, the increase in unreliability caused by a change in a single coverage parameter exceeds the total contribution to that unreliability due to all noncoverage failures. Although in this simple example the unreliability is always extremely small, this relationship between the magnitudes of coverage and noncoverage failures is typical of much more complex and, hence, much less reliable systems as well.

9.5. SUMMARY

It is, of course, obvious that the more reliable a system becomes, the more improbable are the events that cause it to fail. Accordingly, reliability models designed to estimate the reliability of such systems must necessarily take into account effects that could be ignored or only roughly approximated in models designed for less reliable structures. These effects are generally referred to as coverage effects, that is, effects that result in system failure due, not to an exhaustion of resources, but rather to faults that, while circumventable, are not detected and isolated before they have caused the system as a whole to malfunction.

CARE III is designed to allow the user to model coverage effects to a detail heretofore impossible. To take full advantage of this capability, the user must attempt to specify more completely just how the effects of a fault make themselves manifest to the system. In order to estimate the distribution of the time from the occurrence of a fault to its detection, in particular, consideration must be given to the frequency and thoroughness with which the faulty module is tested. If the module is tested every τ seconds, for example, and if the probability is unity that the fault is detected if it is present when the test is conducted, the distribution of the time to detection is well modeled as $d(t) = 1 - t/\tau, 0 \leq t \leq \tau$. If, on the other hand, the module is tested at random intervals with a less than certain outcome even if the fault is present, a distribution of the form $d(t) = e^{-\delta t}$ might be more appropriate. Similar considerations are needed to select the other relevant functions and parameters used in the CARE III coverage model.

In many cases, coverage model parameters may be difficult to determine. Even in these cases, it is felt that CARE III can still play a valuable role for two reasons: (1) it forces the user to examine aspects of a system that might otherwise have been ignored; and (2) more importantly, it provides a means for determining the sensitivity of a system's reliability to assumptions made both about the behavior of faults and about the mechanisms provided to recover from them.

ACKNOWLEDGMENT

Research reported in this chapter was sponsored by the NASA Langley Research Center under Contract NAS1-15072.

REFERENCES

[BJUR76] Bjurman, B. E., et al., "Airborne Advanced Reconfigurable Computer System (ARCS)," Final Report, NASA Contract NAS1-13654, Aug. 1976.

[BOUR69] Bouricius, W. G., W. C. Carter, and P. R. Schneider, "Reliability Modeling Techniques for Self-Repairing Computer Systems," *Proc. 24th Natl. Conf. ACM*, 1969.

[BRYA82] Bryant, L. A., and J. J. Stiffler, *CARE III User's Manual*, NASA Contract NAS1-15072, Mar. 1982.

[CONN77] Conn, R., P. Merryman, and K. Whitelaw, "CAST—A Complementary Analytic-Simulative Technique for Modeling Complex, Fault-Tolerant Computing Systems," *Proc. AIAA Comput. Aerosp. Conf.*, Nov. 1977

[COX68] Cox, D. R., and H. D. Miller, *The Theory of Stochastic Processes*, Methuen, London, 1968.

[FELL64] Feller, W., "On Semi-Markov Processes," *Proc. Natl. Acad. Sci.*, vol. 51, 1964.

[LAND78] Landrault, C., and J. C. Laprie, "SURF—A Program for Modeling and Reliability Prediction for Fault-Tolerant Computing Systems," *Informative Technology*, J. Moneta Ed., North-Holland, Amsterdam, 1978.

[MATH72] Mathur, F. P., "Automation of Reliability Evaluation Procedures through CARE—The Computer-Aided Reliability Estimation Program," *AFIPS Conf. Proc.*, vol. 41, 1972.

[NG77] Ng, Y. W., and A. Avizienis, "ARIES—An Automated Reliability Estimation System," *Proc. 1977 Annu. Reliab. Maintainability Symp.*, Jan. 1977.

[STIF75] Stiffler, J. J., "An Engineering Treatise on the CARE II Dual Mode Reliability and Coverage Models," Final Report, NASA Contract L-18084A, 1975.

[STIF80] Stiffler, J. J. "Robust Detection of Intermittent Faults," *Dig., 10th Annu. Int. Symp. Fault-Tolerant Comput.*, Kyoto, Japan, Oct. 1–3, 1980.

[TRIV82] Trivedi, K. S., *Probability and Statistics with Reliability, Queuing, and Computer Science Applications*, Prentice-Hall, Englewood Cliffs, N.J., 1982.

PROBLEMS

9.1. [TRIV82]

(a) Consider a structure consisting of two identical elements, each having a constant failure rate λ. Their outputs are compared; a miscompare invokes a self-diagnostic routine which, with probability C, correctly identifies the faulty element. The diagnostic routine requires τ seconds of running time, with τ an exponentially distributed random variable with mean $1/\delta$. Thus, if $\delta < < \lambda$ and if the structure is considered operational as long as at least one element is operational and has not been misdiagnosed as faulty, the structure can be modeled as a four-state Markov chain, as shown in Fig. P9.1(a). Find the structure's reliability $R(t)$ using both the differential equation and the combinatorial techniques discussed in Section 9.2.

(b) Show that this same structure can be modeled as a three-state semi-Markov process of the form shown in Fig. P9.1(b). Find expressions for $\lambda_1(t)$ and $\lambda_2(t)$. (*Note:* Since t here is a measure of the elapsed time since entry into the initial state, all transition parameters in this case are functions only of the structure's age; such restricted semi-Markov processes are called nonhomogeneous Markov processes.)

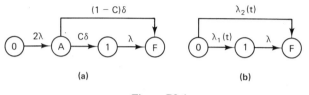

(a)   (b)

Figure P9.1

9.2. Consider a two-out-of-four structure designed to operate as follows. If at most one element has been identified as faulty, the structure's outputs are obtained by passing all remaining element outputs through a majority voter (assumed to be fault-free). If two elements have been identified as faulty, one of the two remaining elements is discarded and the outputs obtained directly from the other. Since a majority voter cannot produce reliable outputs unless more than half its inputs are correct, and since an element's outputs are not ignored until it is found to be defective, show that this structure can be modeled by adding one more state to the semi-Markov model shown in Fig. 9.2.5. Use the technique described in Section 9.2 to derive the structure's reliability when the time between the failure of an element and the detection of that event is a constant τ seconds. Show that this structure is more reliable than the one modeled by Fig. 9.2.5 by the amount $2e^{-\lambda t}(e^{-\lambda \tau} - e^{-\lambda(t-\tau)})^3$ with λ the element failure rate, for all times $t > 2\tau$.

9.3. [STIF80] Consider a generalized version of the single-fault model shown in Fig. 9.3.2 in which the transition rates α and β are allowed to assume the more general forms $\alpha(t)/a(t)$ and $\beta(t)/b(t)$. Assume that $P_A = P_B = 1$ and show that the probability that a fault leads to a system failure is maximized for

$$a(t) = \begin{cases} 1 & t < \tau \\ 0 & t \geq \tau \end{cases}$$

for some τ which depends only on the fault detection rate $\delta(t)/d(t)$. (It is useful to note that, when $P_A = P_B = 1$, the states A_E and B_E in the model of Fig. 9.3.2 can be combined, as can the states A_D and B_D.)

9.4. Consider the double-fault model of Fig. 9.3.3 when the transition rates are all independent of time and of the subscripts $(1, 2)$ and when $P_{A_1} = P_{A_2} = P$.

   (a) Show that, in accordance with this model, the probability of a failure due to a double fault t seconds after the occurrence of the second fault, given that the first fault was initially benign and that $\beta \neq 0$, can be expressed in the form

$$P_F(t) = \frac{\beta + \rho + (1 - P)\delta}{\beta + \rho + \delta} \left[1 - ae^{-\lambda_a t} - be^{-\lambda_b t} \right]$$

   Find a, b, λ_a, and λ_b. (*Hint:* Under the conditions specified, states $A_1 B_2$ and $A_2 B_1$ can be collapsed into a single state.)

   (b) Show that the conditional probability of an eventual failure due to the double fault under consideration is a function of α if and only if $\beta = 0$ (i.e., if and only if the two faults are transient).

Chapter 10

FAULT-TOLERANT SOFTWARE

Herbert Hecht and Myron Hecht

10.1. MOTIVATION FOR FAULT TOLERANCE IN SOFTWARE

Because software does not degrade physically as a function of time or environmental stresses it was long assumed that concepts such as reliability or failure rate were not applicable to computer programs. It is true that a program that has once performed a given task as specified will contine to do so provided that none of the following change: the input, the computing environment, or user requirements. However, because it is not reasonable to expect a program to be constantly operating on the same input data, and because changes in the computing environment and user requirements must be accommodated in most applications, past and current failure-free operation cannot be taken as a dependable indication that there will be no failures in the future. Failure rates and error densities of existing programs are discussed in the following paragraphs. Later topics in this chapter deal with the consequences of failure and with current approaches to increased software reliability.

10.1.1. Failure Experience of Current Software

Every computer professional has experienced software failures, and even the general public is coming to understand that when "the computer is down" it is not always due to a hardware failure. The initial reaction is that the latest software failure is caused by stupidity or worse on the part of a particular programmer, and that it is the "natural" state for software to be perfect and to operate without failure. Unfortunately, there are hard data to indicate that this is not the case, and that existing software products exhibit a fairly constant failure frequency. The key to this finding is that the number of failures must be correlated with the *execution time* that the program has experienced over a given calendar interval. The theoretical basis for using execution time as the denominator for software reliability measurements has been established by John D. Musa [MUSA79].

From a practical point of view, execution-time-based measurements are suitable for assessing software reliability because they (1) show consistency in time for a given program, and (2) show consistency among different programs that are of approximately the same magnitude and at the same life-cycle phase. Consistency in time is illustrated in Fig. 10.1.1, which shows the failure rate obtained by the present author on a FORTRAN program of approximately 20,000 statements while it was being developed [HECH77]. There were sizable variations during the initial development period when the program underwent major changes but starting with the eighth month, when it entered the test phase, the failure rate stayed very close to the trend line. Consistency among programs is indicated by the data of Table 10.1.1, abstracted from a data base compiled by Musa [DACS80].

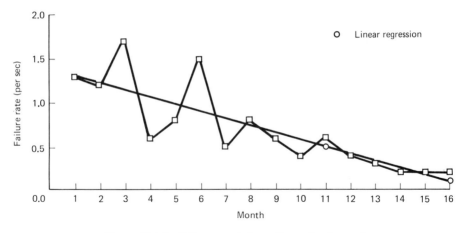

Figure 10.1.1   Failure rate during software development.

TABLE 10.1.1   SUMMARY OF PROGRAM FAILURE RATE DATA

Number of Programs	Life-cycle phase	Size (kilowords)	Range of failures/hour
4	Test	60–2500	0.02–0.2
6	Operation	100–>200	0.01–0.04

Another indication that software faults will always be with us is found in the fault density (the number of faults per 1000 lines of code), which ranges from 10 to 50 for "good" software and from 1 to 5 after intensive test using automated tools [MILL81].

A further reminder of the pervasiveness of faulty software is the well-known fact that operating systems, compilers, and other proprietary programs from reputable vendors are frequently delivered with a listing of "known bugs."

10.1.2. Consequences of Software Failure

Most readers will have personal experience with incorrect billing, lost airline or hotel reservations, and similar mishaps attributed to faulty programs. Most of these will on closer examination be found to be due to a data entry error, but the software cannot be completely exonerated. To cope with the propensity of data entry personnel for making such errors, checking routines or other protection mechanism should have been provided. In these cases the consequences of lack of software reliability are inconvenience to a third party and possibly some loss of business or goodwill to the software user.

More serious errors are occasionally reported in the general press, such as six- or seven-digit government checks being sent to welfare recipients or payroll programs that add the deductions in computing net pay. A report by the General Accounting Office states that overpayments due to computer errors to Navy personnel being discharged amount to $4.2 million per year, and that only 23% of these are ever recovered. When this figure is multiplied by the number of government and private-sector organizations that may be using similar programs, it is seen that very sizable losses due to faulty software arise in just one application.

The most serious consequences of faulty software occur in real-time control systems, where either human life can be endangered or large economic losses can be incurred due to a failure. In spite of the employment of the best available software development techniques and the participation of highly motivated personnel in space-craft control applications, there have been spectacular failures due to software errors, including the launch failure of *Mariner 1* in 1962, the destruction of a French mete-orological satellite in 1968, several problems during the *Apollo* missions in the early 1970s, and a number of malfunctions in the Space Shuttle in 1982. While techniques are being perfected to cope with known sources of errors in these programs, the growth of software complexity continues with a resultant increase in its vulnerability to errors.

Of particular concern in terms of consequences of software failures are applica-tions in the control of passenger aircraft (either on-board flight control or the air traffic control on the ground), in safety systems of nuclear power plants, and in the launch control of strategic missiles. The fault tolerance techniques described in this chapter have been developed primarily for use in critical real-time control applications.

10.1.3. Difficulties in Test and Verification

Although improvements in software development technology can undoubtedly reduce the incidence of software faults, the final line of defense rests on test and verification. The latter term is used here in the sense of a formal verification technique for computer programs, sometimes referred to as *proof of correctness* [ELSP73, ROBI77,

GERH80]. Formal verification has been applied on an experimental basis and usually to small programs. Earlier results have been less than convincing [GERH76], but outright errors in the verification procedures have probably been largely overcome in current verification systems. Still, proof of correctness ultimately rests on mathematical induction and is therefore subject to the shortcomings of that process [DIJK72, REYN76]. Other major limitations are the expense in handling large programs, difficulties in verifying adherence to timing constraints (important for real-time programs), and uncertainty about how well requirements stated in a natural language can be translated into a formal specification that is suitable as the starting point for verification.

The latter problem, the potential for faulty translation of user requirements into the document which forms the basis for fault avoidance or fault tolerance efforts, is common to most of the techniques discussed in this chapter. It is a particularly critical issue with regard to formal verification because the specifications written for this purpose are usually constrained to a rigid syntax and terminology.

Conventional testing is a hit-or-miss activity, consisting largely of functional and performance requirements verification. However, conventional testing generally does *not* include robustness tests (input data outside specifications), limit tests (input data at boundary regions), or tests of all branches and loops. Conventional testing will find some errors, but it is true that "program testing can be used to show the presence of bugs, but never to show their absence" [DIJK72]. Complete testing of any practical programs is impossible because of the vast number of possible input combinations [GOOD80]. Considerable research and development effort has therefore been expended to define equivalence classes of inputs, that is, data sets which will be handled in an exactly equivalent manner by the program such that running a single test case for that set will demonstrate the action of the program for the entire set. The techniques that have been proposed include [HOWD78]:

> *Path testing:* each possible path from input to output is traversed once.
> *Branch testing:* each exit from each node is traversed at least once.
> *Functional testing:* each functional decomposition is tested at least once.
> *Special values testing:* testing for all values assumed to cause problems.
> *Anomaly analysis:* testing for program constructs that can cause problems.
> *Interface analysis:* testing for problems at interfaces of modules.

These techniques are evaluated in [HOWD78] on six practical programs that contained 28 known errors. Pertinent results of that experiment are shown in Table 10.1.2. There was at least one error that could not be found by any technique or combinations of these techniques. These results are fairly consistent with the statement that very extensive testing may reduce fault density by a factor of 10 that was implicit in the analysis from [MILL81] related in Section 10.1.2.

Symbolic execution is a technique that combines elements of formal verification with those of methodical testing [KING75]. By executing a test case with symbolic

TABLE 10.1.2 EFFECTIVENESS OF
TEST STRATEGIES

	Faults found	
Strategy	Total	Percent
Path testing	18	64
Branch testing	6	21
Functional testing	12	43
Special values testing	17	61
Anomaly analysis	4	14
Interface analysis	2	7

rather than actual values, it is assumed that the test results will then be valid for all values of the symbolic variables. Various forms of symbolic execution are also evaluated in [HOWD78] and are found to discover 14 to 17 of the 28 faults (50 to 61%).

It is thus concluded that neither formal verification techniques nor extensive testing can at this time be depended on to provide the degree of reliability that is required for software in critical applications, particularly in real-time control systems.

10.2. DEALING WITH FAULTY PROGRAMS

It was shown in the preceding discussion that any practical program can be presumed to contain faults, and that designers must deal with these faults if a program failure has serious consequences. In this section we describe and classify techniques by which the overall system can be protected from the effects of faulty programs under three headings: robustness, fault containment, and fault tolerance.

10.2.1. Robustness

Robustness has been defined as "the extent to which software can continue to operate correctly despite the introduction of invalid inputs" [IEEE82]. This implies, for example, that the program will properly handle inputs out of range, or in a different type or format than defined, without degrading its performance of functions not dependent on the nonstandard input. As the examples suggest, robustness techniques frequently are used in checking input data. When these are found not to comply with the program specification, a new input may be requested (particularly where this can be supplied by a human operator), the last acceptable value of a variable can continue to be used, or a predefined default value can be assigned. In all cases a flag is usually raised to notify operators of an exceptional program state and to facilitate the handling of the exception condition by other program elements.

Most of the techniques described as *self-checking* software are covered by the definition of robustness above. Self-checking [YAU75] features can include testing of:

The function of a process (e.g., by checks on the output)

The control sequence (e.g., by setting an upper limit on loop iterations)

Input data (e.g., by use of error-detecting code and type checks)

A distinctive feature of the robustness technique is that it provides protection against predefined causes of software problems. In this respect it can be regarded as an implementation of anomaly analysis and interface analysis (see Section 10.1.3) within the program itself. An advantage of this specificity is that errors are usually detected early, before they can contaminate related programs or data sets. On the other hand, robustness cannot usually be depended on to provide complete protection against faulty software because of the possibility of faults for which no checks have been incorporated.

10.2.2. Fault Containment

Fault containment is the methodology that prevents incorrect output due to faults in a given module from affecting other parts of the program. The error-detection capability required for fault containment is therefore more comprehensive than that specified for robustness where only *some* classes of errors need to be detected. Fault containment does not necessarily ensure that the program will continue to run after an error has been detected. Error-detection techniques utilized most frequently are reasonableness tests on the output, watchdog timers, and hardware alarms (overflow, divide by zero, etc.). The typical protective action taken in a program incorporating fault containment is a rollback to the beginning of the affected module, beginning of the program, or initialization of the entire software system.

Where the failure is triggered by a temporary and unusual data value or computer control state, the program can be expected to resume normal operation after rollback or restart. However, if the state that caused the program to enter a faulty execution sequence persists, the restoration of service will not be immediate or automatic. As the name implies, fault containment is aimed primarily at preventing a fault in one section of code from contaminating data values or affecting the execution of other programs. Examples of fault containment can be found in the operating systems of computers that emphasize highly reliable service. The "closed environment" concept incorporated in an advanced microcomputer operating system is an instance of fault containment [DENN76].

10.2.3. Fault Tolerance

Fault tolerance is a programming methodology which provides for (1) explicit or implicit error detection for all fault conditions, and (2) backup routines for continued service to critical functions in case errors arise during operation of the primary software. Fault tolerance provides for uninterrupted operation in the presence of program faults *through multiple implementations of a given functional process.* Although less specific uses of the term "fault tolerance" that include robustness and fault containment sometimes occur, the narrower definition has been used since 1972 [ELME72]. Unlike robustness, fault tolerance (as defined here) provides broad fault coverage to cope with all possible software failure modes in a given program segment. The distinction between fault containment and fault tolerance lies in the absence of backup routines in the former.

Experimental fault-tolerant routines have been documented by Randell [RAND75], Avizienis [AVIZ77], and the authors of this chapter [HECH81]. Design techniques for fault-tolerant software have been described by many others, including [HORN74], [KOPE74], [KIM76], and [TAYL80]. A further classification of software fault tolerance is provided in the following section, and specific design issues are discussed in later parts of this chapter.

10.3. DESIGN OF FAULT-TOLERANT SOFTWARE

Fault-tolerant software design techniques can be classified as either (1) N-version programming or (2) recovery block. These schemes correspond to the major hardware fault-tolerance methods of (1) fault masking (voting) and (2) dynamic redundancy. Major features of N-version programming and recovery block are discussed in the next two subsections.

10.3.1. N-Version Programming

N-version programming is defined as "the independent generation of $N \geq 2$ functionally equivalent programs, called 'versions,' from the same initial specification." "Independent generation of programs" here means that the programming efforts are carried out by N individuals or groups that do not interact with respect to the programming process. Wherever possible, different algorithms and programming languages or translators are used in each effort" [CHEN78].

When $N = 2$, N-version programming can be expected to provide good coverage for error detection but may be found wanting in assuring continued operation of the software. Upon disagreement among the versions, three alternatives are available: (1) retry or restart (in which case fault containment rather than fault tolerance is provided, (2) transition to a predefined "safe state," possibly followed by later retries, or (3) reliance on one of the versions, either designated in advance as more reliable or selected by a diagnostic program (in the latter case the technique takes on some of the aspects of dynamic redundancy). The second alternative may be acceptable for some process control or transportation applications where an infrequently occurring "halt" can be tolerated. However, for the broad class of critical applications none of these options is desirable; hence more than two independent versions must be provided.

For $N \geq 3$ a majority voting logic can be implemented. The results reported by [CHEN78] apply to $N = 3$, presumably the preferred scheme also for future applications. Further discussion is therefore primarily directed at three-version programming, which requires:

1. Three independent programs, each furnishing identical output formats
2. An acceptance program that evaluates the output of requirement 1
3. A driver (or executive segment) that invokes requirements 1 and 2 and furnishes the results to other programs

An important design decision is the frequency with which comparisons are to be carried out (the scope of the fault tolerance provisions). Fault tolerance of large scope (infrequent comparisons) minimizes the performance penalties caused by the fault tolerance procedures and permits a large measure of independence in the program design. On the other hand, it must accommodate a wide divergence of numerical variables because of the large number of independent program steps and may require long wait states for synchronization of results. Fault tolerance of small scope requires commonality of program structures at a detailed level and thus reduces the degree of independence of the individual versions. Also, the overhead required for frequent comparisons may interfere with the throughput objectives. For most applications it will be desirable to aim for the largest scope possible without violating desired tolerances on comparison of variables or incurring excessive wait times.

An evaluation of the fault tolerance capabilities of three-version programming contained in [CHEN78] is synopsized in Table 10.3.1. These results were obtained on the RATE program, a partial differential equation algorithm for estimating temperatures over a two-dimensional region. Each individual version of the program consisted of over 600 PL/I statements, and seven separate versions were available. From these, 12 three-version sets were constructed, and each set was subjected to 32 test cases, yielding the 384 total tests indicated in the table.

TABLE 10.3.1 EXPERIMENT IN THREE-VERSION PROGRAMMING

Number of faulty versions in the set	Number of tests	Correct executions of the set		Incorrect executions of the set	
		Number	Percent[a]	Number	Percent[a]
0	290	290	76	0	0
1	71	59	15	12	3
2	18	0	0	18	5
3	5	0	0	5	1
	384	349	91	35	9

[a]Percentage of the total 384 cases.

Four of the individual versions were programmed by students as part of a graduate seminar assignment while the other three were coded by more senior personnel. Although programming for critical applications in an industrial environment will produce individual versions with fewer faults and more favorable results, the data in

Table 10.3.1 indicate that the technique will need additional development before it can be considered for operational programs. However, it must be noted that comparable data have not been published for other fault tolerance techniques.

Two issues of concern arise from these results: errors of omission and timing of the vote. The authors of [CHEN78] observe in another paper [AVIZ77] that in N-version programming, incidents of omission (e.g., lack of programming to handle exceptional data states) are more likely to be correlated among independently programmed versions than are incidents of commission (i.e., faulty program statements). The second issue of concern is the proportion of test sets that contain one faulty version and two good versions which executed incorrectly at the system level.

The reference notes that in most cases where a single faulty version resulted in incorrect execution, the standard operating system of the computer intervened before the program reached the voting stage. Provision of a watchdog timer that forces a vote after a certain interval would have increased the success ratio for these cases. Although it is conceptually difficult to provide watchdog timers for asynchronous processes, they can be implemented in real-time control applications, the primary candidates for fault-tolerant software. In this application, a "frame" of computational tasks to be repeated within a fixed interval is specified. During each frame, at least one vote must be completed. Thus, setting a watchdog timer at the beginning of the frame for its expected time duration (plus a tolerance) can be used to force the vote.

Because N-version programming will in most cases cause each of the participating computers to be in a different state sequence during the execution of a program it is not easily used in systems that depend on synchronized comparisons for hardware fault tolerance such as the FTMP [HOPK78]. This difficulty does not arise in loosely synchronized fault-tolerant computers such as SIFT [WENS78]; however, it may be necessary to invoke additional diagnostics to establish whether a miscompare is due to a hardware or a software fault in that design. In fault-tolerant computers that employ dynamic redundancy (e.g., FTSC [STIF76]) or in simplex computers, the individual versions will have to be run consecutively with consequent performance penalties. The software design effort required to generate truly independent versions and the hardware resources required to overcome the inherent performance penalties associated with this approach need to be investigated further. Finally, N-version programming does not overcome failure due to a common design specification that results in common failures. However, this shortcoming is shared, at least in principle, by all fault tolerance and fault avoidance techniques.

10.3.2. Recovery Block

The recovery block structure was originated by a group of researchers at the University of Newcastle-upon-Tyne [RAND75] and represents the dynamic redundancy approach to software fault tolerance. It consists of three software elements: (1) a *primary routine,* which executes critical software functions; (2) an *acceptance test,* which tests the output of the primary routine after each execution; and (3) an *alternate routine,* which performs the same function as the primary routine (but may be less capable or slower), and is invoked by the acceptance test upon detection of a failure.

The simplest structure of the recovery block is:

Ensure T

By P

Else by Q

Else Error

where T is the acceptance test condition that is expected to be met by successful execution of either the primary routine P or the alternate routine Q. The structure is easily expanded to accommodate several alternates $Q1, Q2, \ldots, Qn$.

The significant differences from N-version programming are that (1) only a single implementation of the program is run at a time (in the case above either P or Q), and (2) the acceptability of the results is decided by a test rather than by comparison with functionally equivalent alternate versions. In essence there is a comparison involved here also, because the result of either P or Q must compare with the result model contained in T. A more subtle difference between the recovery block and N-version programming is that P and T (and frequently also P and Q) are deliberately designed to be as uncorrelated (orthogonal) as possible, whereas the independence of the N versions depends on the more random differences in programming style among programmers.

Real-time control applications require that the results furnished by a program be both correct and timely. For this reason the recovery block for a real-time program should incorporate a watchdog timer which initiates execution by Q if P does not produce an acceptable result within the allocated time [HECH76]. A flow diagram of the resulting software structure is shown in Fig. 10.3.1. Program flow under direction of the application module is shown in solid lines; timer-triggered interrupts are shown in dashed lines.

The system executive in this example has a status module, a primary routine failure flag A, and an alternate routine execution counter. Prior to entering the recovery block, the status module checks flag A. If A has not been set (i.e., the primary routine has not failed), the status module formats a call to the primary routine and the recovery block proceeds normally. On entering this block, the executive formats calls to both P and Q and sets the timer for the expected maximum run time of P. Control passes to the primary call and process P is executed. After P is complete, the acceptance test is run, and if the results are acceptable and on time, control returns to the executive. The timer is reset (loaded with an appropriate interval for the next operation) and another recovery block is called (or the previous one is repeated with new data).

If the acceptance test rejects the results of P, or if the results are not furnished within the allocated time, a transfer is made to the alternate call. The flag A is set, the timer is reset for the expected maximum duration of Q, and process Q is executed. At

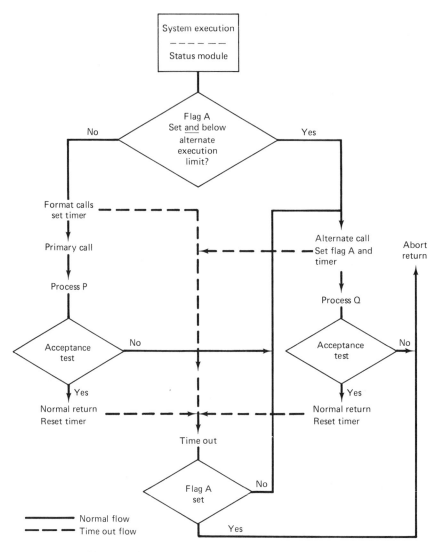

Figure 10.3.1   Recovery block for real-time applications.

the (timely) conclusion of Q, the acceptance test is once again run, and if passed, a normal return to the executive occurs and the timer is reset as described above.

When the flag A has been set, a different entry to the recovery block occurs. The status module of the system executive examines the alternate routine execution counter. If this counter is below an execution limit (which may be either a system-wide fixed value or routine specific), the status module increments the counter and formats a call to the alternate routine. If, however, the alternate execution limit has been exceeded, the status module resets flag A, resets the alternate execution counter, and formats a call to the primary routine. The advantages of this reversion scheme are discussed in Section 10.4.2.

An essential feature of the recovery block structure is that the primary and alternate processes furnish results which can be treated interchangeably by other software elements. The fact that an alternate process was executed may be made known to the executive (e.g., from the state of flag A) but should be transparent to other application programs. If this transparency is not achieved, the execution of subsequent recovery blocks will be affected by the path taken within a prior recovery block. This results in a complex control structure which is difficult to validate and should be avoided for critical applications.

If the acceptance test rejects the results of Q, an abort condition exists and the program exits differently. The abort exit will also be taken if the timer runs out before a result is furnished by Q. The setting of flag A prevents repeated execution of Q when this program does not furnish suitable results within the expected time.

This basic recovery block structure can be augmented in detail as shown in Fig. 10.3.2. The acceptance test is divided into several separate tests which are invoked both before and after execution of the primary routine. The first acceptance test checks on the call format and parameters. If these are not proper, an immediate exit to the alternate routine is taken. The second test, also executed before the primary routine, checks on the validity of the input data. The data test is particularly important because circumstances over which the software designer has no control can so corrupt the data that normal execution of the program is impossible. Where data errors are common, provision of an alternate data source may be considered, and the program can then be structured as shown within the dashed box of Fig. 10.3.2. The final acceptance test is executed after the primary routine (as shown in Fig. 10.3.1), and examines the output data. Failure of any of these tests causes control to pass to the alternate routine as indicated in the figure. Further details on design techniques for these acceptance tests are given in Section 10.5.

The integration of application modules structured as recovery blocks into a fault-tolerant software system is shown in Fig. 10.3.3. The box labeled "Application Modules" and the decision diamond labeled "Return" together represent the structure shown in Fig. 10.3.1. When a normal return is taken, the Task Select function will access the next application module from a task list that has been generated as part of the initialization. In the absence of failures of the recovery blocks, the process will always remain within the inner loop. If an abort exit is taken, the failure is recorded and some diagnostics may be performed. In case of a first failure in a recovery block, a retry may be initiated. If the failure persists, further execution of the task represented by the recovery block is suspended. A new task list is then generated and this replaces the one with which the system had been initialized. If the system has any higher-level standby provisions, such as an emergency control system, these may be activated when an abort condition is encountered.

It is sometimes believed that real-time control situations do not permit the invocation of alternate routines, accessing alternate data sources, or retries because timing constraints inherent in the application will be violated. Actually, the iteration

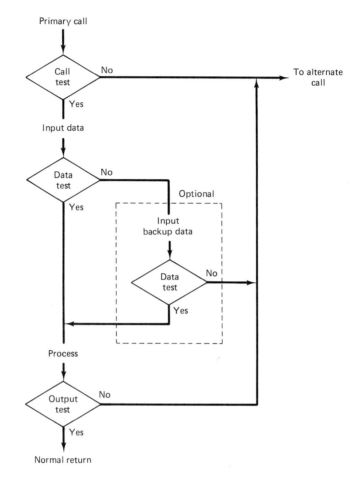

Figure 10.3.2   Internal structure for primary application module.

rates are selected to provide a desired stability margin under the most demanding operating conditions. If a single delay equivalent to an iteration period is encountered, or if a single control output is skipped for several iteration periods, this will at worst result in a transient disturbance from which the system will recover as soon the normal iteration frequency is restored and in most cases it will not result in any noticeable degradation of system performance.

In the recovery block approach a single program is executed at any given time, and therefore no special demands on computer redundancy or computer architecture are made. The performance penalty in normal operation is small (the execution of the acceptance test). Storage requirements are expanded because in addition to the primary application program, the acceptance test and the backup program must also be available in memory. Software development cost will be increased due to the need to generate two programs and the associated acceptance test. However, for critical applications the recovery block approach represents a verifiable increase in reliability

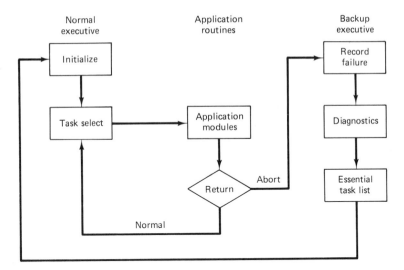

Figure 10.3.3 Executive and applications modules.

that is difficult to duplicate in any other way. The assessment of the reliability achieved by the recovery block is discussed in the following section.

10.4. RELIABILITY MODELS FOR FAULT-TOLERANT SOFTWARE

The preceding sections have provided an overview of the concepts and methods of software fault tolerance, and later sections are devoted to a more detailed discussion of several key areas in the analysis and design of fault-tolerant software. The subject of the present section is reliability modeling. The benefits of fault tolerance techniques, and particularly of the recovery block approach, can be demonstrated very clearly by modeling. The fact that this benefit can be shown by modeling gives recovery blocks a substantial advantage over other approaches to reliability improvement. Section 10.4.1 introduces the terminology used for modeling and the basic software failure model which is subsequently developed into a practical and realistic model for the reliability of fault-tolerant software structures.

10.4.1. Terminology and Software Failure Models

When the output of a computer program produces results that do not meet user requirements (or place the computer into a state that does not support user needs) it has produced an *error*. The execution of the program has resulted in a *failure* or more specifically a *software failure*. To produce this failure, a *fault* must have been present in the software but software *faults* result in a *failure* only when suitable input data or computer states exist. These conditions external to the program which are necessary to *activate* the fault are called *triggers* or, more generically, *external events*.

The basic software failure model of Fig. 10.4.1 illustrates the relations discussed above. The figure also indicates that the error becomes evident only through observation. Some errors may not be observed at all, while others may be manifested in a way that makes determination of the actual failure a difficult matter.

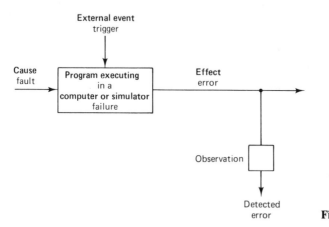

Figure 10.4.1   Basic failure model.

The application of this model at the system level is shown in Fig. 10.4.2. The fault in this example is assumed to be the lack of zero-divide protection in the attitude calculation program of an aircraft flight control system. The external event that activates the fault is the occurrence of a data set that causes a zero denominator to be generated. The immediate error produced is an incorrect attitude value observable only under exceptional conditions (e.g., when extensive data recording is provided as part of a flight test program). The error results in a faulty input to the autopilot, which in turn causes an incorrect control surface deflection. This condition may be observed by an alert pilot, who can prevent propagation of the failure by disengaging the autopilot

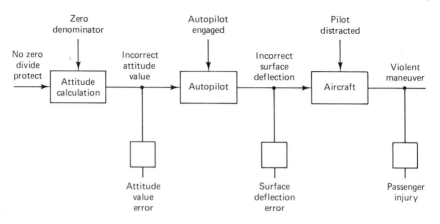

Figure 10.4.2   System failure model.

and taking over manual control. If the pilot is distracted, the surface deflection error will not be observed until the aircraft executes a violent maneuver, possibly causing injury to passengers.

As this example suggests, fault tolerance provisions might be incorporated at several levels in a system. In this case the first level is in the attitude calculation. Had this module been structured as a recovery block, the incorrect attitude value would have been detected internally and would have triggered the invocation of a backup attitude calculation routine. Fault tolerance provisions in the autopilot might have prevented acceptace of the faulty attitude input, or they might have detected that the surface deflection command issued was incorrect.

10.4.2. Reliability Models

Reliability models are intended to illustrate the effect of failures of elements on the overall system, particularly where some elements are redundant or incorporate fault tolerance provisions. In the conventional (hardware) reliability model, shown in Fig. 10.4.3, redundant elements are placed in parallel and all essential functions required for a system are placed in series. The failure probability of a function that consists of two redundant elements, such as C in the figure, is the product of the failure probabilities of the individual elements, here $C1$ and $C2$. If both elements have the same failure pobability, the function failure probability, $F[C]$, is given by

$$F[C] = F[C1]^2 = F[C2]^2 \qquad (10.4.1)$$

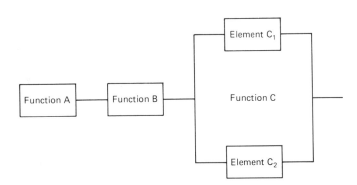

Figure 10.4.3 Conventional reliability model.

The reliability of a system is the product of the reliability of all its functions. In the case Fig. 10.4.3, the system reliability $R[S]$, is given by

$$R[S] = R[A] \cdot R[B] \cdot R[C] \qquad (10.4.2)$$

where $R[x] = 1 - F[x]$.

While this modeling technique can be used to depict the structure of fault-tolerant software, it is not suitable for quantitative evaluation because it does not account for the two most significant factors that contribute to system failure after fault tolerance is implemented in a software package: undetected failures and correlated faults. In *N*-version programming the undetected failures are those that never reach the voter (see Section 10.3.1), while in the recovery block approach they arise from inadequate coverage of the acceptance test. Correlated faults are those present in two or more versions of a program (in the recovery block case failures will result only if the primary and all alternates are faulty).

Figure 10.4.4 is a representation of these potential causes of system failure for a recovery block with a single alternate. A given recovery block can be in one of the following four states:

1. Primary routine operates satisfactorily.
2. A failure in the primary software has been detected.
3. Alternate routine operates satisfactorily.
4. Recovery block fails (abort condition).

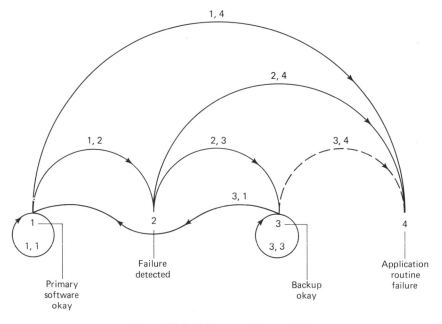

Figure 10.4.4   State transition model.

The possible transitions between these states are shown by the arcs in Fig. 10.4.4. Of particular interest is the arc 3,1, which models reversion to the primary routine after satisfactory operation in the backup mode. This arc represents the capability (not usually present in hardware failure models) of permitting an element that has caused a failure to be returned to service. In software the failure is not due to a physical deterioration. It is due to inability of the primary routine to process correctly a particular data set in a particular machine state. Because the primary routine is presumed to be more efficient or to possess other capabilities superior to those of the backup, it is desirable to return it to service as soon as the data and machine states have changed. This can be done by initially limiting the operation of the alternate to a fixed number of iterations, say 10. If there are repeated failures of the primary after it is returned to service, a longer interval for operation in the backup mode will be allowed.

The system failure probability is represented by the probability of all paths that originate at state 1 and terminate at state 4. These paths are:

1,4: undetected failure of the primary routine

1,2 and 2,4: detected failure of the primary routine and a correlated fault in the alternate that prevents state 3 from being achieved

1,2 and 2,3 and 3,4: detected failure of the primary routine followed by satisfactory operation of the alternate and then followed by an uncorrelated fault in the alternate before reversion to the primary

This latter arc is shown dashed because it represents an extremely small contribution to the probability of failure, as will be seen in the numerical example below. However, this is the only uncorrelated failure of the primary and backup routines modeled in Fig. 10.4.3.

The transition probabilities associated with this model are shown in Table 10.4.1, where the following symbols are used:

c = coverage (error detection capability) of the acceptance test

f = failure probability of the primary routine

s = success probability of the alternate routine

u = probability that no correlated faults exist in the primary and alternate routines

TABLE 10.4.1 TRANSITION PROBABILITIES FOR
THE MODEL OF FIG. 10.4.4.

		\multicolumn{4}{c}{From}			
		1	2	3	4
To	1	$1 - f$	cf	0	$f(1 - c)$
	2	0	0	u	$1 - u$
	3	0^a	0	s	$1 - s$
	4	0	0	0	1

[a]The reversion to state 1 is a deterministic process which is outside the scope of this analysis.

The probability of failure of the recovery block, $P[F]$, is the sum of the probabilities leading to state 4, or

$$P[F] = P[1,4] + P[1,2]P[2,4] + P[1,2]P[1,2]P[2,3]P[3,4]$$
$$= f(1 - c) + cf(1 - u) + cfu(1 - s)$$
$$= f(1 - cus) = f(1 - E)$$

where $E = cus$. E represents the effectiveness of the fault tolerance provisions. When there is no fault tolerance (when any factor contributing to the product cus is 0), the failure probability of the recovery block is identical with the failure probability of the primary routine.

As a means of enabling the reader to gain some experience with this model and to illustrate the reliability improvement possible with the recovery block approach, we consider a software system composed of 10 tasks of approximately equal size and complexity. The software operates 24 h a day and it uses 50% of the CPU time. The execution time is therefore 12 h per day. We assume that the software maintenance cycle for critical programs is 15 calendar days. Thus, between the first detection of a fault and its correction the software will be executed a total of 180 h, and each individual task will be executed 18 h. From Table 10.1.1 it is seen that the best operational software has a failure rate of 0.01 per hour, so that the expected number of failures during the maintenance interval is almost 2 for the entire software and 0.18 for the specific task in which the fault was found.

We now assume that each task is structured as a recovery block with a single alternate. Two implementations of fault tolerance are considered: a standard implementation in which the probability of undetected failures for each acceptance test is 10% ($c = 0.9$) and the probabilty of correlated failures between the primary and the alternate is also 10% ($u = 0.9$), and a very carefully validated implementation which reduces each of these probabilities to 5% ($c = u = 0.95$). The success probability of the alternate software in both cases is assumed to be 0.998. This value is based on the alternate executing only 1% of the time that the primary module is invoked. The resulting failure probabilities are shown in Table 10.4.2.

TABLE 10.4.2 FAILURE PROBABILITIES FOR A SINGLE RECOVERY BLOCK

Condition	Symbol	Probability	
		Standard implementation	Validated implementation
Primary failure	f	0.180	0.180
Coverage	c	0.900	0.950
Uncorrelatedness	u	0.900	0.950
Success of alternate	s	0.998	0.998
Fault tolerance effectiveness	cus	0.808	0.901
Failure of block	$P[F]$	0.034	0.018

The standard implementation reduces the failure probability of the recovery block to slightly less than 20% of the original value, while the validated approach reduces it to 10%. If additional recovery provisions are incorporated at the system level (such as the ones shown in Fig. 10.3.3), it is quite reasonable to expect that one-half of the remaining failures can be avoided. Under the most favorable assumptions used here, fault tolerance techniques can thus reduce the failure probability to about 5% of the level that prevails without their use.

10.5. CONSTRUCTION OF ACCEPTANCE TESTS

This section describes types and selection criteria for acceptance tests, the key element of the recovery block approach described in Section 10.3. There are two levels on which the acceptance tests can be performed. The higher-level acceptance test (i.e., that which tests that the outputs of the program are consistent with the functional requirements) is called a *functional acceptance test*. The lower level is called the *structural acceptance test,* and tests sections of code to ensure that key variables and functions have been properly executed. Functional-level tests are always required. However, for programs under development, the addition of structural tests provides the following benefits:

1. Unexpected behavior of the primary system will be noted even in cases where only a mild degradation is encountered. This aids in program evaluation.
2. Switching to the alternate program is exercised more often under realistic (un-planned) conditions. Realistic testing of the fault tolerance mechanism is a difficult undertaking.
3. As a program matures, it is usually easier to relax acceptance conditions than to make them more restrictive.

10.5.1. Program Characteristics Useful for Acceptance Tests

Most acceptance tests currently used fall into one of the following categories: 1. satisfaction of requirements, 2. accounting tests, 3. reasonableness tests, and 4. computer run-time checks. Although the distinctions between these categories is sometimes blurred, the classifications do serve a useful starting point for the designer confronting a section of critical code.

Acceptance tests may be devised such that they test for what a program *should* do or for what a program *should not* do. For example, acceptance tests in software controlling an automated rail transit system can be written to test for conformance to specified velocities at each location on the route or for violation of safety rules (e.g., the train should not exceed a certain velocity around curves or in the vicinity of a station). Testing for a violation of safety conditions (i.e., testing for what the program should not do) may be simpler and provide a higher degree of independence of the acceptance test from the primary routine than testing for conformance to the pre-planned velocity profile (i.e., what the program should do).

Unfortunately, there is no methodology for deciding on the most appropriate type of test for a given situation. Thus the primary problem facing the software designer is what kind of acceptance test should be used, a choice that is often dictated by run time, storage, and error-detection requirements. Ultimately, one would like to see a classification of acceptance tests that characterize them by these parameters to allow a rational selection for each application. The fact that this stage has not been realized, however, need not deter advancing with practical applications; there is little methodology for the routine testing of software, yet it sometimes yields satisfactory results.

Satisfaction of requirements.   In many cases the problem statement or the specifications of the software impose conditions that must be met at the completion of program execution. These conditions may be used to construct the acceptance tests. The simplest example is inversion of mathematical operations (e.g., squaring the result of a square-root operation to see if it equals the original operand). Another simple illustration of this concept is the sort operation acceptance test described by Randell [RAND75]. At the completion of a sort, the acceptance test checks that the elements are in uniformly descending order and that the number of elements in the sorted set is equal to the number of elements in the original set. This test is not complete: changes in an element during execution would not be detected. An additional component of the test, ensuring that every element in the sorted set appeared in the unsorted set, would make the test exhaustive. However, this component was rejected because of run time requirements.

As noted previously, independence is a crucial consideration in the design of acceptance tests. Devising independent satisfaction of requirements tests may be a difficult and subtle problem. For example, the famous "eight queens" problem requires that eight queens be located on a chess board such that no two queens threaten each other. An acceptance test based on satisfaction of requirements might check that the horizontal, vertical, and two diagonals associated with each queen do not contain the location of any other queen. If the primary routine involves the same check as part of the solution algorithm, this acceptance test is not suitable.

As will be shown in Section 10.5.2, testing for satisfaction of requirements is usually most effective when carried out on small segments of code. Accounting tests and reasonableness tests discussed below can handle larger sections of code, a consideration that may be desirable if capacity or timing constraints prove to be limiting. However, for text editing systems, compilers and simliar programs, tests for satisfaction of requirements constitute the most promising approach at present.

Accounting checks.   Accounting checks are suitable for transaction-oriented applications with simple mathematical operations such as airline reservation systems, library records, and the control of hazardous materials. The simplest form of accounting checks is the checksum. Whenever a large number of records is transmitted or reordered, a tally for both the total number of records and the sum over all records of a particular data field can be compared between source and destination.

The double-entry bookeeping system has evolved over the last 500 years as an effective means of detecting errors due to incorrect transcriptions or information losses in the noncomputerized commercial environment. Such accounting practices have been instituted in financial computing and are applicable in other high-volume transaction applications. A complete description of this procedure may be found in most elementary accounting texts.

When the software involves control of physically measurable inventories such as nuclear material, dangerous drugs, or precious metals, the reconciliation of authorized transactions with the physical inventory can be used as an acceptance test. In many cases, determination of the physical quantity can be automated so that the entire process can be handled without operator intervention.

In the examples described above, discrepancies detected by the acceptance test may be due to either a software failure, deliberate alteration of input or internal data, or actual theft. Thus the dividing line between software reliability and security becomes blurred. Although intellectually distressing, this lack of distinction opens the way for software reliability techniques to be used in computerized security applications, and vice versa.

Reasonableness tests.   Reasonableness tests detect software failures by use of precomputed ranges, expected sequences of program states, or other relationships that are expected to prevail. The difference between satisfaction of requirements tests and reasonableness tests is that the latter are based on physical constraints while the former type are based on logical or mathematical relationships.

Reasonableness tests are suitable in control or switching systems where physical constraints can determine the range of possible outcomes. An illustration of the principle of the reasonableness test is the determination of the true airspeed, a computed quantity, from the indicated airspeed, a sensed quantity, in a flight control system. The first level of acceptance test based on a precomputed range arrived at from physical constraints is that the speed must be within the structural capabilities of the airframe (e.g., 140 to 1100 km/h for a commercial subsonic aircraft). Thus, if the true airspeed is outside this range, there is something wrong with either the sensor or the computer (an additional possibility is that the aircraft is out of control).

Further refinements on the test above would use a reasonable range of *changes* to true airspeed. Thus, if changes between the current airspeed and the previous value indicate accelerations beyond the design limit of the aircraft, an abnormal condition exists. This test is actually considerably more powerful in that much smaller deviation can be detected. For example, if the previous true airspeed is 1000 km/h, and the subsequent calculation, which may occur in the next tenth of a second, results in an airspeed of 1020 km/h, the acceptance test will detect an error: the consequent acceleration is almost 6g!

A second type of reasonableness test is based on progression between subsequent states. For example, in an electronic telephone switching system, it is not reasonable to proceed from a connected state to a ringing state or line-busy state. However, such a test is not exhaustive; it would not detect the premature termination of a connection.

Tests for reasonableness of numerical or state variables are quite flexible and effective for constructing fault-tolerant process control software. They permit acceptance criteria to be modified as a program matures.

Run-time checks.   Run-time checks consist of those provided by most current computers as continuous execution sequences which are often hardware implemented. Such tests detect anomalous states such as divide by zero, overflow, underflow, undefined operation code, end of file, or write-protection violations. Although not specifically designed as such, these run-time tests can serve as additional acceptance tests that cover a much wider area and detect more subtle discrepancies. Upon detection of a run-time condition error, a bit in a status register is set, and transfer to an alternate routine can be effected.

Run-time checks can also incorporate data structure and procedure-oriented tests that are embedded in special support software or in the operating system. Such examples include array value checking or unauthorized entries to subroutines. Stucki [STUC75] and Yau [YAU76, YAU75] describe a number of interesting run-time monitoring techniques.

10.5.2. Fault Trees as a Design Aid

The overall design goal of fault-tolerant software can be briefly stated as preparing for the unexpected. A key step in reaching this goal is the identification of conditions that should trigger invocation of the alternate routine.

Unfortunately, even in principle, there is no way to anticipate all the problems that will be encountered. However, in designing fault-tolerant software, one can have a conception of the general *classes* of failures that can occur. Fault trees can be used as a means of identifying these classes of faults in a top-down manner, and if used as part of a formal design process, can serve as documentation of potential software failures which are covered in the fault-tolerant design. In addition, review of the fault-tolerant aspects of the software is facilitated by the use of the trees: failures that are covered are explicitly listed; uncovered failures do not appear.

Traditionally, fault trees have been used for the evaluation of hardware reliability. The basic notion in this application is that a top event (i.e., failure of the system) is broken down into simpler events (e.g., failures of subsystems or individual circuits) that are characterized as a "yes/no" occurrences. These simpler events are linked together by AND or OR gates.

This process of breaking down complex events into simpler events is continued until the failures of individual components or other events with known probabilities are identified. One then determines the probability of successively higher-level events by combining probabilities of the immediately lower events in the ways dictated by the gates linking them together: addition in the case of an OR gate; multiplication in the case of an AND gate. The final result of this process is an estimation of the probability of the top event as the probabilities of the lower events are combined.

Detailed descriptions on the applications of fault trees to hardware systems reliability can be found in [AEC75].

The application of this technique for software reliability proceeds along similar lines as in hardware. The top event is the failure of a software system, and successive levels describe various types of failures that can occur in the system. The bottom-level events, also known as *primal events,* consist of specific modules or sections of code.

Unlike hardware fault trees, however, these primal events do not have specific failure probabilities. Instead, they represent events whose success or failure can be tested relatively simply and in real time. If it can be shown that all events leading into an OR gate can be tested in such a way, the higher-level event in question is said to be covered by the set of acceptance tests. On the other hand, if any single event leading into an AND gate can be simply tested, the higher-level event is covered (i.e., all inputs to an AND gate must be uncovered in order for the output to be uncovered). If all higher-level events can be covered by acceptance tests on the primal events that have been identified, one can characterize the system as having 100% coverage. Techniques for demonstration of complete coverage in complex trees are available (e.g., complementary cut sets discussed in [US76]. However, even for the relatively complex software systems, the trees may be sufficiently understandable that demonstration of coverage can be shown by means of inspection.

Although fault trees do not guarantee comprehensive coverage, they are an improvement over existing techniques for the placement of acceptance tests, which are basically intuitive and which depend on "reasonable" assumptions and undocumented "truths" about the system as perceived by its designers. Advantages of the fault tree approach include:

A more pictorial method for deriving and placing acceptance tests which is easy to understand

Documentation of all assumptions on anticipated inputs, outputs, and operations

Easier design reviews for verification of completeness, correct reasoning, and proper assumptions

Documentation of deliberate omissions (perhaps on the basis of being "extremely unlikely" or because of a design decision)

Together with these advantages, there are some problems inherent in the use of this methodology. As noted above, the method does not ensure coverage, nor does it guarantee that all flaws will be spotted. Like any graphical method, fault trees tend to take up a lot of space.

The drawing of fault trees is more of an art than a science. A useful, comprehensible fault tree, like a flowchart, is an aesthetically pleasing work which can greatly facilitate the comprehension of a complex computer program. Some research has been done on the automated drawing of fault trees for hardware [LAPP77] and software systems [LEVE83]. However, fault tree usefulness in providing engineering insight into the system under consideration is limited. A thorough understanding of the system and a goal of explicitness are prerequisities for the drawing of coherent, logical, and comprehensive fault trees.

10.5.3. Placement of Acceptance Tests within the Program

The exact form of the fault trees depends on the system requirements. However, one can develop a framework for their general form as shown in Fig. 10.5.1. The module under consideration will perform several operations associated with its overall function. The top event in this case will be failure of the module to meet its overall functional requirements, and beneath that will be failure of the module to fulfill its functional specifications (there may be several levels of OR gates if the functional specifications for the module are subdivided). Development continues until either:

1. A sufficiently detailed and explicit failure is identified which can be tested for and bypassed with an alternate routine, or
2. A predetermined level is reached (perhaps by a separate set of design specifications).

In many cases it may be possible to devise recovery blocks that can both detect and correct errors on the functional requirements level. However, in other cases, development of an acceptance test or a parallel alternate routine may be too complicated, and development of the fault trees below the functional level will provide a simpler alternative.

As shown in Fig. 10.5.1, development of the trees below the functional requirements level involves a description of the structural aspects of subroutines, procedures, or data structures contained within the module. This description will generally involve more detailed documentation than the requirements listings for the functional-level recovery blocks. The documentation may involve some textual material, but for the most part, it will involve the source listings. Structural acceptance tests and alternate routines are developed by examining the input, transformation processes, and output of the component procedures or subroutines. Additional considerations are where particular sections of code sit in the hierarchy of routines, or the execution order.

To illustrate the approach, an example is taken from a module from the operating system of the fault-tolerant multiprocessor computer (FTMP) developed by the C.S. Draper Laboratories [HOPK78]. The FTMP architecture consists of 10 processors configured as three triads and a single spare. The component processors of each triad are tightly coupled (i.e., execute each instruction cycle together), but the triads are more loosely coupled to each other (i.e., synchronization occurs only after a number of tasks have been performed). The software module under consideration is called the dispatcher and is responsible for assigning tasks to each of the triads. The dispatcher also designates one of the triads to restart the task list at periodic intervals and interfaces with a hardware timer to handle interrupts. Following are briefly stated functional requirements for the dispatcher. The dispatcher must:

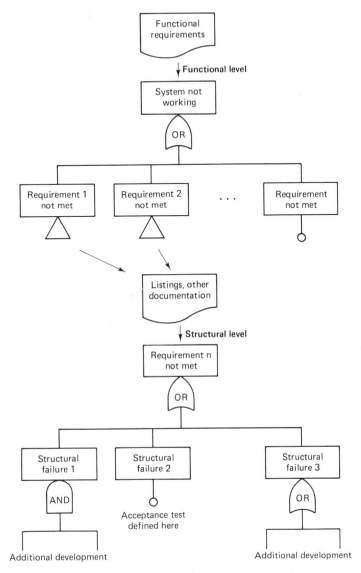

Figure 10.5.1 Development of fault trees for the placement of acceptance tests.

1. Initialize certain variables upon power-up and at the beginning of a new task iteration cycle.
2. Execute tasks at one of three predetermined iteration rates.
3. Recognize the timer interrupt for the start of a new iteration cycle.
4. Provide for retirement of faulty processors and reconfiguration of the system if a hardware fault is detected.
5. Execute a set of data transfer operations at predetermined iteration rates.

A top-level fault tree for the dispatcher based on these requirements is shown in Fig. 10.5.2. The OR gate indicates that failure to meet any of the five requirements listed above is a failure of the system. The term "primary" is used to distinguish this dispatcher from an alternate versions which are called in the event of a failure in the primary. The triangles under the first three failures are transfers to subsequent development; the circles under the last two indicate that this level of detail is sufficient for development of the acceptance tests.

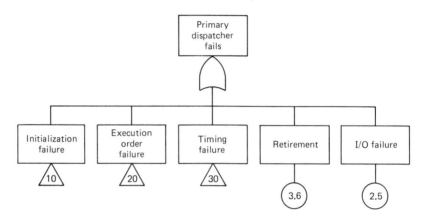

Figure 10.5.2 Top-level fault tree for the FTMP dispatcher.

Figure 10.5.3 shows a further development of transfer 30 of Fig. 10.5.2. The development moves beyond the terminology of the functional specifications into the vocabulary of variable names, procedure failures, and other specific coding implementation details. The tree is terminated once the failure can be detected with a specific acceptance test or is out of the scope of software reliability. Thus the failure "interval timer not loaded" can be detected with acceptance test 1.4, and "clock failure," which is considered to be a hardware failure, is not checked by any acceptance test.

The Boolean properties of the AND and OR gates are employed in the placement of acceptance tests. When an OR gate links the failures, all must be tested, but when an AND gate joins the failure, it is necessary that only one event be tested. Thus, for the "Stuck in R4 Rate Group" failure, the three possible causes, "Stuck in R4 Applications Task," "Stuck in Task Selection," or "Stuck in Uninterruptible ASM Routine" must each be tested for. However, the "Stuck in Applications Routine" failure can occur only when two conditions prevail simultaneously: (1) the interval timer is not set and (2) a design flaw in the applications routine causes a failure to terminate. In this case, only one of these potential failures needs to be covered with an acceptance test. Checking the status of the interval timer is easier than proving the correctness of every applications task for all possible data states and configurations.

As is evident from this example, considerable insight into the operation of the software system is required for the drawing of fault trees. This understanding can be difficult to achieve because of the following three factors:

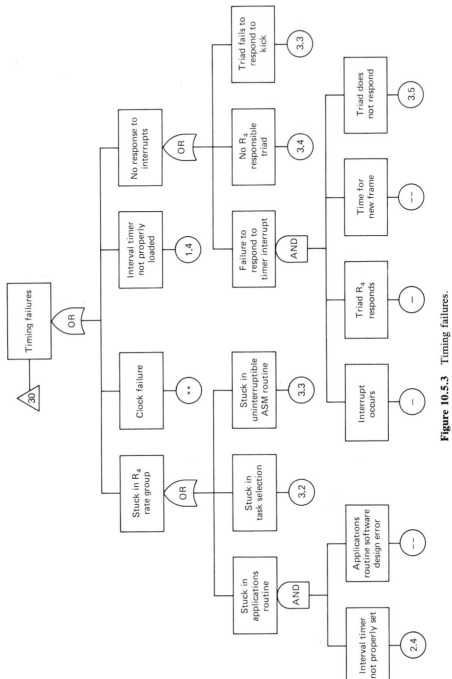

Figure 10.5.3 Timing failures.

1. The system is under development. Thus design specifications, coding, and even requirements are subject to change. It is possible that assumptions used in the derivation of earlier acceptance tests are no longer valid, or that the recovery block itself is no longer appropriate because of changes in design.

2. As a result of the system being under development, documentation is often insufficient (if available at all). The definitive information is the source code. In a disciplined environment, supporting information will be current, complete, and organized. Unfortunately, it is often the case that informal communications are used: excerpts from articles and progress reports, and hastily drawn diagrams produced on lunchtime napkins.

3. From the organizational point of view, it desirable that the primary design and fault tolerance groups communcate only formally to ensure a truly independent assessment of the software vulnerabilities. However, during development, this assessment can be extremely difficult because of frequent and informal interaction between the two groups.

It is thus necessary to balance a variety of concerns (design stability versus ability to adjust to unforeseen developments, resources devoted to documentation versus coding, independence of the design and fault-tolerant groups versus the need for one to explain to the other what it is doing) in the management of the design process.

10.6. VALIDATION OF FAULT-TOLERANT SOFTWARE

Validation serves two purposes: (1) to detect and correct faults in the software design and coding and (2) to provide assurance that the software will properly fulfill its functional requirements. Traditional approaches to producing reliable (but non-fault-tolerant) software have emphasized the validation and test phase of the software development cycle. Indeed, costs for independent verification and validation of software can be as high as the initial development costs.

The general problem of producing fault-free software has been addressed extensively in the literature. Some of the attempts to devise systematic, generic, and automated validation schemes are described in Section 10.1. Unfortunately, these attempts have achieved only limited success and have not become widespread in their use. Indeed, Mills categorically states that it is impossible to definitively prove the correctness of a program [MILS75]. Whether or not this is ultimately true, the current state of software verfication technology tends to support the claim more than to weaken it.

10.6.1. Fault-Tolerant Software Validation

In non-fault-tolerant software it is presumed that faults affecting the ability of a computer program to fulfill its functional requirements will cause a system failure. In fault-tolerant software, such a concession is not made. Instead, it is expected that faults existing in the primary routine will be detected and circumvented (i.e., effectively masked from the rest of the system).

Such an expectation imposes specific validation requirements on the fault tolerance provisions of any software. In the case of recovery blocks the validation procedure must show that:

1. The acceptance test detects all possible primary routine failures and invokes the alternate routine.
2. The acceptance test does not spuriously invoke the alternate routine.
3. The alternate routine executes successfully whenever it is invoked by the acceptance test.
4. The acceptance test does not spuriously move to the abort state if the alternate routine performs its function as specified.

The validation of fault-tolerant software thus poses problems that are quite distinct from the validation of ordinary software. In the latter case, the primary goal is to establish that the *code* meets the user requirements. For fault-tolerant software, the primary goal is to establish that the *fault tolerance* works. This goal poses a unique set of problems which include:

The inability to predict the nature and range of all software failures which should cause the acceptance test to invoke the alternative routine.

The necessity to demonstrate that both the acceptance test and alternate routines will function properly (i.e., detect and correct the error) in the event of a primary failure.

The necessity to ensure that the particular recovery block undergoing evaluation will function properly when other software components have failed or have invoked alternate routines.

10.6.2. Fault Trees as a Validation Tool

Section 10.5.3 describes the use of fault trees for the formulation and placement of recovery blocks within a given software system. The top event of that class of fault trees is the failure of the system as a whole, and the objective of the fault tree development is to define a set of acceptance tests that would detect system failure.

This section discusses the application of fault trees to validation of recovery blocks. The top event of this type of fault tree is the failure of the function in question, and the objective of the fault tree development is to determine a minimal set of test cases which can demonstrate that the function under validation operates correctly in the presence of primary routine design flaws and unforeseen conditions.

The added difficulties described in Section 10.6.1 require a systematic approach; intuitive or semi-intuitive methods are not sufficient. While the fault tree methodology does not conclusively validate the software, it unambiguously documents the range of conditions that were considered, and forces the cataloging of assumptions and "unreasonable" conditions that are not tested. The documentation in graphical form facilitates review and identification of bad assumptions, faulty reasoning, or inadvertent omissions. The weaknesses of the technique are the inability to assure full and complete coverage and the fact that drawing understandable and complete trees is still more of an art than a science.

The top event in the validation fault trees is the failure of a specific recovery block or other fault-tolerant feature. If it can be demonstrated that there are no primal events that, when true, cause the top event to be true, the software is validated *for the scope of faults considered in the fault tree development.*

A complete validation of the software must take into account all possible hardware system configurations, memory environments, ranges of input variables and outputs, timing, and previous software failures. The validation must be performed on both the acceptance test and the alternate routine for all the conditions above.

In the first pass at fault tree construction, all possible values of the parameters given above can be classified into general groups. The structure of the trees facilitates evaluation of which redundant values need and need not be tested for. As a result of these evaluations, most data values and system configurations can be dropped. The remaining primal events form a list of validation test cases. An example of how this elimination may be performed and documented is given later in this section.

Prior to development of the test cases themselves, it is necessary to define a framework for the *classes* of validation tests. In non-fault-tolerant software, validation is concerned only with the primary routine. However, validation of recovery blocks requires consideration of a number of additional types of potential failures as shown in Fig. 10.6.1. Recovery block failure will be due to a failure of any of its three components: the primary routine, the acceptance test, or the alternate routine. Table 10.6.1 describes the validation test objectives for each of the seven sets of failure classes shown in the fault tree of Fig. 10.6.1.

In validation of non-fault-tolerant software, only test cases under transfer A of Fig. 10.6.1 would be developed. Invocation failures under transfer G may or may not be within the scope of the recovery block. If a decision is made to exclude these errors from the analysis (perhaps because these invocations are part of a system which is designed and validated elsewhere), a diamond termination is made in order to explicitly denote their exclusion from the validation.

Figure 10.6.1 has defined the classes of validation test cases to be developed in a logical manner which does not consider operational problems or expenses. Because most exhaustive validations will involve several thousand test cases with resultant large expenditures of both professional hours and computer time, it may be desirable to combine the test runs for several sets of validation objectives. Figure 10.6.2 shows an example of how part of the fault tree shown in Fig. 10.6.1 is restructured to be consistent with this economy measure. A class of validation test cases was developed to validate simultaneously that the acceptance test can detect failures in the primary routine (transfer *B*) and that the alternate routine correctly executes the function when invoked by the acceptance test under these circumstances (transfer *F*).

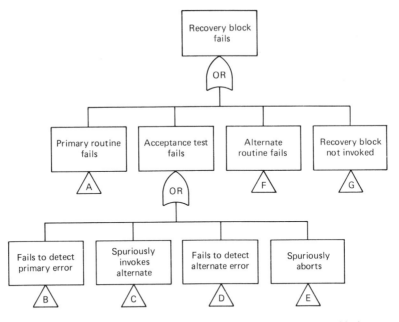

Figure 10.6.1   Generalized top-level tree for validation of recovery blocks.

TABLE 10.6.1   OBJECTIVES OF VALIDATION OF FAULT-TOLERANT SOFTWARE

Transfer	Objective of validation test cases
A	Demonstrate that the primary routine executes correctly (as defined by design specifications)
B	Demonstrate that the acceptance test detects all primary routine errors
C	Demonstrate that the acceptance test properly interprets all correct (as defined by design specifications) primary routine outputs
D	Demonstrate that the acceptance test detects all alternate routine errors
E	Demonstrate that the acceptance test properly interprets all correct (as defined by design specifications) alternate routine outputs
F	Demonstrate that that the alternate routine executes correctly (as defined by design specifications)
G	Demonstrate that the system properly invokes the primary routine, acceptance test, alternate routine, and abort routine

After the top-level tree which defines the validation test classifications has been formulated, subsequent trees are used to develop the actual validation test cases. Figure 10.6.3 shows the general form of a complete development for the transfers shown in Fig. 10.6.1 or 10.6.2. The failures may occur when the system is operational, when previous hardware failures have occurred or previous software failures may have occurred. For each one of these failure histories, a set of all possible memory configurations and data values is considered.

Even for the simplest problems, such a comprehensive validation tree is probably impractical to develop in detail and nearly impossible to test for. However, insight

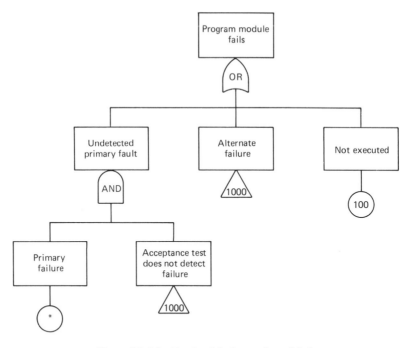

Figure 10.6.2   Top-level fault tree for validation.

into the system, simplifying assumptions, and the decision to disregard certain potential branches will reduce the problem to manageable proportions. It is in this reduction process that fault trees have their main utility. Major assumptions, omissions, and system insights are inevitably documented and available for later review.

Figure 10.6.4, part of a validation fault tree for elements of the SIFT [WENS78] operating system, is an example of how fault trees facilitate the documentation of simplifying assumptions. The recovery block undergoing validation is called the "error reporter," and its function is to detect and report faulty processors to the operating system. Two general failure modes are possible: (1) failure to detect a "disagreeing" (i.e., faulty) processor, and (2) the spurious identification of a functional processor as faulty—the latter fault is developed elsewhere.

The functional specifications of the error reporter required that it detect up to four (out of a total of six) faulty processors. Hence the lower level of the diagram identifies four recovery block failures: inability to identify one, two, three, or four faulty processors. In the bottom level, an important simplifying assumption is made: that failure to detect a given processor as faulty is independent of the number of other processors that have failed. Thus failure to identify two faulty processors is the compound event of failure to identify one processor *and* failure to identify the second processor.

The validation for the failure to identify one faulty processor will consist of six test cases. Each test case will simulate the failure of the primary routine to identify a specific faulty processor. Should the validation demonstrate that the acceptance test

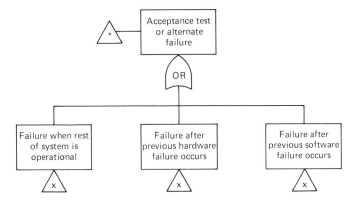

*Transfers A–G from Figure 10.6.1

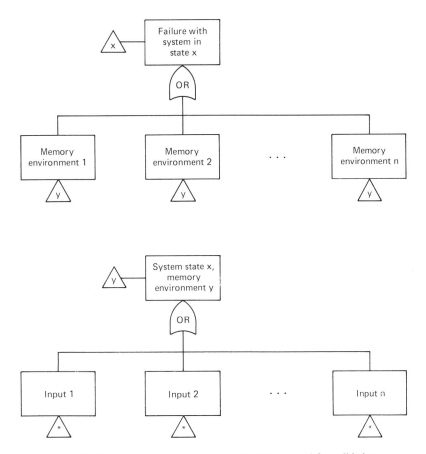

Figure 10.6.3 Subsequent development of fault trees used for validation.

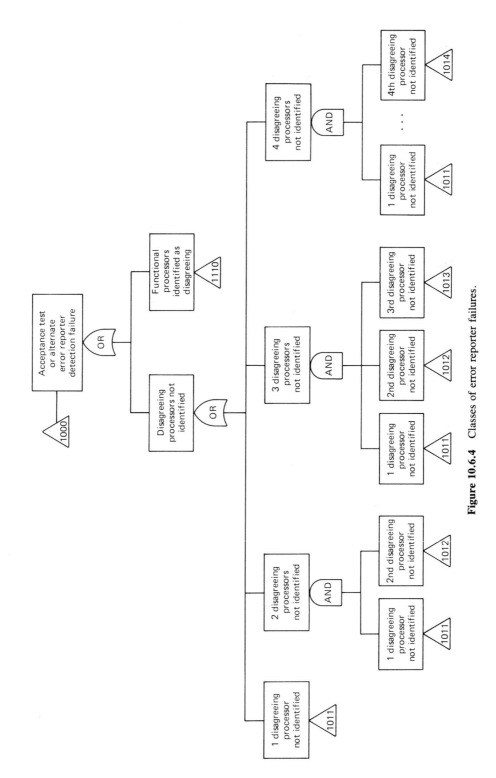

Figure 10.6.4 Classes of error reporter failures.

692

and alternate can detect and correct the primary error reporter failure, the events listed under transfer 1011 would be false. As a result of the simplification noted in the paragraph above, testing for failure to detect two faulty processors will now consist of only *five* test cases, which simulate the failure of the primary routine to detect a *second* processor as faulty. Without the simplification, a total of 30 test cases would be necessary (i.e., a simulation of a primary routine failure to detect any two of the six processors as having failed).

REFERENCES

[AVIZ77] Avizienis, A., and L. Chen, "On the implementation of N-Version Programming for Software Fault Tolerance during Execution," *Proc. COMPSAC'77,* IEEE Cat. 77CH1291-4C, pp. 149–155, Nov. 1977.

[CHEN78] Chen, L., and A. Avizienis, "*N*-Version Programming: A Fault Tolerance Approach to Reliability of Software Operation," *Dig., 8th Annu. Int. Symp. Fault-Tolerant Comput.,* Madison, Wis., IEEE Cat. 78CH1286-4C, pp. 3–9, June 21–23, 1978.

[DACS80] Data and Analysis Center for Software (DACS), "Software Reliability Data Submitted to the DACS by John D. Musa," Jan. 1980.

[DENN76] Denning, P. J., "Fault Tolerant Operating Systems," *Comput. Surv.,* vol. 8, no. 4, pp. 360–389, Dec. 1976.

[DIJK72] Dijkstra, E. W., "Notes on Structured Programming," in *Structured Programming,* Academic Press, New York, 1972.

[ELME72] Elmendorf, W. R., "Fault Tolerant Programming," *Dig. 2nd Annu. Int. Symp. Fault-Tolerant Comput.,* Newton, Mass.,IEEE Cat. 72CH0623-9C, June 19–21, 1972.

[ELSP73] Elspas, B., et al., "An Interactive System for the Verification of Computer Programs," SRI Project 1891, Stanford Research Institute (now SRI International), Sept. 1973.

[GERH76] Gerhart, S. L., and L. Yelowitz, "Observations on the Fallibility in Applications of Modern Programming Methodologies," *IEEE Trans. Softw. Eng.,* vol. SE-2, no. 3, pp. 195–207, 1976.

[GERH80] Gerhart, S. L., et al., "An Overview of AFFIRM: A Specification and Verification System," in *Information Processing 80,* F. H. Lavington, Ed., North-Holland, Amsterdam, 1980.

[GOOD80] Goodenough, J. B., and C. L. McGowan, "Software Quality Assurance: Testing and Validation," *Proc. IEEE,* vol. 68, no. 9, pp. 1093–1098, Sept. 1980.

[HECH76] Hecht, H., "Fault Tolerant Software for Real-Time Applications," *Comput. Surv.,* vol. 8, no. 4, Dec. 1976.

[HECH77] Hecht, H. et al., "Reliability Measurement during Software Development," The Aerospace Corporation, NASA-CR-145205, Sept. 1977.

[HECH81] Hecht, M., and H. Hecht, "Fault Tolerant Software Modules for SIFT," SoHaR, Inc. Rep. TR-81-04, Apr. 1981.

[HOPK78] Hopkins, A. L., et al., "FTMP—A Highly Reliable Fault Tolerant Multiprocessor for Aircraft," *Proc. IEEE,* vol. 66, no. 10, pp. 1221–1239, 1978.

[HORN74] Horning, J. J., et al., "A Program Structure for Error Detection and Recovery," *Proc. Conf. Operat. Syst.: Theor. Pract. Aspects,* IRIA, pp. 174-193, Apr. 1974.

[HOWD78] Howden, W. E., "An Evaluation of the Effectiveness of Symbolic Testing," *Softw. Pract. Experience,* vol. 8, pp. 381–397, 1978.

[IEEE82] IEEE Std 729-1982, "IEEE Glossary of Software Engineering Terminology," The Institute of Electrical and Electronics Engineers, Inc., 1982.

[KIM76] Kim, K. H., and C. V. Ramamoorthy, "Failure Tolerant Parallel Programming and Its Supporting System Architectures," *AFIPS Conf. Proc.,* vol. 45, (NCC 1976), pp. 413–423, Apr. 1976.

[KING75] King, J. C., "A New Approach to Program Testing," *Proc. 1975 Int. Conf. Reliable Softw.,* IEEE Cat. 75 CH0940-7CSR, pp. 228–233, Apr. 1975.

[KOPE74] Kopetz, H., "Software Redundancy in Real-Time Systems," *Proc. IFIP Congr. (Stockholm),* pp. 182-186, 1974.

[LAPP77] Lapp, S. A., and G. J. Powers, "Computer Aided Synthesis of Fault Trees," *IEEE Trans. Reliab.,* Apr. 1977.

[LEVE83] Leveson, N. G. and J. L. Stolzy, "Safety Analysis of Ada Programs," *IEEE Trans. Reliability,* vol. R-32, no. 5, pp. 496-484, December 1983.

[MILL75] Miller, E. F., Jr, and R. A. Melton, "Automated Generation of Test Case Data Sets," *Proc. Int. Conf. Softw. Reliab.,* IEEE Cat. 75CH0940-7CSR, Apr. 1975, p. 51.

[MILL81] Miller, E. F., Jr., et al., "Application of Structural Quality Standards to Software," *Softw. Eng. Stand. Appl. Workshop,* IEEE Cat. 81CH1633-7, pp. 51–57, July 1981.

[MILS75] Mills, H. D., "How to Write Correct Programs and Know It," *Proc. Int. Conf. Softw. Reliab.,* IEEE Cat. 75CH0940-7CSR, Apr. 1975, p. 363.

[MUSA79] Musa, J. D., "Validity of the Execution-Time Theory of Software Reliability," *IEEE Trans. Reliab.,* vol. R-28, no. 3, pp. 1131–1143, Aug. 1979.

[RAND75] Randell, B., "System Structure for Software Fault Tolerance," *IEEE Trans. Softw. Eng.,* vol. SE-1, no. 1, pp. 220–232, June 1975.

[REYN76] Reynolds, C., and R. T. Yeh, "Induction as the Basis for Program Verification," *IEEE Trans. Softw. Eng.,* vol. SE-2, no. 4, pp. 244–252, Dec. 1976.

[ROBI77] Robinson, L., and O. Roubine, "SPECIAL—A Specification and Assertion Language," Tech. Rep. CSL-46, Stanford Research Institute (now SRI International), Jan. 1977.

[STIF76] Stiffler, J. J., "Architectural Design for Near-100% Fault Coverage," *Dig., 6th Annu. Int. Symp. Fault-Tolerant Comput.,* Pittsburgh, Pa., IEEE Cat 76CH1094-2C, pp. 134–137, June 21-23, 1976.

[STUC75] Stucki, L. G., and G. L. Foshee, "New Assertion Concepts for Self-Metric Software Validation," *Proc. 1975 Int. Conf. Reliab. Softw.,* IEEE Cat. 75CH0940-7CSR, Apr. 1975, pp.59–71.

[TAYL80] Taylor, D. J., et al., "Redundancy in Data Structures: Improving Software Fault Tolerance," *IEEE Trans. Softw. Eng.,* vol. SE-6, no. 6, pp. 585–595, Nov. 1980.

[US76] U.S. Atomic Energy Commission, *Reactor Safety Study,* WASH1400, vol. 1, 1976.

[WENS78] Wensley, J. H., et al., "SIFT: The Design and Analysis of a Fault Tolerant Computer for Aircraft Control," *Proc. IEEE,* vol. 66, no. 10, pp. 1040–1054, Oct. 1978.

[YAU75] Yau, S. S., and R. C. Cheung, "Design of Self-Checking Software," *Proc. 1975 Int. Conf. Reliab.,* IEEE Cat. 75CH0940-7CSR, Apr. 1975, pp. 450–457.

[YAU76] Yau, S. S., R. C. Cheung, and D. C. Cochrane, "An Approach to Error-Resistant Software Design," *Proc. 2nd Int. Conf. Softw. Eng.*, IEEE Cat. 76CH1125-4C, Oct. 1976, pp. 429–436.

PROBLEMS

10.1. Classify each of the following practices as (A) fault avoidance, (B)robustness, (C) fault containment, or (D) fault tolerance.
  (a) Structured programming.
  (b) Invocation of alternate routine when primary exceeds time limit.
  (c) Use of checksums on transmittal of data.
  (d) Automatic restart on divide by zero.
  (e) Indication to data entry personnel when data are out of range.
  (f) Proof of correctness for all data manipulation routines.
  (g) Use of default data when data entered are out of range.
  (h) Stopping a program when loop iterations exceed a limit.

10.2. A program consists of 10 independent routines. The probability that a routine is faulty is 0.10 (for each of the routines). It is intended to use three-version programming, with voting to be conducted after execution of each routine. The effectiveness of the voting in eliminating faults is 0.85 when one out of three routines is faulty and 0 when more than one routine is faulty (compare these assumptions with Table 10.3.1). What is the probability of a fault-free program:
  (a) When only a single version is produced and routine testing is conducted?
  (b) When only a single routine is used but extensive testing is conducted that reduces the fault content to 10% of the original level?
  (c) When three-version programming is used?

10.3. Devise acceptance tests for each of the following programs:
  (a) A routine that sorts all orders received in a given day by ZIP code of the originator
  (b) A program that computes sales tax on the same orders
  (c) A program that computes rate of climb increment for aircraft from data supplied by inertial instruments. The basic algorithm is

$$RC = 0.1 \sum_i VA[i]$$

where VA is vertical acceleration in ft/s/s and the summation is conducted over the last 10 samples. Assume that a barometric rate of climb transducer is available and that the accuracy of the data obtained from it is 10% ± 30 ft/s. The data obtained from a correctly operating inertial acceleration algorithm have only negligible error.

10.4. Why are conventional reliability models (e.g., that shown in Fig. 10.4.3) not suitable for software?

10.5. A fault-tolerant software system has been operating satisfactorily for a number of years (i.e., no failures that are significant at the overall system level have occurred). It is now proposed to install a logging routine which will record every failure of the primary software and the number of attempted reversions to the primary program after the backup software has been invoked. The logging routine will impose a 0.5% performance penalty on the system. Do you favor installation of the logging routine, and what are the reasons for your decision?

10.6. The operating system for a spacecraft computer is to be implemented in read-only memory (ROM) which can not be modified after the spacecraft is launched. The expected life of the spacecraft is 7 years, and on the basis of prior experience is is expected that five failures of the operating system will occur during that interval. In case of previous failures, recovery has been possible by shutdown of the computer and restart, but this involves data loss and there is no certainty that it will always be successful. It has therefore been decided to make the operating system fault tolerant. Assume that all failures of the primary operating software will be detected. What is the largest value for correlated failure probability of the back-up software that will permit the expected number of failures during the mission to be reduced to one?

10.7. Construct a fault tree for a program that assigns students to classes. Each class has an attendance limit.

10.8. A fault-tolerant software system that controls fuel flow into a boiler will fail if the primary software fails *and* the backup software is not invoked *and* a special routine fails which shuts off fuel flow when the steam pressure exceeds a certain limit. How many software failures can be sustained before the system fails?

Index

DATE DUE

12-4-89 NSLS			
OCT 27 1990			
APR 27 1992			